SAP® BusinessObjects™ BI Security

SAP PRESS is a joint initiative of SAP and Galileo Press. The know-how offered by SAP specialists combined with the expertise of the Galileo Press publishing house offers the reader expert books in the field. SAP PRESS features first-hand information and expert advice, and provides useful skills for professional decision-making.

SAP PRESS offers a variety of books on technical and business-related topics for the SAP user. For further information, please visit our website: *www.sap-press.com*.

Greg Myers and Eric Vallo
SAP BusinessObjects BI System Administration
2012, 472 pp., hardcover
ISBN 978-1-59229-404-6

Brogden, Sinkwitz, Holden, Marks, and Orthous
SAP BusinessObjects Web Intelligence (2nd Edition)
2012, 591 pp., hardcover
ISBN 978-1-59229-430-5

Ray Li and Evan DeLodder
Creating Dashboards with SAP BusinessObjects (2nd Edition)
2012, 679 pp., hardcover
ISBN 978-1-59229-410-7

Heilig, Kessler, Knötzele, John, and Thaler-Mieslinger
SAP NetWeaver BW and SAP BusinessObjects
2012, 795 pp., hardcover
ISBN 978-1-59229-384-1

Christian Ah-Soon and David François Gonzalez

SAP® BusinessObjects™ BI Security

Galileo Press

Bonn • Boston

Galileo Press is named after the Italian physicist, mathematician, and philosopher Galileo Galilei (1564–1642). He is known as one of the founders of modern science and an advocate of our contemporary, heliocentric worldview. His words *Eppur si muove* (And yet it moves) have become legendary. The Galileo Press logo depicts Jupiter orbited by the four Galilean moons, which were discovered by Galileo in 1610.

Editor Emily Nicholls
Acquisitions Editor Kelly Grace Harris
Copyeditor Pamela Siska
Cover Design Graham Geary
Photo Credit iStockphoto.com/CSA_Images
Layout Design Vera Brauner
Production Graham Geary
Typesetting Publishers' Design and Production Services, Inc.
Printed and bound in the United States of America, on paper from sustainable sources

ISBN 978-1-59229-437-4
© 2013 by Galileo Press Inc., Boston (MA)
1st edition 2013

Library of Congress Cataloging-in-Publication Data
Ah-Soon, Christian.
SAP BusinessObjects BI security / Christian Ah-Soon and David François Gonzalez. —
1st ed.
p. cm.
ISBN 978-1-59229-437-4 — ISBN 1-59229-437-5 1. SAP ERP. 2. Business
intelligence—Data processing. 3. Business intelligence—Computer programs
4. Data protection. 5. Computer security. 6. Computer networks—Security
measures. I. Gonzalez, David. II. Title.
HD38.7.A385 2013
005.8—dc23
2012037440

In memory of our friend and colleague
Marc Ferenczi.

Contents at a Glance

Dear Reader,

Please allow me the pleasure of introducing Christian Ah-Soon, first-time author and data security hero whose debut book is in your hands.

If you think "hero" is too strong a word, it's only because you don't know Christian. After months of collaborating with his knowledgeable co-author, David François Gonzalez, he has produced a comprehensive data security guide of a quality that may even qualify him as a *super* hero. Beyond distributing security rights and enhancing user accountability, Christian can write polished pages under pressure, maintain contact with his editorial team using trusty gadgets, and master publishing steps that far surpass the traditional author role.

Like every champion, Christian's primary objective—protecting SAP BusinessObjects Business Intelligence systems—involves training and entrusting a new generation of safe-keepers with his mission. As his apprentice, you'll find his security insights about functional and data security eminently approachable and his step-by-step instructions and screenshots effectively actionable.

In fact, by purchasing this book from SAP PRESS, you've joined the league of extraordinary security personnel trusted with spreading the word about security. Because you're one of Christian's earliest security trainees, we hope you'll visit *www.sap-press. com* and share your feedback about this first edition. You also may receive requests from admirers for autographs, interviews, and additional information about SAP PRESS resources. Don't be alarmed!

Emily Nicholls
Editor, SAP PRESS

Galileo Press
Boston, MA

emily.nicholls@galileo-press.com
www.sap-press.com

Contents

11   Defining and Implementing a Security Model 507

Appendices 535

Acknowledgments

I would like to thank all the people who helped us write this book. At SAP PRESS, Emily Nicholls and Kelly Grace Harris have been wonderful to support and guide us throughout this writing process. Several people have reviewed parts of the book or have given us some help along the way: Xiaohui, Maheshwar, Loïc, Samuel, Alexandre, Pierpaolo, Didier, Joseph, Kenneth, David, Jérôme, and Greg. They all deserve our gratitude.

I can't forget all the partners, customers, and colleagues I work with on a daily basis, not only on my team in Paris but also in Canada, India, the United States, and China. Working with them makes my job exciting.

Finally, I have a special thought for my friends and family, especially Claire, Inès, and Elisabeth.

Christian Ah-Soon

For the last 13 years, I have had opportunities to move to different teams, and each time I have made the most of it. Most of my knowledge and professional satisfaction come from my exchanges with members of these teams: the Region Implementation Group and the Customer Solution Adaption and Customer Adoption and Enablement teams—especially Romaric Sokhan and Matthias Badaire. I have met inspiring individuals among the consultants from the BI War Room; and the developers, documentation, pre-sales, program managers, support engineers, and testers with whom I work every day.

I would also thank all the customers for whom I helped find solutions who keep me connected with the other side of the mirror.

Last, I would like to thank my wife, Stephanie, for her patience; my mother; my aunt; my school friends; my closer friends for their support; and, of course, my two kids, Eliot and Lola.

David François Gonzalez

Because business intelligence products manage very sensitive data, it is critical that each system is properly secured to give only authorized users access to it.

1 Introduction to Security in SAP BusinessObjects Business Intelligence 4.0

To provide a foundation for a conversation on BusinessObjects security, this chapter first briefly covers business intelligence and common security challenges and then introduces SAP BusinessObjects and SAP BusinessObjects Business Intelligence 4.0. Launching from this introduction, it offers a roadmap for this resource on SAP BusinessObjects security and the chapters ahead.

First, we address the underpinnings of all security concerns: the concept of sensitive data and business intelligence.

1.1 Business Intelligence Overview

Data have always been an organizational asset; it is mandatory to control and analyze data to make better decisions and determine strategic directions for any endeavor. It is natural that computers have been used for these purposes. In the mid-1990s, a new term emerged to categorize tools used to analyze and synthesize data in order to assist company governance through better business decision-making: business intelligence. At that time, the different applications were used to query and report business data.

In the years since, companies have continued to generate and store higher volumes of data. New technologies can answer the need for faster and more pervasive data, and adjectives such as big data, on-demand, mobile, and in-memory are used to describe this flexibility.

With this explosion of data, and the evolution of technical hardware, more complex tasks were requested of these tools. The area once covered by business intelligence has become specialized and has broadened to include the following tools, among others:

► Extract Transform Load (ETL) tools to gather data from different sources and prepare them for data warehousing

► Data Quality tools to cleanse data in order to remove redundancy or corrupted entry

► Enterprise Performance Management (EPM) tools to present data through dashboards and show key performance indicators (KPIs)

► Statistical and Predictive Analysis tools to discover hidden relationships in data, thereby providing the basis for making predictions about future events

Another business intelligence evolution is the democratization of its usage. Initially available to only a few, these tools are now available to a greater audience, thanks to easier user interfaces and new deployment modes. Now anyone with access to individual or corporate data can create reports to analyze it.

1.2   System Security Considerations

These reporting tools are intended to be deployed on top of enterprise databases and data warehouses. By nature, they contain enterprise operational data that may be sensitive. In this context, security is a must-have requirement, ensuring that an unauthorized person cannot see data he is not permitted to see, does not perform an action he is not allowed to take, or does not corrupt data he has been able to access.

But the task of securing this environment has become increasingly difficult. Nowadays, the business intelligence administrator who sets out to define system security must consider numerous constraints:

► The different possible data sources

  ► Internal sources: data warehouse, database, ERP software (such as SAP ERP), personal files, and so on

  ► External sources: Web Services, unstructured data, and so on

▶ The different stakeholders and users involved in the BI system

  ▶ System administrators who are responsible for deploying and managing the overall IT framework

  ▶ Database administrators who create accounts and grant access to the database

  ▶ Database designers who design the database schemas and deploy them

  ▶ BI administrators who are responsible for the Business Intelligence platforms

  ▶ Security administrators who guarantee different security aspects such as authentication, authorization, and vulnerability

  ▶ Metadata designers who design the metadata to be exposed through reporting

  ▶ Report designers who create reports used by users

  ▶ End users who consume reports

  Sometimes one stakeholder may assume several or many of these roles.

▶ The legal compliance rules (such as the Sarbanes-Oxley Act) that impose constraints for data traceability, user visibility, and so on

▶ The existing technical environment

  ▶ Authentication and authorization that are already centralized on security systems like SAP NetWeaver BW, Active Directory, or LDAP

  ▶ Deployment choices such as which web server and application server or desktop vs. web deployment

  ▶ Processes such as the validation phases that move content from development to testing and then to production environments

  ▶ Other corporate rules that impose technical choices such as open source vs. proprietary solutions

Remember that the security of the Business Intelligence system must integrate into this existing environment. For example, SAP BusinessObjects Business Intelligence includes different reporting tools, each of which has specific security requirements.

For these reasons, setting the security of a business intelligence system requires a nuanced understanding of the challenges ahead. Before describing the content of the SAP BusinessObjects Business Intelligence solution, let's review SAP BusinessObjects history, which helps explain some of its technical choices and designs.

1.3 A Brief History of Business Objects

The SAP BusinessObjects Business Intelligence portfolio addresses the need for business intelligence tools. Let's trace the history of BI back to its SAP-independent Business Objects roots.

After its creation in 1990, Business Objects launched Skipper SQL 2.0.x, BusinessObjects v3.0, and BusinessObjects v4.0. Its key products were Designer (the metadata design tool used to create universes), BusinessObjects (the ad hoc reporting tool used to create query and analyze data through universes), and Supervisor (the security tool used to manage groups, users and rights). In 1999, BusinessObjects v5.0 was released. It contained the first version of Web Intelligence, the web version of BusinessObjects that provides reporting capability over the web.

Several years later, in 2003, Business Objects acquired Crystal Decisions. After the respective releases of BusinessObjects Enterprise 6 and Crystal v10, these lines were merged in order to release BusinessObjects Enterprise XI R1. 2005 saw the release of BusinessObjects Enterprise XI R2, which integrated each line better and offered the best of each of them. The resulting suite was based on the Crystal Decisions framework and included Web Intelligence, Desktop Intelligence (the new name for BusinessObjects), and Universe Designer.

Several acquisitions by Business Objects in the mid-2000s expanded its portfolio: Medience in 2005 (Data Federator was released as an independent package in XI 3.x), Infommersion, Inc. in 2005 (which brought Xcelsius into Business Objects' offerings), and Cartesis, a provider of financial reporting tools, in 2007.

In October 2007, SAP announced its intent to acquire Business Objects. In 2008, just after the SAP acquisition, XI Release 3 was launched. This release contained the first version of Web Intelligence Rich Client, OLAP Intelligence (an OLAP analysis tool), Live Office, and BI Widget.

In 2010, SAP BusinessObjects Business Intelligence 4.0—shortened to BI 4.0 in the remainder of this book—entered ramp-up. This release brought better integration with SAP products; its ramp-up phase ended in 2011 when the BI 4.0 Support Package 2 (SP2) Patch 5 was declared generally available.

In 2012, the ramp-up phase of BI 4.0 Support Package 3 (SP3), renamed Feature Pack 3 (FP3), ended after two months and the release of its Patch 6. At the same time, the Support Package 4 (SP4)—which is based on FP3 and contains corrections of issues discovered in ramp-up—was released. It has been recommended for general availability, whereas the FP3 branch remains available for ramp-up customers.

The content of this book has been written based on SP4. However, most of the book's content can apply to all releases of BI 4.0, unless explicitly mentioned for some features introduced in FP3/SP4.

1.4   SAP BusinessObjects Business Intelligence 4.0 Review

Let's spend a moment focusing on BI 4.0, which is an Enterprise BI release that contains clients and server components. From the server installer, you have access to the following:

▶ BI Launch Pad (previously known as InfoView), which acts as the end-user portal

▶ Web Intelligence, a query and reporting tool

▶ Analysis, Edition for OLAP, which is the OLAP analysis tool integrated into BI Launch Pad

▶ BI Workspaces, which is used to create dashboards in BI Launch Pad and is considered to be the successor to XI 3.x Dashboard Builder

▶ The BI 4.0 administrative tools Central Management Console (CMC), Central Configuration Manager (CCM), and Upgrade Management Tool

From the client installer, you can access the following:

▶ Web Intelligence, which is the Desktop mode of Web Intelligence

▶ Widgets, which are applications that can permanently show your favorites reports on your desktop

▶ Query as Web Service Designer, which is the tool used to create queries based on Web Services

▶ The new metadata design tool Information Design Tool, which creates universes that take advantage of New Semantic Layer capabilities

▶ The historical metadata design tool Universe Design Tool, which creates universes similar to the XI 3.x ones

▶ The Data Federator Administration Tool, which is used to manage Data Federator services

- The Translation Management Tool, which translates any resource object in different locales
- The Report Conversion Tool, which converts Desktop Intelligence documents into Web Intelligence documents; note that BI 4.0 no longer contains Desktop Intelligence

BI 4.0 belongs to a larger sequence of releases that make up the SAP Business Intelligence suite. Some of these releases contain products that rely on the BI 4.0 server; others work as standalone tools but can also connect to a platform. In both cases, they benefit from all services provided by this platform: security repository, resources storage, and so on.

Figure 1.1 shows how the following releases piece together:

- SAP Crystal Reports 2011: The classic Crystal Reports reporting tool
- SAP Crystal Reports for Enterprise: The successor to Crystal Reports 2011, this new version of Crystal Reports supports the new features introduced in BI 4.0
- Explorer (previously known as Polestar): A data discovery tool that must be installed on the server side and relies on a BI 4.0 server installation
- Live Office: An extension for Microsoft Office that allows you to run queries from these products; it also relies on a BI 4.0 server installation
- Dashboard Design (previously known as Xcelsius): Can be used as a standalone tool but can also connect to a BI 4.0 server installation
- SAP BusinessObjects Analysis, Edition for Microsoft Office: Allows you to analyze and navigate in your multidimensional databases from within Microsoft Excel and PowerPoint
- SAP BusinessObjects Mobile: A mobile application that can be downloaded from the iOS or Android store to display Web Intelligence or Crystal Reports documents; it cannot work as a standalone tool and must connect to a BI 4.0 server installation
- SAP Predictive Analysis: A statistical analysis and data mining solution used to build predictive models and to discover hidden insights and relationships in data, thereby providing the basis for making predictions about future events
- SAP Visual Intelligence: A new analysis product that doesn't yet connect to BI 4.0 but might soon

In addition, BI 4.0 can also take advantage of SAP StreamWork, an on-demand product that allows collaboration between users.

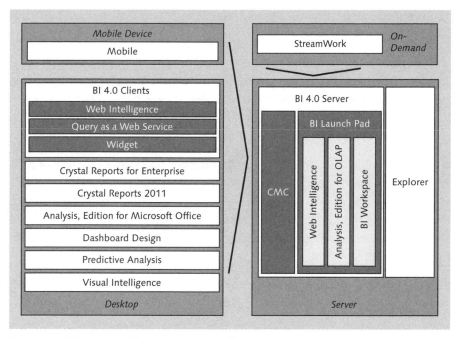

Figure 1.1 SAP BusinessObjects Business Intelligence Suite

1.5 Book Roadmap

This book is intended as a resource for SAP BusinessObjects administrators, security administrators, and universe designers who are tasked with ensuring the security of SAP BusinessObjects data. As a comprehensive guide to keeping an SAP BusinessObjects Business Intelligence system secure, this resource focuses mainly on data and functional security and introduces several products or components, their usage, and corresponding security models, but touches on other important concepts along the way.

Chapter 1 serves as a general introduction to business intelligence, the evolution of Business Objects, and SAP BusinessObjects Business Intelligence 4.0.

Chapter 2 presents a general overview of BI 4.0 architecture and describes security-related architecture concepts. It presents the tool used to administer BI 4.0: the CMC.

Chapter 3 provides an explanation of how users and groups are stored in the Central Management Server (CMS) repository, their properties, and the alias used for external authentication. This chapter then presents how these users can authenticate using different authentication modes and describes how to configure LDAP and Active Directory authentication.

Chapter 4 explains how administrators can use the rights framework to set security rights to users and groups. We define the different concepts attached to this framework and their properties, such as inheritance, owner rights, and access level. The chapter also lists general rights and presents the CMC Security Query and the CMC Relationship Query that can be used to ease rights definitions.

Chapter 5 lists the objects that can be stored in the CMS repository—system objects like users, groups, folders, and connections, or content objects created by reporting tools like reports, dashboards, and analysis. The chapter lists their custom rights and the corresponding impacts if denied. The chapter also enumerates all applications displayed in the CMC: their security model and custom rights, with their impacts if denied.

Chapter 6 reviews the different connection types (relational, OLAP, data sources), covers how to define them, and addresses their different authentication modes.

Chapter 7 presents security (filters, access restrictions, and object access levels) that can be defined for universes created in Universe Design Tool, the historical metadata design tool that is still supported in BI 4.0.

Chapter 8 presents security that can be defined for universes created with Information Design Tool, the new metadata design tool released in BI 4.0. Semantic Layer security brings some new concepts: data security profiles, business security profiles, and user custom attributes.

Chapter 9 addresses how data are filtered during scheduling and publishing. Remember that the ultimate objective of system security and personalization is to make sure that the user receives only the data he is allowed to see.

Chapter 10 covers specificities related to querying data from the SAP NetWeaver BW system. As it can also be used as an external security source, it brings additional workflows in security.

Chapter 11 contains practical recommendations for defining a security model. The security model is quite complex, and some guidelines can be useful to define such a security mode. It also lists all rights to assign in order to run basic workflows and describes how to set up delegated administration.

Finally, **Appendix A** compares security features of universes created with Universe Design Tool and Information Design Tool. It also describes how the security changes when a universe is converted in terms of universe access restrictions, object access levels, CMC rights, and connections.

Now let's turn our attention to the BI 4.0 architecture and the most important security-related architecture concepts that it draws upon.

To understand security of the system, it is important to know some basics about the system architecture, its deployment, and its administration.

2 Administration and Security

The architecture of the BI 4.0 platform, the products and tools that make up the suite, and the various administration workflows are so large that describing them in detail would require a dedicated book. This chapter does not presume to replace such a resource but instead provides insights into some of the concepts about system administration, and security in particular, that are mentioned in the coming chapters.

First we offer an overview of the different components in a BI 4.0 deployment, followed by an explanation of the BI 4.0 installation itself. We cover the different components installed and the parameters you must define at installation time (such as HTTP and CORBA ports and passwords).

Next we tackle the two administration tools—the Central Configuration Manager (CCM) and the Central Management Console (CMC)—and then data storage between the Central Management Server (CMS) repository and the File Repository Server (FRS) file system.

Then we take a look at the role and use of cryptography to encrypt these data and discuss some servers running on the system and the services they host are listed.

Last, we provide an introduction to auditing, which allows you to keep track of user activity on your system.

Note

For more details on the topics covered in this chapter, refer to the SAP BusinessObjects Business Intelligence 4.0 documentation:

▶ Administrator Guide

▶ Installation Guide

The latest versions of these guides can be found at *http://help.sap.com/bobi*.

Let's begin by deconstructing a BI 4.0 deployment into its various components.

2.1 BI 4.0 Deployment

Even if it offers new services and hosts new components, the BI 4.0 architecture relies on the same basis as the XI R2 or XI 3.x architecture.

As shown in Figure 2.1, you can identify two main areas in a BI 4.0 deployment: the server and the client. On the server side, you have the following:

▶ **The corporate data you mean to query**
These include relational databases, multidimensional databases, text files, Web Services, and so on.

▶ **The BI 4.0 server backend—that is, the servers and components you install with the BI 4.0 installer**
These include functional servers used for reporting products (Web Intelligence Processing Server, Crystal Processing Server, Explorer Master Server, and so on) and also administrative servers used to support the system, such as the Central Management Server and File Repository Server.

These servers can be installed and distributed on several machines linked together to make a *cluster*, which allows for load-balancing and fault tolerance.

▶ **The databases used by BI 4.0 servers for their own usage**
These include the CMS repository database, audit, monitoring and version control databases. You can use the ones installed by default or configure the system to use yours.

▶ **The file system used by the File Repository Server to store resources created with BI 4.0 reporting tools and shared in the BI 4.0 repository**
Examples of such resources are reports and universes.

▶ **The external authentication system, if you use one central system across your organization to keep users and authentications**
The central system might be SAP NetWeaver BW, LDAP, Active Directory, and so on.

▶ **The web applications server frontend**
These are the frontend hosts application servers where BI 4.0 web applications have been deployed.

The client side gathers the following different methods for users to access BI 4.0 server capability:

▶ **Thin clients**
These are web applications that are accessed through browser (BI Launch Pad, CMC, Explorer, and so on) and whose processing is done on the server side.

▶ **Thick clients**
These are deployed on machines such as Web Intelligence (Desktop deployment), Crystal Reports 2011, Crystal Reports For Enterprise, Dashboard Design, Universe Design Tool, and Information Design Tool.

▶ **Mobile devices (iOS or Android) where a BI Mobile product has been installed**
These can also connect to the BI 4.0 server for access to documents and reports saved in the repository.

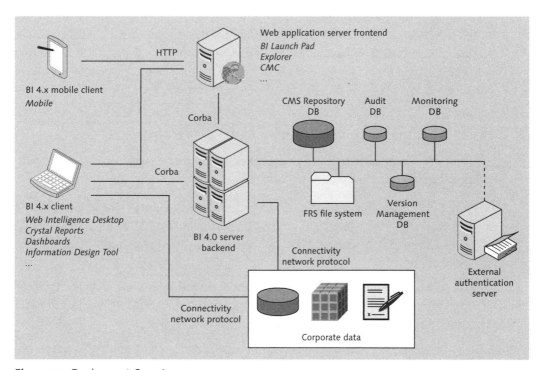

Figure 2.1 Deployment Overview

The options for a BI 4.0 installation are more numerous. Let's explore them now.

2.2 BI 4.0 Installation

For the BI 4.0 platform, you have two installers. One installer is for the BI servers and is available on Windows and UNIX platforms. This installer can run only on 64-bit platforms. The other installer is for the BI client tools and is only available on Windows platforms. This installer can run on 32-bit or 64-bit platforms.

On Windows, even if you can install the BI 4.0 client and server tools on the same machine, this deployment is not recommended on production systems and should be reserved for a development or a sandbox machine for the following reasons:

▶ If you have to patch your system, you have to patch the client and the server.

▶ For database connectivity that has both 32-bit and 64-bit drivers, the 32-bit drivers used by the client tools can be loaded by the server processes that should load only 64-bit drivers.

On UNIX, you can install the BI 4.0 server on the same computer as an XI 3.x installation but with different accounts: one account for the BI 4.0 installation and one for the XI 3.x. On Windows, installation of XI 3.x and BI 4.0 servers on the same machine is not supported.

2.2.1 Components Installed with BI 4.0 Server Installer

During the server installation, you are asked to provide parameters for some components installed during the installation:

▶ The Server Intelligence Agent (SIA) node name and port ("6410" by default): The SIA is a server used to start the BI 4.0 system and monitor the other servers. The SIA port can be changed later in the CCM on Windows, but its name cannot be changed.

▶ The CMS port and cluster key: As described in Section 2.4, the CMS is an important server in the system. Among other tasks, it is responsible for security and resource access.

   ▶ The port is the CORBA port used by this server. It is "6400" by default, but you can modify it in the installer or after the installation in the CCM or CMC.

   ▶ The cluster key is used to encrypt and decrypt the cryptographic keys that encrypt data in the BI 4.0 repository. During installation, you need to define a master key. If you are installing the first node, this cluster key becomes the master key. If later you plan to add another machine with another CMS to your cluster, you must provide the same master key so this new machine can decrypt the cryptographic keys of the existing cluster and be added to the cluster. You can modify this cluster key in the CCM (see Section 2.3).

▶ Administrator password: In the CMS repository, the installer creates the Administrator user that will connect to the system once it is started; you must define his password during installation. Because this user has super-privileges, you must provide a robust password and keep it safe.

▶ The CMS database: The CMS server requires a database to save its data. By default, the Windows installer embeds the SQL Server 2008 Express database and the UNIX installer embeds an IBM DB2 Workgroup 9.7 database. You can select to install and configure this database and use it for the CMS database. If you choose this option, consider these points:

  ▶ On Windows, you need to enter passwords for two accounts: the database administrator (its name is `sa` and cannot be changed) and one for the instance `BOE140` dedicated to the BI 4.0 system. By default, its name is `boeuser` but it can be changed.

  ▶ On UNIX, the name of the data source is `BOE14`.

If you use another database, you need to provide the parameters to access to this database and the name and password for the account used for BI 4.0 in this database. This account must have the rights to create, edit, and drop tables.

▶ Audit database: In BI 4.0, audit is no longer an optional component. It is part of the installation and is configured during the installation workflow. Supported databases for the audit database are the same as those supported by the CMS database. If you install the database embedded by the installer, then the audit database is installed in it as well. On Windows, on the embedded SQL Server 2008 Express database, the name of this instance in the database is `BOE140_AUDIT`. On UNIX, on the embedded DB2 database, the name of this instance is `AUDBOE14`.

If for the audit you select another database, you need to provide parameters to access to this database and the name and password for the account used for BI 4.0 in this database. This account must have the rights to create, edit, and drop tables.

The audit database can be modified after the installation in the CMC. Especially for performance reasons, you may install the audit database in a different database than the one used for the CMS repository.

▶ Version management: BI 4.0 supports a version control system. This requires a Subversion database that is installed and configured during installation. After the installation, you can configure and use another system in the CMC, but, at installation time, you need to define two things:

  ▶ A port for Subversion database ("3690" by default)

  ▶ A password for the LCM account created in Subversion for BI 4.0

▶ SAP Solution Manager (SM) and Introscope Enterprise Manager (IEM) are two frameworks used to analyze, monitor, and troubleshoot BI 4.0 products.

  ▶ SM is a framework released by SAP to monitor and troubleshoot other SAP products. It must be installed on a dedicated machine. To retrieve metrics, SM uses a Solution Management Diagnostic (SMD) agent that can trace only components written in C++. You must install this agent independently on the BI 4.0 server.

  ▶ IEM is a third-party application used to trace components written in Java, such as Adaptive Processing Server. IEM must be installed on another server and relies on an Introscope Java agent, installed by default with BI 4.0 server. IEM can also retrieve metrics sent by the Solution Management Diagnostic agent.

As of BI 4.0, you can integrate your server installation into these frameworks. At BI 4.0 installation time, you can define the ports used by the SMD agent installed on your BI 4.0 server and the host name and port of the IEM server, so the two agents can push their metrics to IEM. These parameters are saved in configuration files that you can modify after the installation in the CMC. SM can be used to connect to IEM, keep track of what has been monitored, and create reports on the system activity.

In addition, starting with BI 4.0, the installer also installs a Derby database used for monitoring, although it is not displayed during installation. You can later modify this database used by monitoring in the CMC.

Make sure you keep all the parameters and passwords you enter during the installation safe for two reasons:

▶ You may have to reuse them later.

▶ They must remain confidential because they provide direct access to the system and give super-privileges to the user.

2.2.2 BI 4.0 Server Installation Workflow

On Windows, you need to run the BI 4.0 server installer with a local administrator account. Once it's installed, you can run the BI 4.0 server with any other local or domain administrator account.

On UNIX, you can perform the installation as `root` or a simple user, but it is recommended that you install as simple user:

1. Launch the setup (`setup.exe` on Windows or `setup.sh` on UNIX).

2. Select the language of the installation.

3. The installer performs checks to validate that some prerequisites have been met, as shown in Figure 2.2:

   ▶ Other products like Information Platform Services (IPS of Data Services), SAP Crystal Reports Server, or a previous version of BI 4.0 are not installed (except for a patch installation).

   ▶ You have the rights to perform the installation: local administrator rights on Windows or default user rights on UNIX.

   ▶ On Windows: Windows .NET Framework 3.5 Service Pack 1 and Windows installation program 4.5 are installed.

   ▶ On Windows: No reboot is requested because of files locked by another application.

   ▶ On UNIX: Enough disk space is available in the temporary directory.

   ▶ You can install the default local CMS database and all the drivers needed to access this CMS database.

   ▶ The machine runs on a supported 64-bit operating system.

In the event of a missing prerequisite, make the requested changes and then retry the installation or just go back and forward in the installer to re-launch the prerequisite checks.

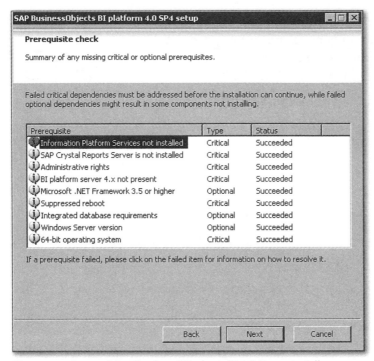

Figure 2.2   Prerequisite Check on Windows BI 4.0 Server Installer

4. Read and accept the license agreement.

5. Enter your name, your organization, and the product keycode.

6. Select the language packs to install.

7. Select the install type:

   ▶ Full: To install all components from the installer

   ▶ Custom/expand: To select the components to install

   ▶ Web Tier: To install only web applications server frontend

   The remainder of this workflow is considered a custom installation, since it covers all components to install for the BI 4.0 server and the databases it requires.

8. Enter the destination folder.

9. Select the components to install. You can check the needed disk space by clicking the DISK COSTING button.

10. If, in the previous step, you selected the CMS from among the components to install, you must choose either to start a new BI 4.0 deployment or to expand an existing one. In the latter case, your installation becomes a node joining onto the existing cluster.

11. Select whether to install the default Apache Tomcat web application server now or later.

12. Select whether you want to use the default Subversion database for Version Management or another existing version control system.

13. Enter the SIA node name and its port.

14. If you want to install a CMS and create a new cluster:

    ▶ Enter the port for the CMS server.

    ▶ Define the Administrator account password and the CMS cluster key, as shown in Figure 2.3. If these keys are not strong enough, you'll receive an error message that will prevent you from moving forward.

    ▶ Choose to use the default database embedded with the installer or your own database.

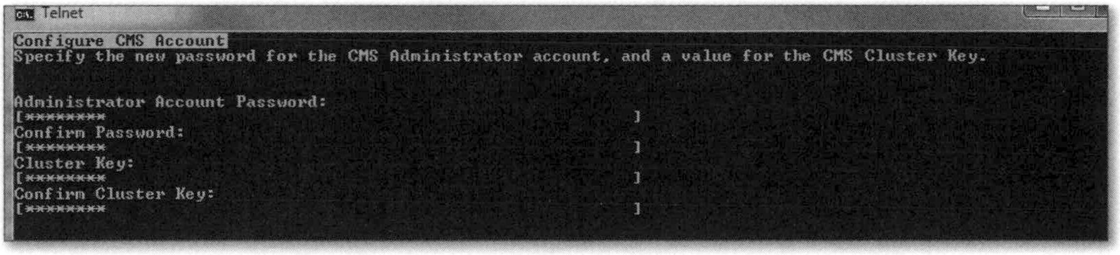

Figure 2.3 Administrator Password and CMS Cluster Key on UNIX BI 4.0 Server Installer

To use the default database, you need to define the database administrative and BI 4.0 accounts (username and password).

If you have chosen to use your own database, you must provide database parameters (middleware and account) for both the CMS repository and Auditing databases.

15. If you have decided to extend a cluster instead of creating a new one, you need to provide some parameters that grant you access to this cluster:

> ▶ The name and the port of the system to join

> ▶ The password of the Administrator account of the cluster

> ▶ The cluster key of this cluster

16. If you have selected to install the default Apache Tomcat web application server, you need to define the ports of the default web application server.

17. If you have selected to install Web Application Container Server (WACS) or RESTful Web Services, you must define the port to use.

18. If you have selected to install and use the default Subversion repository for Version Management, you need to define the port and the password for this repository, as shown in Figure 2.4.

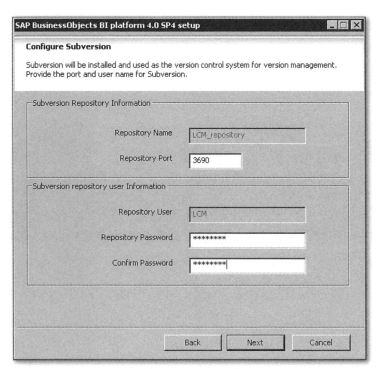

Figure 2.4 Subversion Configuration on Windows BI 4.0 Server Installer

19. Select whether to configure the SMD agent. If you decide to configure it, you need to enter the name of the machine where the SMD agent is running and its communication port.

20. Select whether to configure integration with Introscope Enterprise Manager. If you choose to configure it, you need to enter the name of the machine where the Introscope Enterprise Manager is running and its communication port.

21. Click the START INSTALLATION button.

If you opt to run a full installation, these are the main differences compared to the custom installation:

▶ All components are selected for installation.

▶ You can install only a new cluster. You do not have the option to join an existing cluster.

▶ Audit is installed.

▶ Subversion is installed and configured.

If you choose to install the default embedded Apache Tomcat, then it is installed and the web applications are deployed on it.

If you select to install only Web Tier, then only the binaries and resources for web applications are actually installed. If you opt to use your own application server, then, after the installation, you must run Wdeploy to generate and deploy the web applications on it.

2.2.3 BI Platform Client Tools

The BI 4.0 client tools installer is available only on Windows. You can run it using any local or domain administrator.

The workflow is straightforward, so we do not document it in this chapter. By default, when you run the full install, you install the following products and tools:

▶ Business View Manager

▶ Data Federation Administration Tool

▶ Information Design Tool

▶ Query as a Web Service Designer

▶ Report Conversion Tool

▶ Translation Management Tool

▶ Universe Design Tool

- Web Intelligence Rich Client
- Widgets

Once these client tools are installed, you can connect to the BI 4.0 server if it is also installed and started.

2.2.4 Other BI 4.0 Suite Installers

In addition to the two BI 4.0 installers, other BI 4.0 suite products require their own installers for installation.

On the server side, you can run the SAP Explorer installer. This installer must be run on the same machine as your BI 4.0 server installation.

Other installers are client tools installers that can be run either on the same machine as the one where client tools are installed or on another one:

- SAP Crystal Reports 2011
- SAP Crystal For Enterprise
- SAP BusinessObjects Dashboard Design
- SAP BusinessObjects Analysis, Edition for Microsoft Office
- SAP Predictive Analysis
- SAP Visual Intelligence

To install SAP Mobile, you need to access the corresponding online stores to download and install it on your mobile device.

2.3 Administration Tools

When you install the BI 4.0 server products, you can install three desktop tools:

- Wdeploy: This tool is used to deploy BI 4.0 web applications on web application servers.
- Upgrade Management Tool: This tool allows you to upgrade the XI R2 or XI 3.x CMS repository to BI 4.0. On Windows, you can use it for full or incremental upgrade. Only full upgrade is supported on UNIX.
- Central Configuration Manager (CCM): This tool allows you to manage the BI 4.0 services and to start and stop the SIA. It is available only on Windows.

If you have deployed the web applications, you have access to the Central Management Console (CMC), which is a web application where you can manage the system resources. This section covers the CCM and the CMC because they are the two main administration tools.

2.3.1 Central Configuration Manager (CCM)

On Windows, the CCM tool allows you to define some global parameters and to start and stop the BI 4.0 system.

As with other tools installed on your server, you can start it from START • PROGRAMS • SAP BUSINESSOBJECTS BI PLATFORM 4.0 • SAP BUSINESSOBJECTS BI PLATFORM, using the CENTRAL CONFIGURATION MANAGER.

The CCM is used to perform some critical administrative tasks:

▶ To start and stop the SIA, or the default Apache Tomcat installed with the installer

▶ To modify three cluster parameters, as shown in Figure 2.5:

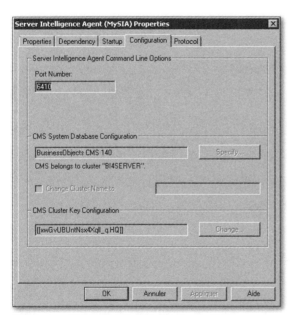

Figure 2.5 SIA Properties Dialog Box in CCM

▶ The SIA port

▶ The cluster name

▶ The cluster key

Recall that the CCM tool is not available on UNIX, so you need to use the following commands to perform the same tasks there:

▶ `startservers`: Starts the system and all BI 4.0 servers, especially the SIA

▶ `stopservers`: Stops the system

▶ `cmsdbsetup.sh`: Configures the CMS repository, changes cluster name, changes cluster key, and reinitializes the CMS repository

▶ `ccm.sh`: Modifies server parameters (start, stop, enable, disable, and so on)

▶ `db2startup.sh`: Starts the default DB2 database used for the CMS repository

▶ `db2shutdown.sh`: Stops the default DB2 database used for the CMS repository

▶ `tomcatstartup.sh`: Starts the default Apache Tomcat web application server installed by the BI 4.0 server installer

▶ `tomcatshutdown.sh`: Stops the default Apache Tomcat web application server installed by the BI 4.0 server installer

These commands are located in the *<INSTALLDIR>/sap_bobj/* directory, where *<INSTALLDIR>* is the directory where you have installed the BI 4.0 server.

2.3.2 Central Management Console (CMC)

The CMC is a web-based tool used to perform most administrative tasks in the CMS repository:

▶ Create and organize users and groups

▶ Configure system authentication

▶ Define and assign security rights and access levels

▶ Enter license keys and review what they cover

▶ Manage resources, their versions and their lifecycle

▶ Start and stop system servers

▶ Audit the system

▶ Monitor the system

▶ Use the resource lifecycle

By default, the URL for the CMC is *http://<servername>:<port>/BOE/CMC*.

After the system installation and start, you can log on to the CMC using the Administrator account and the password you set during installation, as described in Section 2.2.1.

The CMC is organized in tabs; each tab is dedicated to a specific object type or to a specific task. To access a tab, you can:

▶ Click the vertical tab in the left side of the CMC.

▶ Select the area in the dropdown list in the CMC top left.

▶ From the HOME tab, click the link with the name of the tab to open.

Once the tab is open, you can perform your tasks in that tab.

In the next chapters, you are often requested to go in the CMC to perform some security tasks.

2.4   CMS Repository and File Repository Server

During the installation, you need to provide parameters for the CMS repository. With the File Repository Server (FRS) file system, this CMS repository is the location where the BI 4.0 system stores the data it needs. This section details the differences between the InfoObjects saved in the CMS repository and the physical objects saved in the FRS file system, and how InfoObjects, the CMS repository, and the FRS file system are organized.

2.4.1   InfoObjects and Physical Files

The CMS is in fact the name of a process running on the server side. This server (or process) is one of the most important because it takes care of authentication, security rights, access to resources, load-balancing, and other important tasks. The CMS needs to manage different data for the smooth running of the system: both BI resources and also administrative objects such users and servers.

To store these data, the CMS relies on two locations:

▶ A database repository, which by extension is called the *CMS repository*

▶ A file system, for physical files (usually BI resources such as documents and universes)

In the CMS repository, objects are stored as InfoObjects. These are generic models — users, groups, applications, connections, servers, reports, and so on — used to store data. This generic model also enforces a generic security model. Chapter 3 describes the CMS in more detail.

Some InfoObjects are also attached to physical files, as is the case for documents and universes. These physical files are stored in the FRS, but that have also a corresponding InfoObject in the CMS repository that references them.

For example, when you share a Web Intelligence document in the system repository, the system saves the document in the FRS file system and creates an InfoObject that contains its name in the CMS repository, the folder where it is stored, the universe or connection it references, and the name and path of this document in the FRS file system.

In contrast, when you create a connection in the system, all data defining this connection are saved in the InfoObject created for this connection.

2.4.2 InfoObject Structure

An InfoObject is a set of parameters and values. Here are some important parameters:

▶ SI_NAME: The name of the InfoObject. Its main purpose is for the end user to understand. This name is not used by the BI 4.0 system.

▶ SI_ID: The ID of the InfoObject in a cluster. In the same cluster, all objects are linked with this ID, as it is guaranteed to be unique in a cluster.

▶ SI_CUID: The InfoObject Cluster Unique Identifiers. When is it generated, this CUID is statistically unique in the world. The CUID is used each time you want to promote some InfoObjects from one system to another. During a promotion, the BI 4.0 system compares only the CUID and never the ID.

▶ SI_PATH: If the InfoObject is attached to a physical file in the FRS, then this parameter is used for the folder of this object in the FRS.

▶ SI_FILE1: If the InfoObject is attached to a physical file in the FRS, then this parameter is used for this file name in the FRS.

▶ SI_PARENTID: All InfoObjects have one and only one parent, defined in this field.

▶ SI_KIND: This is a tag that identifies the object type: "Webi," "User," "Folder," and so on.

▶ SI_UNIVERSEID: If the InfoObject is a document based on a universe, then this parameter is the SI_ID of this universe.

▶ SI_DATACONNECTIONID: If the InfoObject is a document or a universe based on a connection, then this parameter is the SI_ID of this connection.

> **Note**
>
> User InfoObjects can belong to different groups (see Chapter 3, Section 3.2.3). In this case, the relationships between users and groups are not stored through SI_PARENTID field but through the SI_USERGROUPS field.

Figure 2.6 shows an example where a Web Intelligence document, a universe, and a connection are linked in the CMS repository. The Web Intelligence document and the universe InfoObjects are also linked to the corresponding files saved in the FRS file system. Section 2.4.4 describes the FRS file system in greater detail.

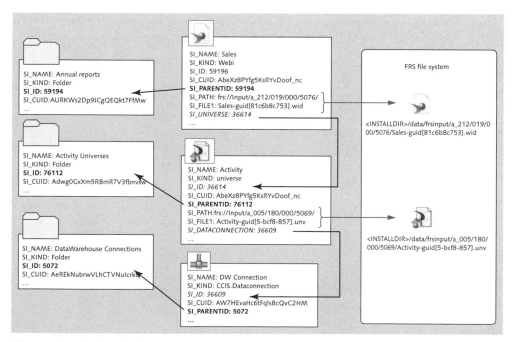

Figure 2.6 InfoObject Links in CMS Repository

In the CMC, you can get some of these InfoObjects parameters by following these steps:

1. Depending on the object type, go to the corresponding CMC tab: Universes, Connections, Users and groups, etc.

2. Use the left pane to navigate in the tree structure and access the object.

3. In the right pane, select the object.

4. In the toolbar, click the Manage the object properties button or right-click this object and in the contextual menu, select Properties to open the Properties dialog box.

5. In this dialog box, the following parameters are displayed, as shown in Figure 2.7:

   ▶ The InfoObject ID and CUID are displayed in the ID, CUID text field.

   ▶ If the InfoObject has an associated object located in the file system, its path is displayed in the File Name text field.

These parameters are read-only and cannot be modified. The dialog box displays other parameters depending on the object type.

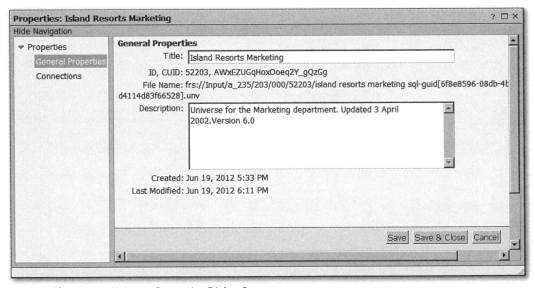

Figure 2.7 Universe Properties Dialog Box

2.4.3 CMS Database Structure

Some the information can be found in the CMC by right-clicking the different InfoObjects, but only the SI_NAME, ID, or the CUID. However, all this information is in the CMS database.

When the installer sets up the CMS repository at install time, it creates the following seven tables used to store all data:

▶ CMS_VersionInfo: This table contains only the version of the BI system.

▶ CMS_InfoObjects7: This is the main table in the repository because it contains all InfoObjects, one InfoObject being stored in each row. In the columns, the different InfoObject parameters (as described in Section 2.4.2) are stored: ObjectID, ParentID, TypeID, SI_CUID, and ObjName. When they are stored in this table, sensitive parameters are encrypted. Section 2.5 discusses encryption in more detail.

▶ CMS_Aliases7: This table maps user aliases to their corresponding users (Chapter 3, Section 3.5 covers aliases and mapped users in detail). Indeed, a user may authenticate to different system repositories, and aliases are created for this user for each different authentication mode. When the user logs on to the system, the CMS must identify the user corresponding to the alias he uses to log on. These mappings are stored in a separate table to enable fast access and reduce logon time.

▶ CMS_IdNumbers7: This small table keeps track of an index used to generate unique object ID (SI_ID) in the cluster. When a new object is created in the cluster, the system takes this index as a reference to assign it an ID and updates it when needed.

▶ CMS_RELATIONS7: This table is used to store relationships between InfoObjects.

▶ CMS_Sessions7: This table stores sessions to the system. When a user logs on, a row is created and it is deleted when the user logs off.

▶ CMS_LOCKS7: This table is used internally by the system for database locking and table management.

> **Warning!**
>
> We recommend that you not modify these tables directly by yourself in the database because you risk corrupting them.

The CMS database can be modified only by BI 4.0 tools, such as the CMC. You can also use the BI 4.0 software development kit (SDK) to access these data. In this case, some virtual tables wrap these tables and expose easier interfaces to them:

▶ `CI_InfoObjects`: This virtual table contains documents, folders, categories, inboxes, etc.

▶ `CI_APPOBJECTS`: This virtual table contains universes, connections, etc.

▶ `CI_SYSTEMOBJECTS`: This virtual table contains system objects, such as users, user groups, servers, events, etc.

2.4.4 FRS File System

In the CMS repository, the system stores data about the objects it handles. However, the BI resources themselves are not stored in the CMS repository but in a file system.

This file system is created at the time of installation. It is by default located on the first machine created in the cluster, although you can change it later in FRS properties in the CMC. To have functional disk accesses, we recommend that you use the Storage Area Network (SAN) or Network Attached Storage (NAS) file system storage. Such systems also provide a backup mechanism.

In this file system, two main folders are created:

▶ Input folders: These folders are used to store file versions of the resources (documents, reports, universes, etc.) saved in the CMS repository.

▶ Output folders: These folders are used to store the output of scheduled documents. If your users schedule a lot of documents, instances are saved here. Make sure you have enough disk space or limit the scheduling capabilities of your users.

In the BI 4.0 backend, two servers are running in order to return objects of these two folders when they are requested. These two servers in fact make up the FRS.

If an InfoObject in the CMS is linked to a file in the FRS file system, then you can see this file path in the CMC, in the object's properties, as shown in Figure 2.7. This file path is saved in the `SI_PATH` and `SI_FILE1` parameters of the InfoObject.

We don't recommend that you modify these files because the FRS content must remain synchronized with the CMS repository. If needed, the Repository Diagnostic Tool can be used to find and fix inconsistencies between CMS repository and FRS file system.

2.5 Cryptography

The BI 4.0 platform uses cryptography to encrypt some parameters of InfoObjects saved in the CMS database (such as user credentials, enterprise passwords, and connection parameters) or some files saved in the FRS file system (such as Crystal Reports documents). Section 2.4 reviewed these files and repositories.

In XI R2/XI 3.x, this encryption is done with a cryptographic key and without the option to modify it. In BI 4.0, you can now revoke this key and generate a new one. Furthermore, you must also enter another key (the cluster key), which is used to encrypt this cryptographic key. Let's explore both options further.

2.5.1 Cluster Key

The CMS cluster key is used to encrypt and decrypt the cryptographic keys that, in turn, are used to encrypt sensitive data saved in the system. You must enter this key when you install and create a first node in the cluster, as shown in Figure 2.8.

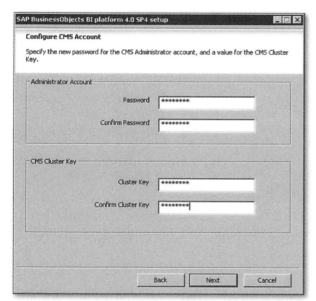

Figure 2.8 Administrator Password and CMS Cluster Key on Windows

If you are installing more than one CMS for a cluster, you must enter the exact same value in the CMS cluster key for all the CMS databases; otherwise, the CMS will not start. When CMS starts, it will try to use the CMS cluster key to decrypt the cryptographic keys (the ones in the CMC) to read the different InfoObjects in CMS database, as some objects in the CMS database are encrypted.

This cluster key is encrypted and stored locally on all machines of the cluster. To change this cluster key, stop all machines to modify it on all machines.

On machines running on Windows, use CCM to modify this cluster key by following these steps:

1. Start CCM.

2. Right-click the SERVER INTELLIGENCE AGENT line and, in the contextual menu, select STOP to stop it.

3. Once it has stopped, right-click the SERVER INTELLIGENCE AGENT line and, in the contextual menu, select PROPERTIES to open the SERVER INTELLIGENCE AGENT PROPERTIES dialog box.

4. Click the CONFIGURATION tab. In the CMS CLUSTER KEY CONFIGURATION section, click the CHANGE button to open the CHANGE CLUSTER KEY dialog box, as shown in Figure 2.9.

5. In this dialog box, you can either automatically generate a random key by clicking the GENERATE checkbox or explicitly type in the cluster key.

6. Click OK to close the dialog box and change the cluster key.

7. Click OK to close the SERVER INTELLIGENCE AGENT PROPERTIES dialog box.

8. Right-click the SERVER INTELLIGENCE AGENT and, in the contextual menu, select START to restart it.

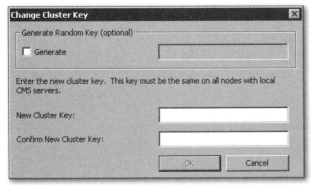

Figure 2.9 Change Cluster Key Panel for Modifying SIA Properties

On machines running on UNIX, use the `cmsdbsetup.sh` command to change this cluster key.

2.5.2 Cryptographic Key

In order to prevent unauthorized data access and data corruption, the system uses a cryptographic key to encrypt the sensitive data it stores. The components that make this encryption framework (encryption libraries and engines) are installed by default on each BI platform deployment.

In order to manage cryptographic key, a new tab (CRYPTOGRAPHIC KEYS) has been introduced in the CMC in BI 4.0. By default, only users in the "Cryptographic Officers" group and the Administrator are allowed to access and open this tab. Management of these keys can be done on a live system, without having to stop it, but modifying the cluster key in the CCM requires stopping the system.

Cryptographic Key States

Figure 2.10 shows the different states a cryptographic key can have.

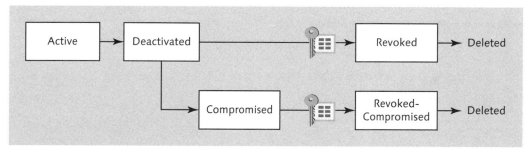

Figure 2.10 Cryptographic Key States

These states are described next:

- *Active*: You can have only one active key at a time in the system. That active key is the one used to encrypt new objects created on the system as needed. It is also used to decrypt the objects it previously encrypted.

- *Deactivated*: When you create a new key, this new key automatically becomes the new active key, and the previous active key is deactivated. The latter is still used to decrypt the objects it has encrypted, but only the new active key is used to encrypt new objects. Once a key is deactivated, you can revoke it or mark it as compromised.

▶ *Revoked*: When you revoke a deactivated key, you re-encrypt objects encrypted by this key with the current active key. Once the key is in this revoked state, objects are no longer encrypted with it and you can delete it.

▶ *Compromised*: This state is more a label to add to a deactivated key. It helps you keep track of the keys that have been deactivated and need to be revoked later. A compromised key is still used to decrypt the objects it has encrypted, but only the new active key is used to encrypt new objects. Once a key is compromised, you can only revoke it. After a key is marked as compromised, the CMC prompts you to revoke it immediately and re-encrypt the objects it has encrypted.

▶ *Revoked-Compromised*: When you revoke a compromised key, you re-encrypt objects encrypted by this key with the current active key. Once a key is in revoked-compromised state, objects in the CMS repository cluster are no longer encrypted with it, and you can delete it.

It is not possible to re-active a deactivated, compromised, or revoked key.

Viewing Encrypted Objects

To view objects encrypted by a key, follow these steps:

1. In the CMC, go to the CRYPTOGRAPHIC KEYS tab.

2. Select a key and right-click it.

3. In the contextual menu, use PROPERTIES to open the PROPERTIES dialog box.

In this dialog box, navigate to the PROPERTIES • OBJECTS LIST section; the objects encrypted by this key are listed in the right pane, as shown in Figure 2.11.

Creating a New Cryptographic Keys

To create a new active key and deactivate the previous active one, follow these steps:

1. In the CMC, go to the CRYPTOGRAPHIC KEYS tab.

2. In the toolbar, right-click the CREATE A NEW CRYPTOGRAPHIC KEY button or select the active key, and, in the contextual menu, select NEW • CRYPTOGRAPHIC KEY.

3. In the CREATE NEW CRYPTOGRAPHIC KEY dialog box, click the CONTINUE button.

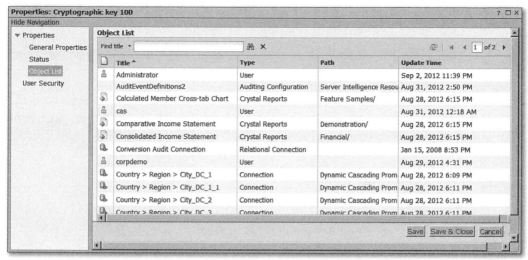

Figure 2.11 List of Objects Encrypted by a Key

4. In the NAME text field, enter a name for the new key.

5. Click OK to close the dialog box and create the new key. This new key has the ACTIVE status in the STATUS column, whereas the old one has the DEACTIVATED status, as shown in Figure 2.12.

Figure 2.12 Active and Deactivated Cryptographic Keys

Setting a Deactivated Cryptographic Key as Compromised

To mark a deactivated key as compromised, follow these steps:

1. In the CMC, go to the CRYPTOGRAPHIC KEYS tab.

2. In the list of keys, select a deactivated key.

3. Right-click it and, in the contextual menu, select MARK AS COMPROMISED.

4. In the MARK AS COMPROMISED dialog box, click the CONTINUE button.

5. When you are asked whether objects must be re-encrypted, click No in order to keep the key marked as compromised and not revoke the key.

The dialog box closes and, in the list of keys, the key now appears with the COMPROMISED status.

If you had answered YES when you were asked to re-encrypt objects, then the objects would have been re-encrypted with the active key, and the key would be be in REVOKED-COMPROMISED status.

Revoking a Cryptographic Key

To revoke a deactivated or compromised key, follow these steps:

1. In the CMC, go to the CRYPTOGRAPHIC KEYS tab.

2. In the list of keys, select a compromised or deactivated key.

3. Right-click it and, in the contextual menu, select REVOKE.

4. In the REVOKE dialog box, click the CONTINUE button to close the dialog box and start the re-encryption.

5. While the re-encryption is processing, the key appears with the COMPROMISED: RE-ENCRYPTION IN PROCESS or DEACTIVATED: RE-ENCRYPTION IN PROCESS status depending on its previous status.

6. Click the REFRESH button when the re-encryption is over. The key appears with REVOKED-COMPROMISED or REVOKED status.

7. Right-click the key and, in the contextual menu, use DELETE to delete it.

2.6   BI 4.0 Servers

With the CMC, you can list the different servers enabled and started on the machines that make up your cluster. As some of these servers are mentioned in the remainder of this book, we describe them here, giving particular attention to the Adaptive Job Server and Adaptive Processing Server.

After you have started the system with the CCM on Windows or the `startserver` command on UNIX, as described in Section 2.3, the Server Intelligence Agent is responsible for starting the different servers that enforce the BI 4.0 backend layer.

Table 2.1 lists some of these servers among the default 20 servers running on your system (that is, 16 servers for BI 4.0 and 4 servers for Explorer).

These servers are started and stopped by the Server Intelligence Agent, which also monitors them and restarts them as necessary. The SIA itself is not listed in the list of servers listed in the CMC, but it can be started from the CCM on Windows or from the `start.sh` or `stop.sh` commands on UNIX.

Server Name	Description
AdaptiveJobServer	This server, which we call Job Server throughout the rest of this book, is used to perform most scheduling actions. It hosts several services described; some services are described in Section 2.6.1.
AdaptiveProcessingServer	This server hosts multiple services. This server has assumed more importance in BI 4.0 since it manages more than 20 services; some are described in Section 2.6.2.
CentralManagementServer	This is the most important server of your BI 4.0 system. This server manages the other servers, users' sessions, and security concepts like authorization and authentication. Having at least one CMS per cluster is mandatory. If your cluster contains several machines, you can add one additional CMS per machine.
ConnectionServer	This server manages access to relational databases. It is the server component equivalent of the Connection Server library.
CrystalReportsProcessing-Server	This server is used for Crystal Reports documents workflows.
ExplorerMasterServer	This server is used by Explorer. It manages other servers used for Explorer and administrates information spaces.
InputFileRepository	This server is used to access the files saved on file system and attached to the InfoObject saved in the CMS repository, as described in Section 2.4.4.
OutputFileRepository	This server is used to access the files saved on file system and that are the results of scheduled objects (documents, LCMBIAR, etc.) as described in Section 2.4.4.
WebiProcessingServer	This server is used for Web Intelligence documents workflows.

Table 2.1 Some BI 4.0 Servers Listed in the CMC

Of these servers, two servers are generic and host several services of BI 4.0 platform: the Adaptive Job Server and Adaptive Processing Server.

2.6.1 Adaptive Job Server

The Adaptive Job Server is the server that hosts all services for scheduling jobs; some of these services are listed in Table 2.2.

Service Name	Description
Authentication Update Scheduling Service	Used to update external users and groups from SAP NetWeaver BW, LDAP, or Active Directory (see Chapter 3 for more details)
Users and Groups Import Scheduling Service	Used to import users and groups through a CSV file (see Chapter 3, Section 3.3.4 for more details)
Visual Difference Scheduling Service	Used to schedule comparison through Visual Difference (see Chapter 5, Section 5.18 for more details)
Web Intelligence Scheduling Service	Used to schedule Web Intelligence documents

Table 2.2 Some Services Hosted by the Adaptive Job Server

To get the list of Adaptive Job Server services started on your system, follow these steps:

1. Go to the SERVERS tab in the CMC.

2. In the left pane, select SERVERS LIST to display the list of servers.

3. In the right pane, in the list of servers, locate the Adaptative Job Server, displayed as <MachineName>.ADAPTIVEJOBSERVER.

4. Right-click it and, in the contextual menu, select EDIT COMMON SERVICES to open the EDIT COMMON SERVICES dialog box, which contains the services started on your system in the AVAILABLE SERVICES list, as shown in Figure 2.13.

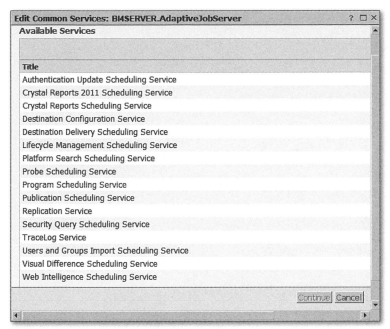

Figure 2.13 Services in the Adaptive Job Server

2.6.2 Adaptive Processing Server

In contrast to the Adaptive Job Server, the Adaptive Processing Server is a server that hosts most services of the BI 4.0 system used to process users and internal requests.

Table 2.3 details some of these services among those supported by the Adaptive Processing Server.

Service Name	Description
Data Federation Service	Used for Data Federation data source and multi-source universe
DSL Bridge Service	Used for New Semantic Layer (see Chapter 8)
Lifecycle Management Service	Used for Promotion Management (see Chapter 5, Section 5.13)
Monitoring Service	Used for monitoring

Table 2.3 Some Services Hosted by the Adaptive Processing Server

Service Name	Description
Publishing Service	Used for publication (see Chapter 9, Section 9.3)
Rebean Service	Used by Web Intelligence (see Chapter 5, Section 5.19)
Security Token Service	Used for SAP authentication for user impersonification (see Chapter 10, Section 10.6)
Translation Service	User for Translation Management Tool

Table 2.3 Some Services Hosted by the Adaptive Processing Server (Cont.)

To get the list of Adaptive Processing Server services started on your system, follow the same steps as for Adaptive Job Server, as outlined in see Section 2.6.1, but for the <MachineName>.ADAPTIVEPROCESSINGSERVER.

> **Note**
>
> Because the Adaptive Processing Server hosts many services, we recommend that you duplicate it and assign some to specific tasks in order to balance the services among different servers to avoid performance issues and bottlenecks.

2.7 Auditing

As opposed to monitoring, which gives you the current status of the system from global metrics point of view (memory usage, number of open sessions, and so on), auditing lets you record your system activity, mainly from a functional point of view.

Auditing records actions initiated by users that log on to your system. From this recorded history, auditing provides you a better insight into SAP BusinessObjects BI 4.0 by helping you identify who has accessed which resources in your system and which actions (view, refresh, schedule, etc.) have been taken on these resources.

This retroactive history can be useful to check that your system is properly secured and that no one accesses resources or perform actions he is not allowed to carry out.

2.7.1 Auditing Database

To audit events, you need to have a database where the system can save them. At installation time (see Section 2.2.1 for an overview of installation), you can choose to use the default database installed for the CMS repository or to use your own database, as shown in Figure 2.14.

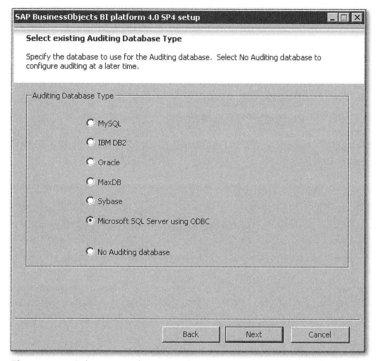

Figure 2.14 Selecting Auditing Database in Windows BI 4.0 Server Installer

In all cases, you can go to the CMC to modify the databases used for auditing after the installation.

In this database, events are stored in the ADS_EVENT table. When an event is logged, some parameters saved in these tables are useful to track what resources users accessed and whether the system has been properly secured:

▶ Event_ID: An identifier for the event

▶ User_ID: The CUID of the user who initiated the event

► User_Name: The name of the user who initiated the event

► Session_ID: The ID of the specific session the user used to perform the operation

► Client_Type_ID: The ID of the client tool or products used to perform the action (the client names can be found in the ADS_APPLICATION_TYPE_STR table: BI Launch Pad, Core Services, Crystal Reports Services, Explorer, Lifecycle Management, Lifecycle Management Service, Open Document, Web Intelligence Services)

► Start_Time: The time (in GMT) when the audited event has happened

► Event_Type_ID: The name of the event logged in the audit (the possible events can be found in the ADS_EVENT_TYPE_STR table, in the Event_Type_Name column: Auditing Modification, Create, Delete, Edit, Logon, Logout, Modify, Page Retrieved, Prompt, Refresh, Rights Modification, Run, Save, Search, View)

► Event Status: The result of the event; for example, whether a report was run successfully or run failed

Usually, an event takes place in a more global workflow, called an *action*. The ADS_EVENT table also contains some parameters that allow you to track all events that take part of the same actions and when they appear in the action:

► Action_ID: An identifier for the action

► Sequence_In_Action: The order of appearance of the event in the action

If applicable, some parameters used to identify the object implied in the event are also audited:

► Object_ID: The CUID of this object in the CMS repository

► Object_Name: The name of this object

► Object_Type_ID: The ID that identifies the object type (possible object types are saved in the ADS_OBJECT_TYPE_STR table, in the Object_Type_Name column: "WebIntelligence," "Calendar," "User"...)

► Object_Folder_Path: The full path of the object in the CMS repository

---

Note

You can create reports from the data saved in the audit database. Audit universe and documents are no longer delivered with the BI 4.0 installer. But you can still find them on the SDN website. At the printing of this book, the URL is *http://scn.sap.com/docs/DOC-6175*.

2.7.2 CMC Auditing Tab

You can manage audit configuration in the AUDITING tab of the CMC. As shown in Figure 2.15, you can run any audit configuration tasks in this single tab:

▶ SET EVENTS: Select the events to audit; the events have been harmonized across all products and you do not need to define the events to audit for each individual process or product.

▶ SET EVENT DETAILS: Select the details of the events that are audited.

▶ CONFIGURATION: Make changes to the auditing database.

Modifications in audit configuration are also audited, so audit information cannot be added, changed, or deleted without being audited as well.

Figure 2.15 Auditing Tab in the CMC

2.8 Summary

The BI 4.0 system follows a classical architecture based on the one used in XI R2 and XI 3.x. The administration of this system includes also security administration, so an overview of architecture concepts is useful to understand how it leverages security:

▶ At installation time, several databases and components are installed and configured. Several ports and passwords are requested.

▶ On the server side, you can use two tools to perform most administrative tasks: the CCM and the CMC.

▶ The system relies on the CMS repository, which stores InfoObjects in a database, and the File Repository Server file system, which stores files.

▶ In the CMC, you can manage the cryptographic key used to encrypt some InfoObjects parameters and files saved in the file system. This cryptographic key is encrypted by the cluster key.

▶ Among the servers run on the system, the Adaptive Processing Server and Adaptive Job Server host some services to process users' requests and manage scheduled tasks.

▶ Auditing can help you monitor who accesses your system, the resources he accesses, and the actions he performs.

Now that we have an idea of the basic security administration concepts, let's turn our focus to functionally securing a system, with an emphasis on the presentation of users and how they authenticate to the system.

The BI 4.0 repository contains users that can log on to the system. These users can either authenticate to the system or to an external system through external authentication.

3 Users and Authentication

As with other secured systems, it's important to modelize users in BI 4.0 in order to grant them access to the system and define their authorizations. In the BI 4.0 system, these users are stored in the CMS repository and are used to enforce the different security concepts described in the next chapters.

This chapter covers the following topics related to users and their authentication in the BI 4.0 system:

▶ The different authentication modes for users—for Enterprise that comes by default after the installation but also the authentications based on external systems

▶ The users and groups model, in the case of Enterprise authentication

▶ The workflows to manage Enterprise users and groups in the CMC

▶ The different methods to implement trusted authentication between the application server and BI 4.0

▶ The aliases used to grant multiple authentications for the same user and the mapped users that are created when authentication is based on an external system

▶ The workflows to manage aliases in the CMC

▶ The workflows to configure the authentication with external systems (LDAP and Active Directory); SAP authentication is described in Chapter 10

3.1   User Authentication

The *user* is identified by his account name and his authentication mode, which are used to log on to the CMS repository. Thus, it is not possible to have two users who have the same account name and the same authentication in the CMS repository. With aliases, which are described in Section 3.5, it is possible to have two users with the same name but different authentication modes.

Note

In the CMS repository, a user is stored as an InfoObject and the user's CUID and ID are also used to internally link it with other objects in the CMS repository.

Authentication defines how users authenticate to log on to Business Objects products, now under the umbrella of SAP. The BI 4.0 platform supports different authentication modes. The main difference between these authentication modes is the external authentication system they use, if any.

The following authentication modes do not rely on an external authentication system:

▶ *Enterprise*: In this authentication mode, all authentication information is stored in the CMS repository.

▶ *Standalone*: In this authentication mode, you don't access any CMS repository or external source and no authentication is requested. This mode is supported only by Web Intelligence Rich Client, Universe Design Tool, and Information Design Tool.

In the case of *external authentication*, the following are the most common supported external sources:

▶ LDAP

▶ Active Directory

▶ SAP NetWeaver BW (described in Chapter 10)

The use of external source allows you to enforce an existing security system without having to duplicate it in the BI 4.0 system and maintain it in two locations. It is updated in one location: the external source.

Let's review these authentication modes in detail, beginning with those that do not rely on an external authentication system.

3.1.1 Enterprise

By default, the BI platform is configured to support Enterprise authentication. The users you create in the CMS repository have the Enterprise authentication; their password is stored in the CMS repository that contains all the data for this user. This is the only available out-of-the-box authentication mode after the BI 4.0 system installation with the standalone mode that in fact does not require a CMS repository and does not need to authenticate.

You can define some parameters for Enterprise authentication:

- The first parameters are related to account and password management and are listed in Table 3.1.

- The ENABLE AND UPDATE USER'S DATA SOURCE CREDENTIALS AT LOGON TIME parameter is used for connection authentication and is described in Chapter 6, Section 6.4.

- The last parameters are used for trusted authentication and are described in Section 3.4.

Name	Description
Enforce mixed-case passwords	When activated, this option forces passwords to contain at least two of the following character classes: numbers, lowercase letters, uppercase letters, or punctuation.
Must contain at least N characters	When activated, this option sets a minimum length for the password string.
Must change password every N day(s)	When activated, this option forces your users to change their passwords every N day(s).
Cannot reuse the N most recent passwords	When activated, this option prevents your users from reusing one the N last passwords.
Must wait N minutes to change password	When activated, this option forces your users to wait N minutes before re-changing their passwords.

Table 3.1 Enterprise Parameters for Password and Account Management

Name	Description
Disable account after *N* failed attempts to log on	When activated, after *N* failed attempts, the user's account is disabled.
Reset failed logon count after *N* minute(s)	When the "Disable account after *N* failed attempts to log on" option is activated, this parameter defines the number of minutes before the number of failed attempts is reset to zero.
Re-enable account after *N* minute(s)	When activated, if the account has been disabled after some failed attempts, this parameter re-enables the account after *N* minutes. If this option is not selected, then users must ask their administrators to enable it.

Table 3.1 Enterprise Parameters for Password and Account Management (Cont.)

3.1.2 Standalone

Only Web Intelligence Desktop (also known as Rich Client; see Chapter 5, Section 5.19.1) and Universe Design Tool support the standalone authentication mode. Other tools do not support it.

This mode is intended to allow users to work in a non-secured environment, so security is not enforced. That means that no authentication is needed to run these tools or to open resources (connections, universes, or reports) created in this mode; the resources created in this mode are saved locally on their physical disks.

Additionally, there is no CMS interaction. You cannot import documents from or export documents to a CMS repository. For testing purposes—or if you do not handle secure data—this mode can be convenient to quickly design universes and reports without having to depend on the CMS repository. But because the standalone mode does not enforce any security, it is not the recommended authentication mode.

Any middleware needed to access database for reporting must be installed locally on the machine.

Let's turn our attention to the most common supported external sources.

3.1.3 LDAP

Lightweight Directory Access Protocol (LDAP) is an application protocol to access a directory service. The directory service structure is organized in a hierarchical structure with entries. An entry has multiple attributes and each attribute has one or more values. Table 3.2 shows various LDAP attributes.

Attribute Abbreviation	Name
DC	Domain Component
O	Organization
OU	Organization Unit
CN	Common Name

Table 3.2 Some LDAP Attributes

Any entry in the hierarchical structure is identified by its *distinguished name* (also called DN); that name can be seen as the concatenation of all attributes and their values of the nodes to follow in the structure to return to the top root. For example, in Figure 3.1, the distinguished name of the user "JIM" is

`CN=JIM,CN=Users,DC=COMPANY,DC=COM`

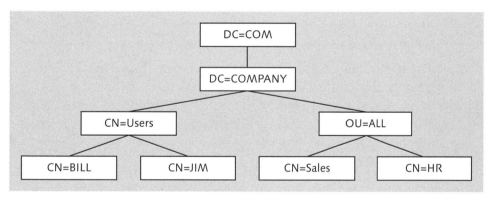

Figure 3.1 LDAP Structure Example

The list of groups containing the user is saved in the user's `memberof` attribute.

LDAP servers have become very popular as security repositories, and BI 4.0 can enforce an LDAP system to authenticate its users. As with any external authentication, you need to configure your CMS repository so it can access the LDAP server. Then you need to map LDAP groups into some groups in the CMS repository. These steps are described in Section 3.7.

3.1.4 Active Directory

Active Directory is the LDAP implementation by Microsoft. It also enforces the Kerberos protocol, which is a secure authentication protocol that relies on the use of tickets and secret keys. As Windows operating systems also support both Active Directory and Kerberos to authenticate, the authentication of BI 4.0 with Active Directory can be done at three levels:

▶ Active Directory authentication, where, like the LDAP authentication, the BI system relies on the Active Directory to store user passwords and to authenticate the users who try to log on to the BI 4.0 platform.

▶ Active Directory authentication with Windows single sign-on. This single sign-on can be configured if the Active Directory authentication has been configured. When Windows single sign-on is configured, if the user has opened his Windows session by authenticating with Active Directory, this session is reused when he connects to the BI platform so he won't have to retype his credentials again.

▶ Active Directory authentication with single sign-on to database. This single sign-on can be configured if both the BI 4.0 platform and the database are configured with Active Directory. The session used to connect to the CMS repository is reused to authenticate to the database where data are retrieved (see Chapter 6, Section 6.3).

Active Directory can also be seen as an LDAP source. But for the BI platform, LDAP authentication is different from the Active Directory authentication. If you connect to the Active Directory server using LDAP authentication, you cannot set up Active Directory authentication with single sign-on to database. You may use the secondary credentials mapping to refresh your data from your database (see Chapter 6, Section 6.3).

As for any external authentication, you need to configure your CMS repository so it can access the Active Directory, and then map Active Directory groups into some groups in the CMS repository. We provide further detail on these steps in Section 3.8, but first let's look at how Enterprise users and groups fit into the big security picture.

3.1.5 Enabling Authentication Selection for BI Launch Pad

By default, when you log on to the thick client, you'll find all of the different authentication modes available to you. This is the same with the CMC; however, with the default configuration of BI Launch Pad, you cannot see the different authentication modes.

To propose other authentication modes, you need to modify the `BIlaunchpad.properties` file saved in the folder containing the BOE web applications on the web application server.

For example, if you are using the Apache Tomcat web application server provided with the BI platform installation, this file is located in the folder

C:\ProgramFiles(x86)\SAP BusinessObjects\Tomcat6\webapps\BOE\WEBINF\config\default

In this `BIlaunchpad.properties` file, set the `authentication.visible` parameter to true, as in

```
authentication.visible=true
```

After you have made this change, restart your web application server. Once it is restarted, you can select the authentication mode when you connect to the BI 4.0 system.

3.2   Enterprise Users and Groups

Once you have installed the BI 4.0 system, the only authentication mode is Enterprise. This is because the standalone mode cannot really be considered as authentication since it does not require a CMS repository and therefore does not need to authenticate.

In the Enterprise authentication, users' parameters are all stored in the CMS repository and do not need external system to log users on to the BI 4.0 system. This section details these parameters and the folders attached to users, how the users are organized in groups, and the predefined users and groups found in the CMS repository. Finally it explains the impact of deleting groups and users.

3.2.1   User Parameters

When users are created, they are stored in the CMS repository with the parameters outlined in Table 3.3.

Name	Description
Account Name	By default, this account name is the user name, used to identify and log the user into the system. But with the use of an alias, it is possible to log on with a name other than the user name (see Section 3.5). This account name is not case sensitive.
Full Name	User's full name.
Email	The user's email can be used for scheduling, publishing, or monitoring.
Description	Provides a description of the user and is for informational use only.
User Attributes	If some user attributes have been defined, then these user attributes and their value for the current user are displayed in this section. For Enterprise user attributes, you can set their value when editing user properties. If the user attribute is retrieved from an external source, the value that has been retrieved is displayed and cannot be changed. See Chapter 8, Section 8.8 for more details.
Password	The user password policies are defined in the Enterprise authentication area. If the authentication mode is Enterprise: ▶ This password is mandatory, but it can be empty. ▶ This password is case sensitive. ▶ When user logs on, the password he provides is checked against the CMS repository.
Password never expires	Select this option if you do not want to limit the user password in time. This option is available only if the authentication mode is Enterprise.
User must change password at next logon	Select this option if you want the user to modify his password next time he logs on to the CMS repository. This option is available only if the authentication mode is Enterprise.
User cannot change password	Select this option if you want to prevent the user from modifying the password. This option is available only in Enterprise authentication mode.

Table 3.3 User's Parameters

Name	Description
Database Credentials—Enable	Enables the user to authenticate with a connection whose authentication mode is secondary mapping (see Chapter 6, Section 6.3).
Database Credentials—Account Name	If the user can authenticate with a connection whose authentication mode is secondary mapping, then this account name is used during authentication (see Chapter 6, Section 6.3).
Database Credentials—Password	If the user can authenticate with a connection whose authentication mode is secondary mapping, then this user password is used during authentication (see Chapter 6, Section 6.3).
Concurrent User/Named User	Depending on your license, you may choose whether, once connected, the account must be counted as a concurrent user or a named user.
Attribute Binding—Import Full Name, Email Address and Other Attributes	In the case of external authentication (see Section 3.5), fills in the user attributes from the external authentication system.
Attribute Binding—Account is Disabled	In the case of external authentication (see Section 3.5), disables the account.
Alias	This parameter outlines the different aliases attached to a user (see Section 3.5.1).

Table 3.3 User's Parameters (Cont.)

In Enterprise authentication, all users can modify their passwords in BI Launch Pad or most client tools, unless an administrator has prevented them from doing so, through the "User cannot change password" parameter. Inversely, the user must change his password the first time he connects if an administrator has set the "User must change password at next logon" parameter.

3.2.2 User Personal Folders

When a user is created in the CMS repository, several folders are automatically created and owned by this user:

▶ My Favorites: This folder contains the user's private folders, such as personal reports and documents.

▶ Inbox: In this folder, the user can receive documents or reports sent by others users through the BI platform mail, scheduling, or publishing capability.

▶ Personal Categories: In this folder, the user can create and organize his categories in order to sort his documents and reports. The user can assign his documents categories and then access them through these categories.

The user can access these folders from the BI Launch Pad or other report tools. For example, in the BI Launch Pad, these folders are available from the DOCUMENTS tab, as shown in Figure 3.2.

Figure 3.2 User's Personal Folders in BI Launch Pad

The user has all rights to these folders and can manage and organize them for his personal use. No one else has access to these personal folders, except administrators, who can see them in the CMC if they have been granted this right.

In the CMC, as an administrator, you can also access and administer these folders. Typically, you can modify these top-root folder rights in order to modify the default security. For example, if you deny the "View objects" right for the Inbox top-root folder to the Everyone group, then you disable your users' ability to access their Inbox folders. The steps for setting rights at the top-root folder are covered in Chapter 4, Section 4.7.

3.2.3 Groups Structure

As in many security systems, in the CMS repository, it is possible to organize users into groups. A *group* is identified by its name, which is unique in each BI 4.0 system. Thus, two groups cannot have the same name, even if they are located in different sub-groups. Internally, a group is also identified by its ID and CUID.

Users and groups in the CMS repository are organized as a directed acyclic graph, in which there are different possible roots. A group or a user can belong to multiple groups. It is not possible to have cyclic inheritance; for example, a group A cannot belong to a group B that also belongs to group A.

As with users, there are two types of groups:

▶ Enterprise groups are the default, out-of-the-box groups that you can create in the CMS repository without having to run extra configuration steps.

▶ Mapped groups are used once you have configured your CMS repository to authenticate to an external system (SAP NetWeaver BW, LDAP, or Active Directory). These groups are detailed in Section 3.5.3.

3.2.4 Predefined Users

By default, the BI platform comes with several *predefined users, as* shown in Table 3.4.

Account Name	Description
Administrator	During the platform installation, you must provide a password for this Administrator user. Keep it safe, because you'll use this account to connect to the CMC and set up other users and groups and, more generally, your CMS repository organization. Later, you can also create other administrator accounts and use them for daily administrative tasks. But the first time you connect to the CMC, you must use the Administrator. The Administrator user belongs to the Administrators and Everyone groups. This administrator has all rights granted; he can log on to all tools and use all the features secured by rights.
Guest	This user belongs to the Everyone group, so the account is granted very few rights. This usually means that he doesn't have the right to use CMC, Universe Design Tool, Information Design Tool, or Crystal Reports for Enterprise, among others. By default, the Guest account is not assigned a password. It is intended to let users connect anonymously and use very basic features of the system that are not confidential. You can assign a password to this account. Users who connect with this account must provide it to log on.

Table 3.4 Predefined Users

Account Name	Description
	By default, this Guest account is disabled in order to prevent unexpected use. If you want your users to use it and connect anonymously, you must explicitly enable it.
SMAdmin	By default, this SMAdmin account is disabled. It must be enabled if you want to use SAP Solution Manager (see Chapter 2, Section 2.2.1), the tool used to carry out analysis and monitoring of SAP products. If enabled, this user account is a read-only account used by the SM server to log on to the CMS and gather data from your deployment, such as server configuration. If you do not use SM, you do not need to enable this account.

Table 3.4 Predefined Users (Cont.)

3.2.5 Predefined Groups

After the installation, the CMS repository contains several *predefined groups*, who have predefined rights assigned.

You can use these groups to quickly assign rights to users by adding them to these groups. Through rights inheritance (see Chapter 4, Section 4.3), these users inherit the rights or access levels assigned to the predefined group. Once you have better defined your security model, you may prefer to create your own groups and assign them your own explicit security, but these predefined groups are a good start to defining security.

Table 3.5 lists the predefined groups.

Account Name	Description
Administrators	This group has Full Control access level on all objects top-root folders, so its users can access all tools and are able to administrate the platform from the CMC.
Cryptographic Officers	This group has Full Control access level on the Cryptographic Keys top-root folder (return to Chapter 2, Section 2.5). It can be used to define users who can administrate these keys.

Table 3.5 Predefined Groups

Account Name	Description
Data Federation Administrator	This group has Full Control access level on the Data Federation public folder. To connect to the Data Federation Administration Tool, a user must have the Full Control access level on this folder.
Everyone	This group contains all users in the CMS, meaning that any rights defined for this group are always inherited by all users. When a user (whatever his authentication mode is) is created, he is automatically added to the Everyone group; it is not possible to remove him from this group.
Monitoring Users	This group can be used to facilitate the broadcasting of monitoring alerts. You can select this group as recipient of these alerts and all users in this group receives these alerts.
QaaWS Group Designer	This group has Full Control access level on the Web Service Query List top-root folder.
Report Conversion Tool Users	This group has Full Control access level on the Report Conversion Tool application.
Translators	This group has Full Control access level on the Translation Management Tool application.
Universe Designers Users	This group has Full Control access level on the Universe Design Tool application and on the Universes and Connections folders. It has also granted advanced rights for Information Design Tool: "Save for all users," "Compute statistics," "Publish universes," "Retrieve universes," "Create, modify, or delete connections," and "Share projects."

Table 3.5 Predefined Groups (Cont.)

After the BI 4.0 installation, the Administrators and Cryptographic Officers groups contain the Administrator user; other predefined groups (except the Everyone group, which always contains all users) do not contain any users.

3.2.6 Deleting Users and Groups

When you delete a *group* in the CMS repository, you do not delete the users or subgroups it contains. When you delete a *user* in the CMS repository, all the personal folders, personal categories, and inboxes linked to this user and the resources they contain are definitively deleted and cannot be accessed any longer, as explained in Section 3.2.2. The other resources owned by this user that do not belong to these personal folders are not deleted, but their ownership is transferred to the Administrator user. Deleting a user deletes the InfoObject that stores the user and his ID. So even if you create a new user with the same name, this new user has a different ID than the previous one and it is not possible to recover that resource's ownership.

For this reason, it is always better to disable the user instead of deleting him. Disabling a user prevents him from logging on to the system but does not delete anything from the CMS repository. If this account needs to access the system in the future, you just have to enable the account. Once you are absolutely sure that the account does not need to be used, you can delete it definitively. Even if a user belongs to multiple groups, when you delete him, he is removed from all groups.

3.3   Managing Users and Groups in the CMC

Users and groups management is done in the CMC, in the USERS AND GROUPS tab. To create your first users and groups, you need to log on to the CMS using the Administrator account, the password you set at installation time, and select the Enterprise authentication mode. You can create additional users, give them administrative rights, and then use these users to re-log on to the CMC.

3.3.1   Viewing Users and Groups

In the CMC, the USERS AND GROUPS left pane contains three entries that correspond to the three ways to display users and groups:

▶ USER LIST displays all users as a flat list in the right pane.

▶ GROUP LIST displays all groups as a flat list in the right pane.

▶ GROUP HIERARCHY displays the group hierarchy in the left pane. Click a group to display its content (users and sub-groups) in the right pane. This view is more convenient to show the structure of your users and groups. Because a group or a user can belong to different groups, the same group or user can appear below different groups.

The content displayed in the left pane is sorted in alphabetical order. If there are too many users and groups to display, they are listed page by page.

Two parameters define the number of objects displayed in the CMC:

▶ The maximum number of objects per page defines the number of users and groups displayed in the right pane. By default, this number is 50. Any user can modify this maximum number applied to him in the CMC PREFERENCES panel. This panel be opened by clicking the PREFERENCES link in the top right of the CMC page, as shown in Figure 3.3.

If you have many users in your CMS repository, you may need to navigate page by page to find a specific user, even if you extend this number. Another way to find your user is to use the FIND TITLE function that can help you to filter objects through different fields (any field, name or description).

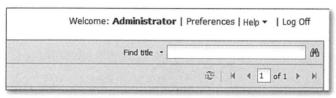

Figure 3.3 Preferences and Find Options in the CMC

▶ By default, the CMC left pane can display a maximum number of 200 objects. If there are more than 200 objects to display in the left pane, the message "Too many objects" is displayed. To display a specific user, use the FIND option.

You can also modify this value by modifying the CmcApp.properties file located in the folder *<webserverinstallation>\webapps\BOE\WEBINF\config\default*.

Edit this file and in the line:

```
max.tree.children.threshold=200
```

Replace 200 by the value that suits you. If you increase this value, run tests to make sure that your browser can handle the load. Note that upper limit cannot exceed 1000 objects.

3.3.2 Creating Enterprise Users

To give a new user access to the BI 4.0 system, you'll need to create a new user account for him in the CMS repository by following these steps:

1. In the CMC, select the USERS AND GROUPS tab.

2. In the left pane, select USER LIST or GROUP HIERARCHY.

3. Right-click USER LIST or GROUP HIERARCHY and select NEW • NEW USER or, from the menu bar, select MANAGE • NEW • NEW USER to open the NEW USER panel.

4. You can enter main parameters of the new user in this panel. Keep ENTERPRISE as AUTHENTICATION TYPE. Refer to Section 3.2.1 for a description of these parameters.

5. Click CREATE to create the new user. The new user is created but the NEW USER panel remains open so you can fill new parameters to create a new user.

6. Click CREATE AND CLOSE to close the NEW USER panel and to create the new user.

3.3.3 Creating Enterprise Groups

To create a new user group in order to organize users, follow these steps:

1. In the CMC, select the USERS AND GROUPS tab.

2. In the left pane, select GROUP LIST or GROUP HIERARCHY.

3. Right-click GROUP LIST or GROUP HIERARCHY and select NEW • NEW GROUP or, from the menu bar, select MANAGE • NEW • NEW GROUP to open the CREATE NEW USER GROUP panel.

4. Type the name of the new group and, if needed, a description of this group.

5. Click OK to create the new group and close the CREATE NEW USER GROUP panel.

3.3.4 Creating Users and Groups from CSV File

Since BI 4.0 FP3, it is possible to use a CSV file in the CMC to do one of two things:

▶ Use a CSV file to import or remove users from the CMS repository. By default, the created users have Enterprise authentication. They are disabled and you need to explicitly enable them in the USER PROPERTIES panel (see Section 3.3.6).

▶ Use a CSV file to import secondary credentials for users.

As the import relies on a job run on the server, you must check in the CMC that you have a Job Server process up and running in this deployment.

To import or remove users, the CSV file must contain lines that fit the syntax

```
Add,<Group>,<Accountname>,<Name>,<Password>,<email>,<Profile>,<Value>
```

to add or update a user. To remove a user, the lines must follow the syntax

```
Remove,<Group>,<Accountname>
```

The fields are described in Table 3.6. For example:

```
Add,Board,jim,Jim,secret,jim@company.com,country,US
Remove,Board,leo
```

Field name	Field description
`<Group>`	When you add a user, this is the group where the user is added. If this group does not exist, it will be created during the import. When you delete a user, this is the group that contains this user. It can be any group. This group is not deleted, even if the eliminated user is the last one in the group.
`<Account name>`	Account name (case sensitive)
`<Name>`	User full name
`<Password>`	Password
`<email>`	Email
`<Profile>`	Profile (see Chapter 9, Section 9.5)
`<Value>`	Value of the profile for this user

Table 3.6   Parameters to Add or Remove a User through a CSV File

To update user database credentials (see Chapter 6, Section 6.3), the file must contain lines that fit this syntax:

```
Add,<Account name>,<DBName>,<DBPassword>
```

The fields are described in Table 3.7.

Field name	Field description
`<Account Name>`	Account name (case sensitive)
`<DBName>`	Secondary user name for database credentials
`<DBPassword>`	Password for database credentials

Table 3.7 Parameters to Add Database Credentials through a CSV File

To import a CSV file from the CMC, follow these steps:

1. In the CMC, select the USERS AND GROUPS tab.

2. In the menu bar, select MANAGE • IMPORT USER GROUP • USER/GROUP/DBCRE-DENTIAL to open the IMPORT USER/GROUP/DBCREDENTIAL panel, as shown in Figure 3.4.

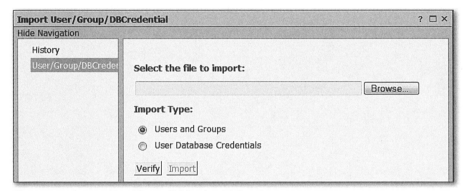

Figure 3.4 Import User/Group/DBCredential Panel

3. Click the BROWSE button to select the CSV file from your file system.

4. Choose one radio button to select if your CSV file contains users and groups to import or user database credentials.

5. Click the VERIFY button to parse and check the file syntax.

6. Once the file has been checked, click the IMPORT button to launch the import. A job is created to import the file and create the users or set the database credentials. When the job is completed, the CMC displays the import result.

7. Click the cross in the header of the IMPORT USER/GROUP/DBCREDENTIAL panel to close it.

> **Note**
>
> Importing users from a text file was already possible in XI 3.x with the Import Wizard tool. The Import Wizard's successor, Upgrade Management Tool, no longer offers this feature, so it has been implemented in the CMC although the file format is different than in XI 3.x.

3.3.5   Editing User Parameters

When creating a new user, you can set only a limited set of its parameters. Once the user has been created, you can modify the user's parameters, except the authentication mode. Table 3.3 lists all these parameters.

You can add or modify the email address or the password (only in Enterprise mode) or the database credential.

To edit user's parameters, follow these steps:

1. Go to the USERS AND GROUPS tab in the CMC.

2. In the left pane, navigate in the USER LIST, GROUP LIST, or GROUP HIERARCHY branch in order to display the list of users or of groups in the right pane.

3. In the menu bar, select MANAGE • PROPERTIES or right-click the user and in the contextual menu, select PROPERTIES. The PROPERTIES panel opens. This panel lists all user's parameters, as well as the ID and CUID assigned to the user.

4. Modify the requested parameters. Note that the options related to aliases are described in more detail in Section 3.6.

5. Click the SAVE & CLOSE button to save your changes and close the PROPERTIES panel.

3.3.6   Enabling/Disabling Users

For security reasons, you may have to disable users. Disabled users can no longer log on to the products, but their resources and their account are not deleted, so you can re-enable them later. To enable or disable a user, follow these steps:

1. Go to the USERS AND GROUPS tab in the CMC.

2. In the left pane, click USER LIST to display the list of users in the right pane.

3. Select the user to enable or disable.

4. In the menu bar, select MANAGE • PROPERTIES or right-click the user and in the contextual menu, select PROPERTIES. The PROPERTIES panel opens.

5. In the ATTRIBUTE BINDING section, select the ACCOUNT IS DISABLED checkbox to disable the user or unselect it to enable it.

6. Click the SAVE & CLOSE button to save your change and close the PROPERTIES panel.

Another way to disable a user is to disable all his aliases. This process is outlined in Section 3.6.4.

3.3.7 Adding Users and Groups to Groups

There are different workflows for adding users or groups to groups. The workflows differ if you want to start from the source (the users and groups) or from the destination group.

To add a user or a group to different groups, follow these steps:

1. Go to the USERS AND GROUPS tab in the CMC.

2. In the left pane, select the user or the group to add.

3. In the menu bar, select ACTIONS • JOIN GROUP to open the JOIN GROUP panel.

4. In the AVAILABLE GROUPS list, select the list of groups where the user or the group must be added.

5. Click the > button to move these groups in the DESTINATION GROUP(s) list.

6. Click OK to close the Join Group panel and add the user or group in the selected groups.

If you prefer to run this workflow starting from the group (group-centric) and want to combine several users or groups into one single group, follow these steps:

1. Go to the USERS AND GROUPS tab in the CMC.

2. In the left pane, select the group where users and groups must be added.

3. In the menu bar, select ACTIONS • ADD MEMBERS TO GROUP to open the ADD MEMBERS TO GROUP panel.

4. In the AVAILABLE USERS/GROUPS list, select the users and groups to add to the target group.

5. Click the > button to move these users and groups in the SELECTED USERS/GROUPS list.

6. Click OK to close the ADD MEMBERS TO GROUP panel and add the selected users and groups to the group.

3.3.8 Removing Users or Groups From Groups

To remove a user—whatever his authentication mode—or a group from a group, follow these steps:

1. Go to the USERS AND GROUPS tab in the CMC.

2. In the left pane, click and expand the GROUP HIERARCHY branch to display the group hierarchy in the left pane.

3. Navigate in this tree in order to reach the group containing the user to remove. Click this group to display the users it contains in the right pane.

4. Select the user to remove from the group.

5. In the menu bar, select ACTIONS • MEMBER OF or right-click the user or the group and in the contextual menu, select REMOVE FROM USER GROUP. A confirmation panel opens.

6. Click YES to remove the selected user or group from the selected group.

Another way to remove a user or a group from another group is to work with the list of groups containing the user or the group. To do so, follow these steps:

1. Go to the USERS AND GROUPS tab in the CMC.

2. In the left pane, click USER LIST to display the list of users in the right pane.

3. Select the user to remove from the group.

4. In the menu bar, select ACTIONS • MEMBER OF or right-click the user and in the contextual menu, select MEMBER OF. The MEMBER OF panel opens. This panel lists the groups that contain this user.

5. Select the groups from which the user or the group must be removed, you may use the ⌈Ctrl⌉ key for multi-selection.

6. Click the REMOVE button in the toolbar to remove the user or the group from the selected groups.

7. Click the cross in the top right header of the MEMBER OF panel to close it.

> **Note**
>
> It is not possible to remove a user from the Everyone group.

3.3.9 Deleting Users

To delete a user, whatever his authentication mode, follow these steps:

1. Go to the USERS AND GROUPS tab in the CMC.

2. In the left pane, click USER LIST to display the list of user in the right pane.

3. Select the user to delete.

4. In the menu bar, select MANAGE • DELETE or right-click the user and in the contextual menu, select DELETE. A confirmation box opens.

5. Click OK to confirm and delete the user.

> **Note**
>
> It is not possible to delete the Administrator and Guest users.

3.3.10 Deleting Groups

You can only delete Enterprise groups from the CMC.

1. Go to the USERS AND GROUPS tab in the CMC.

2. In the left pane, select the group to delete.

3. In the menu bar, select MANAGE • DELETE. A confirmation box is displayed.

4. Click OK to delete the group.

Deleting a group does not delete the users or sub-groups it contains. As for users, it is not possible to recover a deleted group. You may recreate it, but you have to explicitly re-add the users and groups it contained.

> **Note**
>
> It is not possible to delete any predefined group.

3.3.11   Account Manager

In some cases, you may want to set parameters to a large number of users. You can do this manually users by users, but this is time-consuming. Another method is to use the ACCOUNT MANAGER panel. In this panel, you can set some parameters to all users that belong to the same group if you have enough rights. You can modify some parameters related to security and authentication. These parameters are listed in Table 3.8, and their descriptions can be found in Table 3.1.

Category	Parameter
Password	Password
	Password never expires
	User must change password at next logon
	User cannot change password
Database Credentials	Enable database credentials
	Account name
	Password
Alias	Enable Enterprise alias
	Enable third-party alias

Table 3.8   Parameters Supported in the Account Manager Panel

To use the ACCOUNT MANAGER panel:

1. Go to the USERS AND GROUPS tab in the CMC.

2. In the left pane, navigate in the USER LIST, GROUP LIST or GROUP HIERARCHY branch in order to display the list of users or of groups in the right pane.

3. Right-click the user or the group and in the contextual menu, select ACCOUNT MANAGER to open the ACCOUNT MANAGER PANEL, as shown in Figure 3.5. In this panel, you can modify the parameters listed in Table 3.8.

4. Click the CHANGE USER PASSWORDS TO NEW VALUE checkbox to modify passwords settings. If you leave this checkbox unselected, the corresponding parameters are not modified.

5. Click the CHANGE DATABASE CREDENTIALS checkbox to modify database credentials. If you leave this checkbox unselected, the corresponding parameters are not modified.

6. Click the ENABLE/DISABLE USER ALIASES checkbox and its subsidiaries to enable or disable user aliases:

   ▶ Click the ENTERPRISE checkbox to modify the alias based on Enterprise authentication. Select the ENABLED checkbox to enable it or leave it unselected to disable it.

   ▶ Click the THIRD PARTY checkbox to modify all aliases based on external authentications (SAP, Active Directory, or LDAP). Select the ENABLED checkbox to enable all these aliases or leave it unselected to disable them.

   If you leave the ENABLE/DISABLE USER ALIASES checkbox unselected, the corresponding parameters are not modified.

7. Click the SAVE & CLOSE button to set these settings to the selected user or to the users belonging to the selected group and to close the ACCOUNT MANAGER panel.

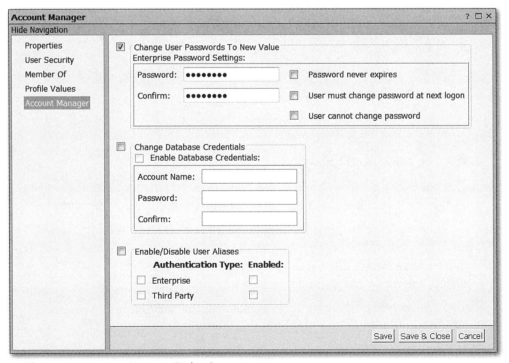

Figure 3.5 Account Manager Dialog Box

When you use Account Manager for a group, these new parameters are pushed to all users that belong to the group. They persist at the user level, but not at the group level, so take the following characteristics into consideration:

▶ If you add another user to this group, this new user does not inherit these settings.

▶ After you have modified some settings through Account Manager, you can modify these settings for any user belonging to this group.

3.3.12 Defining BI Launch Pad Preferences

This feature has been introduced in BI 4.0 in order to easily customize a user's pages in BI Launch Pad. You can define the BI Launch Pad preferences for any group, and all users who belong to this group inherit these preferences. It is not possible to define these preferences at user level.

You can define the following parameters in BI Launch Pad preferences:

▶ The BI Launch Pad start page, which can be one of these options:

   ▶ The HOME tab, which can also be defined through these preferences

   ▶ A tab displaying one of the user's personal folders

   ▶ A tab displaying any public folder content

   ▶ A tab displaying any public category content

▶ The columns displayed in the DOCUMENTS tab

▶ How to display documents in BI Launch Pad (through a new tab or a new window)

▶ The number of objects per page

To define BI Launch Pad preferences for a group, follow these steps:

1. Go to the USERS AND GROUPS tab in the CMC.

2. In the left pane, navigate in the GROUP LIST or GROUP HIERARCHY branch in order to display the list of groups in the right pane.

3. Right-click the group and in the contextual menu, select BI LAUNCH PAD PREFERENCES to open the BI LAUNCH PAD PREFERENCES panel, as shown in Figure 3.6.

4. Modify the parameters as needed.

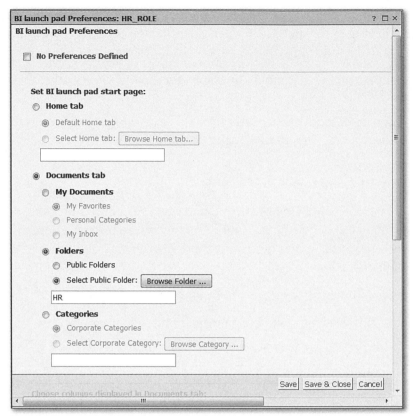

Figure 3.6 Detail of the BI Launch Pad Preferences Panel

5. Click the SAVE & CLOSE button to save these preferences for the selected group and close the BI LAUNCH PAD PREFERENCES panel.

A user with "Change preferences" rights can update his BI Launch Pad preferences in BI Launch Pad. If this is the case, then these preferences apply. If the user has not defined his BI Launch Pad preferences and if he belongs to a group where you have set BI Launch Pad preferences, then the BI Launch Pad preferences defined for this group apply to this user. If no preference has also been defined for this group, then the preferences defined for the parent group of this group apply and so on, until some preferences are found or until the parent group does not belong to any group.

In the event of a conflict in defining the parent group, if the user is member of multiple groups, the user inherits the preferences from the group with the lowest ID.

Example

A user belongs to three groups (Group1, Group2 and Group3) that are his direct parent groups. Group1's ID is 100, Group2's ID is 101 and Group3's ID is 102. BI Launch Pad preferences have been defined for Group2 and Group3. The user inherits the BI Launch Pad preferences defined for Group2 because it has the lowest ID and since no preferences has been defined for Group1.

3.3.13   Setting Enterprise Parameters

To modify the parameters of the Enterprise authentication, follow these steps:

1. Go to the AUTHENTICATION tab in the CMC.

2. The AUTHENTICATION tab lists the different authentication supported by your system. Double-click on the ENTERPRISE line to open the ENTERPRISE panel, which is shown in Figure 3.7.

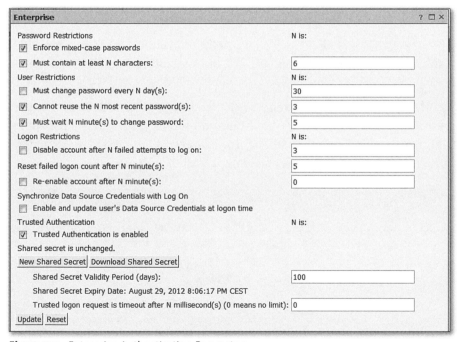

Figure 3.7   Enterprise Authentication Parameters

3. Modify the parameters as needed.

4. Click the UPDATE button to save your changes and close the ENTERPRISE panel.

3.4 Trusted Authentication

If you are using the default Enterprise authentication, there is no single sign-on method that allows you to reuse the session opened in the browser to connect to BusinessObjects web applications. For this reason, you can use trusted authentication to perform single sign-on by relying on the web application server to verify the identity of a user. It can be useful to integrate BusinessObjects portal into a larger portal that controls authentication.

This method of authentication involves establishing trust between the Central Management Server (CMS) and the web application server hosting the BI platform web application. When the trust is established, the system relies on the web application server to check the identity of a user. This authentication does not apply to thick clients.

You need to generate and upload a shared secret (see Section 3.4.1) on all machines running the CMS or application servers, then you configure your system to pass the shared secret (see Section 3.4.2) and the user name to authenticate (see Section 3.4.3).

Setting up trusted authentication requires that you write some code to get the user name from the browser, pass it to the application server, and then use the appropriate protocol to configure the method. In this section, we describe the general concept but not the details to fully implement trusted authentication.

> **Warning!**
>
> Trusted authentication can be seen as a trick to security because it forces the CMS to trust the web application. To control the use of this method, you may:
>
> ► Set up a secure web connection using Secured Sockets Layer (SSL) security
>
> ► Configure the CMS server so it accepts connections only from a specific IP address

Our examples are based on a user whose account name, jim, must be passed to the application server. We also refer to the Tomcat application server provided with BI 4.0, whose files are located, by default, below the folder *C:\Program Files (x86)\ SAP BusinessObjects\Tomcat6*.

3.4.1 Sharing Shared Secret Key

To generate and share the secret key used in trusted authentication, follow these steps:

1. Go to the AUTHENTICATION tab in the CMC.

2. The AUTHENTICATION tab lists the different authentication supported by your system. Double-click on the ENTERPRISE line to open the ENTERPRISE panel.

3. To enable trusted authentication, click the TRUSTED AUTHENTICATION IS ENABLED checkbox in the TRUSTED AUTHENTICATION section.

4. Click the NEW SHARED SECRET button to generate a new shared secret key.

5. Click the DOWNLOAD SHARED SECRET button to open the FILE DOWNLOAD dialog box appears. In this dialog box, select the folder where you are saving `TrustedPrincipal.conf` file containing this shared secret. You must download this file on all machines running the CMS server or the application servers. Thus the shared secret can be used to establish trust between the CMS and the application servers.

6. Select the directory *<INSTALLDIR>\SAP BusinessObjects Enterprise XI 4.0\win64_x64*.

7. Click the SAVE button to close the FILE DOWNLOAD dialog box and save the file.

8. In the SHARED SECRET VALIDITY PERIOD text field, type the number of days of validity for your shared secret.

9. In the TRUSTED LOGIN REQUEST IS TIMEOUT AFTER *N* MILLISECOND(S) text field, type the timeout value for authentication requests. This value defines how long the application waits for the user to log on. If this value is zero, then there is no timeout.

10. Click the UPDATE button to save your changes and close the ENTERPRISE panel.

3.4.2 Passing Shared Secret

You can pass the shared secret using one of two possible methods:

▶ Through the `TrustedPrincipal.conf` file. If you use this method, as these files are already generated, there is no additional step.

▶ Through the web session, the shared secret is passed through a web session defined in a JSP page.

To configure the web session, follow these steps:

1. In the BusinessObjects server installation, copy the `global.properties` file located in *<INSTALLDIR>\Tomcat6\webapps\BOE\WEB-INF\config\default* into the *<INSTALLDIR>\Tomcat6\webapps\BOE\WEB-INF\config\custom* folder. These folders must have been installed in all machines where you have installed the BusinessObjects web application components.

2. The `default` folder contains all web applications' default parameters. When you can copy its content into the `custom` folder and modify these copied files, they overwrite the ones in the `default` folder.

3. Edit this copied `global.properties` file in order to add the following line:

   `trusted.auth.shared.secret=<SecretVariable>`

   where `<SecretVariable>` is the variable used to pass the secret.

4. In the generated JSP page, you can use the following command to explicitly associate the shared secret to the session

   `request.getSession().setAttribute(<SecretVariable>,"<Secret>");`

   where `<Secret>` is the secret copied from the `TrustedPrincipal.conf` file.

   For example:

   `request.getSession().setAttribute(MySecret,"6a1...bdd");`

> **Note**
>
> When you are making changes in the application server, we recommend that you stop, delete the work folder (for example, the one located in *<INSTALLDIR>/Tomcat6/* for the Tomcat application server installed by the installer), and restart it.

3.4.3   Passing User Name

Whatever method you use to create the trust (that is, either shared secret or `TrustedPrincipal.conf` file), you need to pass the user name that authenticates. You have six different methods to pass this user name. You need to define the method to use in the same `global.properties` file created to define which method to pass the shared secret. If you have not yet created it, refer to the Section 3.4.2, then edit it to add the following lines that set these parameters:

```
sso.enabled=true
trusted.auth.user.retrieval=<UserPassMethod>
```

`trusted.auth.user.param=<`**`MethodParameter`**`>`

where:

- `<`**`UserPassMethod`**`>` is one of the following values: `WEB_SESSION`, `HTTP_HEADER`, `COOKIE`, `QUERY_STRING`, `USER_PRINCIPAL`, or `REMOTE_USER`.
- `<`**`MethodParameter`**`>` is a parameter that may be used by some of these methods (see below).

Let's explore each of these methods and the additional steps they require next.

WEB_SESSION

In this method, the user name is set into a variable associated with the web session through a JSP page. The name of this variable is defined in the `trusted.auth.user.param` property of the `global.properties` file. For example, to use the `UserVariable` variable, enter the following:

```
sso.enabled=true
trusted.auth.user.retrieval=WEB_SESSION
trusted.auth.user.param=UserVariable
```

In the JSP page, to set the user name to pass, you can use the method

```
request.getSession().setAttribute(UserVariable,<userName>);
```

HTTP_HEADER

In this method, the user name is passed through the HTTP header. The name of this HTTP header is defined in the `trusted.auth.user.param` property of the `global.properties` file. For example, to use a `UserHTTP`, enter

```
sso.enabled=true
trusted.auth.user.retrieval=HTTP_HEADER
trusted.auth.user.param=UserHTTP
```

COOKIE

In this method, the user name is passed through a cookie. The name of this cookie is defined in the `trusted.auth.user.param` property of the `global.properties` file. For example, to use a cookie named `UserCookie`, enter the following:

```
sso.enabled=true
trusted.auth.user.retrieval=COOKIE
trusted.auth.user.param=UserCookie
```

Then your application server generates the following cookie, which is sent to the client browsers:

```
Name: UserCookie
Content: <userName>
Host: <WebServername>
Path: /
```

QUERY_STRING

In this method, the user name is passed through URL. The name of the variable used in the URL is defined in the `trusted.auth.user.param` property of the `global.properties` file. For example, to use a variable named `UserURL`, enter the following:

```
sso.enabled=true

trusted.auth.user.retrieval= QUERY_STRING
trusted.auth.user.param=UserURL
```

Then to log on to BI Launch Pad, use the URL

```
http://<hostname>:<port>/BOE/BI/logon.jsp?UserURL=<userName>
```

USER_PRINCIPAL/REMOTE_USER

In this method, the user name and password are stored in your application server and are passed to the BI 4.0 server. As an alternative, you may also integrate your application server into an external authentication system on which it can rely, but this section details only the method to pass user name and password.

For this method, you need to modify some files in your installed application server, detailed here:

▶ As in previous methods, you must edit the `global.properties` file in order to add either the parameters

```
sso.enabled=true
trusted.auth.user.retrieval=USER_PRINCIPAL
```

or

```
sso.enabled=true
```

```
trusted.auth.user.retrieval=REMOTE_USER
```

▶ In the `server.xml` file located in the `conf` folder, replace

```
<Realm className="org.apache.catalina.realm.UserDatabaseRealm" ... />
```

with

```
<Realm className="org.apache.catalina.realm.MemoryRealm" .../>
```

▶ In the `tomcat-users.xml` located in the *conf* folder, under the `<tomcat-users>` section, add a line for each user that can connect:

```
<user user name="<userName>" password="<password>" roles="onjavauser"
/>
```

▶ In the `web.xml` file located in the `webapps\BOE\WEB-INF\` folder, add these lines before the `</web-app>` tag:

```
<security-constraint>
 <web-resource-collection>
    <web-resource-name>OnJava Application</web-resource-name>
         <url-pattern>/*</url-pattern>
    </web-resource-collection>
    <auth-constraint>
        <role-name>onjavauser</role-name>
    </auth-constraint>
</security-constraint>
<login-config>
    <auth-method>BASIC</auth-method>
    <realm-name>OnJava Application</realm-name>
</login-config>
```

3.5   Aliases and External Authentications

Trusted Authentication, seen in Section 3.4, is used to implement single sign-on if you use Enterprise authentication. If you use external authentication, you need to map a user in the CMS repository to a user in that external system. This mapping is modelized through aliases. When a user mapped to a user in an external system tries to log on to the BI 4.0 system, BI 4.0 checks that this user belong to an external mapped group and verifies his password to the external system.

In the CMS repository, users contain aliases that define the authentication modes they are granted.

3.5.1 Aliases

An *alias* is defined by a name and an authentication mode.

When you create a user, an alias is created for this user by default. The account name is similar to the alias name. For this user, you can then create other aliases that allow him to authenticate with different names and authentication modes (for example, to different external systems).

In such cases, the user has multiple identities represented by the aliases attached to the user. He can log on to the system using different authentication modes, but because he is connected with the same account name, he can access the same resources in the CMS repository.

You can create an alias for a user in two ways:

► **By explicitly creating a new one**

► **By assigning an alias of another user**
After the assignment, if the initial user owning the alias has no more assigned aliases, then this user is deleted, as well as his personal resources (inboxes, personal folders, and personal categories). Such cases can be used to merge a user with another user, although only the resources of the final user are kept.

Even if the user authenticates with the credentials of the alias, he is logged with his account name. However, for single sign-on to database (see Chapter 6, Section 6.3.4), the credentials that are kept and are sent to the connection for authentication to the database are the alias credentials.

Different combinations of aliases for a user are possible. For example, a user can have one Enterprise alias, one Active Directory alias, two LDAP aliases, and one SAP alias. These combinations are governed by two constraints:

► A user cannot have two Enterprise aliases.

► It is not possible to assign an existing Enterprise alias to a user that does not have one. You need to explicitly create it directly for this user (see Section 3.6.1).

You can also choose how to map a user from an external source when a user with the same name but a different authentication mode already exists in the CMS repository:

► You can either opt to merge the two users and create a new alias for the existing user, or

► You can opt to create a new user. To avoid name conflict, the name of this new user has the suffix 0.

If the users have the same name and same authentication mode, they are considered as being the same user. It is not possible to create users with the same name and the same authentication mode in the CMS repository.

3.5.2 Mapping Users from External Sources

After the platform installation, you can only create users with Enterprise authentication. To create users with external authentication, you first have to configure the CMS repository with the external system. We discuss two external systems in this chapter:

► LDAP (Section 3.7)

► Active Directory (Section 3.8)

The configuration for SAP authentication is described in Chapter 10 because the whole process involves some slight differences.

All external authentications rely on the same principles:

► A mapping must be done between users and groups from the external system and the BI 4.0 system.

► This mapping is first done at group level: A group in BI 4.0 CMS repository is created in order to be mapped with a group from the external system

► All external users belonging to this mapped external group are candidates for being replicated in your BI 4.0 system.

► When created in the CMS repositories, these users are created in the group mapped to the external groups.

You can define when the users are actually created:

► **Only when the user logs on to the BI 4.0 system**
In this case, the first time the user logs on to the BI 4.0 system, it takes longer since the user needs to be created. But the CMS repository stores only the users who are really accessing the platform.

► **By the BI 4.0 system when the aliases update occurs**
All users from the groups to map are created even if they never access the BI

4.0 system. The objective to create all users once is to reduce the workload the first time the user is created. If, after an update, a user is created in the external server, then the user is created in the BI 4.0 repository during the next update.

You can define the type of licences to assign to the users created from the external sources: named users or concurrent users. If you opt to create named users, make sure you have enough licenses, especially if you choose to create all users once.

When these users are imported from Active Directory, LDAP, or SAP NetWeaver BW, they are created in the CMS repository using some name whose syntax is detailed in Table 3.9.

	Object	Name
Enterprise	User	`<Account name>`
	Alias	`secEnterprise:<Account name>`
SAP NetWeaver BW	User	`<SAP System ID>~<SAP client number>/<SAP user name>`

	Alias	`secSAPR3:<SAP System ID>~<SAP client number>/<SAP user name>`
		For example:
		`secSAPR3:PRD~100/hasso`

LDAP	User	`<Account name>`

	Alias	`secLDAP:<Account distinguished name>`
		For example:
		`secLDAD:CN=bill,CN=Users,DC=COMPANY,DC=COM`

Active Directory	User	`<Account name>`

	Alias	`secWinAD:<Account distinguished name>`
		For example:
		`secWinAD:CN=bill,CN=Users,DC=COMPANY,DC=COM`

Table 3.9 Name of Created User and Alias, Depending on Authentication Mode

You can also define how aliases are created:

▶ **Merge accounts if an account with the same name already exists in the CMS repository.**
In this case, when adding a account in the BI 4.0 system, the two accounts are merged, and the external account become an alias of the existing account. If there is no existing account with this name, an account is created with a single alias that authenticates with the external system.

▶ **Always create another account in the CMS repository even if another account with the same name already exists.**
In this case, the created account mapped to the external system is prefixed with the number 0.

For users created from external authentication system, the parameters described in Table 3.3 also apply, except the following parameters related to passwords that cannot be modified since they are stored in the external system:

▶ Password

▶ Password never expires

▶ User must change password at next logon

▶ User cannot change password

Thus, you cannot modify the passwords from the BI 4.0 system—you need to connect to your external source to change it.

In Active Directory, it is possible to force a user to change his password the first time he logs on. If such a user tries to connect for the first time through a BI 4.0 CMS that has configured with this Active Directory, then the Active Directory does not allow him to log on.

It is also possible in SAP NetWeaver BW to force a user to change his password the first time he logs on, but in the same configuration, the SAP NetWeaver BW system does allow him to log on.

Once created, you can add mapped users to other Enterprise groups, although it is better to add the mapped group that contains them in order to maintain group organization. But do not remove them from their mapped group; otherwise, they cannot log on to the CMS repository any longer.

3.5.3 Mapped Groups

During the external authentication configuration, you need to define some external groups that contain external users allowed to log on to the BI 4.0 system. When the configuration is defined, the BI 4.0 system connects to the external system in order to read these groups from the external system and to create them in the CMS repository. When they are created, these take some name whose syntax is detailed in Table 3.10.

	Name

SAP NetWeaver BW	`<SAP System ID>~<SAP client Number>/<SAP role>`
	 For example:
	 `PRD~100/Designers`

LDAP	`<Group distinguished name>`
Active Directory	For example: `CN=Board,CN=Groups,DC=COMPANY,DC=COM`

Table 3.10 Name of Created Group, Depending on Authentication Mode

It is not possible to have two groups mapped to two LDAP or Active Directory servers groups that have the same distinguished name.

Once they are created, you can use add or move these to other groups and assign security to them. However you cannot add some Enterprise users to them. Their only specificity is their mapping to an external group that is used by mapped users to connect. For this reason, if you remove a mapped user from his mapped group:

▶ If the option is to create an alias when the user logs on to BI 4.0 (see Section 3.5.2), then he is recreated the next time he tries to log on.

▶ Otherwise, it is recreated during the next update, and he can't log on in the meantime.

3.5.4 Updating Groups and Users

Changes may occur in the external system used for authentication. Since these mapped users and groups have been created from this system, these changes impact this mapping. On the other hand, if some users created from the external system are deleted from the CMS repository, then with the group mapping in place, the user can still reconnect.

These cases are described in the following two sections.

Changes in the External System

If a new user is added in the external system into a group that is mapped into the CMS repository, then this user is created the CMS repository:

▶ If a groups and users update occurs before this user logs on to the CMS repository and if the option is to create new aliases during this update (see Section 3.5.2), then the user is created during the update.

▶ Otherwise, the user is created in the CMS repository the first time he logs on to BI 4.0.

If a mapped group is deleted in the external system, the corresponding group is not deleted in the CMS repository and the mapped users can still log on. If an update happens...

▶ After a groups update, then the mapped group is deleted in the CMS repository and the mapped users can no longer log on.

▶ After a groups and users update, then both the mapped group and users are deleted in the CMS repository. The users can no longer log on.

If a mapped user is deleted in the external system, then he can no longer log on to the CMS repository since the BI 4.0 system can't authenticate him against the external system. If an update happens...

▶ After a groups update, then there is no change for the user since it updates only the group, not their users.

▶ After a groups and users update, the user—along with his personal folders, inboxes, and so on—is deleted from the CMS repository.

Changes in the CMS Repository

It is not possible to directly delete a group mapped to an external group from the CMC. Instead, you need to go to the authentication configuration page and remove the mapping.

Once the group mapping is deleted, the mapped users can no longer log on since this mapping no longer exists. If an update happens...

▶ After a groups update, then the group is deleted, but not the mapped users that belong to this group. These users still can't log on since the group that supported their mapping no longer exists. If you recreate the group mapping, and run a groups update, the mapped users can reconnect again and access their personal folders.

▶ After a users update, then the users the group contained are deleted. As users are deleted, so are their personal folders and the resources they contain.

Deleting a mapped user in the CMC deletes the user only in the BI 4.0 repository. Of course, all his personal resources (personal folders, inboxes, and so on) are deleted as well.

But if the mapped group of this user still exists in the BI 4.0 repository, then:

▶ If the option is to create the alias when the user logs on to BI 4.0 (see Section 3.5.2), then he is recreated the next time he tries to log on.

▶ Otherwise, it is recreated during the next update, and he can't log on in the meantime.

In both cases, when the user is recreated, the user is new and has empty personal folders and a different CUID.

3.5.5 Scheduling Groups and Users Update

As described in Section 3.5.4, you can update group or user mapping on demand. You can also schedule this update to be run when the system is less used to avoid workload during peak activities. Furthermore, by defining a schedule frequency, you can make sure your system is regularly synchronized with the external system.

The scheduling recurrence options are the same as the ones supported by the BI platform to schedule a report. To define and run these schedules, you need to have a Job Server up and running in your servers.

You can schedule both a group update or an update for groups and users. A scheduled update uses the same options defined for an on-demand update and proceeds in the same way, with similar output.

3.6 Managing Aliases in the CMC

Managing aliases is done in the CMC, in the user's properties panel. Let's explore the various tasks involved in managing aliases—creating, assigning, reassigning, enabling and disabling, and deleting the alias, as well as enabling authentication selection for the BI Launch Pad.

3.6.1 Creating an Alias

You can only create an alias for a user that already exists in the CMS repository. Furthermore, it is not possible to create an Enterprise alias for a user who already has one. This alias can only be an alias to an external system, with which the BI 4.0 system has been configured. You must also have mapped a group from this external system to a group in the CMS repository.

To create an alias, follow these steps:

1. Go to the USERS AND GROUPS tab in the CMC.

2. Select the user to assign a new alias.

3. In the menu bar, select MANAGE • PROPERTIES, or right-click the user and in the contextual menu select PROPERTIES. The PROPERTIES panel opens to display the aliases in the ALIAS section on the bottom of this panel, as shown in Figure 3.8.

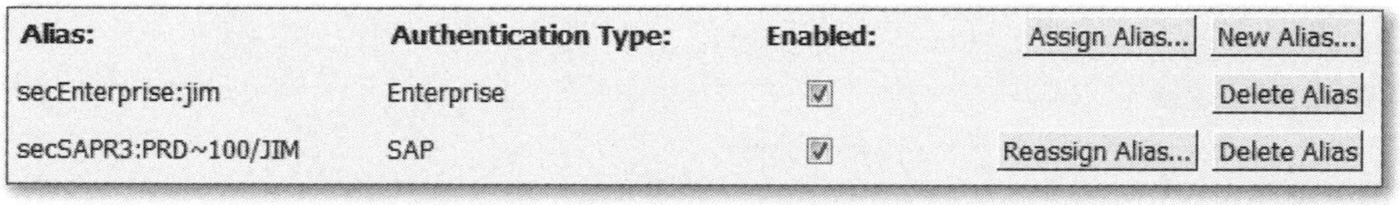

Alias:	Authentication Type:	Enabled:		
			Assign Alias...	New Alias...
secEnterprise:jim	Enterprise	☑		Delete Alias
secSAPR3:PRD~100/JIM	SAP	☑	Reassign Alias...	Delete Alias

Figure 3.8 Alias Section in the User's Properties Panel

4. Click the NEW ALIAS button to enter the new alias details.

5. In the AUTHENTICATION TYPE dropdown menu, select the new alias authentication mode: SAP NetWeaver BW, LDAP or ACTIVE DIRECTORY.

6. In the ACCOUNT text field, enter the reference of the user in the external system, using the syntax described in Table 3.9:

   ▸ For LDAP or Active Directory, enter the user's distinguished name.

   ▸ For SAP, use `<SAP System ID>~<SAP client number>/<SAP user name>`.

7. Click the UPDATE button to create the alias. The new alias is displayed in the ALIAS section.

8. Click the SAVE button to save these changes and close the PROPERTIES panel.

3.6.2 Assigning an Alias

When you assign an alias to a user following these steps, you move a third-party alias from another user to the user you are currently viewing.

1. Go to the USERS AND GROUPS tab in the CMC.

2. Select the user to assign a new alias.

3. In the menu bar, select MANAGE • PROPERTIES or right-click the user and select PROPERTIES from the contextual menu. The PROPERTIES panel opens. The aliases are displayed on the bottom of this panel, in the ALIAS section.

4. Click the ASSIGN ALIAS button to assign the alias.

5. In the CHOOSE WHICH ALIASES SHOULD BE ADDED TO text field, type the user name associated with the alias to assign, and not the alias itself.

6. Click the SEARCH button. All aliases that can be assigned to the user are displayed in the AVAILABLE ALIASES list, as shown in Figure 3.9.

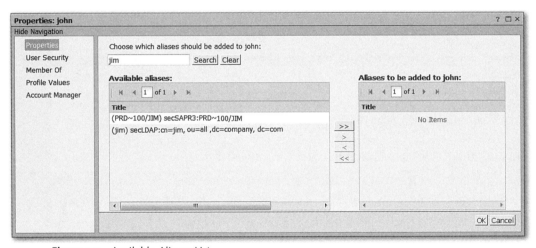

Figure 3.9 Available Aliases List

7. In the AVAILABLE ALIASES list, select the alias to assign. You can select multiple aliases by using the ⌷Ctrl⌷ key.

8. Click the > button to move the selected alias(es) to assign into the ALIASES TO BE ADDED TO list.

9. Click OK to validate.

10. Click OK to confirm and assign the selected alias(es).

11. Click the SAVE & CLOSE button to close the PROPERTIES panel.

3.6.3   Reassigning an Alias

It is possible to remove an alias from a user in order to attach it to another user. This is typically useful when you need to merge users. To reassign an alias, follow these steps:

1. Go to the USERS AND GROUPS tab in the CMC.

2. In the left pane, click USER LIST to display the list of users in the right pane.

3. Select the user associated with the alias to reassign.

4. In the menu bar, select MANAGE • PROPERTIES or right-click the user and select PROPERTIES from the contextual menu. The PROPERTIES panel opens. The aliases are displayed on the bottom of this panel, in the ALIAS section.

5. Click the REASSIGN ALIAS button in the same line as the alias to assign. It is not possible to assign an alias whose authentication mode is already Enterprise.

6. If this alias is the last one for this user, a message will ask you to confirm this task before deleting this user to reassign his alias.

7. After your confirmation, the panel lets you create a new Enterprise user to host this alias or assign the alias to another user that must have an Enterprise alias (as shown in Figure 3.10).

   ▶ Click the ASSIGN THE ALIAS TO A NEW USER link to create a new Enterprise for the user.

   ▶ To assign the alias to another existing Enterprise user, select the user among the ones listed in the AVAILABLE USERS list. You can type a name in the LOOK FOR text field and click the FIND NOW button to filter the AVAILABLE USERS list.

8. Click OK to assign the alias to the selected user and display this user's properties, including his new alias.

9. Click the SAVE & CLOSE button to save your changes and close the PROPERTIES panel.

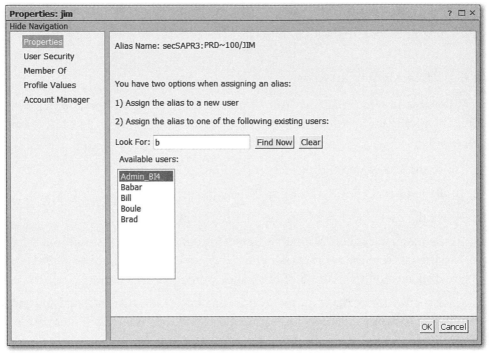

Figure 3.10 Different Options for Reassigning an Alias

3.6.4 Enabling/Disabling an Alias

You can disable an alias to prevent a user from logging on using the name and the authentication mode of this alias. If all aliases of a specific user are disabled, then the user can no longer log on. You can re-enable an alias later.

To disable or enable an alias, follow these steps:

1. Go to the USERS AND GROUPS tab in the CMC.

2. In the left pane, click USER LIST to display the list of users in the right pane.

3. Select the user associated with the alias to disable.

4. In the menu bar, select MANAGE • PROPERTIES or right-click the user and select PROPERTIES from the contextual menu. The PROPERTIES panel opens.

5. In the ALIAS section, unselect the checkbox in the ENABLED column to disable the alias, or select this checkbox to enable the alias.

6. Click the SAVE & CLOSE button to save this change and close the PROPERTIES panel.

3.6.5 Deleting an Alias

To delete an alias, follow these steps:

1. Go to the USERS AND GROUPS tab in the CMC.

2. In the left pane, click USER LIST to display the list of users in the right pane.

3. Select the user associated with the alias to delete.

4. In the menu bar, select MANAGE • PROPERTIES or right-click the user and select PROPERTIES in the contextual menu. The PROPERTIES panel opens. The aliases are displayed on the bottom of this panel, in the ALIAS section.

5. Click the DELETE ALIAS button next to the alias to delete. A confirmation windows opens.

6. Click OK to confirm and delete the selected alias.

7. Click the SAVE & CLOSE button to close the PROPERTIES panel.

When you delete an alias, the user cannot log on using this alias. He can log on only with the remaining aliases.

> **Warning!**
>
> A user must always have at least one alias. If you delete all aliases of a user, then the user itself is deleted.

3.7 Managing LDAP Authentication in the CMC

To set up LDAP authentication, the LDAP wizard in the CMC guides you through the different configuration steps.

3.7.1 Configuring LDAP Parameters

To configure the LDAP authentication, follow these steps:

1. Go to the AUTHENTICATION tab in the CMC.

2. The AUTHENTICATION tab lists the different authentication plug-ins available in your system. Double-click on LDAP to open the LDAP panel.

3. Click the START LDAP CONFIGURATION WIZARD button to start the configuration wizard.

4. In the next panel, enter your the LDAP hostname and port in the LDAP HOST (HOSTNAME:PORT) text field. If your LDAP server uses the default LDAP port (389), then you do not need to enter it.

5. Click the ADD button to add your LDAP server to the list, as shown in Figure 3.11.

   This LDAP server is considered the primary server. You can identically add other LDAP servers if you want to have a failover deployment. These additional LDAP servers are considered secondary.

Figure 3.11 Enter LDAP Hostname and Port

6. When you have entered your LDAP servers, click the NEXT button to define your LDAP server type.

7. In the LDAP SERVER TYPE dropdown menu, select the type of your LDAP server among the ones that are supported, as shown in Figure 3.12.

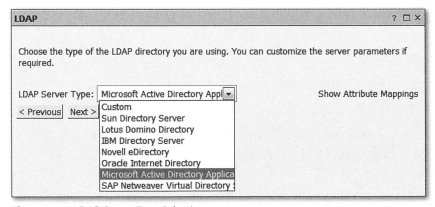

Figure 3.12 LDAP Server Type Selection

8. Click the SHOW ATTRIBUTE MAPPINGS link to display the attribute names exposed by your LDAP server and modify them if it does not use the default ones, as shown in Figure 3.13.

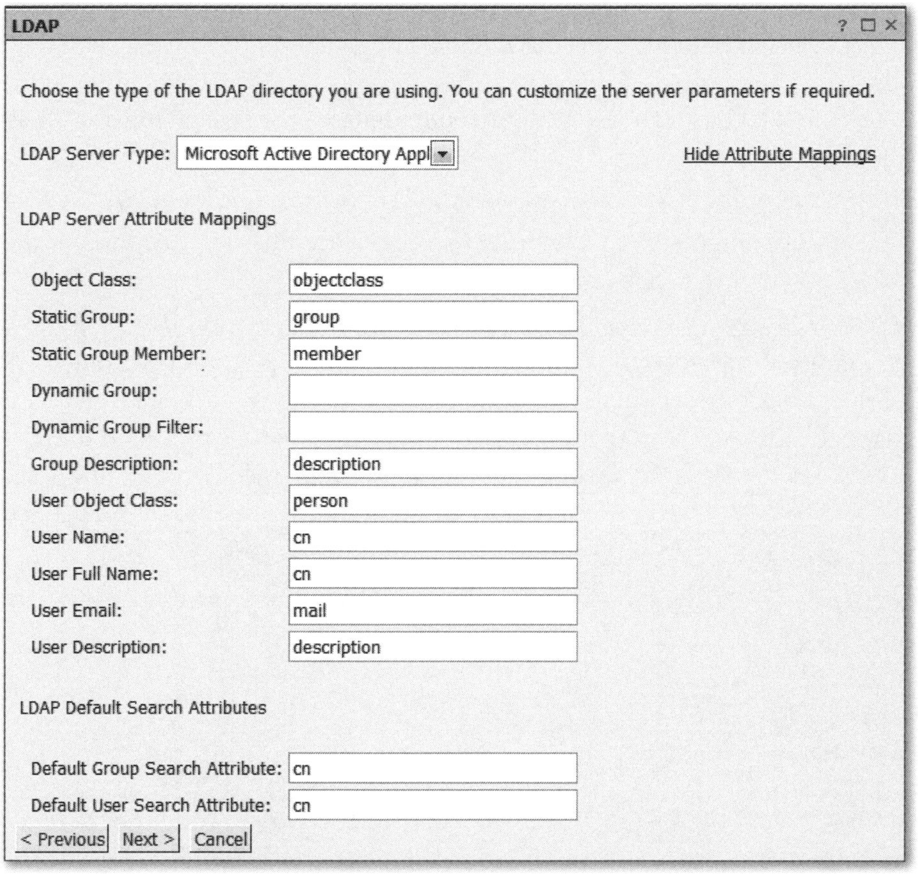

Figure 3.13 LDAP Attribute Mappings

9. Click the NEXT button to define your LDAP Base distinguished name.

10. In the BASE LDAP DISTINGUISHED NAME text field, enter the distinguished name of LDAP entry to consider as the top-level structure. In our example, it is DC=COMPANY,DC=COM, as shown in Figure 3.14.

Figure 3.14 Defining Base LDAP Distinguished Name

11. Click the NEXT button to define the account used to retrieve data from the LDAP server.

12. If your LDAP server allows anonymous logon, you do not need to fill the LDAP SERVER ADMINISTRATION CREDENTIALS section since BI 4.0 can connect to the LDAP server using anonymous logon.

    Otherwise, we recommend that you create in the LDAP server a dedicated account to be used by the BI platform to retrieve information from the LDAP server. If needed, ask your LDAP administrator to help you to create this LDAP user, then type the distinguished name of this user and his password into the LDAP SERVER ADMINISTRATION CREDENTIALS section, as shown in Figure 3.15.

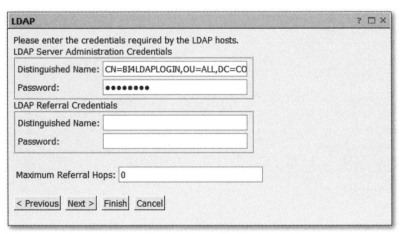

Figure 3.15 LDAP Account Used to Connect to the LDAP Server

13. If your LDAP server uses referrals, then in the LDAP REFERRAL CREDENTIALS section, type the credentials of this referral. A *referral* is a reference to another LDAP server that may contain an object (or information on this object) that has been requested but does not belong to the LDAP server.

14. In the MAXIMUM REFERRAL HOPS field, type the number of referral server to contact. If you maintain the value 0, no referral server is contacted.

15. Click the NEXT button to define SSL option.

16. In the TYPE OF SSL AUTHENTICATION dropdown menu, select one of the following SSL options (see Figure 3.16):

   ▶ BASIC (NO SSL): This is the least secure protocol since the logon and the password are sent through the network.

   ▶ SERVER AUTHENTICATION: The logon and password are also sent through the network, but they are encrypted using SSL before being sent. However, the LDAP server's identity is not verified.

   ▶ MUTUAL AUTHENTICATION: This is the most secure protocol; it is similar to the previous authentication, but the LDAP server's identity is verified.

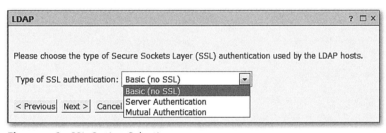

Figure 3.16   SSL Option Selection

17. Click the NEXT button.

18. If you have selected SERVER AUTHENTICATION or MUTUAL AUTHENTICATION, you need to define SSL options.

   Select one of the radio buttons, as shown in Figure 3.17 to define when the application accepts certificate. Java applications accept a server certificate only if it comes from a trusted Certificate Authority. For other applications, you can also select to always accept certificates or to accept a certificate *only* if it comes from a Certificate Authority *and* if the CN attribute of the server certificate exactly matches the hostname of the LDAP host you supplied at the beginning of the wizard.

   ▶ Click the NEXT button to enter the hosts of your deployment (see Figure 3.18).

   ▶ In the SSL HOST text field, enter a hostname and click the ADD button to add it to the list.

▶ In the list of hostnames, click the one you have added. In the corresponding text fields, enter the path to the certificate and key database files, the password for the key database and the nickname for the client certificate in the certificate database. To use any default value, click the USE DEFAULT VALUE checkbox.

▶ Repeat these steps to add each machine.

▶ To define the default values, in the hostname list, click the [default] line. Type the default values for each parameter.

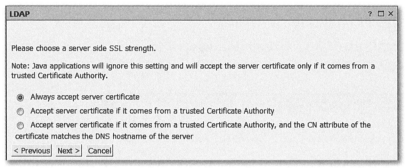

Figure 3.17 SSL Strength Options

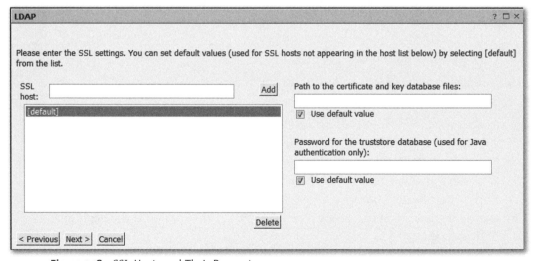

Figure 3.18 SSL Hosts and Their Parameters

19. Click the NEXT button to define the SSO option.

20. The AUTHENTICATION dropdown menu contains two options, as shown in Figure 3.19:

    ▶ BASIC (NO SSO): Users have to enter their logon and password in the logon page.

    ▶ SITEMINDER: Used to enforce SSO to the LDAP server through SiteMinder.

    Since we do not cover SiteMinder here, select the BASIC (NO SSO) option.

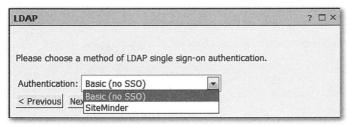

Figure 3.19　Select LDAP SSO Option

21. Click the NEXT button to display the panel shown in Figure 3.20 and to select the aliases creation options. The impact of these options are described in Section 3.5.4.

22. In the NEW ALIAS OPTIONS section, select one radio button to define how aliases are created from the LDAP system:

    ▶ Select the ASSIGN EACH ADDED LDAP ALIAS TO AN ACCOUNT WITH THE SAME NAME radio button to create the alias and to merge it to a user with the same name but a different authentication, if such user already exists in the CMS repository. Otherwise, if such a user does not exist, then a new user with the LDAP alias is created.

    ▶ Select the CREATE A NEW ACCOUNT FOR EVERY ADDED LDAP ALIAS radio button to always create another user with an LDAP alias in the CMS repository, even if another user with the same name already exists. In this case, the name of this new created user is suffixed with the number 0.

23. In the ALIAS UPDATE OPTIONS section, select one radio button to define when new aliases corresponding to external users not yet created in the BI 4.0 system are created:

▶ Select the CREATE NEW ALIASES WHEN THE ALIAS UPDATE OCCURS radio button to automatically create them from the LDAP system into the BI 4.0 system during a batch update.

▶ Select the CREATE NEW ALIASES ONLY WHEN THE USER LOGS ON radio button to create a new alias only when the user is accessing the BI 4.0 platform for the first time.

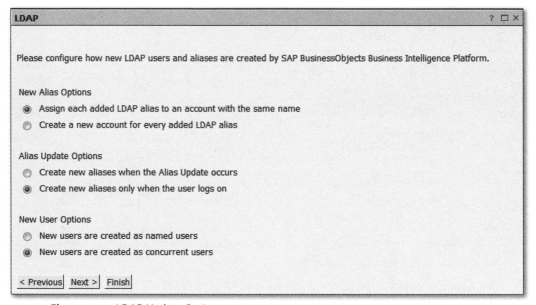

Figure 3.20 LDAP Update Options

24. In the NEW USER OPTIONS section, select the radio button to define the type of licences to assign to the users created from the LDAP server—named users or concurrent users.

25. Click the NEXT button to display the last screen of the LDAP panel.

26. Click the FINISH button.

At this point, the LDAP configuration is completed, and you can access the LDAP configuration parameters panel used to modify these LDAP parameters (see Section 3.7.2). In this panel, you need to enter the mapped groups to update.

3.7.2   Editing LDAP Authentication Parameters

The LDAP parameters panel lists all parameters related to LDAP authentication configuration. You may change any LDAP authentication parameters you have entered in the LDAP configuration wizard, but you can also edit the list of mapped groups and run or schedule an update of users and groups.

You enter this LDAP parameters panel after you have completed the LDAP configuration wizard. You can also open it by following these steps:

1. Go to the AUTHENTICATION tab in the CMC.

2. Double-click on the LDAP line to open the LDAP panel.

3. Modify the configuration parameters.

4. Click the UPDATE button to save your changes and close the LDAP panel.

In this panel, you may also run or schedule a groups or users update.

Updating Users and Groups

When configuring the LDAP authentication in the LDAP wizard, you do not enter the groups to map. After the configuration, you can enter this list of mapped groups in this LDAP PARAMETERS panel. To do so, follow these steps:

1. In the MAPPED LDAP MEMBER GROUPS section, add the distinguished name of the LDAP group to map and containing the LDAP users to import.

2. Click the ADD button to add this group to the list of groups to map, as shown in Figure 3.21.

Figure 3.21   Adding LDAP Group to Map

3. You may run an update on demand in the ON-DEMAND LDAP UPDATE section by following these steps:

▶ To update only groups, select the UPDATE LDAP USER GROUPS NOW radio button.

▶ To update groups *and* aliases, select the UPDATE LDAP USER GROUPS AND ALIASES NOW radio button.

▶ If you do not need to update these mappings, select the DO NOT UPDATE LDAP USER GROUPS AND ALIASES NOW radio button.

4. Click the UPDATE button to save your changes and to close the LDAP panel. The groups and/or aliases update you selected will be run.

Scheduling Users and Groups Update

You can schedule users and groups update. As schedules rely on the Job Server, check that you have a Job Server process up and running on your deployment. Then follow these steps:

1. To schedule an aliases update, in the LDAP ALIAS OPTIONS section, click the SCHEDULE button. The SCHEDULE: UPDATE AUTHENTICATION GROUP MEMBERSHIP panel opens.

2. Set the recurrence options for this schedule, as shown in Figure 3.22.

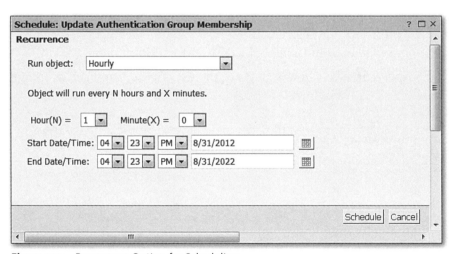

Figure 3.22   Recurrence Option for Scheduling

3. Click the SCHEDULE button to save your schedule and close the SCHEDULE: UPDATE AUTHENTICATION GROUP MEMBERSHIP panel.

4. You can identically schedule a groups update by clicking the SCHEDULE button in the SCHEDULE USER'S LDAP GROUP UPDATES section.

5. If you have no more parameters to set for the LDAP authentication, click the UPDATE button to close the LDAP panel.

If you have scheduled an update, you can cancel it by clicking the CANCEL SCHEDULED UPDATES button in the LDAP ALIAS OPTIONS or SCHEDULE USER'S LDAP GROUP UPDATES section.

3.8   Managing Active Directory Authentication

The Active Directory authentication configuration is more complex and error-prone than the LDAP configuration recently described, so make sure you have properly completed each step before moving to the next.

As described in Section 3.1.4, the objective of the Active Directory authentication is to map Active Directory groups to groups located in your CMS repository.

The configuration consists of the following abbreviated steps, which we walk through in this section:

1. Create two dedicated accounts on the Active Directory.

2. Configure the BI 4.0 servers to run with one of this account.

3. In the CMC, configure the system to authenticate with Active Directory.

4. In the CMC, configure the system to use Kerberos.

5. For Java applications to support Kerberos, you need to:

    ▶ Create Kerberos configuration files (`krb5.ini` and `bscLogin.conf`).

    ▶ Add Kerberos options in their Java command line.

Because Active Directory is tightly integrated with Windows, you may also benefit from setting up single sign-on with a Windows session. For this, you need to run some additional steps:

1. Create a keytab file.

2. Increase header size.

121

3. Configure web applications.

4. Set up a password in the keytab file.

5. Configure the browsers.

We illustrate these steps, using the following examples:

▶ The Active Directory domain name is `COMPANY.COM`.

▶ The Active Directory controller hostname is `ADSERVER`.

By default, all Kerberos files are saved in the *C:/WINNT* folder. You can use another folder. In this case, in the next workflows details, you should replace the folder *C:/WINNT* by the folder where you have saved these files.

3.8.1 Creating Dedicated Active Directory Accounts

To configure Active Directory authentication, we recommend that you create two accounts dedicated to this authentication in the Active Directory server:

▶ One used to run the BI 4.0 servers; in our example, this account is `bi4adservice`.

▶ One used by the BI platform only to query information from the Active Directory; it is used for every transaction with the Active Directory, so it must be always valid. In our example, this account is `BI4ADLOGIN`.

Open the PROPERTIES dialog box for these two accounts to set parameters, as shown in Figure 3.23:

▶ In the ACCOUNT EXPIRES section, select the NEVER radio button to make sure the accounts remain valid.

▶ If you are using Windows 2003 or 2008 for the domain controller, do not check the USE DES ENCRYPTION TYPES FOR THIS ACCOUNT checkbox since the RC4 encryption must be used.

Once these accounts are created, you need to give a Service Principal Name to the one used to run BI 4.0 servers. This Service Principal Name is the name used by Kerberos to identify this account. In our example, we name this Service Principal Name `BI4ADPRINCIPAL/COMPANY`.

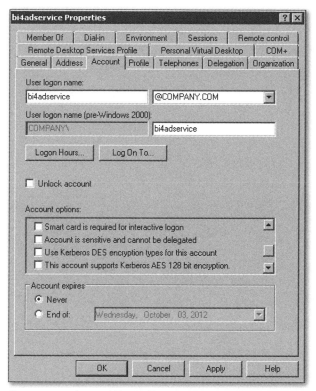

Figure 3.23 Account Properties

To give this Service Principal Name, you need to have installed `setspn.exe`, a Microsoft support tool that can be downloaded from the Microsoft website. Then run the following command on the domain controller, as shown in Figure 3.24 for our example:

```
setspn.exe -A <SPN>/<Domain Name> <Serviceaccount>
```

```
C:\Windows\system32\cmd.exe

C:\Users\Administrator>setspn.exe -A BI4APRINCIPAL/COMPANY.COM bi4adservice
Registering ServicePrincipalNames for CN=bi4adservice,OU=ALL,DC=COMPANY,DC=COM
        BI4APRINCIPAL/COMPANY.COM
Updated object

C:\Users\Administrator>
```

Figure 3.24 Running setspn Command

This Service Principal Name must be unique in your Active Directory forest. Most of the problems in this configuration are due to duplicated Service Principal Name. Check that this is not the case by launching the `ldifde` command

```
ldifde -l serviceprincipalname -r "(serviceprincipalname=<pattern>)" -f
C:\spn.txt
```

in which `<pattern>` is a regular expression used to find the Service Principal Name. It can be the complete Service Principal Name (`BI4ADPRINCIPAL/COMPANY`) or a string containing * characters as mask, as shown in Figure 3.25 for our example.

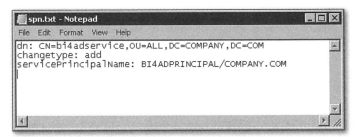

Figure 3.25 Running ldifde Command

As shown in Figure 3.26, the result file (`C:\spn.txt` in our example) must contain only one Service Principal Name, which is the one you have assigned to the account. If this is not the case, try to assign another Service Principal Name that is not yet assigned.

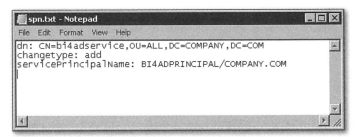

Figure 3.26 Result of ldifde Command

Once the Service Principal Name in Active Directory has been defined, you need to grant Kerberos delegation for this user, by following two steps:

1. Open the account PROPERTIES dialog box and click the DELEGATION tab.

2. Select the TRUST THIS USER FOR DELEGATION TO ANY SERVICE (KERBEROS ONLY) checkbox.

> **Note**
>
> This DELEGATION tab is available only after you have run the setspn command to associate the account with a Service Principal Name.

3.8.2 Starting BI 4.0 with Dedicated Account

Once the account dedicated to running BI 4.0 servers (in our example bi4adservice) has been created and attached to a Service Principal Name, you must declare it as an administrator on all machines running BI 4.0 servers and give it extra rights. Let's explore this process next:

1. Run the Computer Management application. Usually, you can open it by right-clicking the icon representing your computer on your Windows desktop and selecting MANAGE.

2. In the Computer Management application, go to CONFIGURATION • LOCAL USERS AND GROUPS • GROUPS.

3. In the left pane containing all groups, right-click ADMINISTRATORS, then select the ADD TO GROUP from the contextual menu to open the ADMINISTRATORS PROPERTIES dialog box.

4. Click the ADD button to open the SELECT USERS, COMPUTERS, SERVICE ACCOUNTS OR GROUPS dialog box.

5. Enter the logon name of the service account to run BI 4.0 (in our example, COMPANY\bi4adservice).

6. Click the CHECK NAMES button to check that the user is properly found. If it is not found, a dialog box called NAME NOT FOUND opens.

7. Click OK to close the SELECT USERS, COMPUTERS, SERVICE ACCOUNTS OR GROUPS dialog box. The user must appear in the MEMBERS list, as shown in Figure 3.27.

8. Click OK to close the ADMINISTRATORS PROPERTIES dialog box.

9. Exit the Computer Management application.

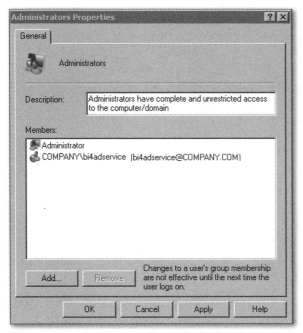

Figure 3.27 Administrators Properties Dialog Box

Now that this account is in the Administrators group, you need to give him some rights by following these steps:

1. On your Windows desktop, select START • ADMINISTRATIVE TOOLS • LOCAL SECU-RITY POLICY in order to run the Local Security Policy application.

2. In the left pane, select LOCAL POLICIES • USER RIGHTS ASSIGNMENT to display the list of rights.

3. In this list, double-click ACT AS PART OF THE OPERATING SYSTEM to open the ACT AS PART OF THE OPERATING SYSTEM PROPERTIES dialog box.

4. Click the ADD USER OR GROUP button to open the SELECT USERS OR GROUPS dialog box.

5. Enter the name of the account intended to run BI 4.0 (in our example, COMPANY\bi4adservice).

6. Click the CHECK NAMES button to check that the user is properly found. If it is not found, a dialog box called NAME NOT FOUND opens.

7. Click OK to close the SELECT USERS OR GROUPS dialog box.

8. Click OK to close the ACT AS PART OF THE OPERATING SYSTEM PROPERTIES dialog box.

9. Exit the Local Security Policy application.

You must now configure the BI 4.0 servers to start with this account.

1. On your Windows desktop, select START • PROGRAM • SAP BUSINESSOBJECTS BI PLATFORM 4 • SAP BUSINESSOBJECTS BI PLATFORM • CENTRAL CONFIGURATION MANAGER to start CCM, the application used to define some BI 4.0 server properties (see Chapter 2, Section 2.3.1).

2. In the servers list, right-click the SERVER INTELLIGENCE AGENT (SIA) line and in the contextual menu, select STOP to stop this agent.

3. Once it is stopped, right-click it again and in the contextual menu, select PROPERTIES to open the SERVER INTELLIGENCE AGENT PROPERTIES dialog box.

4. On the PROPERTIES tab, in the LOG ON AS section, unselect the SYSTEM ACCOUNT checkbox.

5. In the USER text field, enter the logon name of the service account who runs BI 4.0 (in our example, COMPANY\bi4adservice) and in the PASSWORD text field, the password you have set for this account (see Figure 3.28).

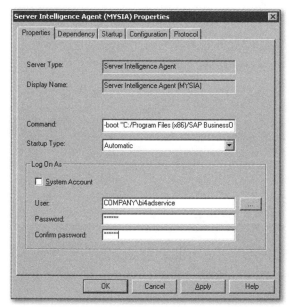

Figure 3.28 Server Intelligence Agent Properties Dialog Box

6. Click OK to close the SERVER INTELLIGENCE AGENT PROPERTIES dialog box.

7. In the servers list, right-click the SERVER INTELLIGENCE AGENT (SIA) line and, in the contextual menu, select START to restart it.

8. Once it is restarted, exit the CCM.

At this point, we have only started BI 4.0 on all machines with the account we have dedicated for Kerberos. The authentication is not yet in place and if you try to log on to any BusinessObjects tools, only the Enterprise authentication will be available. Any issue in these steps is usually due to the user rights. In case of a problem, on all machines, check the account validity and that all rights have been properly set (the "Administrators membership" and "Act as part of the operating system properties" rights).

3.8.3   Configuring AD Authentication into a BI 4.0 System

To set up the Active Directory authentication:

1. Log on to the CMC.

2. Go to the AUTHENTICATION tab.

3. The AUTHENTICATION tab lists the different authentications supported by your system. Double-click on the WINDOWS AD line to open the WINDOWS ACTIVE DIRECTORY panel.

4. In the WINDOWS ACTIVE DIRECTORY panel, click the " " hyperlink following the AD ADMINISTRATION NAME label, as shown in Figure 3.29.

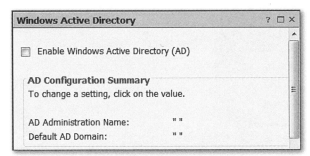

Figure 3.29   Windows Active Directory Panel

5. Click OK in the confirmation windows.

6. In the AD ADMINISTRATION CREDENTIALS section, enter the name and password of the account created to query information from the Active Directory (as shown in Figure 3.30).

   When you enter this name, you must follow this syntax:

   ```
   <Account name>@<DNS_domain_name>
   ```

7. In the DEFAULT AD DOMAIN text field, enter the default Active Directory domain (in our example COMPANY.COM).

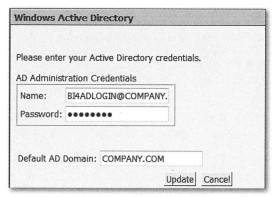

Figure 3.30 Windows Active Directory Credentials

8. Click the UPDATE button to return to the previous panel.

9. In the MAPPED AD MEMBER GROUPS section, in the ADD AD GROUP (DOMAIN\ GROUP) text field, enter an Active Directory group to map to a group in the CMS repository. You must follow the syntax <domain>\<group name> (for example, COMPANY\BI4ADGROUP).

10. Click the ADD button to add this group in the list of mapped groups, as shown in Figure 3.31. This group is displayed using the user's distinguished name.

11. Repeat these steps for all Active Directory groups to map in the CMS repository.

Mapped AD Member Groups
Add AD Group (Domain\Group): [   ] [Add]
secWinAD:CN=BI4ADGROUP,OU=ALL,DC=COMPANY,DC=COM [Delete]

Figure 3.31 Active Directory Group to Map

12. In the On-Demand AD Update section, you may select whether an update must be run at the end of the configuration:

    ▶ To update only groups, select the Update AD Groups now radio button.

    ▶ To update groups and aliases, select the Update AD Groups and Aliases now radio button.

    ▶ To update these mappings later, select the Do not update AD Groups and Aliases now radio button.

13. You can now define some options for the users and groups mapping. The impact of these options is described in Section 3.5.4. In the New Alias Options section, select one radio button to define how aliases are created from Active Directory:

    ▶ Select the Assign each added AD alias to an account with the same name radio button to create the alias and to merge it to a user with the same name but a different authentication, if such user already exists in the CMS repository. Otherwise, if such user does not exist, then a new user with the Active Directory alias is created.

    ▶ Select the Create a new account for every added AD alias radio button to always create another user with an Active Directory alias in the CMS repository, even if another user with the same name already exists. In this case, the name of this new created user mapped to Active Directory is suffixed with the number 0.

14. In the Alias Update Options section, select one radio button to define when new aliases corresponding to external users not yet created in the BI 4.0 system are created:

    ▶ Select the Create new aliases when the Alias Update occurs radio button to automatically create them from Active Directory into the BI 4.0 system during a batch update.

    ▶ Select the Create new aliases only when the user logs on radio button to create a new alias only when the user is accessing the BI 4.0 platform for the first time.

15. In the New User Options section, select the radio button to define the type of licences to assign to the users created from the Active Directory—named users or concurrent users.

16. Click the Update button.

At this point, you can only log on to Web Intelligence Rich Client and Universe Design Tool using Active Directory authentication. However, single sign-on with Windows is not yet activated because you must select WINDOWS AD in the AUTHENTICATION dropdown menu and provide your credentials to log on to the application.

3.8.4 Configuring BI 4.0 with Kerberos

Follow these steps to configure BI 4.0 to use with Kerberos:

1. Log on to the CMC.

2. Go to the AUTHENTICATION tab in the CMC.

3. The AUTHENTICATION tab lists the different authentication plug-ins available in your system. Double-click the WINDOWS AD line to open the WINDOWS ACTIVE DIRECTORY panel.

4. In the AUTHENTICATION OPTIONS section (Figure 3.32), select the USE KERBEROS AUTHENTICATION checkbox. The other option (NTLM) is supported only by a sub-set of BusinessObjects products: Universe Design Tool, Web Intelligence Rich Client, and Crystal Reports 2011. It is not supported by BusinessObjects web applications since they are written in Java. For the same reason, it is not supported by Information Design Tool, Translation Management Tool, Data Federator Administration Tool, Crystal Reports for Enterprise, or Query as a Web Service.

5. In the SERVICE PRINCIPAL NAME text field, enter the account and domain of the service account you created in the Active Directory (see Section 3.8.1).

   ▶ If you have only one Active Directory, you can use the User Principal Name too, in the format `BI4ADPRINCIPAL@COMPANY.COM`.

   ▶ To allow users from other domains than the default domain to log on, you must provide the Service Principal Name you mapped earlier (in our example, `BI4ADPRINCIPAL/COMPANY.COM`, as shown in Figure 3.32).

6. If you plan to use single sign-on to database (see Chapter 6, Section 6.3), then select the checkbox CACHE SECURITY CONTEXT (REQUIRED FOR SSO TO DATABASE).

7. Keep the ENABLE SIGN ON FOR SELECTED AUTHENTICATION MODE selected.

8. Click the UPDATE button to confirm your changes.

Figure 3.32 Authentication Options

3.8.5 Creating krb5.ini

The `krb5.ini` file is used to configure Kerberos. It defines which Windows domains to trust, so it must be created on any machine that must authenticate through Kerberos:

▶ Those that are running web application servers

▶ Those on which client tools (Information Design Tool, Translation Management Tool, and Data Federation Administration Tool) have been installed

This file can be stored in any folder; in our examples, we've saved it under the *C:\WINNT* folder, which is the default Windows location.

This file must contain the following lines:

```
[libdefaults]
   default_realm = <Active Directory domain name>
   dns_lookup_kdc = true
   dns_lookup_realm = true
   default_tgs_enctypes = rc4-hmac
   default_tkt_enctypes = rc4-hmac
[realms]
   <Active Directory domain name> = {
   kdc = <Hostname of domain controller>
   default_domain = <Active Directory domain name>
   }
[domain_realms]
   .company.com = <Active Directory domain name>
   company.com = <Active Directory domain name>
```

In this file, replace two parameters:

▶ `<Active Directory domain name>` by the Active Directory domain name, entered in Fully Qualified Domain Name format and in uppercase. In our example, it is `COMPANY.COM`.

▶ `<Hostname of domain controller>` by the hostname of the Domain Controller. In our example, it is `ADSERVER.COMPANY.COM`.

If your deployment contains several Active Directory domains, enter one entry for each domain below the `[realms]` section. Under the `[libdefaults]` section, the `default_realm` value may be any of the domains, but we recommend using the domain with the greatest number of users.

3.8.6   Creating bscLogin.conf

To configure the BusinessObjects platform to authenticate to Kerberos, you need to provide a configuration file called `bscLogin.conf`. Like the `krb5.ini`, you need to create this file on any machine that must authenticate through Kerberos (both clients and servers). Do this by following these steps:

1. If it does not already exist, create a file called `bscLogin.conf`, and store it in the *C:\WINNT* folder.

2. Add the following code to this `bscLogin.conf` configuration file:

```
com.businessobjects.security.jgss.initiate {
   com.sun.security.auth.module.Krb5LoginModule required;
};
```

If you want to enable the debug mode, add the following code:

```
com.businessobjects.security.jgss.initiate {
   com.sun.security.auth.module.Krb5LoginModule
      required debug=true;
};
```

3. Save and close the file.

3.8.7   Modifying the Java Options for Kerberos

To allow Java applications to authenticate to Kerberos, you need to modify the Java options. For example, to modify these options in a Tomcat application server that runs web applications (such as BI Launch Pad or CMC) or desktop applications based on Web Services (Crystal Reports for Enterprise or Query as a Web Services), proceed as follows:

1. From the START menu, select PROGRAMS • TOMCAT • TOMCAT CONFIGURATION.

2. Once this dialog box is open, click the JAVA tab.

3. As shown in Figure 3.33, add the following lines in the JAVA OPTIONS text field:

   ```
   -Djava.security.auth.login.config=C:\WINNT\bscLogin.conf
   -Djava.security.krb5.conf=C:\WINNT\krb5.ini
   ```

4. Click OK to close the APACHE TOMCAT PROPERTIES dialog box.

5. Restart Tomcat.

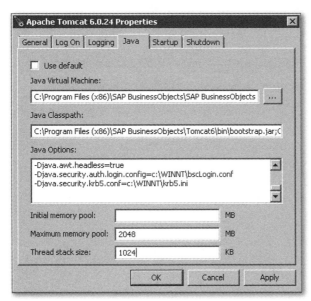

Figure 3.33 Apache Tomcat Properties Dialog Box

The exact workflow depends on the application server you use. Refer to its documentation for more details.

For BusinessObjects desktop applications that run with Java, you need to set these options in their initialization file. For example, do the following for the Information Design Tool:

1. Edit the file `InformationDesignTool.ini` located in *<INSTALLDIR>/win32_x86*. By default:

C:\Program Files\SAP BusinessObjects\SAP BusinessObjects Enterprise XI 4.0\win32_x86

2. Add the following parameters at the end of the Java command line:

```
-Djava.security.auth.login.config=C:\WINNT\bscLogin.conf
-Djava.security.krb5.conf=C:\WINNT\krb5.ini
```

3. Save the file.

For Translation Management Tool, you need to repeat the same steps in the `Trans-Mgr.ini` file. For Data Federator Administration Tool, this file is `DFAdministation-Tool.ini`.

After making these changes, you can log on to the BI Launch Pad, CMC, or any BusinessObjects Java application using WINDOWS AD authentication and by providing your Active Directory user name and password.

3.8.8   Creating a Keytab File

In order to log on to BI 4.0 products with single sign-on, you need to generate the keytab file. This file contains encrypted keys derived from the password and is used to authenticate the user to the web application without having to request his credentials.

1. Run the `ktpass` command with the following arguments (see Figure 3.34):

```
ktpass -mapuser <account> -pass <accountPWD> -princ <SPN> @<domainName>
-crypto <encryption> RC4-HMAC-NT -ptype KRB5_NT_PRINCIPAL -out <key-
tabFile> -kvno 255
```

where:

▸ `<account>` is the name of the account created to run BI 4.0 servers, in our example `bi4adservice` (see Section 3.8.1).

▸ `<accountPWD>` is this account's password.

▸ `<SPN>` is the Service Principal Name associated with this account. In our example, it is `BI4ADPRINCIPAL/COMPANY.COM`.

▸ `<domainName>` is the Active Directory domain name.

▸ `<encryption>` is the encryption associated with the service account you created for Vintela single sign-on for Java. For DES encryption, use `DES-CBC-MD5`. For RC4 encryption, use `RC4-HMAC-NT`.

▸ `<keytabFile>` is the name of the keytab file to generate.

135

Figure 3.34 Running ktpass Command

2. Copy the generated keytab file into the *C:\WINNT* folder of the Java application machine.

You can check the keytab file with the following command, as shown in Figure 3.35.

```
ktpass -in C:\WINNT\host.keytab
```

Figure 3.35 Running ktpass to Check Keytab File

If the file has been properly generated, it will return the parameters you have entered in the `ktpass` command.

> **Note**
>
> Although not recommended because this method is less secure, it is possible to explicitly provide the password directly in Tomcat instead of using the keytab file.

1. In the Java Tomcat options (see Section 3.8.7), add the following options:

```
-Dcom.wedgetail.idm.sso.password=<accountPWD>
```

2. Increase header size, as described in Section 3.8.9.

3. Configure web applications as described in Section 3.8.10, but do not add the following parameter:

```
idm.keytab=C:\WINNT\host.keytab
```

4. Configure your browsers, as described in Section 3.8.11.

3.8.9   Increasing Header Size

Active Directory creates a Kerberos token that is used in the authentication process. This token is stored in the HTTP header. Your Java application server has a default HTTP header size. To make sure the Kerberos token does not exceed this header size, set the size to 16384 bytes.

Refer to the documentation of your web application server to modify this header size. For Tomcat, for example, follow these steps:

1. On the server running Tomcat, open the `server.xml` file. On Windows, this file is located at *<Tomcat Installation folder>/conf*. If you are using the version of Tomcat installed with SAP BusinessObjects Enterprise on Windows and did not modify it, the Tomcat installation folder is *C:\Program Files (x86)\SAP Business-Objects\Tomcat6*.

2. In this file, find the corresponding `<Connector ... />` tag for the port number you have configured. For example, if you use the default port 8080, find the `<Connector ... />` tag containing the `port="8080"` setting:

```
<Connector URIEncoding="UTF-8" acceptCount="100" connectionTimeout="20000"
debug="0"  disableUploadTimeout="true"  enableLookups="false"
maxSpareThreads="75" maxThreads="150" minSpareThreads="25" port="8080"
redirectPort="8443" />
```

3. Add the following `maxHttpHeaderSize="16384"` setting within the `<Connector ... />` tag. For example:

```
<Connector URIEncoding="UTF-8" acceptCount="100" connectionTimeout="20000"
debug="0"  disableUploadTimeout="true"  enableLookups="false"
maxSpareThreads="75"  maxThreads="150"  maxHttpHeaderSize="16384"
minSpareThreads="25" port="8080" redirectPort="8443" />
```

4. Save and close the `server.xml` file.

5. Restart Tomcat.

3.8.10 Configuring Web Applications

Kerberos settings must also be specified for the web applications to accept single sign-on logon. When configured, users do not need to authenticate to log on to these web applications because they can reuse the Windows session. To configure this single sign-on:

1. In the BusinessObjects server installation, copy the `global.properties` and the `BIlaunchpad.properties` files located in *<INSTALLDIR>\Tomcat6\webapps\BOE\ WEB-INF\config\default* into the *<INSTALLDIR>\Tomcat6\webapps\BOE\WEB-INF\ config\custom* folder. These folders must have been installed in all machines where you have installed the BusinessObjects web application components.

   The `default` folder contains all web applications' default parameters. You can copy the folder's content into a `custom` folder and modify these copied files. The web application server prioritizes these files over the ones located in the `default` folder.

2. Edit the `global.properties` file copied in the `custom` folder to add the following parameters with these values:

   ```
   vintela.enabled=true

   idm.realm=<DefaultRealm>

   idm.princ=<SPrincipalN>

   idm.allowUnsecured=true

   idm.allowNTLM=false

   idm.logger.name=simple

   idm.logger.props=error-log.properties

   idm.keytab=C:\WINNT\host.keytab
   ```

   where:

   ▶ `<DefaultRealm>` is the realm you have defined as the `default_realm` in the `krb5.ini` file (see Section 3.8.5). In our case, it is `COMPANY.COM`.

   ▶ `<SPrincipalN>` is the Service Principal Name associated with the account used to run the BI 4.0 servers. In our case, it is `BI4ADPRINCIPAL/COMPANY.COM`.

3. Save and close this file.

4. In the same directory, edit the copied file `BIlaunchpad.properties` and set the default authentication mode to Active Directory in these two lines:

```
authentication.default=secWinAD
```

```
cms.default=<CMS name>:<CMS port number>
```

This file is used for BI Launch Pad configuration.

5. Restart your web application server.

To have Kerberos delegation set up at the website level, you need to associate in the Active Directory the URL used to access the web application to the account used to run BI 4.0. To do so, run the following command for each possible URL:

```
setspn -A HTTP/<URL> <account>
```

where:

▶ `<URL>` is the URL to access BI Launch Pad

▶ `<account>` is the account name used to start BI 4.0 (see Section 3.8.1).

For example, you can run these commands, as shown in Figure 3.36:

```
setspn -A HTTP/BI4SERVER.COMPANY.COM bi4adservice
setspn -A HTTP/BI4SERVER bi4adservice
setspn -A HTTP/10.11.12.13 bi4adservice
```

Figure 3.36 Running setspn Command

3.8.11 Configuring Browsers

To support single sign-on on BI Launch Pad web applications, you must configure the browsers on the client machines in order to enable integrated Windows authentication and add the URL of these BusinessObjects applications to the trusted sites. To do it on Internet Explorer, for example, follow these steps:

1. On the client machine, run Internet Explorer.
2. On the TOOLS menu, select the INTERNET OPTIONS button to open the INTERNET OPTIONS dialog box.
3. Click the ADVANCED tab.
4. Scroll to SECURITY and click the ENABLE INTEGRATED WINDOWS AUTHENTICATION button.
5. Click the APPLY button.
6. Click the SECURITY tab.
7. Select the LOCAL INTRANET icon.
8. Click the SITES button to open the LOCAL INTRANET dialog box.
9. In the LOCAL INTRANET dialog box, click the ADVANCED button.
10. In the ADD THIS WEBSITE TO THE ZONE text field, enter the URL of the server running BusinessObjects web applications. You can enter the full domain name of the site, for example

    `http://BI4SERVER.COMPANY.COM`.
11. Click the ADD button to add this URL into the WEBSITES list.
12. Click the CLOSE button.
13. Click OK to close the LOCAL INTRANET dialog box.
14. Click OK to close the INTERNET OPTIONS dialog box.
15. Exit and restart Internet Explorer browser window for these changes to take effect.

Repeat these steps on all browsers that may connect to BI Launch Pad.

After these changes, you can do two things:

▸ You can log on to BI Launch Pad without having to go through the logon page.

▸ You can log on to Web Intelligence Rich Client by selecting WINDOWS AD as the authentication mode then click the LOG ON button. You do not need to provide your Windows credentials.

3.8.12   Editing Active Directory Configuration

After the Active Directory configuration, you may need to modify some of its parameters. These parameters are quite similar to the ones you may set for LDAP authentication. To modify these parameters, follow these steps:

1. Go to the AUTHENTICATION tab in the CMC.

2. Double-click on the WINDOWS AD line to open the WINDOWS ACTIVE DIRECTORY panel.

3. Modify the configuration parameters.

4. Click the UPDATE button to save your changes and close the WINDOWS ACTIVE DIRECTORY panel.

In this panel, you may also run or schedule a groups or users update, as described next.

Updating Users and Groups

You may run an update on demand in the ON-DEMAND AD UPDATE section:

▶ To update only groups, select the UPDATE AD GROUPS NOW radio button.

▶ To update groups and aliases, select the UPDATE AD GROUPS AND ALIASES NOW radio button.

The update is run when you select the UPDATE button to save your changes and to close the WINDOWS ACTIVE DIRECTORY panel.

If you do not need to update these mappings, select the DO NOT UPDATE AD GROUPS AND ALIASES NOW radio button, which prevents the update from running when you leave this panel.

Scheduling Users and Groups Update

You can schedule users and groups update. As schedules rely on Job Server, check that you have a Job Server process up and running on your deployment. Then follow these steps:

1. Go to the AUTHENTICATION tab in the CMC.

2. Double-click on the WINDOWS AD line to open the WINDOWS ACTIVE DIRECTORY panel.

3. To schedule an aliases update, in the AD ALIAS OPTIONS section, click the SCHEDULE button. The SCHEDULE: UPDATE AUTHENTICATION GROUP MEMBERSHIP panel opens.

4. Set the recurrence options for this schedule, as shown in Figure 3.22.

5. Click the SCHEDULE button to save your schedule and close the SCHEDULE: UPDATE AUTHENTICATION GROUP MEMBERSHIP panel.

6. You can identically schedule a groups update by clicking the SCHEDULE button in the AD GROUP OPTIONS section.

7. If you have no more parameters to set for the Active Directory authentication, click the UPDATE button to close the WINDOWS ACTIVE DIRECTORY panel.

If you have scheduled an update, to cancel it, in the AD ALIAS OPTIONS or AD GROUP OPTIONS section, click the CANCEL SCHEDULE button.

3.9 Summary

To allow your users to log on to the BI 4.0 system, you need to define them in CMS repository. These users can be organized in groups for easier management.

You have different authentication modes for these users:

▶ Enterprise (default) authentication: All authentication info is saved in the CMS repository.

▶ External authentication: Authentication is indirectly done against an external system such as SAP NetWeaver BW, LDAP, or Active Directory.

Some tools also support the standalone mode, in which no CMS repository is required and in which users do not need to authenticate.

External authentication relies on the creation of mapped groups and users. A group from the external system is mapped to a group created in the CMS repository. All users from this external group can log on to the BI 4.0 system. Once they are authenticated against the external system, they are created in the CMS repository as mapped users.

With aliases, it is possible to allow the same user to authenticate into the CMS repository using different names and authentication modes.

External authentication requires some configuration steps to identify the BI 4.0 system against the external system and to authenticate users of this external system. In the case of Active Directory, you can also configure the Windows single sign-on, which allows the Windows session opened by the user to be re-used to automatically log him on to the BI 4.0 system.

Once users are created in the CMS repository, you can use the rights framework described in Chapter 4 to define what they are allowed to do or restricted from doing.

In the CMS repository, you can define for all objects a set of general and—depending on the object—specific rights. This rights framework supports group and folder inheritance and custom access levels, which are predefined sets of rights.

4   Rights Framework

Recall from Chapter 2 that all resources (such as applications, users, groups, folders, documents, universes, servers, categories, and so on) are stored as InfoObjects in the CMS repository. Any InfoObject follows the same security model based on rights and access control lists, which are collections of rights and specific values (either granted or denied) for those rights.

This chapter describes this rights framework model and the different concepts supported by these rights that work to secure your BI resources in the CMS repository, including the following:

▶ An introduction to assigned rights

▶ A comparison of general and specific rights

▶ An description of the rights inheritance model

▶ A description of all general rights, for application and for objects, and an explanation of how to administrate them in the Central Management Console

▶ An explanation of how to define and assign access levels—the recommended way to set security

Let's begin by exploring the concept of assigned rights, which will help lay the foundation for a discussion of the rights framework model.

4.1   Assigned Rights

Each right grants or denies a basic action. Each object stored in the CMS repository supports a set of rights. That list of rights is predefined and depends on the object type, meaning that the set of rights of this object *assigned* to a user or a group defines what this user or group can do with this object.

A right that is not explicitly granted or denied is not specified, meaning that it has no explicit value defined for this user or this group. However, a right can be inherited and, accordingly, granted or denied if it has been assigned to one of the parent folders or groups. In this case, different aggregation rules are applied in order to define the effective value of the right. If the effective value of this right remains unspecified, then it is denied for this user.

As explained in Chapter 2, users and groups can be nested within other groups. Rights can be assigned to these groups; different aggregation and inheritances rules define the effective value of a right for a user. The resulting value for this right, called the *effective right*, can be granted or denied.

There are two ways to assign a right for an object to a user or a group:

▶ Explicitly setting rights at a granular level is called setting *advanced rights*.

▶ Using an *access level* grants or denies a predefined set of rights.

The model is object-oriented, so the object that has been secured lists the denied and granted rights.

4.2   General and Specific Rights

In the CMS repository, there are three different categories of InfoObjects, which is the generic CMS container used to store any resources and data:

▶ *Application* InfoObjects: These InfoObjects represent applications, such as BI Launch Pad, Web Intelligence, Information Design Tool, or the Central Management Console (CMC).

▶ *System* InfoObjects: These InfoObjects are CMS repository core objects, such as users, groups, connections, universes, calendars, or events. Some, such as universes InfoObjects, reference a file saved in the FRS file system.

▶ *Content* InfoObjects: These InfoObjects are non-core objects, such as Web Intelligence reports, Crystal Reports documents, text files, and so on. They typically contain BI resources or users' content, and reference a file saved in the FRS file system.

From a security point of view, the CMS considers all objects types of the same category identically and enforces a set of basic possible actions (view, delete, edit, etc.) that are common to all object types of the same category. These actions are secured by rights; rights common to all objects in the same categories are called *general rights*.

These general rights have more or less the same meaning for all objects in the same category. For example, the "Log into and see this object in the CMC" right is a general right that allows the user to log on to the CMS repository through this application and to manage this application in the CMC. The "View objects" right is a system and content general right because it applies equally to system objects such as users or connections and to content objects such as reports or text files. Sections 4.5 and 4.6 provide an exhaustive list of general rights.

General rights are always enforced by the CMS repository, and an application cannot override the CMS repository behavior. However, an application can also enforce these rights by itself.

Example

If your "Edit objects" right on a report is denied, then any attempt to modify or send a new version of this report to the CMS repository raises an error message. But the reporting tool used to create this report may check this right and prevent you from modifying this report before sending it back to the CMS repository.

In addition to these general rights, each type of object may support an additional set of rights that apply only to that object type and that is specific to that object type. For example, the "Refresh the report's data" right applies only to report objects.

These *specific rights* can be divided into three different categories, one category per InfoObject category: system, content, or application. But remember that the object type defines the list of specific rights that applies to the object. This list of rights secures the features supported by the application or the object.

All specific rights for applications and objects are detailed in Chapter 5.

Figure 4.1 shows an example of rights assigned to a user and groups. Two rights of the Web Intelligence report (Sales.wid) have been assigned to the user vishal:

▶ The general right "View objects" has been explicitly granted.

▶ The specific right "Refresh data" has been explicitly denied.

The group `ITPublishers` has been explicitly granted two rights for the application CMC:

► The general right "Log on to the CMC…"

► The specific right "Allow access to Instances Manager"

The group `Presales` has been explicitly granted some rights for the folder EMEA.

It is important to note that only rights explicitly granted or denied are stored. Other rights are considered not specified, so they are denied by default or inherited.

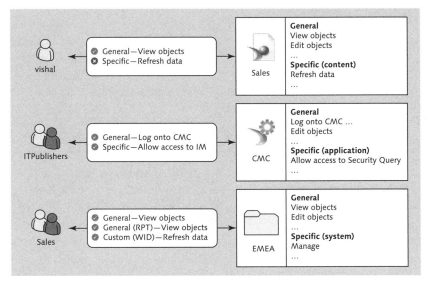

Figure 4.1 Rights of Different InfoObjects Assigned to User and Groups

4.3   Inheritance

Inheritance, which allows you to set security at a higher level and cascade it downward, is a very common capability in security. Inheritance provides the following key benefits, among others:

► It eases maintenance and administration because you do not need to set rights to each individual object. You can define them at a parent level, which is sufficient to have it applied to all objects.

▶ It reduces CMS repository storage because you no longer need to store the rights values for each individual object and user in the CMS repositories.

The BI platform supports two inheritance mechanisms, which provide you a flexible framework to design security:

▶ From groups to the users and sub-groups they contain

▶ From folders to the objects and sub-folders they contain

Let's first look at group inheritance.

4.3.1 Group Inheritance

As you learned in Chapter 3, in the CMS repository, you can organize users in groups and sub-groups. The main advantage of this organization is the rights inheritance. This allows some rights assigned to a group to be also inherited by the users and sub-groups it contains. As groups are often created to categorize users who have similar roles, using group inheritance to define rights may ease administration and maintenance.

When a right is assigned to a group for an object, then all users and sub-groups of this group inherit of the value of this right, unless inheritance has been broken (this topic is discussed in Section 4.3.5). However, if a right is explicitly assigned to a group or a user, then this individualized right overrides the right that can be inherited by his parent group, as shown in Table 4.1.

		The right for the parent group is ...		
		Explicitly granted	Explicitly denied	Not specified
The right for the user or the group is ...	Explicitly granted	Granted	Granted	Granted
	Explicitly denied	Denied	Denied	Denied
	Not specified	Granted	Denied	Not specified, and thus denied

Table 4.1 Effective Right, Depending on Right Assigned to a User or a Group and its Parent Group

For example, imagine a user or a group that belongs to two groups. If the same right has been defined for these two parent groups, then aggregation rules define the final inherited right. Table 4.2 describes the value of a right inherited by a user or a group, depending of the value of the same right assigned to its two parent groups.

		The right for Parent Group 1 is...		
		Explicitly granted	Explicitly denied	Not specified
The right for the Parent Group 2 is...	Explicitly granted	Granted	Denied	Granted
	Explicitly denied	Denied	Denied	Denied
	Not specified	Granted	Denied	Not specified

Table 4.2 Aggregation of Rights Inherited from Two Parent Groups

These aggregation rules are associative and commutative, and can be extended to more groups.

4.3.2 Folder Inheritance

Recall from Chapter 2 that you can organize objects into folders in the CMS repository. These folders also support rights inheritance, which can be useful when defining security that must apply similarly to a set of objects.

These folders are organized into a tree structure. The object types determine the root folder, as follows:

▶ Access Levels: For access levels (see Section 4.8)

▶ Connections: For connections (see Chapter 6)

▶ Categories: For categories used to classify and sort objects saved in public folders

▶ Calendars: For all system calendars

▶ Cryptographic Keys: For keys used for encryption (see Chapter 2, Section 2.5)

▶ Events: Contains all system events

- ▶ Remote Connections: Contains all connections to other CMS system; used for Federation (see "Replicate content" right in Section 4.5.1)

- ▶ Groups: Contains all the user groups created in the CMS repository

- ▶ Folders: Top-root folder of Public Folders

- ▶ Inboxes: Contains all users' inboxes

- ▶ Personal Categories: Contains all users' personal categories

- ▶ Personal Folders: Contains all users' personal folders

- ▶ Profiles: For the profiles used in publications (see Chapter 9, Section 9.5)

- ▶ Replication Lists: Contains the list of objects to be synchronized through Federation (see "Replicate content" right in Section 4.5.1)

- ▶ Servers: Contains all the servers running on the deployment

- ▶ Server Groups: Contains all the server groups created to gather several servers

- ▶ Temporary Storage: Contains the system temporary folders

- ▶ Universes: Contains universes created by Universe Design Tool and Information Design Tool

- ▶ Users: Contains all the users created in the CMS repository

Rights assigned to any of these root folders are called *top-level security* rights and, by default, they are inherited by all objects that belong to this object tree. This mechanism is useful to define a common security for all objects of the same type.

Folders are organized as a tree structure, in which an object can belong only to one folder, so you don't need to take aggregation from different parent folders into consideration.

By default, the rights assigned for a folder to a user or to a group are inherited by all objects of this folder. Thus, for all these objects, the same security applies to the user or the group. If this folder contains also sub-folders, then these rights are also inherited by these sub-folders.

However, as mentioned in Section 4.3.1, if a right is explicitly assigned to an object or a folder, then this explicit right overrides the right inherited by its parent folder. This is shown in Table 4.3, which presents a matrix for group inheritance similar to that in Table 4.1.

		The right for the parent folder is ...		
		Explicitly granted	**Explicitly denied**	**Not specified**
The right for the object or folder is ...	**Explicitly granted**	Granted	Granted	Granted
	Explicitly denied	Denied	Denied	Denied
	Not specified	Granted	Denied	Not specified, and thus denied

Table 4.3 Effective Right, Depending on Right Assigned to an Object or a Folder and its Parent Folder

In addition to this general rule defined by Table 4.3, various folder inheritance options can modify these rules. But before detailing them, let's review the different rights that can be set at the folder level.

4.3.3 General and Type-Specific Rights

A folder may contain different types of objects; each type of object supports different rights. To be exhaustive when defining rights inherited by objects saved in a folder, you must assign at the folder level any general and specific rights for all objects that can be saved in this folder.

All general rights are supported by all objects. In order to provide more flexibility in folder inheritance, this security model lets you set at the folder level different general rights:

▶ **Global general rights inherited by default by all objects in the folder**

▶ **General rights specific to each object type**
For each object type (Web Intelligence, Crystal Reports, and so on), you can define general rights that are inherited only by objects of this type located in this folder and its sub-folders. In this case, these rights override the global general rights.

▶ **Specific rights for any object type**
These rights are available for specific object types only. For example, the right to export a report's data appears for Crystal Reports documents but not for text files.

By using global and specific general rights, you can define security at the folder level that depends on the object type. Global and specific general rights are inherited by objects in the folder, unless scope of right (see Section 4.3.4) or breaking inheritance (see Section 4.3.5) has been used.

In the example depicted in Figure 4.2, the user jim is granted the general "View objects" right. However, he is denied the Crystal Reports-specific general "View objects" right. Thus, he can see the Web Intelligence documents and any other document types saved in this folder *except* the Crystal Reports documents.

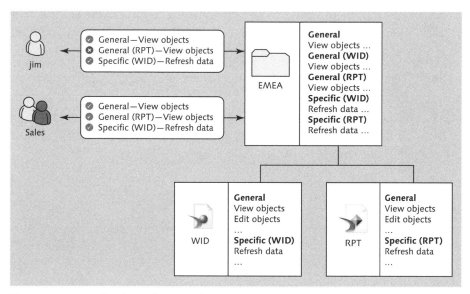

Figure 4.2   Example of Specific General Rights Inheritance

4.3.4   Scope of Rights

When you set rights at the folder level, you can also define the scope of each individual right you assign. This scope of right is a way to control how a right is inherited by the objects of this folder. You have the options to define whether this right applies to only the folder itself, the objects and folders located *in* this folder, or both (the default option).

Example

A possible application of the scope of right is to grant the "Add objects to this folder" right to a user but to limit its scope to the folder itself, and not its sub-objects. Thus, the user can create new sub-folders in this folder. But, because this right does not apply to this sub-folder, he cannot create a new sub-folder in it. This limits the sub-folder depth to only one level.

Note that the same behavior can also be implemented by granting the "Add objects to this folder" general right but denying the "Add objects to this folder" general folder-specific right for this folder (see Section 4.3.3 for more information on this topic).

The scope of right can be defined for any individual right you can set at the folder level: global general rights, specific general rights, or specific rights for each different type of object the folder can contain.

The scope of right also applies to objects that behave like folders, such as inboxes, Favorites folders, object packages, or Crystal Reports documents. A Crystal Reports document saved in the CMS repository can be considered a container, and thus the scope of right defines whether the rights must also apply to objects saved below another Crystal Reports document.

4.3.5 Breaking Inheritance and Overriding Rights

The security model in XI R2 is less flexible than the one in BI 4.0. For example, when a right is denied for a folder to a user or a group in XI R2, if you grant the right to an object in this folder, then it remains denied. An object cannot have more rights than its parent.

The only way to work around this behavior is to break inheritance. Thus, when defining rights for a user or a group for an object, you can decide to disable inheritance from any of the following groups:

▶ **From the parent groups**
All rights assigned or inherited by the parent groups are no longer propagated to the user or the group.

▶ **From the parent folder**
All rights assigned or inherited by the folder containing the object are no longer propagated by the object.

▶ **From both the parent groups and the parent folder**

When disabled, all rights inherited from the parent groups or parent folder (the final option) are no longer inherited and they become not specified for the object. Thus, breaking inheritance has two drawbacks:

▶ It applies to all rights of the objects and it is not possible to individually select the rights that are not inherited.

▶ All rights become not specified, and so by default are considered denied, and you have to redefine them.

In XI 3.x, the rights framework behavior has been modified with the introduction of rights override, which is still how rights are computed in BI 4.0. By default, an explicit right overrides the rights inherited by the parent groups or folder:

▶ A right assigned for an object to a user overrides the corresponding right assigned for this object to the groups containing the user, as described in Section 4.3.1.

▶ A right assigned for an object to a user overrides the corresponding right assigned for the object's parent folder to the user, as described in Section 4.3.2.

Similar to scope of rights, which lets you define how individual rights are inherited, rights override makes breaking inheritance less interesting: You can grant a previously denied inherited right without having to lose all other inherited rights.

But although they are less useful, breaking inheritance options are still available in BI 4.0 and you can still use them if you have specific reason to do so. Note that if you break folder inheritance, then sub-object scope of rights no longer applies.

4.4   Non-Owner and Owner Versions of Rights

Every right, both general and specific, exists in fact in two versions:

▶ A *non-owner* version (such as "View objects" and "Edit objects")

▶ An *owner* version (such as "View objects that the user owns" and "Edit objects that the user owns")

The owner version of the right is intended to give more flexibility when assigning right to folders that can contain objects belonging to different owners. The owner of an object is the user who has created it. If this user is deleted, then the object is owned by the Administrator user.

The right owner version can also be used to secure folders or reports that can have several instances owned by different owners. In this case, you may want to define security that could indifferently apply to all users, without the need to assign different rights to different users. If you set a non-owner version of a right to the Everyone group, this right is applied for all users for all objects in this folder or for all instances of this object.

By using the owner version of the right, you can define a different value for this right for the user that owns the object.

The owner version of a right secures the same workflows and capabilities than the non-owner version of the right. It applies only to the user who owns the object, and it overrides the value of the non-owner version of the right if it is denied or not specified. Table 4.4 shows whether you are granted or denied an action, depending on the object owner and on the values of the right's non-owner and owner version.

		Owner version of the right	
		Granted	Denied
Non-owner version of the right is granted	You own the object	Granted	Granted
	You do not own the object	Granted	Granted
Non-owner version of the right is denied	You own the object	Granted	Denied
	You do not own the object	Denied	Denied

Table 4.4 Non-Owner and Owner Rights Combination Matrix

For example, in Figure 4.3, you assign the following rights for the folder `Common-Reports` to the `Everyone` group:

▶ View objects: Granted

▶ Add objects to the folder: Granted

▶ Edit objects: Denied

▶ Delete objects: Denied

▶ Edit objects that the user owns: Granted

▶ Delete objects that the user owns: Granted

With these rights, any user can create a document and add it in the folder. Any user can view it, but only its owner—the user who has created it—can edit or delete it. For example, `bill` has created a document called `patent.wid`; `jim` can see it, but only `bill` can edit or delete it. Identically, `jim` has created a document called `sales.wid`, which `bill` can view, but only `jim` can edit or delete.

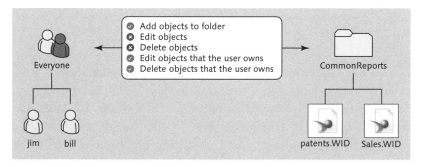

Figure 4.3 Example of Owner-Version Rights

The owner version of a right is usually named by adding "…that the user owns" to the name of the non-owner version of the right.

4.5 Objects General Rights

General rights are rights defined for all objects and enforced by the BI system itself. Depending on the application, there are two philosophies about enforcing this right if it is denied:

- The application prevents you from running the action.
- The application lets you try the action, but the BI system returns an error message when the client tool commits these changes in the CMS repository.

Section 4.5.1 covers the following general rights:

- Add objects to the folder
- View objects
- Edit objects
- Delete objects
- Translate objects
- Copy objects to another folder
- Modify the rights users have to objects
- Securely modify rights users have to objects
- Securely modify rights inheritance settings
- Use access level for security assignment
- Replicate content

Some general rights are supported only by objects that can be scheduled (Crystal Reports, Lifecycle Manager Job, Object Package, Program, Publication, and Web Intelligence reports) or that are file formats for instances of scheduled objects (Adobe Acrobat, Microsoft Excel, Microsoft Word, Rich Text, and Text). It is not possible to set some rights individually to each instance, but these rights can control the actions allowed on all instances. They are used to control scheduling capabilities.

Section 4.5.2 covers the following rights:

- Define server groups to process jobs
- Delete instances
- Pause and resume document instances
- Reschedule instances
- Schedule document to run
- Schedule on behalf of other users
- Schedule to destinations
- View document instances

4.5.1 General Rights in Detail

Let's discuss important details about all these general rights.

Add objects to the folder

This right lets you add objects to a folder. It is mandatory if you want to save or schedule an object (report, universe…) in this folder.

It also applies to objects that behave like folders, such as inboxes, Favorites folders, object packages, or Crystal Reports documents. A Crystal Reports document saved in the CMS repository can be considered a container, and thus this right secures the ability to add a Crystal Reports document in another Crystal Reports document.

View objects

This mandatory right must be granted to you in order to apply an action to an object. If you have this right denied for an object, you won't be able to see or access it. In fact, the CMS repository behaves as if that object did not exist for you. In the remainder of this document, we do not specify that this "View objects" right is needed to apply any other action.

If the right is denied at the folder level, by the rules of inheritance, it applies also to the objects contained in this folder. Thus, both the folder and the objects it contains are not accessible to the user. Even if you grant the "View objects" right to an object in this folder, you are not able to access it since you cannot view the folder. However, if you have a direct link to the object, you can directly open it.

Edit objects

This right allows you to make a change to the object saved in the CMS repository:

▶ The object data or metadata, saved in the InfoObject (name, keywords, description, properties, and so on)

▶ If any, the corresponding file saved in the FRS file system (Web Intelligence or Crystal Report document, universe, and so on)

▶ The links between this object and other objects

Delete objects

This right allows you to delete the object from the CMS repository. When you delete an object, you also delete both the InfoObject saved in the CMS repository and any corresponding files saved in the FRS file system.

Deleting an object cannot be undone.

Translate objects

This right allows you to translate any object using the Translation Management Tool. If this right is denied, then you are not able to extract the strings to translate from the object or to re-import its translated strings.

Copy objects to another folder

This right lets you create copies of objects and place them in other folders in the CMS repository. To do this, you also require the "Add objects to the folder" right on the destination folder.

When you copy an object:

▶ The advanced rights or the access levels assigned to it are not copied. The new object inherits only the rights assigned to its parent folder.

▶ Its instances, if any, are not copied either.

Modify the rights users have to objects

The right allows you to modify any right—for any user—on that object. Note that this right is very powerful because once this right is granted to you for this object, you can then grant yourself—or anyone else—any right on that object and thus gain the full control over the object by granting all the missing rights. For this reason, it is more secure to use the "Securely modify the rights users have to this object" right.

Securely modify the rights users have to objects

This right is similar to but more restrictive than the "Modify the rights users have to objects" because it limits the list of rights and users you can assign.

If you have this right on an object, you can grant or deny only the rights that you are already granted. For example, if you have the "View objects" and "Securely modify the rights users have to objects" rights on an object, you cannot give yourself more rights and can give or take away those two rights only.

Table 4.5 defines in which cases you can grant or deny a right, depending on the "Modify the rights users have to objects" and "Securely modify the rights users have to objects" rights.

		Modify the rights users have to objects	
		Granted	Denied
Securely modify the rights users have to objects	Granted	You can grant or deny any right.	You can grant a right only if it is granted to you. You can deny any right.
	Denied	You can grant or deny any right.	You cannot grant or deny any right.

Table 4.5 Modify Rights Combination Matrix

Use access level for security assignment

Even if this right is a general right, it applies in fact only to an access level object. For other objects, it has no effect.

If this right is denied to you for an access level (see Section 4.8), then you cannot assign this access level to an object.

Replicate content

This right allows you to replicate objects to another system in a federated deployment. A federated deployment consists of several CMS repositories located in different geographical places. To synchronize the content between the CMS repositories, you need to define in the CMC a Federation job that defines the objects to be synchronized between the CMS repositories and the synchronization frequency. But if this right is denied, you cannot select this object on which the right is denied when defining a Federation job.

4.5.2 General Rights Related to Scheduling

Define server groups to process jobs

This right is supported only by object types that can be scheduled and for which you can specify processing servers (Crystal Reports, Object Package, Program, Publication, and Web Intelligence). The server group is one of the scheduling parameters you can set when defining the scheduling of an object in the CMC or BI Launch Pad.

Delete instances

This right is supported only by object types that can be scheduled. It allows you to delete object instances in the CMC or in the BI Launch Pad. If you already have the "Delete objects" right, you do not need this right to delete instances. (But usually, you deny the "Delete objects" right but grant the "Delete instances" right so the user can delete only instances but not the object itself.)

Pause and resume document instances

This right is supported only by object types that can be scheduled. In the CMC or BI Launch Pad, it lets you pause or resume object instances that are running.

Reschedule instances

This right is supported only by object types that can be scheduled. In the CMC or BI Launch Pad, it lets you reschedule object instances. When rescheduling, you do not need to retype prompts.

Schedule document to run

This right is supported only by object types that can be scheduled. In the CMC or BI Launch Pad, it lets you schedule objects.

Schedule on behalf of other users

This right is supported only by object types that can be scheduled. In the CMC or BI Launch Pad, it lets you schedule objects for other users or groups. The user or group that you schedule the object for becomes the owner of the object instance. Chapter 9 provides more details about this right.

To schedule an object for other users or groups, you also need the "Schedule document" right on the object.

Schedule to destinations

This right is supported only by object types that can be scheduled. It lets you modify the default destinations specified for scheduling and schedule objects to other destinations than the current object location.

To schedule the object to destinations, you also need the following rights:

- ▶ The "Schedule document" right on the object that you want to schedule
- ▶ The "Add objects to the folder" right on the recipient inbox (if you want to schedule to an inbox destination)
- ▶ The "Copy objects to another folder" right on the object that you want to schedule (if you want to send a copy to an inbox destination instead of a shortcut)

The owner version of this right is "Schedule objects that the user owns to destinations."

View document instances

This right is supported only by object types that can be scheduled. It is a basic right that is required for all tasks on instances. It lets you view object instances but is also required to perform some tasks on these instances, such as deleting, rescheduling, pausing, and resuming them.

4.6   Application General Rights

Like the object general rights listed in Section 4.5, applications, which can cover tools, products, or even components, are also listed in the CMC. You can get rights for them too.

In this section, we discuss the four general rights that are supported by applications. Applications may also support specific rights, but they are described in Chapter 5.

> **Note**
>
> In the CMC, some applications may be improperly tagged as system or content InfoObject instead of application InfoObject. In such cases, they support general rights that can be defined for any system or content InfoObject (see Section 4.5). Consider these equivalences between rights:
>
> ▶ "View objects" is equivalent to "Log on to ... and view this object in the CMC."
>
> ▶ "Edit objects" is equivalent to "Edit this object."
>
> ▶ "Modify the rights users have to this object" and "Securely modify rights users have to objects" are equivalent to the same rights supported by InfoObjects.
>
> The other general rights you may set are meaningless.

Log on to ... and view this object in the CMC

This right allows you to log on to the application in connected mode and administrate this application in the CMC.

If this right is denied, two things happen:

▶ When you log on to the CMC, you do not see this application in the APPLICATIONS tab. You cannot set security for this application or modify its parameters.

▶ In the application itself, after you have provided a valid username and password in the application logon page or window to authenticate to the CMS repository, an error message is displayed and you cannot connect to the CMS with this application.

Edit this object

If the application has some properties that can be defined in the CMC, then this right allows you to modify these properties.

If this right is denied, then, in the CMC, all parameters in the PROPERTY tab of the application are disabled and cannot be edited.

Modify the rights users have to this object

This right is similar to the right supported by object and was described in Section 4.5. It allows you to modify any right, for any user on that application. This right is very powerful because once this right is granted to you for this application, you can grant yourself, or anyone else, any right on that object and thus gain the full control over the application by granting all the missing rights. For this reason, it is more secure to use the "Securely modify the rights users have to this object" right.

Securely modify rights users have to objects

This right is similar to the right supported by object and was described in Section 4.5. It is more restrictive than the previously described "Modify the rights users have to this object" because it limits the list of rights and users you can assign.

If you have a right on that application, you can grant or deny only the rights that are already granted to you. For example, if you have the rights "View objects" and "Securely modify the rights users have to objects" granted on that application, you cannot give yourself more rights and can give or take away those two rights only.

4.7   Managing Rights in the CMC

You manage object rights in the CMC. In the CMS repository, the security is object-oriented and the assigned rights are attached to the object itself. For this reason, any task related to rights is done from the object. For example, to assign a right for an object to a user or a group, you need to start your workflow from the object to secure, and not from the user or the group. In this section, we cover viewing rights, assigning advanced rights both to a user or group and to a top-root folder, and also unassigning advanced rights.

> **Note**
>
> The CMC often uses the word *principal* to indifferently reference a user or a group.

4.7.1   Viewing Rights

To view the rights assigned to a user or a group for an object:

1. In the CMC home page, select the object category, and use the dropdown menu or use the vertical tab in order to access the objects type management page. In this page, all objects of this type are displayed.

2. Select the object for which you want to view assigned rights.

3. In the menu bar, select MANAGE • USER SECURITY or, in the toolbar, click on MANAGE USER SECURITY. The USER SECURITY panel opens for the selected object, with all rights or access levels already assigned to any user or group for this object, as shown in Figure 4.4.

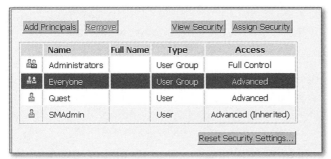

Figure 4.4 List of Rights and Access Levels Assigned to an Object

4. Select any group or user, and then click the VIEW SECURITY button. The PERMISSION EXPLORER panel opens for the selected object.

5. You can click the BROWSE button near the PRINCIPAL text field to change the user or group for which you need to view security.

6. The PERMISSION EXPLORER panel lists all rights for this object and this user. The following columns are shown in the panel:

  ▶ COLLECTION: The right category (GENERAL, APPLICATION, SYSTEM or CONTENT)

  ▶ TYPE: If the right is global general, then GENERAL; otherwise, for specific general right or specific right, the InfoObject type

  ▶ RIGHT NAME: The name of the right

  ▶ STATUS: An icon representing the right status (see Table 4.6)

  ▶ APPLY TO: An icon representing the scope of right (see Table 4.6)

  ▶ SOURCE: How the right has been assigned (GRANULAR if it has been explicitly assigned, or the name of the access level if the right is assigned through an access level)

Icon	Description
✓	Right status: Granted
✕	Right status: Denied
?	Right status: Not specified
▯	Scope of right: Apply to object
▯	Scope of right: Apply to sub-objects
▯	Scope of right: Apply to object and sub-objects

Table 4.6 Icons Used When Displaying Rights

7. You may select in the COMMON FILTER SETTINGS dropdown list a filter to display the rights. The possible options are:

   ▶ NO FILTERS: To list all rights without any filter

   ▶ ASSIGNED RIGHTS: To display only rights explicitly assigned (granted or denied)

   ▶ GRANTED RIGHTS: To display only rights that are explicitly granted

   ▶ UNASSIGNED RIGHTS: To display only rights that are not specified

   ▶ SORT BY TYPE: To list all rights, sorted by their type (GENERAL or the InfoObject type)

   ▶ SORT BY RIGHT NAME: To list all rights, sorted by their name

   ▶ FROM ACCESS LEVEL: To display only rights assigned through access levels

8. You may also use an additional filter on status:

   ▶ In the STATUS column header, click the FILTER icon to open a menu where you can select some right status (GRANTED, DENIED or NOT SPECIFIED).

   ▶ Click OK to close this menu. The list of rights is filtered and only the rights with the selected status are displayed.

9. Click OK to close the PERMISSION EXPLORER panel and return to the USER SECURITY panel.

10. Click CLOSE to close the USER SECURITY panel.

4.7.2 Assigning Advanced Rights

There are two methods for assigning rights for an object to a user or group: through an access level (see Section 4.8) or by explicit assignment of these rights. In this last case, this assignment is shown in the CMC as ADVANCED.

To assign advanced rights to an object for a user or a group, follow these steps:

1. In the CMC home page, select the object category, and use the dropdown menu or the vertical tab in order to access the objects type management page. In this page, all objects of this type are displayed.

2. Select the object for which you want to assign advanced rights.

3. In the menu bar, select MANAGE • USER SECURITY or select MANAGE USER SECURITY from the toolbar. The USER SECURITY panel opens for the selected object, with all rights or access levels already assigned for this object.

4. If the user or group has not already been assigned advanced rights or access level and is not displayed in the USER SECURITY panel, then click the ADD PRINCIPALS button to open the ADD PRINCIPALS panel, as shown in Figure 4.5.

5. In the ADD PRINCIPALS panel, select the user or group in the list of users and groups.

   ▸ Click the > button to move the selected user or group into the SELECTED USERS/ GROUPS list.

   ▸ Click the ADD AND ASSIGN SECURITY button to open the ASSIGN SECURITY panel.

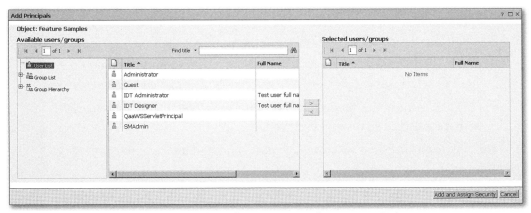

Figure 4.5 Add Principals Panel to Select User/Group for Assigning Rights

If the user or group has already been assigned advanced rights or access level, then select this user or this group, and click the Assign Security button to open the Assign Security panel for this user or group.

6. Once in the Assign Security panel, click the Advanced tab, as shown in Figure 4.6. This tab lists the rights assigned to the user or group. Its user interface and behavior are very similar to the Permission Explorer (see Section 4.7.1).

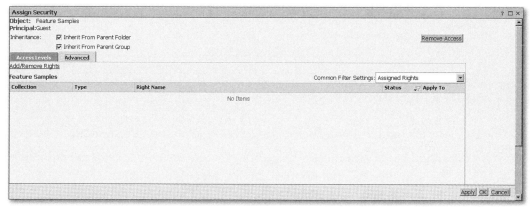

Figure 4.6 Assign Security Panel Listing Advanced Rights

7. To break inheritance, unselect the Inherit From Parent Folder or/and Inherit From Parent Group checkboxes.

8. Click the Add/Remove Rights link to open the Add/Remove Rights panel. This panel contains all rights that can be set for the selected object. Depending on the object type, the rights are sorted in the General, System, Application, or Content section.

   If you set rights for a folder, then you can define the rights for any object type the folder may contain, as shown in Figure 4.7. In the left pane, in the General section, you can set global general rights, whereas in the Content or System section, by selecting an InfoObject type, you can set general and specific rights.

9. Select a category or an InfoObject type in the left pane to display the corresponding rights in the right pane.

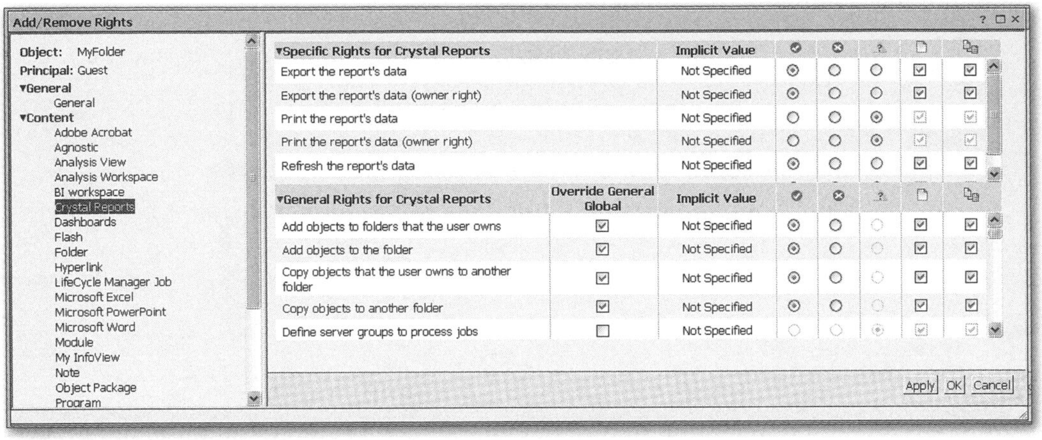

Figure 4.7 ADD/REMOVE RIGHTS Panel for a Folder

10. For each right to modify, select the values to set in the corresponding columns:

   ▶ Right value: You can set the right's value by selecting one of the radio buttons in the GRANTED, DENIED, or NOT SPECIFIED columns.

   ▶ Scope of right: If you have explicitly granted or denied the right, you can define its scope of right by selecting the checkbox in the APPLY TO OBJECT or APPLY TO SUB-OBJECT columns. At least one of these checkboxes must be selected.

   ▶ If the right is a specific general right, you must first click the OVERRIDE GENERAL GLOBAL checkbox before defining a new value for this right, which overrides the corresponding global general right.

11. Click OK to validate your changes and return to the ASSIGN SECURITY panel, which now displays the rights you have added.

12. Click OK to return to the USER SECURITY panel. In the list of rights defined for the object, the user or group is listed with ADVANCED in the ACCESS column.

13. Click CLOSE to close the USER SECURITY panel.

> **Note**
>
> If you have the "Securely modify the rights users have to objects" right granted and the "Modify the rights users have to objects" right denied, then you cannot modify the rights that are denied to you. In the ADD/REMOVE RIGHTS panel, the rights that are denied to you are disabled and cannot be modified, which prevents you from granting yourself or someone else these rights.

4.7.3 Assigning Advanced Rights to a Top-Root Folder

It is possible to define security at top-root folders, which can be useful to define common security for all objects of the same type. Return to Section 4.3.2 to see a list of these top-root folders.

To assign rights at the top root of one of these objects:

1. In the CMC home page, select the object category, and use either the dropdown menu or the vertical tab to access the objects type management page.

2. In the menu bar, select MANAGE • TOP-LEVEL SECURITY • ALL <OBJECT TYPE>. The USER SECURITY panel opens.

This USER SECURITY panel is similar to the one described in Section 4.7.2 and is used to assign rights to any object. You can use it to assign rights at the top-root folder.

4.7.4 Unassigning Advanced Rights

To simply remove all rights assigned to an object for a user or a group, you may unassign rights assigned for an object to a user or a group. To do so, follow these steps:

1. Open the ASSIGN SECURITY panel for the corresponding object:

   ▶ If the object is a top-root folder, repeat the steps described in Section 4.7.3.

   ▶ Otherwise, repeat the steps described in Section 4.7.2.

2. In the ASSIGN SECURITY panel, select the user or group in the list of users or groups who have assigned security for this object.

3. Click the REMOVE button for this user or this group. The security is no longer assigned to this user or this group.

4.8 Access Levels

Setting advanced rights has the advantage of letting you define in detail how to set each individual right and how these rights are inherited. But if you need to define the same set of rights for different users or groups, setting advanced rights for each user and group in the CMC as described in Section 4.7 can become time-consuming and error-prone since the same configuration must be replicated for each user or group.

To manage these drawbacks and easily assign rights, use access levels to ease your administrative tasks. An access level defines a set of granted and denied rights and their scope. These rights can be on any InfoObject type or on any applications. By setting this access level to a user or a group, you directly assign this set of rights to this user or group rather than setting these rights individually.

In this section, we describe the historical five access levels that are predefined and available and we then explore the ability—introduced with XI 3.x—to create your own access levels.

4.8.1 Predefined Access Levels

By default, five access levels are predefined in the CMS repository. These access levels define a set of rights for any object and can be used to assign rights to a user or a group for an object. Table 4.7 details these predefined access levels.

Access Level Name	Description
View	Defines a predefined set of rights to view a document.
View On Demand	Defines a predefined set of rights to view and refresh a document.
Schedule	Defines a predefined set of rights to view, refresh, and schedule a document.
Full Control	In Full Control access level, all rights for all objects or applications are granted. A right granted by Full Control access level can be overridden. For example, if it is inherited by a user that belongs to another group where this right has been explicitly denied, then aggregation rules deny this right to this user.
Full Control (owner)	Similar to the Full Control access level, but all owner rights version of rights are granted whereas the non-owner version of rights remain not specified.

Table 4.7 Predefined Access Levels

You cannot modify the rights defined in a predefined access level. But you can copy a predefined access level in order to create a custom access level.

As opposed to previous releases, it is no longer possible to directly assign the "No Access" access level. In this access level, all rights are set to unspecified. This access level is assigned to a user for an object if, when you are defining advanced rights, you break both folder and group inheritances and you do not set any rights.

> **Note**
>
> Access levels have initially been designed for Crystal Reports documents. The names of these access levels come from Crystal Reports terminology and their meanings fit Crystal Reports behavior. When access levels have been extended to other object types, the values access levels define for object rights are defined to fit the access level meaning.

4.8.2 Custom Access Levels

When you define security, you very quickly reach the limit of the five predefined access levels outlined in the previous section. Those access levels may not necessarily fit your exact requirements. In this case it is still possible to set advanced rights in order to explicitly define a set of rights for a user or a group.

However, unless you use folder or group inheritance, you have to set these advanced rights for all users and groups that need to be assigned the same set of rights. Because the security model is object-oriented, it can be tedious to set up rights for different objects. Furthermore, once defined, any changes in the security policy or any maintenance tasks are very complex and hard to update.

To overcome these drawbacks, custom access levels have been introduced. Like a predefined access level, a custom access level is a named set of granted or denied rights, including global general rights, specific general rights for any object or application, and specific rights for any object or application

When you set a right in a custom access level, you can define two things:

▶ Its value: Granted, denied, or unspecified

▶ Its scope of rights: Itself or sub-objects

You do not need to define a value for all rights. The rights that you do not specify are set to unspecified, so they do not impact final aggregation.

As a predefined access level, it is easy to use a custom access level to directly assign rights to a user or a group for an object. But compared to the predefined access levels, the custom access level has the following advantages:

▶ It is dynamic. If you can modify the rights it contains, then all users or groups assigned this access level immediately benefit of these changes.

▶ An access level can be copied from any other access level—even the predefined access level—and edited, which makes it easy to create new access level.

Figure 4.8 shows the same example as in Figure 4.2 but implemented through custom access level for the user jim.

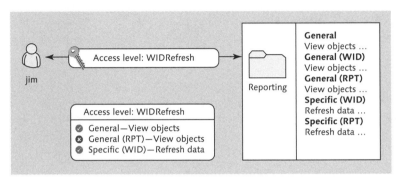

Figure 4.8 Example of Rights Assigned through Access Levels

Access levels are also stored as InfoObject in the CMS, so you can define security rights on them (see Chapter 5).

4.8.3 Aggregation

When different access levels are assigned to a user for an object, the user is assigned the rights defined by all the access levels. In the event of conflicts, the aggregation rules defined in Table 4.2 apply.

But a right can also be assigned simultaneously through advanced right, access level, and inherited. In such cases, the general rule takes two things into consideration:

▶ The value set explicitly through advanced right takes priority over the value set by the access level.

▶ The value set by the access level takes priority over the inherited value.

These relationships are described in Table 4.8.

Advanced right is	Inherited right is	Access level		
		Granted	Denied	Not specified
Granted	Granted	Granted	Granted	Granted
	Denied	Granted	Granted	Granted
	Not specified	Granted	Granted	Granted
Denied	Granted	Denied	Denied	Denied
	Denied	Denied	Denied	Denied
	Not specified	Denied	Denied	Denied
Not specified	Granted	Granted	Denied	Granted
	Denied	Granted	Denied	Denied
	Not specified	Granted	Denied	Not specified, and thus denied

Table 4.8 Effective Value of a Right, Depending on Value Explicitly Set, Value Set by Access Level and Inherited Right

4.9 Managing Access Level in the CMC

In the CMC, one tab is fully dedicated to managing access levels. This section presents the different possible actions for managing these levels. Assigning an access level is very similar to assigning advanced rights, which was presented in Section 4.7.2.

4.9.1 Creating an Access Level

To create a new access level, follow these steps:

1. Go to the ACCESS LEVELS tab in the CMC.

2. In the menu bar, select MANAGE • NEW • CREATE ACCESS LEVEL or click CREATE A NEW ACCESS LEVEL in the toolbar. The CREATE NEW ACCESS LEVEL panel appears.

3. Enter a name and a description for this access level.

4. Click OK to create the new access level and display it in the access levels list.

4.9.2   Setting Access Level Rights

Once you have created the access level, follow these steps to modify it or define the rights enforced by this access level:

1. Go to the ACCESS LEVELS tab in the CMC.

2. Select this access level in the list.

3. In the menu bar, select ACTIONS • INCLUDED RIGHTS or right-click the access level and select INCLUDED RIGHTS in the contextual menu. The INCLUDED RIGHTS panel appears for this access level. As shown in Figure 4.9, this panel is similar to the PERMISSION EXPLORER panel used to display assigned rights (see Section 4.7.1).

   It displays the rights with some details listed in different columns:

   ▶ COLLECTION: The right category (GENERAL, APPLICATION, SYSTEM or CONTENT)

   ▶ TYPE: If the right is a global general right, then this column displays GENERAL; otherwise, for specific general right or specific right, this column displays the InfoObject type

   ▶ RIGHT NAME: The name of the right

   ▶ STATUS: An icon representing the status defined by the access level for this right (see Table 4.6)

   ▶ APPLY TO: An icon representing the scope of right defined by the access level for this right (see Table 4.6)

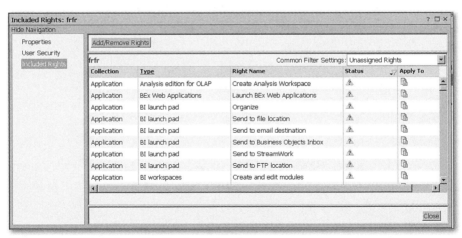

Figure 4.9   Rights Enforced by the Access Level

4. Select in the COMMON FILTER SETTING dropdown list a filter to display the rights. You have the following options:

    ▶ NO FILTERS: To list all rights without any filter

    ▶ ASSIGNED RIGHTS: To display only rights explicitly assigned (granted or denied) by this access level

    ▶ GRANTED RIGHTS: To display only rights explicitly granted by this access level

    ▶ UNASSIGNED RIGHTS: To display only rights that are not specified in this access level

    ▶ SORT BY TYPE: To list all rights, sorted by their type (GENERAL or the InfoObject type)

    ▶ SORT BY RIGHT NAME: To list all rights, sorted by their name

5. Click the ADD/REMOVE RIGHTS button to modify the values for the rights that this access level includes. The panel is updated and displays in its left pane the list of rights categories (GENERAL, CONTENT, APPLICATION, SYSTEM) and the objects in each category.

6. Select a category and an object for which the access level must include rights. The list of rights in this category is displayed in the right pane.

7. For each right, select the value GRANTED, DENIED, or NOT SPECIFIED by selecting the corresponding radio button. If you have explicitly set the GRANTED or DENIED value for a right, you can also select the corresponding checkboxed to define if that right must apply to the object and/or to sub-objects.

8. Repeat until you have defined all rights to include in this access level.

9. Click OK to save the included rights for this access level.

10. Click the CLOSE button to close the INCLUDED RIGHTS panel.

> **Note**
>
> It is not possible to modify the rights included in any of the five predefined access levels (described in Section 4.8.1).

4.9.3 Copying an Access Level

Copying an access level allows you to create a new access level based on an existing one and to modify only some rights, which means you can avoid entirely redefining the access level. To copy an access level, follow these steps:

1. Go to the ACCESS LEVELS tab in the CMC.

2. Select an access level in the access levels list. This can be one of the five predefined access levels (see Section 4.8.1).

3. In the menu bar, select ORGANIZE • COPY or right-click this access level and select ORGANIZE • COPY from the contextual menu.

    The new access level is created and displayed in the access levels list. The name of this new access level is the name of the source access level suffixed by an increment number.

Once an access level is created, you can then edit the rights it includes (see Section 4.9.2) or rename it in order to personalize it (see Section 4.9.4).

4.9.4 Renaming an Access Level

Renaming an access level does not modify the rights it includes or the objects or users and groups it is assigned to—it simply gives it a new name. To rename an access level, follow these steps:

1. Go to the ACCESS LEVELS tab in the CMC.

2. Select an access level in the access levels list.

3. In the menu bar, select MANAGE • PROPERTIES or right-click this access level and select PROPERTIES in the contextual menu. The PROPERTIES panel appears for this access level.

4. Type a new name in the TITLE field.

5. Click the SAVE AND CLOSE button. The panel closes and the access level is displayed with its new name in the access levels list.

> **Note**
>
> Even if it were possible to select one of the five predefined access levels (see Section 4.8.1) and modify its name, this name change is in fact not saved in the CMS repository. It is not possible to modify these predefined access levels.

4.9.5 Assigning an Access Level to an Object

To assign an access level for an object to a user or a group, follow these steps:

1. In the CMC home page, go to the tab dedicated to this object type.

2. Select the object for which you want to assign an access level.

3. In the menu bar, select MANAGE • USER SECURITY or in the toolbar, click the MANAGE USER SECURITY button. The USER SECURITY panel opens for the selected object, with all rights or access levels already assigned for this object.

4. If the user or group has not already been assigned advanced rights or access level and is not displayed in the USER SECURITY panel, click the ADD PRINCIPALS button to open the ADD PRINCIPALS panel.

   ► In the ADD PRINCIPALS panel, select the user or group in the list of users and groups.

   ► Click the > button to move the selected user or group into the SELECTED USERS/ GROUPS list.

   ► Click the ADD AND ASSIGN SECURITY button to open the ASSIGN SECURITY panel.

   If the user or group has already been assigned advanced rights or access level, then select this user or this group, and click the ASSIGN SECURITY button to open the ASSIGN SECURITY panel for this user or group.

   Once in the ASSIGN SECURITY panel (see Figure 4.10), if you want to break inheritance, unselect the INHERIT FROM PARENT FOLDER or/and INHERIT FROM PARENT GROUP checkboxes.

5. Select one or several access levels in the AVAILABLE ACCESS LEVEL list and then click the > button in order to move them into the ASSIGN ACCESS LEVELS list.

6. Click OK to return to the USER SECURITY panel. In the list of rights defined for the object, the user or group is listed with the name of selected access levels in the ACCESS column.

7. Click CLOSE to close the USER SECURITY panel.

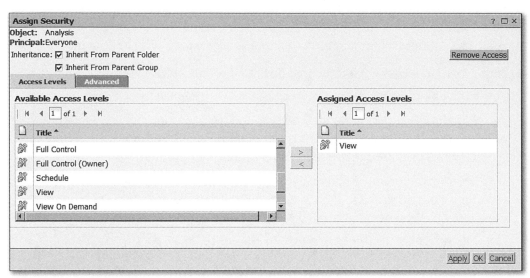

Figure 4.10   Assign Security Dialog Box Listing All Available Access Levels

4.9.6   Deleting an Access Level

You may delete an access level if you do not use it anymore. When an access level is deleted, it no longer secures the objects and the users or groups to which it was assigned. To delete an access level, follow these steps:

1. Go to the ACCESS LEVELS tab in the CMC.

2. Select an access level in list of access levels, except one of the five predefined access levels (see Section 4.8.1) that cannot be deleted.

3. In the menu bar, select MANAGE • DELETE ACCESS LEVEL or right-click this access level and select DELETE in the contextual menu.

4. The DELETE ACCESS LEVEL panel is displayed with the list of objects and users and groups that are impacted by this access level deletion. Review this list to make sure it will have no unexpected or unintended consequences.

5. Click the DELETE button to close the DELETE ACCESS LEVEL panel, delete the access level, and remove it from the access levels list.

4.10   Running Administration Queries in the CMC

By design, CMS repository organization is InfoObjects-centric. This is the case for security assigned for objects are stored at object level.

Identically, most workflows in the CMC are object-centric and start from the object point of view. In some cases, you may need to have a more user-centric view, for example, if you are looking for all objects whose rights are granted or denied to a specific user or group.

This section covers how to run a security query or a relationship query in the CMC for such requests.

4.10.1   Running a Security Query

A security query is a query sent to the CMS repository that looks for all objects for which a user or a group has some specific rights you may define. To run the security query, follow these steps:

1. In the CMC, go to the QUERY RESULTS tab.

2. Select the SECURITY QUERIES branch in the tree, as shown in Figure 4.11.

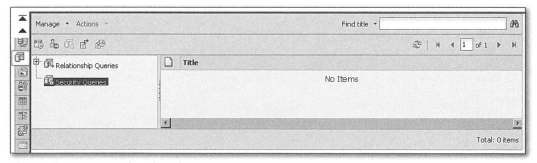

Figure 4.11   Query Results Tab in the CMC

3. Right-click SECURITY QUERIES and select NEW • CREATE SECURITY QUERY; you can also select MANAGE • NEW • CREATE SECURITY QUERY in the menu bar to open the CREATE SECURITY QUERY panel, as shown in Figure 4.12.

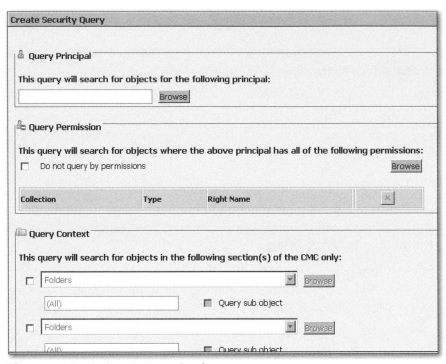

Figure 4.12   Create Security Query Panel

4. In the QUERY PRINCIPAL section, click the BROWSE button to select the user or group that is concerned by the query to run. The BROWSE FOR QUERY PRINCIPAL panel opens.

5. Select the user or group for which you are running the query and then click OK.

6. If you want to search all objects that are secured for this user or group, through access levels or advanced rights, select the DO NOT QUERY BY PERMISSIONS checkbox in the QUERY PERMISSION section. In this case, you do not need to define the rights to look for in the query and can directly define the QUERY CONTEXT.

7. Otherwise, if you want to define some rights for the query, you need to add these rights and their values. In the QUERY PERMISSION section, click the BROWSE button to open the BROWSE FOR QUERY PERMISSION panel. This panel displays in its left pane the list of rights categories (GENERAL, CONTENT, APPLICATION, SYSTEM) and the object types in each category. When you select a category and an object type in this category, the list of rights in this category and for this object type are displayed in the right pane. For the different rights you want to

add in the query, click the radio button in the Granted, Denied, or Not Speci-fied column to define the value you look for this right, as shown in Figure 4.13.

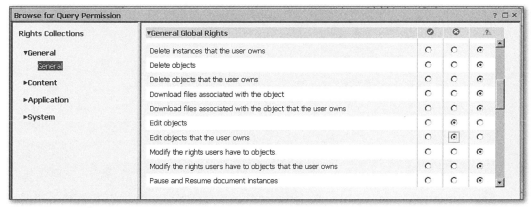

Figure 4.13 Defining Search Criteria Based on Rights Values

8. Click OK to close the Browse for Query Permission panel. The selected rights are displayed in the Query Permission section. To remove a right, click the X button at the far-right end of the corresponding right, as shown in Figure 4.14.

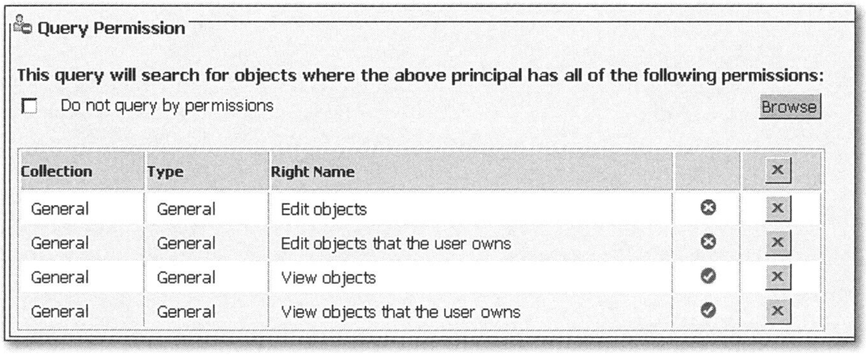

Figure 4.14 Search Criteria

9. In the Query Context section, define the folders where the search is run. You can define a maximum of four folders. Click a checkbox in front of one of the dropdown menus.

10. In the dropdown menu, select the top-root folder where the search must be run.

11. Click the BROWSE button to open the BROWSE FOR QUERY CONTEXT panel. In this panel, you can select a sub-folder below the top-root folder to restrict the query.

12. Click OK to close the BROWSE FOR QUERY CONTEXT panel. The selected folder is displayed below the selected top-root folder.

13. Click QUERY SUB-OBJECT to include sub-folders in the query.

14. Repeat these steps to add other folders in the query.

15. Click OK to run the query. The CREATE SECURITY QUERY panel closes and the objects that fit your search criteria are displayed in the right pane. Click an object to display the PERMISSION EXPLORER for this object and the selected user or group, as shown in Figure 4.15.

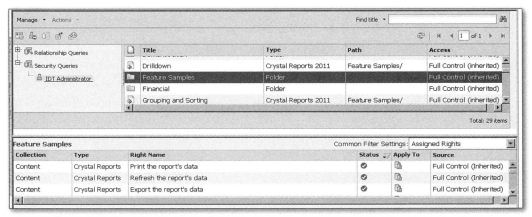

Figure 4.15 Security Query Results

If you run several queries, the results of each query is kept until logoff, which cleans this history.

4.10.2 Running a Relationship Query

In the CMS repository, some objects are linked. For example, a universe relies on a connection, or an access level is assigned for an object. To find these relationships between objects, the CMC offers the ability to find the objects linked to a specific object.

To run a relationship query that lists all objects that have relationships with a specific object, follow these steps:

1. Select any object in the CMC.

2. Right-click this object and select TOOLS • CHECK RELATIONSHIPS or select MANAGE • TOOLS • CHECK RELATIONSHIPS from the menu bar.

3. The CMC switches to the QUERY RESULTS tab and displays the list of objects that are related to the selected object, as seen in Figure 4.16.

If you run several queries, the results of each query is kept until logoff, which cleans this history.

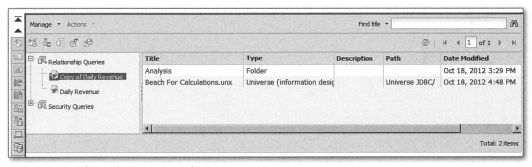

Figure 4.16   Relationship Query Results

4.11   Summary

This chapter has covered the rights framework used to secure objects saved in the CMS repository. In this framework, each InfoObject type supports a set of general rights and, depending on the object, specific rights. General rights are used to secure generic behaviors enforced in the platform, whereas the specific rights can secure functionalities specific to the object type.

This rights framework supports group-to-user and folder-to-object inheritances. The objects that can inherit from rights can be limited by scope of inheritance or the break inheritance option.

Each right exists in two versions: an owner version that applies to objects *you* own and non-owner version for objects you don't own.

Recall that this framework also offers access levels, which are sets of granted or denied rights. You can either use one of the predefined access levels or create your own. Because they can be reused as needed, access levels ease rights management.

Rights and access levels are all defined and managed in the CMC. In order to help you accomplish these tasks, the CMC offers you two tools: the security query, used to run queries based on assigned rights, and the relationship query, used to find relationships between InfoObjects.

This rights framework is used by applications and objects in order to support their specific rights. These specific rights are all listed in next chapter.

Web Intelligence, Crystal Reports, Dashboard, and Analysis are some of the products released within BI 4.0. These products enforce some specific functional rights that are listed, along with their impact on the products.

5   Applications and Rights Reference

Chapter 4 describes the security rights framework that applies to objects stored in the CMS repository and enforced by the BI 4.0 platform. Depending on the object type, this framework offers various sets of general rights that can apply to all applications and to all objects.

In addition to these general rights, each application and object can also support a set of specific rights to secure specific features it enforces. This chapter describes these specific rights for all applications and all objects supported in BI 4.0. Furthermore, this chapter describes specific applications' security models.

Section 5.1 lists and gives a brief introduction to all applications displayed in the CMC APPLICATIONS tab. Each application that supports specific rights or has specific security workflows is detailed later in a dedicated chapter section.

Sections 5.2 and 5.3 list all system InfoObjects and all content InfoObjects supported by the CMS repository, respectively. The bulk of this chapter—Sections 5.4 to 5.19—focuses on specific applications. For each application, a security overview is presented. Then its specific rights are described, as well as the list of specific rights of the resources it generates. Additionally, these sections offer information about what happens if specific rights are denied.

Finally, Sections 5.20 to 5.23 focus on some InfoObjects not covered in previous sections and the specific rights they support.

5.1 Applications List

Figure 5.1 shows the CMC APPLICATIONS tab, which houses the list of applications. *Application* is a broad term that covers the following concepts that can be administrated in the Central Management Console (CMC):

▶ Products: The SAP BusinessObjects reporting tools, such as Web Intelligence, Crystal Reports, Dashboards, or Explorer

▶ Tools: The utilities tools, such as Information Design Tool or the CMC itself

▶ Capabilities or features: Features included in another tool, such as Version Management or Promotion Management that are included in the CMC

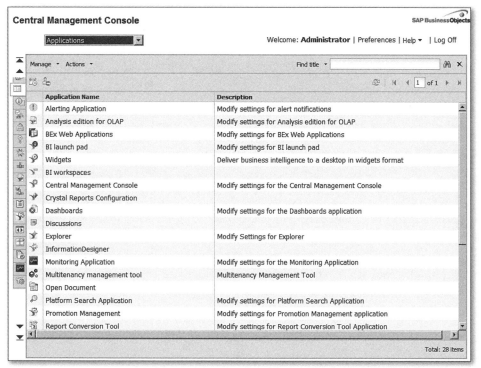

Figure 5.1 Applications Tab in CMC

In the CMS repository, these applications are saved as system InfoObjects.

The CMC offers a generic framework where the applications display the parameters and security rights they leverage. This flexible framework allows different possible configurations in regard to rights:

- **The application does not support any right.**
  Either it does not need to leverage any rights and offers only parameters (such as Discussions), or it is a feature that has been displayed as an application in the CMC APPLICATIONS tab (such as Monitoring Application).

- **The application supports only application general rights** (see Chapter 4, Section 4.6).
  These general rights can be slightly different from the four different rights defined for an application, but at least they are more or less mapped to these general rights. Three of the four general rights (the login right is excluded) are enforced only by the CMC since they secure administration of this application in the CMC.

- **The application supports both general and specific rights.**
  In addition to general rights, the application enforces specific rights. These specific rights are described in Sections 5.4 to 5.19.

The applications are listed in the CMC in the following order, which is almost the alphabetical one (Widgets was known as BI Widgets in previous releases, which explains its place in the list):

- **Alerting Application**
  This application is used to set alerting properties (recipients, mail format, and so on). It supports only general rights, but the "Log on to..." right is replaced by the "Subscribe to alerts and view this object in the CMC" right.

- **Analysis, Edition for OLAP** (see Section 5.4)
  This product, previously known as Voyager, is the OLAP analysis tool available in BI Launch Pad. It supports general and specific rights.

- **BEx Web Applications** (see Section 5.5)
  This is the capability to deploy BEx web applications in the application server hosting SAP BusinessObjects applications and to use BI Launch Pad as a portal from which you can run these BEx web applications. This avoids the deployment of the SAP J2EE web application server. It supports general and specific rights.

- ▶ **BI Launch Pad** (see Section 5.6)
  This web application, previously known as InfoView, is the default BI 4.0 portal. It supports general and specific rights.

- ▶ **Widgets** (see Section 5.7)
  This product, previously known as BI Widgets, runs on your machine in order to show the most common documents visuals from your desktop. It supports general and specific rights.

- ▶ **BI Workspaces** (see Section 5.8)
  This tool, which is seen as the successor of XI R3 Dashboard Builder, is used to organize your content in BI Launch Pad. It generates workspaces, which are the equivalent of dashboards. BI Workspaces supports general and specific rights.

- ▶ **Central Management Console** (see Section 5.9)
  The web application used by administrators to manage their BI 4.0 systems. The CMC supports general and specific rights.

- ▶ **Crystal Reports Configuration** (see Section 5.10)
  This application is used to set some Crystal Reports parameters. It supports only general rights and one specific right.

- ▶ **Dashboards**
  Formerly the Xcelsius product, this application is used to generate dashboards. In BI 4.0, two InfoObjects types are associated with and supported by this application:

  - ▶ Xcelsius: The former file format used by Xcelsius product in XI 3.x

  - ▶ Dashboards: The new file format supported by Dashboard in BI 4.0 (this new file format includes both the previous Xcelsius file format and the generated Flash file)

  Dashboards and its two associated file formats support only general rights.

- ▶ **Discussions**
  This application lets you create a discussion thread between users for any object that supports it in BI Launch Pad. By default, this capability is disabled since collaboration can also be done through SAP StreamWork. If you want to use it, you need to enable it in the CMC, in the BI Launch Pad application's property.

  Discussions application itself does not support any rights, but you can set rights supported by the Note InfoObjects to objects that support them (see Section 5.22).

▶ **Explorer** (see Section 5.11)
This is the data discovery product formerly known as Polestar. Explorer must be installed through its own installer on top of a BI 4.0 installation. When deployed, Explorer appears in the list of applications in the CMC; its two associated InfoObjects—information space and exploration view set— are recognized by the CMC.

Explorer and information space support general and specific rights, whereas the exploration view set supports only general rights.

▶ **Information Design Tool** (see Section 5.12 and Chapter 8)
This is the new metadata design tool introduced in BI 4.0 to generate new universes. Both Information Design Tool and the universes it generates support general and specific rights.

▶ **Monitoring Application**
This new feature is available in the CMC and allows you to monitor server activities and metrics, functional metrics, and so on. It has been introduced in BI 4.0. This application doesn't support any rights.

▶ **Multitenancy Management Tool**
This new tool was introduced in BI 4.0 FP3 to manage multi-tenant deployment. It is a command-line tool installed on the server side that allows you to duplicate resources templates (universes, connections, reports, etc.) and to customize them on the fly. It supports only general rights.

▶ **Open Document**
This application object is used to set parameters for the open document function. It does not support any rights.

▶ **Platform Search Application**
This application object is used to set parameters for the indexing used for Search: index location, weights to assign for index scoring, types of objects to index, list of indexing failures, etc. It supports only application general rights, except the "Log on to..." right.

▶ **Promotion Management** (see Section 5.13)
This feature is used to promote resources from one CMS repository to another one and to export and import LCMBIAR files. In previous releases, this capability was part of Lifecycle Management web application that needed to be deployed on its own. In BI 4.0, it was also deployed with the CMC, but was accessible

through another URL. In BI 4.0 FP3, it has been directly integrated into the CMC. Promotion Management supports general and specific rights.

▶ **Report Conversion Tool**
This is the tool used to convert Desktop Intelligence documents into Web Intelligence documents. If these documents are stored in a XI R2 or XI 3.x repository, then you must have two accounts:

- ▶ One to connect to the XI R2 or XI 3.x repository where the documents to convert are stored. Security is enforced in this repository: this account must have the Report Conversion Tool "Log on to..." right granted and only documents this account is allowed to view can be converted.

- ▶ One to connect to the BI 4.0 CMS repository where the converted Web Intelligence documents are saved.

Report Conversion Tool supports only general rights.

▶ **RESTful Web Service**
This application object is used to manage RESTful Web Service in general like the entry URL and security. It supports only general rights, even if the "Log on to..." right is renamed "View" because there is no restriction against logging on using RESTful Web Service.

▶ **SAP BusinessObjects Mobile** (see Section 5.14)
The mobile application for iOS and Android to display Web Intelligence and Crystal Reports documents. It supports general and specific rights.

▶ **SAP StreamWork** (see Section 5.15)
This is the new SAP on-demand collaboration product. Its integration has been introduced with BI 4.0 FP3. It supports only general rights.

▶ **Translation Management Tool** (see Chapter 4, Section 4.5)
This tool is used to translate any translatable resources into any locale. It supports only general rights but can only translate objects whose "Translate objects" right is granted.

▶ **Universe Design Tool** (see Section 5.16 and Chapter 7)
This historical BusinessObjects metadata design tool is used to generate universes (UNV). Both Universe Design Tool and the universes it generates support general and specific rights.

▶ **Upgrade Management Tool**
This tool is used to upgrade CMS repositories from previous releases. The Upgrade Management Tool can be seen as one successor to XI R2 and XI 3.x Import Wizard (the other successor being Promotion Management), but it supports migration only from XI R2 SP2 (or higher) and XI 3.x releases. It does not support upgrades from earlier releases or from BusinessObjects 5x/6x. From these releases, a two-step migration is needed.

When you connect to a XI R2 CMS repository, you need to provide the Administrator account credentials. When it connects to a XI 3.x CMS repository, you need to provide the credentials of an account in the Administrators group. This account is used to compute rights on the source system, but you can upgrade only objects that this account is allowed to view. The Upgrade Management Tool supports only general rights.

▶ **Version Management** (see Section 5.17)
This feature is used for version control of BI resources saved in the CMS repository. In previous releases, this capability was part of Lifecycle Management web application that needed to be deployed on its own. In BI 4.0, it was also deployed with the CMC, but was accessible through another URL. In BI 4.0 FP3, it has been directly integrated in the CMC. Version Management supports general and specific rights.

▶ **Visual Difference** (see Section 5.18)
This new generic framework released in BI 4.0 is intended to support comparison of different types of BI resources and to be the successor of Delta Viewer and Report Comparison Tool. In BI 4.0, it supports comparison of only LCMBIAR files and LCMBIAR jobs you can create with Promotion Management (see Section 5.13). It supports general and specific rights.

▶ **Web Intelligence** (see Section 5.19)
This is the SAP BusinessObjects product for query, ad hoc reporting, and analysis. It is available both as a three-tier application or from the BI Launch Pad. It generates Web Intelligence documents; both the Web Intelligence application and documents support general and specific rights.

▶ **Web Service**
This application object is used to manage Web Service in general, such as the entry URL and security. It supports only general rights, even if the "Log on to…" right is renamed as "View" because there is no restriction against logging on using Web Service.

In addition to application InfoObjects, the CMS repository also supports system InfoObjects—the core objects used by the BI 4.0 system.

5.2   System Objects List

All these objects—except connection, relational connection, Data Federator data source, event, universe, universe (Information Design Tool), and users who also support specific rights—support only general rights. System InfoObjects cannot be scheduled, so they don't support the scheduling rights set (see Chapter 4, Section 4.5). The only exception is Replication Job InfoObject, which does support scheduling rights.

The following are system InfoObjects:

▶ **Access Level** (see Chapter 4, Sections 4.5 and 4.8)
This is the InfoObject used for access levels. You can set the "Use access level for security assignment" general right to any system or content InfoObject, but access level is the only one to truly enforce it.

▶ **Calendar**
This InfoObject defines dates for any publishing jobs or any tasks that can be scheduled.

▶ **Category**
This InfoObject has been introduced in XI R2 in order to support customers migrating from BusinessObjects 5x/6x. In these release, it was possible to store a document in different categories. Nevertheless, categories are not evenly used: some products, like Web Intelligence or BI Mobile, use these categories to classify documents, but other products do not.

▶ **Connection**
The InfoObject used by Crystal Reports to save its connections. It supports general and specific rights (see Section 5.21.4).

▶ **Data Federation Parameters**
There is only one object of this type in the CMS repository. It is stored in the "Public folders/Data Federation" folder and is used only to store Data Federation parameters. It must be edited only by the Data Federation Administration Tool.

▶ **Data Federator Data Source**
This InfoObject is used to store data sources enforced by Data Federation:

relational SAP NetWeaver BW and SAS connection. It supports general and specific rights (see Section 5.21.3).

▸ **Event**

This InfoObject is used to modelize system alert. Events support general and specific rights.

▸ **Favorites Folder**

This InfoObject is a folder used to modelize users' personal folders.

▸ **Inbox**

This InfoObject is a folder used to modelize users' inboxes.

▸ **OLAP Connection**

This InfoObject is used for OLAP connections created in Information Design Tool and the CMC (see Section 5.21.2).

▸ **Personal Category**

As the name suggests, the Personal Category is used to categorize objects in personal folders.

▸ **Profile**

This InfoObject is used for publishing, by filtering data depending on a user (see Chapter 10).

▸ **Relational Connection**

This InfoObject is used for relational connections created by Universe Design Tool and Information Design Tool. It supports specific rights (see Section 5.21.1).

▸ **Remote Connection**

This InfoObject is used for cluster federation. It references another CMS repository to be synchronized with the current CMS repository.

▸ **Replication Job**

Replication Job is used to define scheduling jobs for cluster federation. Note that it is the only system InfoObject to support scheduling rights set.

▸ **Replication List**

This InfoObject is used to define the objects to synchronize with another CMS repository through cluster federation.

▸ **Server**

The Server InfoObject is used to set parameters or rights to a server.

▸ **Server Group**

This InfoObject is used to gather several servers, which eases management of these servers in the CMC.

▶ **Universe**
The InfoObject is used for universes created by Universe Design Tool. These universes support general and specific rights, which are described in Section 5.16.2. More details on how universes are secured by Universe Design Tool can also be found in Chapter 7.

▶ **Universe (Information Design Tool)**
This InfoObject is used for universes created by Information Design Tool. These universes support general and specific rights, as described in Section 5.12.2. More details on how universes are secured by Information Design Tool can also be found in Chapter 8.

▶ **User**
The User InfoObject stores users (see Chapter 3). In addition to general rights, it is among the few (with User Group) to support specific general rights (see Section 5.20). It also supports one specific right.

▶ **User Group**
The User Group InfoObject stores a user group (see Chapter 3). For inheritance, it supports the same specific general rights supported by User.

5.3   Content Object List

The CMS repository supports the content InfoObjects shown next. All these Info-Objects support general rights. Except when explicitly mentioned, these content InfoObjects do not support general rights related to scheduling (see Section 5.23) or specific rights.

Most content InfoObjects support rights attached to Note InfoObjects (see Section 5.22).

▶ **Adobe Acrobat**
This InfoObject used for PDF file format supports general rights related to scheduling.

▶ **Agnostic**
The InfoObject used for any other object type that does not have its dedicated InfoObject. It supports general rights related to scheduling.

▶ **Analysis View** (see Section 5.4)
This InfoObject is used for workspace created by Analysis, Edition for OLAP.

▶ **Analysis Workspace** (see Section 5.4)
The InfoObject is used for workspace created by Analysis, Edition for OLAP.

▶ **BI Workspace** (see Section 5.8.2)
The InfoObject is used for workspace created in BI Workspace.

▶ **Crystal Reports** (see Section 5.10)
This InfoObject is used for Crystal Reports 2011 and Crystal Reports for Enterprise documents. It supports general rights related to scheduling and specific rights.

▶ **Dashboard**
This InfoObject is used for the new file format introduced in BI 4.0 for Dashboards, formerly Xcelsius.

▶ **Exploration View Set**
The InfoObject is used for Explorer exploration view set (see section 5.11). This object is available in the CMC only after the installation of Explorer.

▶ **Flash**
This InfoObject used for Adobe Flash files.

▶ **Hyperlink**
This InfoObject is used to store in the CMS repository a URL hyperlink.

▶ **Information Space**
This InfoObject is used for Explorer information space. This object is available in the CMC only after the installation of Explorer (see Section 5.11). It supports general rights (without scheduling) and specific rights.

▶ **Lifecycle Manager Job**
This InfoObject is used to define Promotion Management jobs (see Section 5.13). It supports general rights related to scheduling.

▶ **Microsoft Excel**
This InfoObject is used for Microsoft Excel files. It supports general rights related to scheduling.

▶ **Microsoft PowerPoint**
This InfoObject is used for Microsoft PowerPoint files.

▶ **Microsoft Word**
This InfoObject is used for Microsoft PowerPoint files. It supports general rights related to scheduling.

▶ **Module** (see Section 5.8.3)
Modules are containers that can be shared among several BI workspaces.

▶ **Note** (see Section 5.22)
This InfoObject is used for discussion threads. It supports general rights related to scheduling.

▶ **Object Package**
This InfoObject is used to gather objects. It supports general rights related to scheduling.

▶ **Program**
This InfoObject supports general rights related to scheduling.

▶ **Publication**
This InfoObject is used for publication (see Chapter 9). It supports general rights related to scheduling.

▶ **Rich Text**
This InfoObject is used for Rich Text files. It supports general rights related to scheduling.

▶ **Shortcut**
This InfoObject is used to modelize a shortcut to another object in the CMS repository.

▶ **Text**
This InfoObject is used for Text files. It supports scheduling rights set.

▶ **VisualDiff Comparator** (see Section 5.18)
This InfoObject is used in Visual Difference in order to save a comparison and to re-run it later.

▶ **Web Intelligence** (see Section 5.19.5)
This InfoObject is used for Web Intelligence documents. It supports general rights related to scheduling and specific rights.

▶ **Xcelsius**
The Xcelsius file format supported in XI 3.x. It is still available in BI 4.0, along with the Dashboard InfoObject.

Chapter 4, Section 4.5 describes the general rights supported by these objects. Except for some cases, the meaning of these rights is adapted to the application user interface, so the following sections do not discuss their impact on the user interface.

The specific rights supported by these content InfoObjects are described with their corresponding applications from Section 5.4 to Section 5.19, except for Note and file formats that can be scheduling output and that have dedicated sections (see Section 5.22 to Section 5.23).

5.4   Analysis, Edition for OLAP

Analysis, Edition for OLAP (Voyager in XI 3.x) is an analysis tool dedicated to multidimensional databases. It is launched from the BI Launch Pad portal, in contrast to its pendant (Analysis, Edition for Microsoft Office), which can be launched from Microsoft Office tools (Excel and PowerPoint).

During your navigation, you see the multidimensional database through an *analysis* that defines a specific sub-set of data. You can save the current state of your analysis, called *Analysis view*, in the CMS repository. Analysis view can thus be shared with other products of the suite: Analysis, Edition for Microsoft Office, Crystal Reports, and Web Intelligence.

Finally, you can define an *Analysis workspace,* which can gather several analyses. These analyses can even be based on several different multidimensional databases.

> **Note**
>
> Don't confuse an Analysis workspace with a BI workspace created with BI Workspaces.

5.4.1   Analysis, Edition for OLAP Rights

Analysis, Edition for OLAP supports only one general right ("Modify the rights users have to this object") and one specific right described next.

Create Analysis Workspace

This right allows you to create Analysis workspace.

If the right is denied

▶ In BI Launch Pad home page, the ANALYSIS, EDITION FOR OLAP icon in the MY APPLICATIONS section is no longer displayed.

▶ In BI Launch Pad APPLICATIONS dropdown list, the ANALYSIS, EDITION FOR OLAP choice is no longer displayed.

▶ In BI Launch Pad, launch Analysis, edition for OLAP by opening an existing Analysis workspace. In the toolbar, the CREATE A NEW WORKSPACE button is disabled, preventing you from creating a new Analysis workspace.

5.4.2   Analysis View and Analysis Workspace Rights

Both Analysis view and Analysis workspace support only general rights.

5.5   BEx Web Applications

The BusinessObjects web application server can be used as the web application for BEx Web Applications and BI Launch Pad as a portal from which you can run these BEx Web Applications. This capability is secured in the CMC by only one general right, "Modify the rights users have to this object," and one specific right, "Launch BEx Web applications," described next.

Launch BEx web applications

This right allows you to launch BEx web applications in BI Launch Pad.

If the right is denied

▶ In BI Launch Pad home page, the BEx WEB APPLICATIONS icon in the MY APPLICATIONS section is no longer displayed.

▶ In BI Launch Pad APPLICATIONS dropdown list, the BEx WEB APPLICATIONS choice is no longer displayed.

5.6   BI Launch Pad

BI Launch Pad (remember that this was called InfoView in XI 3.x) is the default web-based interface where you and your end users can access their BI resources. Through this portal, you can create, modify, view, schedule, and organize documents created with BusinessObjects reporting products. You can also keep track of different instances of scheduled or published instances of these reports.

In BI Launch Pad, you can use BI Workspaces to organize your content through tabs, pages, menus, and sections (see Section 5.8 for more information on BI Workspaces). From BI Launch Pad, you can also launch the other reporting products (Web Intelligence, Crystal Reports, Explorer, and Analysis, Edition for OLAP).

By default, the BI Launch Pad URL is *http://<server>:<port>/BOE/BI*.

BI Launch Pad supports the four general application rights and some specific rights. We look at these rights next.

Organize

This right allows you to manage objects in BI Launch Pad: to cut, copy, and delete objects and create shortcuts to objects.

If the right is denied

In the DOCUMENTS tab, select an object:

▶ Right-click the object; ORGANIZE is not displayed in the contextual menu.

▶ In the MORE ACTIONS menu, ORGANIZE is not displayed.

Send to BusinessObjects Inbox

This right allows you to send objects to users through the BI platform mailbox.

If the right is denied

In the DOCUMENTS tab, select an object:

▶ Right-click the object; SEND • BI INBOX is not displayed in the contextual menu.

▶ In the SEND menu, BI INBOX is not displayed.

Send to email destination

This right allows you to send objects to users through their internet email.

If the right is denied

In the DOCUMENTS tab, select an object:

▶ Right-click the object; SEND • EMAIL is not displayed in the contextual menu.

▶ In the SEND menu, EMAIL is not displayed.

Send to file location

This right allows you to save objects to a file location. It is enforced only by Crystal Reports documents.

If the right is denied

Open a Crystal Reports document in BI Launch Pad. In the toolbar, FILE • SEND TO • FILE LOCATION is not displayed.

Send to FTP location

This right allows you to save objects to an FTP location.

If the right is denied

▶ Open a Crystal Reports document in BI Launch Pad. In the toolbar, FILE • SEND TO • FTP LOCATION is not displayed.

▶ Open a Web Intelligence document in BI Launch Pad:

  ▶ In the Rich Internet Application interface toolbar, SEND TO • SEND TO FTP has no effect.

  ▶ In the Web interface toolbar, SEND TO • SEND TO FTP is disabled.

Send to StreamWork

This right allows you to share objects and comments to SAP StreamWork.

If the right is denied

You cannot interact with SAP StreamWork from BI Launch Pad.

5.7   Widgets

This product is a client application you install on your desktop to display frequently used documents or content stored in the CMS repository. You can configure a Widgets refresh rate so displayed data are always up to date.

Use Alert Inbox

This right is deprecated and no longer in use.

Use Explorer

This right allows you to browse the content of all connected BI 4.0 system CMS repositories using the DOCUMENT LIST EXPLORER.

If the right is denied

In your Windows desktop, right-click the BI Widgets icon in the task bar. In the menu, you'll see that Document List Explorer is disabled.

Use search

This right allows you to search across content in the CMS repositories of all connected BI 4.0 system using the Content Search.

If the right is denied

In your Windows desktop, right-click the BI Widgets icon in the task bar. In the menu, Content Search is disabled.

5.8 BI Workspaces

BI Workspaces is an application builder integrated into BI Launch Pad. These applications, saved as BI workspaces objects, are available from BI Launch Pad as customized tabs, pages, and sections where you organize your content. A BI workspace defines the structure of the application.

You can then fill your BI workspace with content such Web Intelligence, Analysis, Dashboards, and Crystal Reports documents. You can also add modules (containers) that can be shared among several BI workspaces. These modules can embed also Web Intelligence, Crystal Reports, or Dashboards documents, or simpler objects, such as web page, text, or viewer. As modules can be shared by several BI workspaces, any change done in a module is seen by all BI workspaces that include it.

5.8.1 BI Workspaces Rights

BI Workspaces supports the application general rights (except the "Log on to..." right) and the two specific rights described next.

Create and edit BI workspaces

This right allows you to create BI workspaces in BI Launch Pad, through BI Workspaces. Depending on the "Edit BI workspaces" right, you may be able to edit BI workspaces, as seen in Table 5.1.

	"Edit BI workspaces" right is granted	"Edit BI workspaces" right is denied
"Create and edit BI workspaces" right is granted	Edit is granted.	Edit is granted.
"Create and edit BI workspaces" right is denied	Edit is granted.	Edit is denied.

Table 5.1 Edit BI Workspaces Authorization Depending on "Create and Edit BI Workspaces" and "Edit BI Workspaces" Rights

Even if these two rights defined at application level grant you the right to edit BI workspace, you can edit a BI workspace only if the "Edit objects" right at BI workspace level is also granted.

If the right is denied

You are not able to create a BI workspace:

▶ In BI Launch Pad home page, the BI WORKSPACE icon in the MY APPLICATIONS section is no longer displayed.

▶ In BI Launch Pad APPLICATIONS dropdown list, the BI WORKSPACE choice is no longer displayed.

▶ If the BI workspaces "Edit BI workspaces" right or if the BI workspaces "Edit objects" right is also denied, then you cannot edit the BI workspace. If you open the BI workspace, you'll see that the EDIT BI WORKSPACE button is not displayed in the upper right of the BI workspace, preventing you from editing the workspace.

Create and edit modules

This right allows you to create modules in BI Launch Pad.

If the right is denied

▶ In BI Launch Pad home page, the MODULE icon in the MY APPLICATIONS section is no longer displayed.

▶ In BI Launch Pad APPLICATIONS dropdown list, the BI WORKSPACE choice is no longer displayed.

► When you open a module, the EDIT, SAVE, and SAVE As links are no longer displayed.

Edit BI workspaces

As Table 5.1 shows, this right allows you to edit BI workspaces if the "Create and edit BI workspaces" right is denied to you. You also need to have the "Edit objects" right granted for a BI workspace to edit it.

If the right is denied

Open a BI workspace. In the upper right of the BI workspace, the EDIT BI WORKSPACE button is not displayed, preventing you from editing the workspace.

5.8.2   BI Workspace Rights

BI Workspaces enforces only general rights, without the ones related to scheduling. It also supports the Note rights (see Section 5.22). BI Workspaces enforces the general rights by following their general meaning. Among these two general rights, two have specificities: "Add objects to this folder" and "Edit objects."

Add objects to the folder

This right allows you to add new tabs to a BI workspace. A BI workspace is considered a container where new tabs are stored. These new tabs are stored as BI workspaces as well.

This right does not prevent you from adding modules or other objects to the BI workspace. To add a tab to the BI workspace, you also require the "Edit BI workspaces" right.

If the right is denied

Open a BI workspace. Click EDIT BI WORKSPACE in the upper right of the BI workspace to switch to edit mode. Click the ADD A NEW TAB tab. Click the EXIT EDIT MODE button. After the confirmation message, an error message is displayed.

Edit objects

This right lets you modify a BI workspace: edit tabs, properties, and content. To edit a BI workspace, you must also have the rights to "Create and edit BI workspaces" or "Edit BI workspaces."

If the right is denied

Open a BI workspace. In the upper right of the BI workspace, the EDIT BI WORKSPACE button is not displayed, preventing you from editing the workspace.

5.8.3 Module Rights

Modules enforce only general rights, without the scheduling rights set. They also support the Note rights (see Section 5.22). They enforce the general rights by following their general meaning.

If the "Edit objects" right of a module is denied, then when you open a module in BI Launch Pad, the EDIT and SAVE links are disabled, but not the SAVE As link. This prevents you from modifying a module but not from creating a new module you can edit from this one.

5.9   Central Management Console

The CMC is the web application used by administrators to manage their BI 4.0 system. It has already been discussed in Chapter 2 and it is detailed in most chapters of this book since many tasks related to authentication, rights, and security are managed in the CMC.

By default, the CMC URL is *http://<server>:<port>/BOE/BI*

The CMC supports the four application general rights and three specific rights that are described next.

Allow access to Instance Manager

This right allows you to view the different instances of an object.

If the right is denied

You do not have access to the Instance Manager in the CMC.

Allow access to Relationship Query

This right allows you to use the Relationship Query, described in more detail in Chapter 4, Section 4.10.

If the right is denied

In the CMC, depending on the object type, go to the tab corresponding to a top-root folder: UNIVERSES, CONNECTIONS, FOLDERS. Select an object:

▸ In the menu bar, the MANAGE • TOOLS • CHECK RELATIONSHIPS menu is not displayed.

▸ Right-click the object; in the contextual menu, TOOLS • CHECK RELATIONSHIPS is not displayed.

Allow access to Security Query

This right allows you to use the Security Query, described in more detail in Chapter 4, Section 4.10.

If the right is denied

In the CMC, select the QUERY RESULTS tab:

▸ In the left pane, right-click the SECURITY QUERIES branch; no contextual menu opens to allow you to create a new query.

▸ In the menu bar, the MANAGE • NEW sub-menu does not exist.

5.10   SAP Crystal Reports

In the BI 4.0 suite, two versions of Crystal Reports are released and supported:

▸ Crystal Reports 2011, the successor of Crystal Reports 2008

▸ Crystal Reports for Enterprise, the new version of Crystal Reports that supports new BI 4.0 features

Both applications can save their documents in the CMS repository. When these documents are saved in the CMS repository and accessed through BI Launch Pad, security rights apply to them.

Documents saved in the CMS repositories are secured by rights. But once they are retrieved from the CMS, they are no longer secured. For this reason, the "Download files associated with the object" right can be used to grant or deny the retrieval of Crystal Reports documents from the CMS repository.

> **Note**
>
> Business views are the historical metadata layer implemented by Crystal Reports. It is not covered in this book since it is not supported by Crystal Reports for Enterprise, which supports universes created with Information Design Tool and offers almost the same functionalities as business views.

5.10.1 Crystal Reports Configuration Rights

In the APPLICATIONS tab, the Crystal Reports Configuration application allows you define some parameters for Crystal Reports and to set its security. It supports the four general application rights and one specific right described next.

Launch Crystal Reports for Enterprise from BI Launch Pad

This right allows you to run Crystal Reports for Enterprise from BI Launch Pad if you have installed it on your desktop.

If the right is denied

From the BI Launch Pad home page, it is not possible to launch Crystal Reports for Enterprise:

▶ In the APPLICATIONS dropdown list, the CRYSTAL REPORTS FOR ENTERPRISE choice is not displayed.

▶ In the MY APPLICATIONS sections, the Crystal Reports for Enterprise icon is not displayed.

5.10.2 Crystal Reports Document Rights

Crystal Reports supports general rights, including the ones related to scheduling. It also supports Note rights (see Section 5.22) and the rights of possible schedules output (see Section 5.23): Adobe Acrobat, Microsoft Excel, Microsoft Word, Rich Text, and Text.

It also supports an additional general right named "Download files associated with the object" and specific rights discussed next.

They apply to documents created by Crystal Reports 2011 and Crystal Reports for Enterprise.

Download files associated with the object

This right allows you to retrieve the report from the CMS repository and save it locally. When it is saved locally, rights do not apply any more to the report.

If the right is denied

In the CRYSTAL REPORTS toolbar, the EXPORT button is disabled, preventing you from opening the EXPORT dialog box and exporting the report data into other file formats.

Export the report's data

This right allows you to save a report data into another file format.

If the right is denied

In BI Launch Pad, open the report. In CRYSTAL REPORTS toolbar, the EXPORT button is disabled, preventing you from opening the EXPORT dialog box and exporting the report data into other file formats.

Print the report's data

This right allows you to print the report.

If the right is denied

In BI Launch Pad, open the report. In CRYSTAL REPORTS toolbar, the PRINT button is disabled, preventing you from printing the report.

Refresh the report's data

This right allows you to refresh Crystal Reports document.

If the right is denied

In BI Launch Pad, open the report. In CRYSTAL REPORTS toolbar, the REFRESH REPORT button is disabled, preventing you from refreshing report data.

5.11   Explorer

Explorer is a data discovery product that allows you to quickly navigate and analyze data that have been retrieved directly from your data sources and saved on information spaces. In order to understand the rights enforced by Explorer, the following sections first describe Explorer workflows and then detail the application specific rights and the specific rights of the InfoObjects it generates (information space and exploration view set).

5.11.1 Explorer Overview

To explore data, Explorer relies on *information spaces* that index data, metadata, or both from your data sources:

▶ **Relational universes created with Information Design Tool**

▶ **SAP HANA and SAP NetWeaver BW Accelerator**
In these two cases, the indexing done for universes and Excel files to index metadata and data is used only for metadata. Because these two data sources are already in memory, they do not need to be accelerated.

▶ **Excel files**

To define an information space, you select from the data source the objects or metadata you want the information space to index and on which the users are able to explore. Explorer then indexes the list of values of these objects into facets. Thanks to this indexation, navigation in the information space is fast.

When you explore an information space, you can focus on a specific piece of data and save it as an *exploration view*. In an exploration view, you can organize, format and filter data exposed by information space. You can then organize exploration views into *exploration view sets*, which may contain exploration views based on different information spaces.

You can schedule the information space indexing. But as this schedule does not rely on the Job Server process, when you create such a schedule, you need to provide credentials used by the schedule to run this indexing.

Explorer shares the same repository as BI 4.0, especially the users and their authentication mode. You can launch Explorer from BI Launch Pad. In this case, the session used to open BI Launch Pad is reused and you do not need to re-authenticate to Explorer. You can also open Explorer directly by accessing typing this URL into your browser: *http://<server>:<port>/explorer*

In this case, you need to authenticate to access Explorer. The Explorer HOME tab contains two buttons:

▶ INFORMATION SPACES: Click it to list all information spaces.

▶ EXPLORATION VIEW SETS: Click it to list all exploration view sets.

In the displayed list, click the link with the name of an information space or an exploration view set to open it in a dedicated tab.

5.11.2 Information Space Security

If the information space is based on a universe, then, when it is indexed, the security that applies at query time for the user who has scheduled the indexing applies:

▶ Data retrieved through the connection credentials of the user

▶ Data or business security profiles defined for this universe (see Chapter 8)

Thus, for indexing, we recommend that you use an account that has larger authorization so it can retrieve more data sets in the information space.

Then you can restrict objects and data in information space to users who explore the information space using two methods:

▶ **Universe object access level, if it is based on a universe**
Access level is a property that can be set to objects of universe (dimensions, measures, attributes) and that defines level of confidentiality: public (the default value and the least confidential), controlled, restricted, confidential, or private (the most confidential).

A user or a group can be assigned an access level for a universe. When a user explores an information view based on this universe, he can see only objects of this universe whose access level is lower than or equal to his own access level. Other objects are not displayed, and thus the corresponding data are also not displayed. Universe object access levels are also covered in Chapter 8, Section 8.7.

▶ **Information space personalization**
Personalization is used to filter the data in facets users can see. To put information space personalization in place, you need to create an information space dedicated to security that is used to return for a dimension the values granted to your different users. This dedicated information space is used to personalize your business information space.

When these users navigate in the personalized information space, they can see in the secured facet only the values they are allowed to see. But if the security information space does not grant them any value, then an error message is displayed.

For example, you may filter the list of countries users can see in a personalized information space. The dedicated information space must contain at least two facets—one for the list of users and another for the granted values.

Consider the example shown in Figure 5.2. When you personalize your information space, you need to map the following:

▶ Its `User name` dimension to the `Users` dimension in the information space dedicated to security

▶ Its `Country` dimension to the `Granted Countries` dimension in the information space dedicated to security

This way, when `bill` explores the business information space, he can see only the data for the country US, whereas `jim` can see the countries Denmark and France, as shown in Figure 5.2.

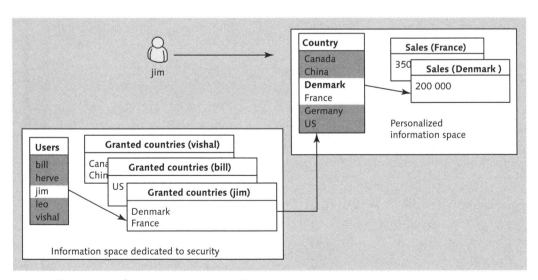

Figure 5.2 Information Space Personalization

To personalize an information space, follow these steps:

1. Create a data source that contains the facet values granted for your users. It can be an Excel file you upload in the CMS repository and on which you create the security information space.

2. Click the MANAGE SPACES button to open the MANAGE SPACES tab.

3. Create an information space on top of this data source and index it.

4. This information space is used for security purpose. For this reason, in the MANAGE INFORMATION SPACES page, in its properties, you can unselect the SHOW ON HOME PAGE checkbox to hide it in the Explorer HOME page.

5. Navigate in the SOURCES tree and select the data source (SAP HANA, universes created with Information Design Tool, Excel files, etc.) of the information space to secured. The INFORMATION SPACES list displays all information spaces based on this source.

6. Select the information space to secure.

7. In the ACTION column, in the dropdown menu, select CONFIGURE to open the EDIT INFORMATION SPACE dialog box.

8. In this dialog box, click the PERSONALIZATION tab. This tab displays a table containing the USER NAME line and the list of objects in the information space.

9. In this tab, click the PERSONALIZE INFORMATION SPACE checkbox.

10. In the dropdown list, select the security information space.

11. In the table, in front of the USER NAME line, select in the dropdown menu the object in the information space used to return users for which security has been defined.

12. In the table, in front of the object to select, select in the dropdown menu the object in the security information space used to return granted values for this object.

13. Click OK to save these personalizations and close the dialog box.

14. Index the information space in order to take this security information space into consideration. If it is based on an in-memory technology (SAP HANA or SAP NetWeaver BW Accelerator) and has already been indexed, this indexing step is useless: Metadata has already been indexed and security is enforced through data retrieved from in-memory.

   Your information space is now secured.

5.11.3 Explorer Rights

When you install Explorer on top of BI 4.0, some servers are added to the CMC. Also, Explorer is added to the APPLICATIONS tab and two new content InfoObjects types to the CMS repository: information space and exploration view set.

The Explorer application supports the application general rights plus the specific rights that are described next.

Browse content

This right allows you to explore information spaces and exploration view sets. In practice, if this right is denied to you, you can only manage information spaces, even if you've been granted other rights ("Explore information spaces," for example).

If the right is denied

In Explorer HOME tab, the SEARCH text field and all buttons are disabled, preventing you from exploring information spaces and exploration view sets. The list of information spaces is also not displayed.

Exploration view sets: Create exploration view set

This right allows you to create new exploration view set. To create an exploration view set, you also need the "Browse content" right.

If the right is denied

▶ Open an information space. In its tab, the CREATE VIEW SET button is not displayed in the toolbar, preventing you from saving a new view set from this information space.

▶ Open an exploration view set. In its tab, the SAVE AS button is not displayed in the toolbar, which prevents you from creating a new exploration view set by duplicating an existing one.

▶ In the HOME tab, select an information space and click the SHOW PROPERTIES button to display this information space's properties. In the right pane that opens, the CREATE VIEW SET button is not displayed, preventing you from saving a new view set from this information space.

Exploration view sets: Delete exploration view set

This right allows you to delete an exploration view set. To edit an exploration view set, you also need the "Browse content" right.

If the right is denied

In the HOME tab, click the EXPLORATION VIEW SETS button to list all exploration view sets. Click the SHOW PROPERTIES button to display exploration view set properties. In the right pane that opens, the DELETE button is not displayed, preventing you from deleting the selected exploration view set.

Exploration view sets: Edit exploration view set

This right allows you to edit exploration views in an exploration view set: adding or removing an exploration view or modifying its position in the exploration view set. This right does not prevent you from opening it, exploring its data, and saving or copying it. To edit an exploration view set, you also need the "Browse content" and "Exploration view sets: Open exploration view set" rights.

If the right is denied

Open an exploration view set. In its tab, you cannot modify the exploration views it contains:

▶ The VISUAL ELEMENTS panel that allows you to add new element is not displayed.

▶ Clicking the EXPLORE button in the exploration view header does not open the exploration panel.

▶ You cannot drag and drop exploration views in the tab to modify their position.

▶ You cannot click the cross icon in an exploration view header to remove it from the exploration view set.

Exploration view sets: Open exploration view set

This right allows you to open a view set, to view or modify it. To open an exploration view set, you also need the "Browse content" right.

If the right is denied

▶ In the HOME tab, click the EXPLORATION VIEW SETS button to list all exploration view sets. Click one; its editor tab does not open.

▶ In the Home tab, select an information space. Click the Show Properties button to display this information space's properties. In the right pane that opens, click an exploration view; its editor tab does not open.

Exploration view sets: Save exploration view set

This right allows you to save an exploration view set. This right does not prevent you from exploring or modifying its data.

If the right is denied

Open an exploration view set or create a new one. In the toolbar of its tab, the Save and Save As buttons are not displayed, preventing you from saving any changes you may make.

Explore information spaces

This right allows you to open an information space or to explore its data.

If the right is denied

▶ In the Home tab, click the Information Spaces button to display the list of information spaces. Click an information space; its tab does not open.

▶ Open an exploration view set. Its tab opens but it does not contain any exploration view and an error message is displayed.

Explore information spaces: Export to bookmark/email

This right allows you to add, in your browser's bookmark, a link to this information space with the current exploration view or to email this link. To bookmark or mail this exploration view, you also need the "Browse content" and "Explore information spaces" rights.

If the right is denied

In the toolbar, the Bookmark this view in your browser and Share this view by email buttons are disabled.

Explore information spaces: Export to CSV/Excel

This right allows you to export data of your exploration view as a CSV or Excel file. For this export, you also need the "Browse content" and "Explore information spaces" Explorer rights and the "Explore information spaces: Export to CSV/Excel" right for the selected information space.

If the right is denied

Open an information space. In its tab, in the toolbar, click the EXPORT button to open the EXPORT TO dialog box; the DATA and EXCEL buttons are disabled, preventing you from generating a picture from the exploration view.

If the option to export to all possible formats (CSV/Excel, image, Web Intelligence) is denied to you, in the toolbar, the EXPORT button is disabled, preventing you from opening the EXPORT TO dialog box.

Explore information spaces: Export to image

This right allows you to export data in your exploration view as an image. For this export, you also need the "Browse content" and "Explore information spaces" Explorer rights and the "Explore information spaces: Export to CSV/Excel" right for the selected information space.

If the right is denied

Open an information space. In its tab, in the toolbar, click the EXPORT button to open the EXPORT TO dialog box; the IMAGE button is disabled, preventing you from generating a picture from the exploration view.

If the option to export to all possible formats (CSV/Excel, image, Web Intelligence) is denied to you, then in the toolbar, the EXPORT button is disabled, preventing you from opening the EXPORT TO dialog box.

Explore information spaces: Export to Web Intelligence

This right allows you to create a WEB INTELLIGENCE document on the same universe used by the current information space. This Web Intelligence document can only be created with information space based on a universe. It is created by generating the corresponding query on this universe and by using the same filters as your exploration view.

For this export, you also need the "Browse content" and "Explore information spaces" Explorer rights and the "Explore information spaces: Export to CSV/Excel" right for the selected information space and the same rights needed to create a Web Intelligence document (see Chapter 11, Section 11.6).

If the right is denied

Open an information space. In its tab, in the toolbar, click the Export button to open the Export to dialog box; the Web Intelligence button is disabled, preventing you from generating a Web Intelligence document from the exploration view.

If the option to export to all possible formats (CSV/Excel, image, Web Intelligence) is denied to you, then in the toolbar, the Export button is disabled, preventing you from opening the Export to dialog box.

Manage information spaces

This right allows you to create, modify, delete, and index information spaces.

If the right is denied

The Manage Spaces link in top of the Explorer interface is disabled, preventing you from opening the Manage Spaces tab.

Manage information spaces: Calculated measures

This right allows you to create a measure in the information space based on the measures already in the information space and simple operators (addition, subtraction, multiplication, division). This measure becomes available in the information space after you re-index it. The "Manage information spaces" and "Manage information spaces: Modify an information space" rights must also be granted to you in order to edit the information space.

If the right is denied

Click the Manage Spaces button to open the Manage Spaces tab. Navigate in the Sources tree to reach an information space source and click it. The Information Spaces list displays all information spaces based on this source. In the Action column, in the dropdown menu, click Configure to open the Edit Information Space dialog box. Click the Objects tab. In the dropdown menu attached to the New button, Calculated Measure is disabled, preventing you from opening the Add Calculated Measure dialog box.

Manage information spaces: Create a new information space

This right allows you to create a new information space. The "Manage information spaces" right must also be granted to you in order to access the MANAGE SPACES tab.

If the right is denied

Click the MANAGE SPACES button to open the MANAGE SPACES tab. In this tab, the NEW button is disabled, preventing you from creating new information space.

Manage information spaces: Launch indexing

This right allows you to index information space. The "Manage information spaces" right must also be granted in order to access the MANAGE SPACES tab.

If the right is denied

Click the MANAGE SPACES button to open the MANAGE SPACES tab. Navigate in the SOURCES tree to reach the information space source (SAP HANA, universes created with Information Design Tool, Excel files) and click it. The INFORMATION SPACES list displays all information spaces based on this source. In the ACTION column, in the dropdown menu, INDEX NOW is disabled, preventing you from indexing the information space.

Manage information spaces: Modify an information space

This right allows you to modify the parameters of an information space:

▶ Its general properties: its name, description, the folder where it is saved, by default in your "Personal Folders" folder

▶ The objects/metadata contained in the information space

▶ Scheduling parameters, to schedule the information space indexing

▶ Personalization, to secure data users can see through the information space (see Section 5.11.2)

The "Manage information spaces" right must also be granted to you in order to access the MANAGE SPACES tab.

If the right is denied

As described for the "Manage information spaces: Launch indexing" right, open the information space ACTION dropdown menu. In this menu, CONFIGURE is disabled, preventing you from opening the EDIT INFORMATION SPACE dialog box.

Manage information spaces: Schedule indexing

This right allows you to schedule the indexing of information space. Scheduling information space is used to refresh data contained in the information space to be updated with the data from the data source. The "Manage information spaces" and "Manage information spaces: Modify an information space" rights must also be granted to you in order to edit the information space.

If the right is denied

As described for the "Manage information spaces: Launch indexing" right, open the information space ACTION dropdown menu and select CONFIGURE to open the EDIT INFORMATION SPACE dialog box. Select the SCHEDULING tab; all is content is disabled, preventing you from modifying the index scheduling parameters.

Manage information spaces: Upload external files

This right allows you to upload local Excel files in order to explore data they contain as information space. These Excel files must be simple, with data organized in columns.

If the right is denied

In the HOME tab, the UPLOAD A SPREADSHEET TO EXPLORE section is not displayed, preventing you from uploading external files.

Search content

This right allows you to search within information spaces content.

If the right is denied

In the HOME tab, the SEARCH text field and button are disabled, preventing you from searching among information space.

5.11.4 Information Space Rights

Information space InfoObject is available in the CMC after Explorer has been installed. Information space supports general InfoObject rights, except the rights related to scheduling. It also supports some specific rights, which are described next, and Note rights (see Section 5.22).

Explore information spaces: Export to CSV/Excel

This right is identical to the Explorer application "Explore information spaces: Export to CSV/Excel" right (see Section 5.11.3), but it applies to a specific information space. Therefore, to export an exploration view as an image, you must have the two rights granted: both at Explorer and at information space level.

Explore information spaces: Export to image

This right is identical to the Explorer application "Explore information spaces: Export to image" right (see Section 5.11.3), but it applies to a specific information space. Therefore, to export an exploration view as an image, you must have the two rights granted: at Explorer and at information space level.

Explore information spaces: Export to Web Intelligence

This right is identical to the Explorer application "Explore information spaces: Export to Web Intelligence" right (see Section 5.11.3), but it applies to a specific information space. Therefore, to export an exploration view as an image, you must have the two rights granted: at Explorer and at information space level.

5.11.5 Exploration View Set Rights

Exploration view set is available in the CMC after Explorer has been installed. Exploration view set supports general InfoObject rights, except the scheduling rights set, but does not support specific rights. It also supports Note rights (see Section 5.22).

5.12 Information Design Tool

Information Design Tool is the successor to Universe Design Tool. Chapter 8 is entirely dedicated to this tool and provides details about the security profiles. The following sections focus only on Information Design Tool and its universes' rights.

5.12.1 Information Design Tool Rights

Information Design Tool application rights are inspired by Universe Design Tool. But it leverages only the rights related to the CMS repository, when a session has been opened. Universe Design Tool rights related to authoring have not been ported because, in Information Design Tool, authoring is done on local projects, and thus without rights being applied (see Appendix A for more details on how these rights are converted from Universe Design Tool). Several sessions can be opened in parallel, but when dealing with resources from a CMS repository, the rights that apply are the ones computed for the account used to open the session.

Administer security profiles

This right allows you to use the Security Editor to create, administrate, and assign universes' data and business security profiles (see Chapter 8).

If the right is denied

In the toolbar, click the SECURITY EDITOR icon or in the menu bar, select the WINDOWS • SECURITY EDITOR menu in order to connect to the Security Editor. The logon page opens. After you have selected the system to log on to and entered your credentials, an error message is displayed.

Compute statistics

This right allows you to launch the STATISTICS MANAGEMENT dialog box used to select tables and columns to calculate and publish the statistics used by Data Federator for multi-source universe or universes based on a relational SAP NetWeaver BW or SAS data source.

If the right is denied

In the Repository Resources view, COMPUTE STATISTICS is disabled in the universe right-click menu.

Create, modify, or delete connections

This right allows you to create and administrate secured connections in the CMS repository. To create a secured connection, you also need the "Add objects to this object" right granted for the connection folder where the connection is created. To edit a secured connection, you also need the "Edit objects" right for this connection and the "Delete objects" right to delete it.

If the right is denied

You cannot create a secured connection or publish a local connection into a CMS repository:

▶ In the Repository Resources view toolbar, INSERT • INSERT RELATIONAL CONNECTION and INSERT • INSERT OLAP CONNECTION is disabled.

▶ In the Repository Resources view, select a connection. In the toolbar, the OPEN and DELETE icons are disabled.

▶ In the Repository Resources view, if you right-click a connection folder, INSERT RELATIONAL CONNECTION and INSERT OLAP CONNECTION are disabled.

▶ In the Repository Resources view, if you right-click a connection, OPEN and DELETE CONNECTION are disabled.

▶ In a local connection contextual menu, right-click a connection and select PUBLISH CONNECTION TO A REPOSITORY. After you have authenticated to the CMS repository, an error message is displayed.

▶ The drag and drop of local connection into the Repository Resources view is disabled.

▶ In the Repository Resources view, double-clicking a connection does not open the editor of this connection

▶ In the menu bar, FILE • PUBLISH • PUBLISH CONNECTION TO THE REPOSITORY is disabled.

Publish universes

This right allows you to publish a universe in the CMS repository. To publish a universe, you also need the "Add objects to this folder" right for the folder where the universe is published and the data foundation or business layer must be based on a connection shortcut that references a connection in the CMS repository.

If the right is denied

In the Local Projects view, right-click a business layer. In the contextual menu, select PUBLISH • TO A REPOSITORY.

▶ If a session to the CMS repository containing the secured connection(s) on which the data foundation or business layer rely is already open, then an error message is displayed.

▶ If such session is not yet open, the OPEN SESSION dialog box opens so you can authenticate to open it. Enter your credentials and click OK; an error message is displayed.

Retrieve universes

This right allows you to retrieve a universe from a CMS repository in order to edit locally its data foundation and business layer. To retrieve a universe, you must also have the "Retrieve universe" right at universe level.

If the right is denied

▶ In the Repository Resources view, if you right-click the universe, in the contextual menu, RETRIEVE UNIVERSE is disabled.

▶ In the Local Projects view, select a local project. In the menu bar, select FILE • RETRIEVE A PUBLISHED UNIVERSE • FROM A REPOSITORY to open the OPEN SESSION dialog box. Select or create a session to the CMS repository. Click OK; an error message is displayed.

Save for all users

You cannot retrieve the corresponding data foundation (if any) and business layer from a universe published in the CMS and save them locally as unsecured resources. To save a universe for all users, you need also to have the "Retrieve universes" and the "Retrieve universe" universe rights.

If the right is denied

When you retrieve a universe from the CMS repository, the data foundation (if any) and business layer are always saved secured: in the Repository Resources view, right-click a universe. In the contextual menu, select RETRIEVE UNIVERSE. In the SELECT A LOCAL PROJECT dialog box, the SAVE FOR ALL USERS checkbox is not selected. It is disabled and cannot be selected.

Share projects

This right allows you to create shared projects and to synchronize objects in these shared projects.

If the right is denied

▶ In the Local Projects view, right-click a local project. In the contextual menu, select NEW SHARED PROJECT to open the OPEN SESSION dialog box. Select or create a session to the CMS repository. Click OK; an error message is displayed.

▶ In the Project Synchronization view, click the CHANGE SESSION button to open the OPEN SESSION dialog box. Select or create a session to the CMS repository. Click OK; an error message is displayed.

5.12.2 Universe Rights

In Information Design Tool, when you edit a universe through its data foundation or its business layer, no security rights apply. But when you merge these resources to publish the universe in the CMS repository, the rights described next apply to the generated universe. These rights apply only in Information Design Tool, except "Create and edit queries based on the universe" and "Data access," which impact the reporting tools that consume the universe.

If the universe was already published, when you republish it and replace the previous universe, two previously assigned rights are kept: the users and groups to which they were assigned and their values.

Assign security profiles

This right allows you to assign or un-assign this universe's security profiles to a user or a group.

If the right is denied

▶ In the SECURITY EDITOR, in universe-centric view, the <, >, and >> buttons are disabled.

▶ In the user-centric view, the checkboxes in front of data and business security profiles used to assign the security profile to the user or group selected in the user or group browsers are disabled and cannot be modified.

Create and edit queries based on the universe

This right allows you to create or edit queries based on this universe. It is enforced both in Information Design Tool and in reporting tools that support these universes. This right is useful if you want your users to be able to refresh reports based on this universe but without being able to create new queries.

If the right is denied

In Information Design Tool, you cannot run a query based on this universe:

► In the Repository Resources view, when you right-click this universe, RUN QUERY is disabled in the contextual menu.

► In the Security Editor, in the universe-centric view, when you right-click this universe, RUN QUERY is disabled in the contextual menu.

► In reporting tools, you are not allowed to create or edit a query based on this universe.

Data access

This right allows you to query data through this universe. This right secures data only and does not cover metadata.

If the right is denied

In Information Design Tool, you cannot query data from this published universe:

► In the Repository Resources view, when you right-click this universe and select RUN QUERY to open the query panel, the REFRESH button is not displayed.

► In the Security Editor, in the universe-centric view, after you select RUN QUERY to open the query panel, the REFRESH button is not displayed.

In reporting tools that may support universe created with Information Design Tool, any workflows that retrieve data through this universe fail. For example, in Web Intelligence or Crystal Reports for Enterprise, when you try to create a new document from this universe, after you have created your query with the query panel and try to run it, an error message is displayed.

Edit security profiles

This right allows you to create, edit, or delete data or business security profiles and modify aggregation options.

If the right is denied

In the Security Editor's universe-centric view:

- Select a universe:

  - Its aggregations options cannot be modified in the dropdown lists.

  - In the tool bar, the INSERT DATA SECURITY PROFILE, INSERT BUSINESS SECURITY PROFILE, CHANGE DATA SECURITY PROFILE PRIORITY, OPEN, and DELETE buttons are disabled.

- Right-click a universe or a security profile; in the contextual menu, INSERT DATA SECURITY PROFILE, INSERT BUSINESS SECURITY PROFILE, and CHANGE DATA SECURITY PROFILE PRIORITY are disabled.

- Right-click a data security profile. In the contextual menu:

  - INSERT DATA SECURITY PROFILE, INSERT BUSINESS SECURITY PROFILE, CHANGE DATA SECURITY PROFILE PRIORITY, and DELETE DATA SECURITY PROFILE are disabled.

  - EDIT DATA SECURITY PROFILE is not displayed.

- Right-click a business security profile. In the contextual menu:

  - INSERT DATA SECURITY PROFILE, INSERT BUSINESS SECURITY PROFILE, and DELETE BUSINESS SECURITY PROFILE are disabled.

  - EDIT BUSINESS SECURITY PROFILE is not displayed.

- Double-click a security profile. The security profile editor does not open.

In user-centric view, select a universe:

- Right-click a data security profile. In the contextual menu, EDIT DATA SECURITY PROFILE is not displayed and DELETE DATA SECURITY PROFILE is disabled.

- Right-click a business security profile. In the contextual menu, EDIT BUSINESS SECURITY PROFILE is not displayed and DELETE BUSINESS SECURITY PROFILE is disabled.

- In the toolbar, INSERT DATA SECURITY PROFILE, INSERT BUSINESS SECURITY PROFILE, EDIT DATA SECURITY PROFILE, EDIT BUSINESS SECURITY PROFILE, CHANGE DATA SECURITY PROFILE PRIORITY, and DELETE buttons are disabled.

- Double-click a security profile. The security profile editor does not open.

Retrieve universe

This right allows you to retrieve a universe and edit its data foundation (if any) and business layer locally. To retrieve a universe, you must also have the Information Design Tool's "Retrieve universes" right granted.

If the right is denied

In the Repository Resources view, right-click a universe. In the contextual menu, RETRIEVE UNIVERSE is disabled.

5.13 Promotion Management

Promotion Management is the CMC feature used to promote resources from CMS repositories and generate LCMBIAR files. The following sections present an overview of Promotion Management, detail how security is promoted, and describe the different Promotion Management specific rights.

Promoting CMS repository was done in previous releases through a web application called Lifecycle Management that needed to be installed separately. In BI 4.0 SP3/FP4, it has been integrated into the CMC as Promotion Management, and you can promote CMS repositories with the CMC without having to install a separate web application.

Promotion Management is useful to promote resources of CMS repositories from one environment to another, for example from a development environment to a test environment before going to production environment. These CMS repositories must have the same major version (BI 4.0).

It can also be used to generate LCMBIAR files that are archive files where you can back up BI content, including their security. Typically, when you are re-designing security, it can be useful to back up your existing security settings (users, groups, folders, access levels, and so on) in an LCMBIAR file so you can restore it if needed. When you generate an LCMBIAR file, you can also secure it with a password that is requested when you re-import this LCMBIAR file.

Only LCMBIAR files generated from BI 4.0 CMS repository can be imported (same major version). LCMBIAR files generated with Upgrade Management Tool or from CMS repository from previous releases cannot be imported.

5.13.1 Promoting Security

When objects are promoted, you have several different options for promoting rights security assigned for these objects to users and groups:

▶ **No security promotion**
No security is promoted. If the object already exists in the destination repository, then the object is promoted, but the rights assigned for this objects are not changed in the target repository. If the object did not exist in the destination repository, then it simply inherits the rights of the folder in which it is created.

▶ **Promote object security**
This option includes rights assigned for this object. You select this option to promote the immediate security assigned for this object, through advanced rights or access levels assigned to the object or its parent folders.

  ▶ If the corresponding users, groups, and access levels do not exist yet in the destination CMS repository, they are promoted as well to promote these assigned rights.

  ▶ If the corresponding users, groups, and access levels do not exist yet in the destination CMS repository, they are not updated from the source CMS repository, but the assigned rights are.

You can check the impacted users, groups and access levels by clicking the View Security button in the Include Security panel.

▶ **Promote user security**
This option is available if you have selected to promote object security. It is similar to the "Promote object security" option, but it promotes as well the other rights and access levels assigned to the users and groups that are promoted because they have security assigned to them for objects selected for promotion. However, this option does not include or promote rights assigned for applications.

▶ **Include application rights**
This option is available if you have selected to promote object and user security. It is similar to the "Promote user security" option, but it promotes all security, including the one assigned for applications.

When a universe is promoted, then the security defined for this universe (access restrictions if created with Universe Design Tool, and security profiles if created with Information Design Tool, is always migrated, even if no security promotion option has been selected.

If you have selected the "Promote object security" option, their assignments to users and groups are promoted in the destination CMS repository:

▶ If the corresponding users, groups, and access levels do not exist yet in the destination CMS repository, they are promoted as well to promote the assignment to the universe access restrictions or security profiles.

▶ If the corresponding users, groups, and access levels already exist in the destination CMS repository, they are not updated from the source CMS repository, but their assignment to the universe access restrictions or security profiles is updated.

You can check and select what users and groups have been assigned this universe access restrictions or security profiles in the MANAGE DEPENDENCIES dialog box.

5.13.2 Promotion Management Rights

Promotion Management supports the four general application rights, except the "Log on to…" right. Indeed, to use it, you need to have the "View objects" right on the "Public Folders/LCM/Promotion Jobs" folder that stores the promotion jobs. If this right is denied, when you open the Promotion Management tab in the CMC, it remains empty and you cannot run any action. Promotion jobs are saved through the "Lifecycle Manager Job" content InfoObject type. This InfoObject supports only general rights, including the scheduling rights set.

Promotion Management also supports the specific rights described next that secure the different actions that can be done: create a job, create an LCMBIAR file, promote or edit a job, and so on.

To connect and authenticate to the source and/or target repositories, you need to provide credentials of user of these repositories. Promotion Management enforces the general objects rights "View objects," "Add objects to folders," and "Edit objects" in these repositories to control the objects you can promote.

Allow access to edit overrides

This right allows you to define overrides. Overriding is the capability to modify some system parameters saved in promoted objects, such as connection, that depend on the CMS repositories. For example, in a configuration with two databases, one for the source environment and one for the target environment, if you promote a connection that references the source database, in the target environment, the promoted connection still references the source database. With override, you can modify the connection parameters on the fly so the connection references the target database after it is promoted.

If the right is denied

In the PROMOTION JOBS tab, in the toolbar, the OVERRIDE SETTINGS button is disabled, preventing you from opening the PROMOTION MANAGEMENT FOR SAP BUSINESS-OBJECTS ENTERPRISE–OVERRIDES panel and defining overrides.

Allow access to include security

This right allows you include security settings when promoting content or generating LCMBIAR files (see Section 5.13.1).

If the right is denied

In the PROMOTE dialog box, in the SECURITY SETTINGS section, the PROMOTE SECURITY radio button is disabled, preventing you from defining security to promote.

Allow access to LCM administration

This right allows you to define some parameters for Promotion Management:

▶ The list of systems defined in Promotion Management

▶ The systems that can be rolled back

▶ Jobs parameters, to manage the jobs instances

▶ Parameters to integrate with CTS, the SAP transport tool

This right does not cover the other parameters in Promotion Management properties panel, reachable from the CMC APPLICATIONS tab.

If the right is denied

In the PROMOTION JOBS tab, in the toolbar, the SETTINGS button is disabled, preventing you from opening the menu attached to this button and from modifying some Promotion Management parameters.

Allow access to manage dependencies

This right allows you to view and to select objects related to objects in the job. Promotion Management displays a dependent object only if the corresponding Promotion Management "View and select <object type>" right is also granted.

If the right is denied

When you create or edit a job, in the job panel editor, in the toolbar, the MANAGE DEPENDENCIES button is disabled, preventing you from opening the MANAGE DEPENDENCIES dialog box and from viewing and selecting objects related to objects in the job.

Create job

This right allows you to create a new job in Promotion Management.

If the right is denied

In the PROMOTION JOBS tab toolbar, the NEW JOB button remains disabled, preventing you from creating a new one.

Delete job

This right allows you to delete any job created in Promotion Management.

If the right is denied

In the PROMOTION JOBS tab, select a job. The DELETE button remains disabled in the toolbar, preventing you from deleting it.

Edit job

This right allows you to edit job parameters: its name, description, keywords, and the objects it promotes. This right does not prevent you from promoting the job and modifying promotion option: schedules, security options (see Section 5.13.1).

If the right is denied

In PROMOTION JOBS tab, in the right pane, select a job:

- ▶ In the toolbar, the EDIT button is disabled.
- ▶ Right-click it; in the contextual menu, EDIT is not displayed.

Edit LCMBIAR

This right is not used.

Export as LCMBIAR

This right allows you to run immediately or to schedule a promotion job whose destination system is an LCMBIAR file.

If the right is denied

In the PROMOTION JOBS tab, in the right pane, select a job whose destination is an LCMBIAR file. Open the PROMOTE dialog box for this job; the EXPORT and SCHEDULE buttons are not displayed.

To open the PROMOTE dialog box, you can either:

▶ Click the PROMOTE button in the toolbar or right-click the job and, in the contextual menu, select PROMOTE.

▶ Or, if you have the EDIT JOB right, click the EDIT button or right-click the job and, in the contextual menu, select EDIT. In the job editor tab, click the PROMOTE button.

Import LCMBIAR

This right allows you to import an LCMBIAR file or overrides saved in an LCMBIAR file into a CMS repository.

If the right is denied

In PROMOTION JOBS tab, in the toolbar, the IMPORT button is disabled, preventing you from opening the attached dropdown menu and from opening the IMPORT FROM FILE dialog box.

Promote job

This right allows you to run immediately or to schedule a promotion job whose destination system is a BI 4.0 repository.

If the right is denied

In PROMOTION JOBS tab, in the right pane, select a job whose destination is a BI 4.0 repository. Open the PROMOTE dialog box for this job; the PROMOTE and

SCHEDULE buttons are not displayed. But you can still test the promotion in the TEST PROMOTE section.

To open the PROMOTE dialog box, you can either:

▶ Click the PROMOTE button in the toolbar or right-click the job and, in the contextual menu, select PROMOTE.

▶ Or, if you have the EDIT JOB right, click the EDIT button or right-click the job and, in the contextual menu, select EDIT. In the job editor tab, click the PROMOTE button.

Rollback job

This right allows you to roll back the last run of a promotion job. The objective of a rollback is to restore the destination system to its previous state. It can be rolled back only if:

▶ Its target is another BI 4.0 CMS repository, not an LCMBIAR file.

▶ In the settings, rollback for this system has been granted.

▶ And, in the last execution of this job, promotion was successful.

If the right is denied

In PROMOTION JOBS tab, select a job in the right pane. If the job last run was successful and if its target is another BI 4.0 CMS repository, then you cannot open the ROLLBACK dialog box and rollback this last run to restore the destination system to its previous state:

▶ The ROLLBACK button remains disabled.

▶ In the right-click menu, the ROLLBACK button remains disabled.

View and select BOMM objects

If SAP BusinessObjects Metadata Management has been installed and uses the CMS repository as its repository, then this right allows you to view the objects it generates and promote them in Promotion Management.

If the right is denied

It is not possible to add a metadata object created by Metadata Management into a promotion job:

▶ In the ADD OBJECTS dialog box, the DATA SERVICES and INFORMATION STEWARD branches are not displayed.

▶ In the MANAGE DEPENDENCIES dialog box, you can see these metadata objects as dependencies, but their checkboxes are disabled, preventing you from selecting or unselecting them.

View and select business views

This right is similar to the "View and version BOMM objects" right but applied to connections, business views, and metadata foundations created and published in the CMS repository by Business View Manager and used by Crystal Reports 2011. In the ADD OBJECTS dialog box, these objects are located in the BUSINESSVIEWS branch.

View and select calendars

This right is similar to the "View and version BOMM objects" right but applied to calendars. In the ADD OBJECTS dialog box, these calendars are located in the CALENDARS branch.

View and select connections

This right is similar to the "View and version BOMM objects" right but applied to connections created by Universe Design Tool, Information Design Tool, and CMC. In the ADD OBJECTS dialog box, these connections are located in the CONNECTIONS branch.

View and select profiles

This right is similar to the "View and version BOMM objects" right but applied to profiles used for publications (see Chapter 10 for more information on publishing). In the ADD OBJECTS dialog box, these profiles are located in the PROFILES branch.

View and select QaaWS

This right is similar to the "View and version BOMM objects" right but applied to profiles used for queries used by Queries as a Web Service. In the ADD OBJECTS dialog box, these queries are located in the QAAWS branch.

View and select report objects

This right is similar to the "View and version BOMM objects" right but applied to content of the "Public Folders" top-root folder. In the ADD OBJECTS dialog box, this content is located in the ALL FOLDERS branch.

View and select security settings

This right is similar to the "View and version BOMM objects" right but applied to users, groups, and access levels. In the ADD OBJECTS dialog box, these objects are located in the USERS, USER GROUPS, USER GROUP HIERARCHY, and ACCESS LEVELS branches.

View and select universes

This right is similar to the "View and version BOMM objects" right but is applied to universes created by Universe Design Tool and Information Design Tool and Information Design Tool shared projects. In the ADD OBJECTS dialog box, these objects are located in the UNIVERSES and PROJECTS branches.

5.14 SAP BusinessObjects Mobile

You can use SAP BusinessObjects Mobile to view Crystal Reports and Web Intelligence documents on your mobile device. You can download it for iOS and Android platforms. Once it is installed, you can connect to CMS repository without having to install or configure anything on the server side.

SAP BusinessObjects Mobile does not support any general rights and only the four specific rights described next.

Log on to SAP BusinessObjects Mobile application

This right allows you to log into the CMS repository through SAP Business Objects Mobile. The right can be seen as the equivalent of the general right "Log on to…"

If the right is denied

On your device, after you have provided your credentials to the CMS repository, an error message is displayed.

Save documents to the local store of a device

This right is not yet implemented in BI 4.0 SP4. You can always save documents on your device. Once it is implemented, denying this right should prevent this.

Send documents from device as an email

This right is not yet implemented in BI 4.0 SP4. You can always send a report by mail. Once it is implemented, denying this right should prevent this.

Subscribe to documents alerts

This right is not yet implemented in BI 4.0 SP4. You can always subscribe and receive document alerts. Once it is implemented, denying this right should prevent this.

5.15 SAP StreamWork

SAP StreamWork is the SAP on-demand collaboration tool. Its integration has been introduced with BI 4.0 FP3. It enables you to send a document to StreamWork, add a StreamWork feed into a BI workspace or open and follow discussion on document in SAP StreamWork. As a prerequisite, you must have subscribed to SAP StreamWork and get an ID and a logon to SAP StreamWork Admin Console. Furthermore, you need to have set up and run an SAP StreamWork Enterprise Agent to connect to SAP StreamWork.

In order to use it, you need to enable it (by default, it is disabled) and configure SAP StreamWork to work with BI 4.0. To do so, follow these steps:

1. In the APPLICATIONS tab, right-click SAP STREAMWORK.

2. In the contextual menu, select SAP STREAMWORK INTEGRATION CONFIGURATION to open the SAP STREAMWORK INTEGRATION CONFIGURATION dialog box.

3. In this dialog box, select the ENABLE STREAMWORK INTEGRATION checkbox.

4. In the UNIQUE IDENTITY PROVIDER ID, type the ID that was given to you when you subscribed to SAP StreamWork.

5. Click REGENERATE to generate a certificate in the IDENTITY PROVIDED BASE64 CERTIFICATE.

6. Copy this string. Do not type anything in the OAUTH CONSUMER KEY text field.

7. Log on to SAP StreamWork Admin Console and enter this certificate to to create a trusted SAML IDP and get a consumer key.

8. Return to the SAP STREAMWORK INTEGRATION CONFIGURATION dialog box in the CMC and enter this key in the OAUTH CONSUMER KEY text field.

9. If you use a proxy, click the CONNECTING USING PROXY checkbox and enter the proxy parameters.

10. Click SAVE AND CLOSE to close the dialog box and save the SAP StreamWork configuration.

11. Log into SAP StreamWork Admin Console and configure the SAML TRUSTED IDENTITY PROVIDER page as described in SAP StreamWork documentation.

When your users log on to BI 4.0, they are asked to provide the credentials of an SAP StreamWork user to map to the BI 4.0 account.

5.16 Universe Design Tool

Universe Design Tool is the historical BusinessObjects metadata design tool. It is still released and supported in BI 4.0, although it is recommended that you use Information Design Tool for new projects. Chapter 7 is entirely dedicated to this tool, especially the access restrictions. This section focuses only on Universe Design Tool and universe rights.

5.16.1 Universe Design Tool Rights

In BI 4.0, Universe Design Tool rights are similar to XI R2 and XI 3.x Universe Designer rights. It supports the application general rights and specific rights. These specific rights are mainly inspired by BusinessObjects 5x/6x Designer and Supervisor. They are enforced in Universe Design Tool when you are logged on to a CMS.

Apply universe constraints

This right allows you to manage access restrictions on universes stored in the CMS repository. To manage access restrictions, you also need the "Edit access restrictions" right for the universe.

If the right is denied

You cannot open the dialog boxes related to access restrictions:

▶ In the TOOLS • MANAGE SECURITY menu, MANAGE ACCESS RESTRICTIONS and PREVIEW NET ACCESS RESTRICTIONS are disabled.

▶ In the EDITING toolbar, the CREATE, MODIFY OR DELETE, OR APPLY ACCESS RESTRICTIONS button is disabled.

Check universe integrity

This right allows you to verify universe integrity. This integrity check is used to find errors in the universe, such as universe structure, invalid SQL in object or join condition, joins cardinalities and so on. Because it generates some traffic with the database, you may secure its use by using this right.

If the right is denied

In the TOOLS menu or the EDITING toolbar, the CHECK INTEGRITY button is disabled, preventing you from opening the INTEGRITY CHECK dialog box and running the check integrity.

Create, modify, or delete connections

This right allows you to do several things:

▶ Create, edit, and delete secured connections. To edit a connection, you must also have its "Edit objects" right granted to you. To delete a connection, you must also have its "Delete objects" right granted to you.

▶ Edit and delete personal or shared connections.

This right does not cover the creation of personal or shared connections.

If the right is denied

In the menu bar, in the TOOLS menu, select CONNECTIONS or, in the STANDARD toolbar, click the CONNECTIONS button to open the CONNECTION PANEL dialog box. In this dialog box:

▶ The EDIT CONNECTION, EDIT DESCRIPTION, REMOVE, CUT, COPY, and PASTE buttons are disabled, preventing you from editing or deleting connections.

▶ Click the NEW CONNECTION button to open the DEFINE A NEW CONNECTION dialog box. In this dialog box, the CONNECTION TYPE dropdown list does not contain the SECURED choice, preventing you from creating secured connection.

Link universe

This right allows you to manage *linked universes* in Universe Design Tool. A linked universe is the capability to reference a universe, called a *core universe*, into another universe, called *derived universe*. The core universe is not copied into the universe, but when reporting tools access the derived universe, it behaves as if it were. Because core universe can be used by several derived universes, this capability allows you to factorize some common objects.

If the right is denied

▸ In the FILE menu, select PARAMETERS or, in the STANDARD toolbar, click the PARAMETERS button to open the UNIVERSE PARAMETERS dialog box. In this dialog box, select the LINKS tab; the ADD LINK... button is disabled, preventing you from opening the UNIVERSE TO LINK dialog box and from creating linked universe. However, the REMOVE button is not disabled, meaning that you can still remove the link between linked universes.

▸ In the EDIT menu, LINKS is disabled, preventing you from opening the LINKS tab of the UNIVERSE PARAMETERS dialog box.

▸ In the INSERT menu, UNIVERSE is disabled, preventing you from opening the OPEN dialog box and creating a linked universe.

Refresh structure window

This right allows you to update the universe content if the database tables or columns used by the universe have been modified: added or removed columns, removed or renamed tables, etc.

If the right is denied

In the VIEW menu, REFRESH STRUCTURE is disabled, preventing you from updating the universe with database changes.

Use table browser

This right allows you to navigate in the tables and the columns of the database referenced by the universe connection and to insert these tables in the universe.

If the right is denied

You are not able to open the TABLE BROWSER dialog box, preventing you from navigating in the database tables and columns:

▸ In the INSERT menu, TABLES is disabled.

▸ In the EDITING toolbar, the TABLE BROWSER button is disabled.

▸ Double-click anywhere in the STRUCTURE WINDOW; this dialog box does not appear.

▸ Right-click anywhere in the STRUCTURE pane; in the contextual menu; TABLES is disabled.

5.16.2 Universe Rights

These rights apply only in Universe Design Tool, except the "Create and edit queries based on universe" and "Data access" rights, which impact the reporting tools that consume the universe.

If the universe was already published, when you republish it and replace the previous universe, two previously assigned rights are kept: the users and groups to which they were assigned and their values.

Create and edit queries based on universe

This right allows you to create or edit queries based on this universe. It is enforced in reporting tools that support these universes. This right is useful if you want your users to refresh reports based on this universe, but without being able to create new queries.

If the right is denied

In reporting tools, you are not allowed to create or edit a query based on this universe.

Data access

This right allows you to query data through this universe. This right secures data only and does not cover metadata. To refresh a query from this universe, you also need at least the connection "Data access" right. Depending on the reporting tool that consumes the universe, you may require additional rights to query data through this universe (see Chapter 11, Section 11.6).

If the right is denied

This right has no impact on Universe Design Tool. For example, it is still possible to view table values even if the right is denied.

In reporting tools that may support universe created with Universe Design Tool, any workflows that retrieve data through this universe fail. For example, in Web Intelligence, when you create a new document from this universe, after you have created your query with the query panel and try to run it, an error message is displayed.

Edit access restrictions

This right allows you to create, modify, and assign access restriction (see Chapter 7, Section 7.4). To manage access restrictions, you also need the Universe Design Tool "Apply universe constraints" right.

If the right is denied

You cannot open the MANAGE ACCESS RESTRICTIONS dialog box:

▶ In the TOOLS menu, MANAGE SECURITY • MANAGE ACCESS RESTRICTIONS is disabled.

▶ In the EDITING toolbar, the CREATE, MODIFY OR DELETE, OR APPLY ACCESS RESTRICTIONS button is disabled.

New list of values

This right allows you to associate a new list of values with an object or edit an existing one. This right does not prevent the creation of a cascading list of values.

If the right is denied

▶ In the TOOLS menu, select LISTS OF VALUES • EDIT A LIST OF VALUES. In the LISTS OF VALUES dialog box, select an object. The EDIT, PURGE, and REFRESH buttons and the CORPORATE DATA (QUERY PANEL) and PERSONAL DATA radio buttons are disabled.

▶ In the left pane, select an object. In the EDIT menu, select OBJECT PROPERTIES or right-click the object and in the contextual menu and select OBJECT PROPERTIES. In the EDIT PROPERTIES dialog box that opens, select the PROPERTIES tab. Notice that the following elements are disabled:

- ▸ The Associate a List of Values checkbox
- ▸ The List Name text box
- ▸ The Restore Default and Edit buttons

Print universe

This right allows you to print a universe or preview it before printing it.

If the right is denied

- ▸ In the File menu, Page Setup, Print, and Print Preview are disabled.
- ▸ In the Standard toolbar, the Print and Print Preview buttons are disabled.

Show table or object values

This right allows you to view the values of a table or of an object.

If the right is denied

Open a universe; in the Structure pane, follow these steps:

- ▸ Select a table. In the View menu, Table Values is disabled.
- ▸ Right-click a table. In the contextual menu, Table Values is disabled.
- ▸ Right-click a column of a table. In the contextual menu, Column Values is disabled.
- ▸ Double-click anywhere outside a table in the Structure pane or right-click anywhere in the Structure pane and, in the contextual menu, select Tables or, in the Insert menu, select Tables, or, in the Editing toolbar, click the Table Browser button. In the Table Browser dialog box that opens:
  - ▸ Right-click a table. In the contextual menu, View Table Values is disabled.
  - ▸ Right-click a column of a table. In the contextual menu, View Column Values is disabled.
- ▸ In the left pane, select an object. In the Formula Bar toolbar, click the Object Properties button or right-click the object and in the contextual menu and select Object Properties or, in the Edit menu, select Object Properties. In the Edit Properties dialog box that opens, select the Properties tab. The Display button is disabled, preventing you from opening the List of Values dialog box that displays possible values for this object.

This right has no impact on the Quick Design Wizard that helps you to create universe because this right is set at universe level. During universe creation, the universe does not already exist; thus, this right is not applicable.

Unlock universe

This right allows you to unlock a universe locked by another user in the CMS repository.

If the right is denied

In the FILE menu, select IMPORT to open the IMPORT UNIVERSE dialog box. A locked universe is displayed with a lock icon in front of its name. Double-click it. If it is locked by another user, an error message is displayed.

5.17   Version Management

In previous releases, content versioning was available in the Lifecycle Management tool. In BI 4.0, with the integration of this tool into the CMC, Version Management has also been added to the CMC. It can be accessed in the CMC through the VERSION MANAGEMENT tab. Version Management can also be accessed from Promotion Management, but it is the only application where it is integrated.

Versioned content is stored by default in a separate Subversion repository that you can install when you install BI 4.0 server tools (see Chapter 2, Section 2.2.1). But you can choose another source management tool and configure Version Management to use it.

In the CMC, the Version Management application can be used to define its parameters, such as the Subversion parameters, but also some rights. Version Management supports three general application rights (it does not need the "Log on to..." right since it is integrated to the CMC) and some specific rights described next.

These specific rights apply at application level. It is not possible to set them individually on objects, but you can secure object type through the "View and version <object type>" right, where <object type> represents a type of object.

Version Management enforces the objects general rights: you can version an object only if you have "View objects" right granted for it. You can replace an object by one of its versioned copy if you have the "Edit objects" right granted.

Allow check-in

This right allows you to check in resources into the Version Management repository.

If the right is denied

▶ The ADD TO VM button is disabled, which prevents you from adding a new object in the Version Management repository.

▶ The CHECKIN button is disabled, which prevents you from adding a new version of an object already versioned in the Version Management repository.

▶ In the CMC PROMOTION MANAGEMENT tab, in the toolbar, in the dropdown menu attached to the VMS ACTIONS button, ADD TO VM and CHECKIN are not displayed.

▶ In the CMC PROMOTION MANAGEMENT tab, right-click a job; in the VMS ACTIONS sub-menu, ADD TO VM and CHECKIN are not displayed.

Allow create copy

This right allows you to create a copy of any version saved the Version Management repository of the selected resource. This copy is saved in the same folder as the selected resource, but it is not versioned. This right does not prevent you from replacing the resource with a specific version (see "Allow get revision" right).

If the right is denied

▶ In the Version Management toolbar, the CREATE COPY button is disabled.

▶ Select a versioned resource by selecting its checkbox, then click the HISTORY button to open the HISTORY dialog box that lists all versions of this resource. In this dialog box, clicking the GET COPY OF VERSION button has no effect.

▶ In the CMC PROMOTION MANAGEMENT tab, in the toolbar, in the dropdown menu attached to the VMS ACTIONS button, CREATE COPY is not displayed.

▶ In the CMC PROMOTION MANAGEMENT tab, right-click a job; in the VMS ACTIONS sub-menu, CREATE COPY is not displayed.

Allow delete revision

This right allows you to delete all versions of a resource from the Version Management repository (but the resource is not deleted from the "Public Folders"). This resource is no longer considered versioned and you need to add it back to Version Management before being able to reversion it.

If the right is denied

In the Version Management toolbar, the DELETE button is disabled.

Allow get revision

This right allows you to retrieve a specific version of a resource to replace the current version in the CMS repository. This right does not prevent you from creating a copy of a version (see "Allow create copy" right).

If the right is denied

▶ In the VERSION MANAGEMENT toolbar, the GET LATEST VERSION button is disabled.

▶ Select a versioned resource by selecting its checkbox, then click the HISTORY button to open the HISTORY dialog box that lists all versions of this resource. In this dialog box, clicking the GET VERSION button has no effect.

▶ In the CMC PROMOTION MANAGEMENT tab, in the toolbar, in the dropdown menu attached to the VMS ACTIONS button, GET LATEST VERSION is not displayed.

▶ In the CMC PROMOTION MANAGEMENT tab, right-click a job; in the VMS ACTIONS sub-menu, GET LATEST VERSION is not displayed.

Allow lock and unlock

This right allows you to lock and unlock resource stored in the Version Management repository. You typically lock a resource when you need to modify it. While it is locked, you can check out the resource, modify it, and then re-save a new version without anyone else being able to modify it. When you have locked an object, you are the only one who can unlock it.

If the right is denied

In the VERSION MANAGEMENT toolbar, the LOCK and UNLOCK buttons are disabled.

View and version BOMM objects

If SAP BusinessObjects Metadata Management has been installed and uses the CMS repository as its repository, this right allows you to view these objects and version them in Version Management.

If the right is denied

In Version Management's left pane, the DATA SERVICES and INFORMATION STEWARD branches are not displayed.

View and version business views

This right allows you to version connections, business views, and metadata foundations created and published in the CMS repository by Business View Manager and used by Crystal Reports 2011.

If the right is denied

In Version Management's left pane, the BUSINESSVIEWS branch is not displayed.

View and version calendars

This right allows you to version calendars.

If the right is denied

In Version Management's left pane, the CALENDARS branch is not displayed.

View and version connections

This right allows you to version connections created with Universe Design Tool, Information Design Tool or the CMC.

If the right is denied

In Version Management's left pane, the CONNECTIONS branch is not displayed, preventing you from selecting any connection saved in the "Connections" top-root folder.

View and version profiles

This right allows you to version profiles used for publications (see Chapter 9, Section 9.5).

If the right is denied

In Version Management's left pane, the PROFILES branch is not displayed.

View and version QaaWS

This right allows you to version queries used by Queries as a Web Services.

If the right is denied

In Version Management's left pane, the QAAWS branch is not displayed.

View and version report objects

This right allows you to version resources in the "Public Folders" folder.

If the right is denied

In Version Management's left pane, the ALL FOLDERS branch is not displayed, preventing you from selecting any content published in the "Public Folders" folder.

View and version security objects

This right allows you to version users, groups, and access levels (see Chapter 3).

If the right is denied

In Version Management's left pane, the following branches are not displayed:

▶ USERS, USER GROUPS, and USER GROUP HIERARCHY, which allow you to select users and groups

▶ ACCESS LEVELS, which allows you to select access levels

View and version universes

This right allows you to version universes created with Universe Design Tool and Information Design Tool and resources saved in Information Design Tool's shared projects (see Section 5.12).

If the right is denied

In Version Management's left pane, the following branches are not displayed:

▶ UNIVERSES, which contains universes and universes sub-folders

▶ PROJECTS, which contains folders created for Information Design Tool's shared projects

View deleted resources

This right allows you to view resources deleted from the CMS repository. If a resource has been versioned in Version Management, even if it has been deleted, the Version Management repository still stores its different versions and unless they have been explicitly removed from the Version Management repository, you can view them.

If the right is denied

In the VERSION MANAGEMENT toolbar, the VIEW DELETED RESOURCES button is disabled.

5.18 Visual Difference

Visual Difference is a framework available in the CMC used to compare different versions of an object. To access Visual Difference, go to the VISUAL DIFFERENCE tab in the CMC.

To compare objects, you need to define a list of objects to compare. These objects can be located in different repositories: CMS repository, Version Management repository (see Section 5.17), or a file system. In BI 4.0, only LCMBIAR files and LCMBIAR jobs are supported and can be compared.

Once the comparison is created, you can run it and see the differences between the compared objects through an interface called the Visual Difference Viewer. You can also save the comparison if you have a Job Server up and running in your system, in order to schedule it and run it the BI 4.0 scheduling framework.

Visual Difference generates "VisualDiff Comparator" content InfoObject that can be saved only in the "Public Folders/Visual Difference/VisualDiff Comparator" folder. You cannot directly assign rights for these objects but you can assign them for the folder that contains them. This type of objects supports only general rights, except the scheduling rights set.

Visual Difference supports three general application rights (it does not need the "Log on to..." right since it is integrated to the CMC) and some specific rights described next.

Create comparison

This right allows you to create a comparison.

If the right is denied

In the Visual Difference right pane, the NEW COMPARISON button is disabled, preventing you from opening the VISUAL DIFFERENCE – COMPARISONS dialog box and create new comparison, scheduled or not.

Delete comparison

This right allows you to delete a scheduled comparison.

If the right is denied

In the Visual Difference right pane, select a scheduled comparison job; in the toolbar, the DELETE button remains disabled, preventing you from deleting it.

Re-run comparison

This right allows you to re-run a scheduled comparison immediately.

If the right is denied

In the Visual Difference right pane, select a scheduled comparison job; in the toolbar, the RERUN button remains disabled, preventing you from running it at once.

View comparison

This right allows you to view the result of a scheduled comparison. It does not cover the right to create a comparison, run it, and see its results.

If the right is denied

In the Visual Difference right pane, select a scheduled comparison job whose result is successful; in the toolbar, the VIEW DIFFERENCE button remains disabled, preventing you from opening the Visual Difference Viewer.

5.19   Web Intelligence

Web Intelligence is an analysis and reporting product designed to work over the web or as a desktop product. It is the successor to historical Desktop Intelligence, which is no longer supported in BI 4.0.

Web Intelligence has different deployment options, which are described in Section 5.19.1. The desktop offline mode has typically some impact on connection security, as detailed in Section 5.19.2. As a Web Intelligence document may contain sensitive data, it is possible to purge or refresh it; we cover this in Section 5.19.3. Finally, the specific rights supported by this product and its documents are described in Sections 5.19.4 and 5.19.5.

> **Note**
>
> In Web Intelligence terminology, Web Intelligence creates a *document*. That document contains *reports*, which are represented by tabs at the bottom of the interface when you open the document in Web Intelligence.

5.19.1 Deployment Options

You can launch Web Intelligence from BI Launch Pad. The three deployment options map possible interfaces:

- ▶ **Rich Internet Application**
  Windows is implemented as a Java applet. You need to have Java installed on your desktop and the applet is downloaded from BI Launch Pad. This interface looks similar to the Web interface, but it offers more options and finer control.

- ▶ **Desktop**
  This mode is available on Windows only. This Desktop interface is the Java applet used in Rich Internet Application but installed on your desktop as a standalone tool. Because it is installed on your desktop, you can also launch directly it from the Windows START menu, without having to go in BI Launch Pad. Compared to the Rich Internet Application, the Desktop version is enhanced to support specific desktop workflows.

- ▶ **Web**
  This mode does not require any download or installation. It was reintroduced in BI 4.0 FP3 and supports only universes as a data source. Typically, it does not support SAP Direct Access (see Chapter 10, Section 10.3). This interface is implemented using DHTML technology.

> **Note**
>
> In the remainder of this chapter, *rich interfaces* refers to both Rich Internet Application and Desktop, since these interfaces are almost identical. *Rich Client* is also used to refer to the Desktop interface.

Web Intelligence Desktop can be installed in two ways:

▸ If it is not already installed on your desktop, you can directly download and install it on your desktop by requesting it from BI Launch Pad. In this mode, communication with the CMS repository is done in HTTP.

▸ You can install it directly from the BI 4.0 client tools installer.

Once installed, you can run Web Intelligence Desktop from the BI Launch Pad or from the Windows START menu.

When you run it from the Windows START menu, you can choose three connection modes:

▸ *Connected*: In this mode, you need to provide credentials that are checked against the CMS repository, which returns a list of your rights.

▸ *Offline*: Credentials are also needed, but they are not required to be connected to the CMS repository. Credentials are checked against a cache that returns the rights saved from a previous log on to the CMS repository (see Section 5.19.2).

▸ *Standalone*: No credentials are needed to log on in this mode. Anyone can log and no rights apply. Nevertheless, only documents that have been saved with the "Save for all users" option can be opened in this mode.

These modes are inherited from Desktop Intelligence, which supported them.

Once you have launched Web Intelligence, you can choose between two working modes:

▸ *Reading*, in which you can view, refresh, and analyze data of your document

▸ *Design*, in which you can design the document and create and edit its query

When you work from BI Launch Pad, you can select which user interface to use.

In reading mode, you can select Web, Rich Internet Application, or Desktop. When you have started Web Intelligence in one of these user interfaces, if you switch to design mode, you remain in the same user interface. In reading mode, you also have the PDF option, but you have only a static version of the report, with no possible interaction.

When you directly start Web Intelligence in design mode, you can also select you user interface: Web, Rich Internet Application, or Desktop.

You select these modes in the BI Launch Pad PREFERENCES page, in the WEB INTELLIGENCE section, as shown in Figure 5.3.

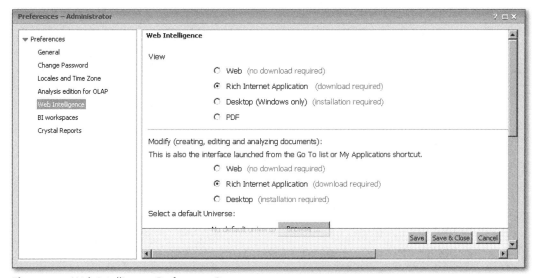

Figure 5.3 Web Intelligence Preferences Page

5.19.2 Offline Mode

One of the advantages of the Desktop offline mode is the ability to work on documents retrieved from the CMS repository but without having to be connected. When you connect to the CMS repository with Desktop interface, it keeps the Web Intelligence report, its universe, and the following data on caches in your machine:

▶ Web Intelligence application rights

▶ Web Intelligence report rights

▶ Universe restriction (if created with Universe Design Tool) or security profiles (if created with Information Design Tool)

▶ Universe rights

▶ Connection parameters

▶ Connection rights

This means that to work with offline mode, you need to have used at least once Web Intelligence Desktop in connected mode with the CMS repository to have downloaded these data on your machine. If you have never connected to this CMS repository, then you cannot log onto Web Intelligence Desktop in offline mode. Offline mode does not work with multi-source universes since they require access to the Data Federator Query Server.

As of BI 4.0 FP3, to retrieve connection parameters of a relational connection based on Connection Server, you need to explicitly grant the "Download connection locally" right for the connection.

If this right is denied, the connection sensitive parameters are kept on the server and are never downloaded on your desktop:

▶ In connected mode, queries to the database through this connection are always run server-side, even if you are using the Desktop interface.

▶ In offline mode, it is not possible to use this connection since it has not been saved in the cache.

To use this connection in offline mode, you need to explicitly grant this right. Thus connection can be saved in the cache, and Desktop interface can use it and run queries with local middleware.

This right is not implemented for OLAP connections and Data Federator data sources:

▶ You can always use offline mode with OLAP connection, through SAP direct access or universes created with Information Design Tool.

▶ You cannot use offline mode for Data Federator data source since it needs access to the Data Federator Query Server.

5.19.3 Purge and Refresh on Open

When you save a Web Intelligence report after it has been refreshed, it contains data that have been retrieved with your profile. It is possible to secure retrieved data so you can see only data you are authorized to access through the following methods:

▶ Through connection authentication (Chapter 6 covers connections and database authentication)

▶ If the report is based on a universe, through universe security:

  ▶ Access restrictions, if the universe has been created with Universe Design Tool (Chapter 7)

  ▶ Security profiles, if the universe has been created with Information Design Tool (Chapter 8)

When you save this document, it contains data retrieved for you, with this security applied to you. If you share the document in the CMS repository so someone else can use it, anyone allowed to open the document can see the data you have retrieved, even if the connection or universe security has been assigned to him and prevents him from seeing it. This security applies only at query time, so anyone can see your data because opening the report only displays its content.

To let other people access your report for their own uses, but prevent them from seeing your data, you have two options:

▶ Purge the report before saving it. This purge removes all data previously retrieved from a refresh. The report contains only the query to run, the formatting, and other parameters, except the data. To use the report, a user who opens the report must refresh it, and the security assigned to him is applied during this refresh.

▶ Force the "Refresh on open" option. This option purges the report before it is saved. In addition, when a user opens the report, it is automatically refreshed. Any connection and universe security assigned to this user is applied during the refresh. Thus, the report contains only data filtered with his security and he is allowed to see it.

Example

A country manager creates a document based on a universe. This universe enforces security to grant users to see figures only for their geographical area. When the country manager refreshes the document, it contains figures for the country. When he saves this document in the CMS repository, he sets the "Refresh on open" option. Thus, when a city manager opens the document, it is refreshed and the security that applies at query time filters the data returned in the document. As a result, the city manager can see only the figures for his city.

To purge a document, switch to design mode. Then, before saving the document, in the Data Access tab, in Data Providers toolbar, click the Purge button to purge data from all queries of the document. You can select to purge only one query:

open the dropdown menu attached to this button and select the query whose data must be purged.

To set the "Refresh on open" option, when you save the document, select the REFRESH ON OPEN checkbox.

You can also force to refresh all documents when they are opened by:

▶ Denying the Web Intelligence application "Documents: Disable automatic refresh on open" right (see Section 5.19.4) for the user.

▶ Selecting the CHECK THE "DISABLE AUTOMATIC REFRESH ON OPEN FOR ALL DOCU-MENTS" SECURITY RIGHT parameter in the CMC, in the Web Intelligence PROPER-TIES panel, as shown in Figure 5.4.

When a user opens a document, it is automatically refreshed, even if it has been saved without this option.

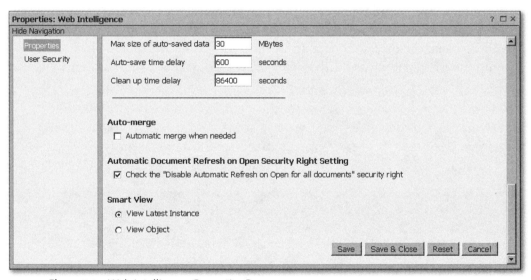

Figure 5.4 Web Intelligence Properties Page

5.19.4 Web Intelligence Rights

Web Intelligence supports the four application general rights (see Chapter 4, Section 4.6). The name of the general right that allows you to log on in Web Intelligence is named "Log on to Web Intelligence."

In addition, Web Intelligence application leverages many specific rights that finely secure its features. In order to clarify and simplify them, some rights have been renamed, added, or removed between XI 3.x and BI 4.0. However, they are properly kept and converted when you upgrade your XI R2 or XI 3.x CMS repository with Upgrade Management Tool.

These rights are now classified into the following categories:

▶ Data: Rights related to data tracking

▶ Desktop interface: Rights specific to Desktop interface; they secure document workflows between local machine and CMS repository

▶ Documents: Rights to create a new document, to enable automatic refresh and save, and to publish a report item as web services

▶ General: Rights to secure user's preference and right-click menu use

▶ Interfaces: Rights to secure the different deployment modes and interfaces

▶ Left pane: Rights to secure the use of the left pane

▶ Query script: Rights to view and edit the generated query script

▶ Reporting: Rights to secure changes to the report specification in design mode

When you connect with Web Intelligence Desktop in offline mode, these rights apply if you have already connected to Web Intelligence Desktop in connected mode, the right being saved in Web Intelligence local cache (see Section 5.19.2).

Data: Enable data tracking

This right allows you to track data changes between two refresh. When enabled, data from the last refresh are compared to data coming from a referenced refresh. This comparison gives you a view of how the data have evolved between references.

If the right is denied

▶ In Web interface reading mode, the TRACK button is disabled in the toolbar, which prevents you from opening the DATA TRACKING dialog box to activate/deactivate it or from modifying its option.

▶ In Rich interfaces reading mode, the TRACK button is disabled in the toolbar, which prevents you from:

  ▶ Clicking on it to open the DATA TRACKING dialog box if data tracking is disabled or disabled it if it is enabled.

> ▸ Opening the TRACK DATA CHANGES dropdown menu dialog to activate or deactivate data tracking or modify its option.

> ▸ In all interfaces design mode, in the ANALYSIS tab, in the DATA TRACKING tab, the TRACK button is disabled in the toolbar. This prevents you from opening the DATA TRACKING dialog box if data tracking is disabled or disabled it if it is enabled.

Data: Enable formatting of changed data

This right allows to modify the formats (colors, fonts) used to display changes found by data tracking. You may define different formats depending on the type of changes: inserted or removed values for dimension, changes for details, increased and decreased values and threshold for measures or numerical details. If you do not modify the formats, the default ones are defined in the CMC, in Web Intelligence parameters page.

If the right is denied

In all user interfaces, in the DATA TRACKING dialog box, in the OPTIONS tab, all controls are disabled, preventing you from modifying data tracking format. To open this dialog box:

> ▸ In reading mode, in the toolbar, in the TRACK dropdown menu, select DISPLAY OPTIONS.

> ▸ In design mode, in ANALYSIS tab, in DATA TRACKING tab, in the SHOW CHANGES dropdown menu, select DISPLAY OPTIONS.

To modify these settings, you also need to have the "Data: Enable data tracking" right; otherwise, you cannot open the DATA TRACKING dialog box.

Desktop interface: Enable local data providers

In Desktop interface, this right allows you to create a document based on a custom data provider (TXT, CSV, or Excel file) or edit the query of a document based on a local data provider. This right does not prevent you from viewing or refreshing the document if the file is available on the local file system.

If the right is denied

In Desktop interface, any workflow where you can create a query based on a local data provider fails:

▶ From the welcome page, if you are already connected to the CMS repository, in the NEW DOCUMENT section, select to create a document from a text of Excel file. In the CUSTOM DATA PROVIDER dialog box, the NEXT button remains disabled or if you browse the file system to select a file by clicking the BROWSE button, an error message is displayed.

▶ In design mode, in DATA ACCESS tab, in DATA PROVIDERS tab, click the NEW DATA PROVIDER button and in the attached dropdown menu, select FROM EXCEL or FROM TEXT. The CUSTOM DATA PROVIDER dialog box opens but, as previously, you cannot go forward.

▶ In the QUERY PANEL toolbar, click the ADD QUERY button and in the attached dropdown menu, select FROM EXCEL or FROM TEXT. The CUSTOM DATA PROVIDER dialog box opens but, as previously, you cannot go forward.

Open a document based on a custom data provider. In design mode, in the DATA ACCESS tab, in the DATA PROVIDERS tab, click the EDIT button: the query panel opens, but it is disabled, preventing you from editing the query on the local data provider.

Desktop interface: Enable Web Intelligence Desktop

This right allows you to use Web Intelligence Desktop interface.

If the right is denied

▶ In the BI Launch Pad PREFERENCES dialog box, in the WEB INTELLIGENCE section, the DESKTOP radio buttons are not displayed in the VIEW and MODIFY sections.

▶ When you try to log on to the CMS repository with Desktop interface, after you have provided your credentials, an error message is displayed.

Desktop interface: Export documents

This right allows you to publish your Web Intelligence documents to the CMS repository using Desktop interface.

If the right is denied

In Desktop interface, in reading mode toolbar, and in design mode FILE tab toolbar:

▸ In the SAVE dropdown menu, SAVE TO ENTERPRISE is disabled.

▸ In the SAVE dropdown menu, select SAVE AS to open the SAVE DOCUMENT dialog box. The button for the current CMS repository is disabled, preventing you from publishing your document in the CMS repository.

Desktop interface: Import documents

This right allows you to retrieve Web Intelligence documents from the CMS repository using Desktop interface.

If the right is denied

▸ In Desktop interface, in reading mode toolbar, and in design mode FILE tab toolbar, in the OPEN dropdown menu, OPEN FROM is disabled.

▸ In Desktop interface, when you are connected in the CMS, from the WELCOME page, in the OPEN DOCUMENT section, click the BROWSE links. In the OPEN A DOCUMENT dialog box, the button for the current CMS repository is disabled, preventing you from retrieving document from it.

Desktop interface: Install from BI Launch Pad

This right allows you to download and install Web Intelligence Desktop from BI Launch Pad. It does not prevent you from launching it if it is already installed.

If the right is denied

In the BI Launch Pad PREFERENCES dialog box, in the WEB INTELLIGENCE section, the INSTALLATION REQUIRED links are not displayed after the DESKTOP radio buttons. When they are enabled, you can use these links to download the Web Intelligence Desktop installer.

Desktop interface: Print documents

This right allows you to print a Web Intelligence document through Rich interfaces. This right does not cover:

▸ Printing the Web interface since it is in fact an export to PDF

▸ Printing the document summary from the left pane

If the right is denied

In Rich interfaces, the PRINT button is disabled in the reading mode toolbar and in design mode FILE tab toolbar. This prevents you from opening the PRINT dialog box and printing the document.

Desktop interface: Remove document security

This right allows you to save a document locally, without its security. By doing this, users can open it without having to authenticate to the CMS repository, and the document can be seen in standalone mode. This capability is possible only in Desktop interface.

If the right is denied

In Desktop interface, in reading mode toolbar or in design mode FILE tab, in the SAVE dropdown menu, select SAVE AS to open the SAVE dialog box. In this dialog box, the REMOVE DOCUMENT SECURITY checkbox is unselected and disabled, which prevents you from selecting this option.

Desktop interface: Save document for all users

This right allows you to save a document locally, for all users. Any user who has an account in the CMS repository can open it, but he needs to have authenticated to the CMS repository first. This capability is possible only in Desktop interface.

If the right is denied

In Desktop interface, open the SAVE dialog box as described previously. In this dialog box, the SAVE FOR ALL USERS checkbox is unselected and disabled, which prevents you from selecting this option.

Desktop interface: Save documents locally

This right allows you to save locally on your machine a document retrieved from the CMS repository. This right applies only to Rich interfaces since it is not possible to save a document locally through the Web interface.

If the right is denied

In Rich interfaces, in the SAVE dialog box, if you select a local folder to save your document, then an error message is displayed. To open this dialog box:

► In reading mode toolbar, in the Save dropdown menu, select Save As.

► In design mode, in the File tab, in the Save dropdown menu, select Save As.

Desktop interface: Send by mail

This right allows you to send a document by email through Desktop interface. It does not cover sending Web Intelligence document from BI Launch Pad.

If the right is denied

In Desktop interface, in the reading mode toolbar and in the design mode File tab toolbar, the Send by E-mail attachment button is disabled, preventing you from opening its dropdown menu and sending the document by email.

Documents: Disable automatic refresh on open

This right is used to force a document to be automatically refreshed when users open it (see Section 5.19.3), even if the document has been saved without this option. To do this, you must have first set the property Check the "Disable automatic refresh on open for all documents" security right parameter in the CMC. Then, if this right is denied, even if the "Refresh on open" has not been set, the document is always refreshed on opening.

If the right is denied

This right has no impact on the user interface since you can still save a document with or without the "Refresh on open" option. But when you open it, it is refreshed anyway, if the Check the "Disable automatic refresh on open for all documents" security right parameter has been set in the CMC.

Documents: Enable auto-save

This right allows you to benefit of the auto-save feature. The auto-save parameters (enabled/disabled, auto-save delay time, and so on) are set in the CMC in Web Intelligence application's properties. If auto-save has been enabled, then your document is regularly saved in your "My Favorites/~WebIntelligence" folder. If you lose your connection to BI Launch Pad, you can recover it from this folder. This option is available only when you launch Web Intelligence from BI Launch Pad, both in Web or Rich Internet Application interfaces since BI Launch Pad has some session time-out.

If the right is denied

Your document is not auto-saved.

Documents: Enable creation

This right allows you to create a new Web Intelligence document, but does not cover saving an existing document with a new name.

If the right is denied

- ▶ In Web interface, you can click the NEW icon in the toolbar and select a new data provider. But then an error message is displayed.
- ▶ In Rich interfaces, in both reading and design modes, the NEW button in the toolbar is disabled.
- ▶ In Desktop interface, when you are connected to the CMS repository, from the WELCOME page, in the NEW DOCUMENT section, click the BLANK DOCUMENT button or select a data provider: an error message is displayed.

General: Edit 'My Preferences'

This right allows you to change Web Intelligence preferences in BI Launch Pad.

If the right is denied

No option is displayed in the WEB INTELLIGENCE section of the BI Launch Pad's PREFERENCES dialog box (see Figure 5.3).

General: Enable right-click menus

This right allows you to use the right-click button in design mode in order to open the contextual menu that contains shortcuts for most common commands.

If the right is denied

In Web interface, in design mode, right-click any item in a report. The contextual menu does not open.

Interfaces: Enable Rich Internet Application

This right allows you to use Web Intelligence Rich Internet Application user interface (see Section 5.19.1).

If the right is denied

In the WEB INTELLIGENCE section of the BI Launch Pad's PREFERENCES dialog box, the RICH INTERNET APPLICATION radio buttons are not displayed in VIEW and MODIFY sections.

Interfaces: Enable web query panel

This right is deprecated. It is still used in BI 4.0, but it should be removed in upcoming releases. It allows you to open the Web Intelligence Web interface directly in design mode.

If the right is denied

In the WEB INTELLIGENCE section of the BI Launch Pad's PREFERENCES dialog box, the WEB radio button is not displayed in the MODIFY section. This prevents you from selecting it and launching this Web interface in design mode directly from BI Launch Pad.

Interfaces: Enable web viewing interface

This right allows you to open the Web user interface for Web Intelligence for viewing.

If the right is denied

In the WEB INTELLIGENCE section of the BI Launch Pad's PREFERENCES dialog box, the WEB radio button is not displayed in the VIEW section. This prevents you from selecting it and launching this Web interface in reading mode directly from BI Launch Pad.

Left pane: Enable document structure and filters

This right allows you to display the document structure and filters in Web Intelligence left pane. When you are in design mode, this shows in a hierarchical tree the list of reports, report items, and filters that make the document.

If the right is denied

In all user interfaces, in design mode, it is not possible to display the document structure. In the left pane:

▶ In the dropdown menu, the DOCUMENT STRUCTURE AND FILTERS option is not displayed.

▶ The DOCUMENT STRUCTURE AND FILTERS vertical tab is not displayed.

Left pane: Enable document summary

This right allows you to display the document summary in the left pane. This document summary displays some general data about the current document, some statistics, and some of its main parameters. In design mode, you can also modify some of these parameters.

If the right is denied

In all user interfaces, in both reading and design modes, it is not possible to display the document summary. In the left pane:

▶ In the dropdown menu, the DOCUMENT SUMMARY option is not displayed.

▶ The DOCUMENT SUMMARY vertical tab is not displayed.

Furthermore, in design mode, in the PROPERTIES tab, the DOCUMENT button is disabled, which prevents you from opening the DOCUMENT SUMMARY dialog box, where you can modify some of the document parameters.

Query script: Enable editing (SQL , MDX, ...)

If the document is based on a universe, this right allows you to modify the script generated to query the database. Depending on the data source, this script is expressed as an SQL or MDX expression. You also need the document rights "Edit query" and "View SQL" to view and edit the script.

This right must be granted with care, since modifying the script includes the ability to modify the script generated after the universe security has been applied and thus bypassing this security.

If the right is denied

▶ In Web interface query panel, if you have the "Query script: Enable viewing (SQL, MDX...)" right granted, click the VIEW SCRIPT button in the toolbar to open the Query Script viewer. You can select the USE CUSTOM QUERY SCRIPT radio button and modify the script. But when you click the SAVE button, an error message is displayed.

▶ In Rich interface query panel, if you have the "Query script: Enable viewing (SQL, MDX...)" right granted, click the VIEW SCRIPT button in the toolbar to open the Query Script viewer: the USE CUSTOM QUERY SCRIPT radio button is disabled, which prevents you from modifying the script.

Query script: Enable viewing (SQL , MDX, ...)

If the document is based on a universe, this right allows you to view the script generated to query the database, if the data source is a universe. Depending on the data source, this script can be expressed using SQL or MDX expression. In the case of SAP Direct Access (see Chapter 10, Section 10.3), you cannot see this script. You also need the document rights "Edit query" and "View SQL" to view the script.

If the right is denied

▶ In Web user interface, in the query panel, when you click the VIEW SCRIPT button in the Query Panel toolbar, an error message is displayed.

▶ In Rich interfaces, in the query panel, the VIEW SCRIPT button in the QUERY PANEL toolbar is disabled, which prevents you from opening the QUERY SCRIPT VIEWER.

Reporting: Create and edit breaks

This right allows you to create break when viewing a report.

If the right is denied

▶ In all user interfaces, in design mode, in the REPORT ELEMENT tab, in the TABLE LAYOUT toolbar, the BREAK button is disabled and cannot be clicked to open the MANAGE BREAKS dialog box.

▶ In all user interfaces, in design mode, when you right-click a cell, BREAK is disabled in the contextual menu and cannot be selected to open its sub-menu.

Reporting: Create and edit conditional formatting rules

This right allows you to create, modify and organize conditional formatting. This allows you to define a cell format (text font, background, border, etc.) depending on the cell content. Creating and modifying these rules can only be done in Rich interfaces, whereas applying them or modifying the order in which their condition is evaluated can be done in all interfaces.

If the right is denied

▶ In Web interface, in design mode, it is not possible to apply formatting rules or change the order in which their condition is evaluated:

  ▶ In ANALYSIS tab, in CONDITIONAL tab, the FORMATTING RULES button is disabled.

  ▶ In the right-click menu, FORMATTING RULES is disabled.

▶ In Rich interfaces, in design mode, in ANALYSIS tab, in CONDITIONAL tab, the FORMATTING RULES or NEW RULE buttons are disabled, preventing you from opening the CONDITIONAL FORMATS and FORMATTING RULE EDITOR dialog boxes.

Reporting: Create and edit input controls

This right allows you to create and modify a document input controls. Input controls can be seen as report filters since they allow you to filter data displayed in a report element (a section, a table, etc.) to which it is attached. As input control can be represented as interface controls such as a button, dropdown menu or even a table or a chart of the report, you can interactively modify these filters.

This right does not control the use of input controls: in both reading and design mode, you can filter data in the document even if this right is denied. Input control can also be used as input to create report filters.

If the right is denied

In Web user interface, in design mode, in the left pane, in the INPUT CONTROLS tab:

▶ The NEW and arrow buttons are not displayed in the toolbar, which prevents you from creating a new input control and from modifying their order.

▶ In an input control header, the EDIT and REMOVE buttons are not displayed.

In Desktop interface, in design mode, in the left pane, in the INPUT CONTROLS tab:

▶ The NEW button is disabled in the toolbar, which prevents you from creating a new input control.

▶ In an input control header, the EDIT and REMOVE buttons are disabled.

Reporting: Create and edit predefined calculations

In design mode, this right allows you to insert predefined calculations. This is a simple method to add a new cell to a column, a row, or both containing standard calculation (sum, count, min, max, average) that applies to the values in the column, the row, or both.

If the right is denied

In all interfaces design mode, you cannot include predefined calculations:

- ▶ In the ANALYSIS tab, in the FUNCTIONS tab, all buttons and dropdown menus (SUM, COUNT, MORE) are disabled.

- ▶ Right-click a report. In the contextual menu, SUM, COUNT, AVERAGE, MIN, MAX and PERCENTAGE are disabled.

Reporting: Create and edit report filters and consume input controls

This right allows you to create and edit report filters used to filter displayed data. These filters may be based on input controls or not. A report filter does not modify the data included in the document; it is just a visual filter that hides some data.

If the right is denied

In all interfaces, in reading mode, in the toolbar, the FILTER BAR button is denied, which prevents you from opening the FILTER BAR.

In all interfaces, in design mode, you cannot create report filters:

- ▶ In the ANALYSIS tab, in the FILTER tab, the FILTER button is disabled; which prevents you from opening the REPORT FILTER dialog box and from adding, editing, and removing filters.

- ▶ In the ANALYSIS tab, in the INTERACT tab, the FILTER BAR button is disabled, which prevents you from opening the FILTER BAR.

- ▶ When you right-click a cell or a chart in the report, in the right-click menu, FILTER is disabled, which prevents you from opening the REPORT FILTER dialog box and from adding, editing, and removing filters.

- ▶ In the left pane, in the DOCUMENT STRUCTURE AND FILTERS tab, right-click a filter; REMOVE FILTER and EDIT FILTER are disabled.

Reporting: Create and edit sorts

This right allows you to sort data in your reports, either through standard sorts (alphabetical, numerical) or custom ones.

If the right is denied

In all interfaces, in design mode, you cannot add and remove sorts or open the MANAGE SORTS dialog box to manage them and also create custom sorts.

▶ In the ANALYSIS tab, in the DISPLAY tab, the SORT button is disabled.

▶ When you right-click a cell or a chart in the report, in the right-click menu, SORT is disabled.

Reporting: Create formulas and variables

This right allows you to create and edit formulas and variables. They allow you to use advanced calculations in your reports by giving you access to functions and operators.

If the right is denied

In design mode, you cannot edit formula or create, edit or remove variables:

▶ In Web interface, you cannot edit any formula in the FORMULA BAR.

▶ In Web interface, when you right-click a cell, in the contextual menu, EDIT FORMULA is disabled, which prevents you from opening the FORMULA EDITOR dialog box.

▶ In Rich interfaces, you can type a new formula in the FORMULA BAR, but when you try to validate it, an error message is displayed.

▶ In Rich interfaces, right-click a cell, and select EDIT FORMULA in the contextual menu. Edit the formula, but when you try to save it, an error message is displayed.

In Web interface design mode, in the left pane, in the AVAILABLE OBJECTS tab:

▶ Right-click the VARIABLES folder and select NEW in the contextual menu. The CREATE NEW VARIABLE dialog box opens, but when you try to save the new variable, an error messages is displayed.

▶ Right-click a variable and in the contextual menu, select:

  ▶ EDIT: The EDIT VARIABLE dialog box opens, but when you try to save it, an error message is displayed.

  ▶ REMOVE: When you confirm, an error message is displayed.

In Rich interfaces design mode, in the left pane, in the AVAILABLE OBJECTS tab:

▶ Right-click the VARIABLES folder. NEW VARIABLE is disabled.

▶ Right-click a variable and in the contextual menu:

  ▶ Select EDIT. The VARIABLE EDITOR opens, but when you try to save your changes, an error message is displayed.

  ▶ Select RENAME. After you have typed the new name, an error message is displayed.

  ▶ Select REMOVE. An error message is displayed.

Reporting: Enable formatting

This right allows you to modify the report specification, which is the case when you drill, fold, or modify formatting of the report. This right is mandatory to do any changes in the report specification. Thus, even if a "Reporting: ... " right is granted, the features it secures are not available if the "Reporting: Enable formatting" right is denied.

If the right is denied

▶ In BI Launch Pad, select a document. In the toolbar, select MORE ACTIONS MODIFY or right-click it and select MODIFY in the contextual menu; the document is opened in reading mode.

▶ In Web interface reading mode, in the toolbar, the TRACK, DRILL, FILTER BAR, OUTLINE buttons are disabled. Furthermore, the DESIGN button that allows you to switch to design mode is disabled.

▶ In Rich interfaces reading mode, in the toolbar, click the DRILL, FILTER BAR, OUTLINE buttons: an error message is displayed. Furthermore, the DESIGN and DATA buttons are disabled.

Reporting: Enable merged dimensions

This right allows you to create merged dimensions. Merged dimensions are useful when you have two queries in Web Intelligence that share the same object dimension (see Chapter 7, Section 7.1). Creating a shared dimension allows the queries to aggregate their data.

If the right is denied

▶ In all interfaces, in design mode, in the DATA ACCESS tab, in the DATA OBJECTS toolbar, the MERGE button is disabled, which prevents you from opening the AVAILABLE OBJECTS dialog box.

▶ In all user interfaces, in design mode, when you right-click a cell, MERGE is disabled in the contextual menu.

Reporting: Insert and remove reports, tables, charts, and cells

This right allows you to modify the document structure by adding or removing any element: reports, tables, charts, sections and cells.

If the right is denied

In all interfaces, in design mode, all commands to add or to remove report elements are disabled:

▶ In the REPORT ELEMENTS tab, all buttons that allow you to add a table, a cell, a section, a chart, a column or a row are disabled.

▶ Right-click a report tab at the bottom of the application. In the contextual menu, ADD REPORT, DUPLICATE REPORT, and REMOVE REPORT are disabled.

▶ In FILE tab, in the toolbar, PASTE is disabled.

▶ In a report, right-click a cell, a table, a chart, a column or a row. PASTE, INSERT, DELETE, and MERGE are disabled.

▶ In the left pane, in the DOCUMENT STRUCTURE AND FILTERS tab:

  ▸ Right-click the document; ADD REPORT is disabled.

  ▸ Right-click a report; ADD REPORT, DUPLICATE REPORT and REMOVE REPORT are disabled.

  ▸ Right-click a cell, a table, a chart or a section; DELETE is disabled.

▶ Dragging and dropping an object from the left pane AVAILABLE OBJECTS tab does not create a new element in the report.

5.19.5 Web Intelligence Documents Rights

Web Intelligence documents support general rights, including the scheduling rights set. It also supports Note rights (see Section 5.22) and the rights of possible schedules output (see Section 5.23): Adobe Acrobat and Microsoft Excel.

If a document's general right "Edit objects" is denied, you can still open and modify the document. But when you try to save it, an error message is displayed, preventing you from modifying it. If you want to keep your changes, you need to save it with another name.

It also supports specific rights described next.

Edit query

This right allows you to edit the document query. This right is mandatory if, in the query, you also want to view or edit the generated script.

If the right is denied

In design mode, it is no longer possible to open the query panel:

► In Web interface, in the DATA ACCESS tab, in DATA PROVIDERS toolbar, the NEW DATA PROVIDER button is not displayed and the EDIT button is disabled.

► In Rich interfaces, in the DATA ACCESS tab, in DATA PROVIDERS toolbar, the NEW DATA PROVIDER and the EDIT buttons are disabled.

Export the report's data

This right allows you to export document data into a CSV, PDF, or Excel file. If this right is granted, then it is always possible to save in these file formats. If this right is denied, then export to these file formats if the corresponding "Save as CSV," "Save as Excel," or "Save as PDF" right is granted. Table 5.2 summarizes whether you can export to a file format depending on the "Export the report's data" and "Save as <file type>" rights.

	"Save as <file type>" right is granted	"Save as <file type>" right is denied
"Export the report's data" right is granted	Granted	Granted
"Export the report's data" right is denied	Granted	Denied

Table 5.2 Availability of File Format Export Depending on Rights' Value

If the right is denied

The impact of this right depends on the "Save as <file type>" rights. If one of these rights is granted, it is still possible to export the document in the corresponding file format. If this right is denied, see the description of the "Save as <file type>" rights to get a description of its impact on user interfaces.

Refresh list of values

This right allows you to refresh list of values. List of values can be found for example in prompts when you need to filter a query. The possible values for a dimension can be retrieved from the database and prompted to the user.

To refresh list of values, you also need the "Use lists of values" right in order to first access this list.

If the right is denied

When using list of values, you cannot refresh this list from the database. As explained in the "Use lists of values" right description, you need to open the LIST OF VALUES dialog box. In this dialog box, the REFRESH button is disabled.

Refresh the report's data

This right allows you to refresh the document data by running the query to retrieve the data from the documents data providers.

If the right is denied

In Web interface reading mode, click the REFRESH button in the toolbar; an error message is displayed.

In Web interface design mode:

▶ In the FILE tab, click the REFRESH button or any command dropdown menu attached to it; an error message is displayed.

▶ In the DATA ACCESS tab, in the DATA PROVIDERS tab:

    ▶ Click the REFRESH button or any command dropdown menu attached to it; an error message is displayed.

    ▶ Click the EDIT button. In the QUERY PANEL that opens, click the RUN QUERY or REFRESH buttons; an error message is displayed.

In Rich interfaces view mode, the REFRESH button in the toolbar is disabled.

In Rich interfaces design mode:

- In the FILE tab toolbar, the REFRESH button is disabled.
- In the DATA ACCESS tab, in the DATA PROVIDERS tab:
  - The REFRESH button is disabled.
  - Click the EDIT button. In the query panel that opens, the RUN QUERY button is disabled.

Save as CSV

If the "Export the report's data" right is denied for this document, then this right allows you to save the Web Intelligence document data as a CSV file.

If the right is denied

- In Web interface, in reading mode toolbar and in design mode, in the FILE tab toolbar, EXPORT DATA TO CSV in the EXPORT menu is disabled, preventing you from opening the SAVE AS CSV OPTIONS dialog box.
- In Rich Client, in reading mode toolbar and in design mode, in the FILE tab, in the toolbar, CSV (DATA ONLY) in the SEND BY EMAIL ATTACHMENT menu is disabled, preventing you from sending by email data of this document as a CSV file.

Save as Excel

If the "Export the report's data" right is denied for this document, then this right allows you to save the Web Intelligence document data as an Excel file format.

If the right is denied

- In Web interface, in reading mode toolbar and in design mode, in the FILE tab toolbar, open the EXPORT • EXPORT DOCUMENT AS or EXPORT • EXPORT CURRENT REPORT AS menus; EXCEL, EXCEL 2007, and TEXT are disabled, preventing you from saving document or report data in these file formats.
- In Rich Interface Application, in reading mode toolbar and in design mode, in the FILE tab toolbar, select SAVE AS in the dropdown menu attached to the SAVE button to open the SAVE DOCUMENT dialog box. In this dialog box, click the MY

DESKTOP, MY DOCUMENTS, or MY COMPUTER buttons. In the FILES OF TYPE dropdown list, the EXCEL, EXCEL 2007, and TXT FILE options are not displayed.

▶ In Rich Interface Application, in reading mode, in the toolbar, select SAVE As in the dropdown menu attached to the SAVE button to open the SAVE DOCUMENT dialog box. In this dialog box, click the MY DESKTOP, MY DOCUMENTS, or MY COMPUTER buttons. In the FILES OF TYPE dropdown list, the EXCEL, EXCEL 2007, and TXT FILE options are not displayed.

▶ In Rich Interface Application, in reading mode toolbar and in design mode, in the FILE tab toolbar, select SAVE As in the dropdown menu attached to the SAVE button to open the SAVE DOCUMENT dialog box. In this dialog box, click the MY DESKTOP, MY ANALYSIS, MY DOCUMENTS, or MY COMPUTER buttons. In the FILES OF TYPE dropdown list, the EXCEL, EXCEL 2007, and TXT FILE options are not displayed.

▶ In Desktop interface, in reading mode toolbar and in design mode, in the FILE tab toolbar, EXCEL in the SEND BY EMAIL ATTACHMENT menu is disabled, preventing you from sending the document data in this format.

Save as PDF

If the "Export the report's data" right is denied for this document, then this right allows you to save the Web Intelligence document data as a PDF file format.

If the right is denied

▶ In Web interface, in reading mode toolbar and in design mode, in the FILE tab toolbar, open the EXPORT • EXPORT DOCUMENT AS or EXPORT • EXPORT CURRENT REPORT AS menus; PDF is disabled, preventing you from saving document or report data in this file format.

▶ In Rich Interface Application, in reading mode toolbar and in design mode, in the FILE tab toolbar, select SAVE As in the dropdown menu attached to the SAVE button to open the SAVE DOCUMENT dialog box. In this dialog box, click the MY DESKTOP, MY DOCUMENTS, or MY COMPUTER buttons. In the FILES OF TYPE dropdown list, the PDF option is not displayed.

▶ In Rich Interface Application, in reading mode, in the toolbar, select SAVE As in the dropdown menu attached to the SAVE button to open the SAVE DOCUMENT dialog box. In this dialog box, click the MY DESKTOP, MY DOCUMENTS, or MY

COMPUTER buttons. In the FILES OF TYPE dropdown list the PDF option is not displayed.

▶ In Desktop interface, in reading mode toolbar and in design mode, in the FILE tab toolbar, select SAVE AS in the dropdown menu attached to the SAVE button to open the SAVE DOCUMENT dialog box. In this dialog box, click the MY DESKTOP, MY ANALYSIS, MY DOCUMENTS, or MY COMPUTER buttons. In the FILES OF TYPE dropdown list, the PDF option is not displayed.

▶ In Desktop interface, in reading mode toolbar and in design mode, in the FILE tab toolbar, PDF in the SEND BY EMAIL ATTACHMENT menu is disabled, preventing you from sending the document data in this format.

Use lists of values

This right allows you to use lists of values. Lists of values can be found, for example, in prompts when you need to filter a query. The possible values for a dimension can be retrieved from the database and prompted to the user.

If the right is denied

When editing the document query, you are not able to choose prompts as a possible option for prompts: in any interface, open the document in design mode. In the DATA ACCESS tab, select the DATA PROVIDERS tab. Click the EDIT button to open the query panel. In the query panel, select an object and drag and drop it in the QUERY FILTERS section in order to create a filter from this object. In the new created filter, open the dropdown menu DEFINE FILTER TYPE for operand type and select the VALUE(S) FOR LIST option: an error message opens instead of the LIST OF VALUES dialog box.

View SQL

This right allows you to view the script generated to query the database through a universe: in SQL for a relational universe or in MDX for a multidimensional universe. To view this script, the document "Edit query" right and the Web Intelligence application "Query script: Enable viewing (SQL, MDX, ...)" right must also be granted.

If the right is denied

In all user interfaces, in the query panel, click the VIEW SCRIPT button; an error message is displayed.

5.20   Users and Groups

Users and groups InfoObjects support general rights, without the ones related to scheduling. These general rights are enforced by following their general meaning (see Chapter 4, Section 4.5). But compared to other InfoObjects, users and groups, InfoObjects support additional general rights: "Change preferences," "Change user password," and "Subscribe to objects." When these rights are assigned to a group, they are inherited by all users it contains, following the inheritance rules (see Chapter 4, Section 4.3).

Users InfoObjects also supports one specific right: "Add or edit user attributes."

Change preferences

When granted to your own account, this right allows you to change your BI Launch Pad preferences.

If the right is denied

In BI Launch Pad, the PREFERENCES link is not displayed, preventing you from modifying your preferences.

Change user password

This right allows you to modify the password of a user. This right does not control the password restrictions options ("Password never expires," "User must change password at next logon," "User cannot change password"), or the user's database credentials (see Chapter 6, Section 6.3). To change a user password, you also need the "Edit objects" right granted for this user.

If the right is denied

If it is denied, it prevents you from changing any parameter for the user, including the password. So the "Change user password" right is typically denied when the "Edit objects" right is granted, to prevent you from changing any user settings, except its password.

If this right is denied to you for your own account, then you are not allowed to modify your password in the tools where you can change it: Web Intelligence Desktop, Universe Design Tool, BI Launch Pad, CMC, and so on.

If the right is denied

Go to the CMC USERS AND GROUPS tab and select a user. Double-click this user or, in the toolbar, select the MANAGE OBJECT PROPERTIES button to open the user's PROPERTIES panel. In the ENTERPRISE PASSWORD SETTINGS section, the PASSWORD and CONFIRM text fields are disabled and cannot be modified.

Subscribe to objects

If it is assigned to a user, this right allows you to add or exclude it into any publication's list of recipients or excluded recipients. If it is assigned to a group, this right allows you to add or remove it from any publication's list of recipients.

If the right is denied

It is not possible to add the user or the group in the list of Enterprise recipients of a publication.

In the BI Launch Pad:

▶ In the DOCUMENTS tab, right-click a publication and in the contextual menu, select PROPERTIES, or, in the menu bar, select VIEW PROPERTIES. The PROPERTIES dialog box opens. In this dialog, in the left pane, select the ENTERPRISE RECIPIENTS section.

 ▶ If the right applies to a user or a group not yet a recipient or the publication, select the user or group name in the AVAILABLE list. Click the > button to move it in the SELECTED or EXCLUDED list. Click the SAVE or SAVE AND CLOSE button; an error message is displayed.

 ▶ If the right applies to a user already select or explicitly excluded from the list of the publication recipient, select the user name in the SELECTED or EXCLUDED list. Click the < button to move it in the AVAILABLE list. Click the SAVE or SAVE AND CLOSE button: an error message is displayed.

 ▶ If the right applies to a group already select or explicitly excluded from the list of the publication recipient, select the user name in the SELECTED or EXCLUDED list. Click the < button to move it in the AVAILABLE list. Click the SAVE or SAVE AND CLOSE button: an error message is displayed.

▶ If the user for which the right is denied is your own account (through direct assignment or inheritance from a group), you cannot add or remove yourself from a publication's recipients. Right-click a publication:

▶ In the contextual menu, select SUBSCRIBE. An error message is displayed, unless you were already recipient of the publication.

▶ In the contextual menu, select UNSUBSCRIBE. An error message is displayed.

In CMC, in the FOLDERS tab, use the left pane to navigate to a folder containing a publication.

▶ Right-click a publication and, in the contextual menu, select PROPERTIES to open the PROPERTIES dialog box. In this dialog box, the impact is similar to that in BI Launch Pad, described previously.

▶ If the user for which the right is denied is your own account (through direct assignment or inheritance from a group), you cannot add or remove yourself from a publication's recipients. The behavior when you right-click a publication is similar to that in BI Launch Pad, described previously.

Add or edit user attributes

This right allows you to edit the value of user attributes for this user (see Section 8.9). To change user attributes, you also need the "Edit objects" right granted for this user. If it is denied, it prevents you from changing any parameter for the user, including these user attributes.

If the right is denied

If you have defined some user attributes for your system, go to the CMC USERS AND GROUPS tab and select a user. Double-click this user or, in the toolbar, select the MANAGE OBJECT PROPERTIES button to open the user's PROPERTIES panel. User attributes are displayed in this panel in the ADDITIONAL USER PROPERTIES section; they are disabled and you cannot modify them.

5.21   Connections

The CMS repository relies on different connections that are saved in the CMS repository as the following system InfoObjects:

▶ Relational Connections: for relational connections created in Information Design Tool or both OLAP and relational connections created in Universe Design Tool

▶ OLAP Connections: for OLAP connections created in Information Design Tool and CMC

▶ Connections: for connections created in Business View Manager for Crystal Reports 2011

▶ Data Federator data sources: for relational SAP NetWeaver BW or SAS connections created in Information Design Tool and based on Data Federator Query Server

These connections are more fully described in Chapter 6. This section focuses only on the rights they enforce.

5.21.1 Relational Connection Rights

This connection is created in Universe Design Tool and Information Design Tool. It supports general rights (without the scheduling rights set) and specific rights described next.

Data access

This right allows you to retrieve data from the database defined in this connection.

If the right is denied

Any workflow that needs to query data from the database referenced by the connection fails, both in metadata design tools and reporting tools. For example:

▶ Information Design Tool: Any workflow that queries data from the database fails. For example:

  ▶ In the connection editor, open the SHOW VALUES tab. You can see the database structure but cannot display database values.

  ▶ In a data foundation based on this connection, COUNT ROWS, SHOW TABLE VALUES, PROFILE COLUMN VALUES, and SHOW COLUMN VALUES are disabled.

  ▶ In a business layer based on this connection, right-click an object of this business layer. In the contextual menu, SHOW VALUES is disabled.

  ▶ In the REPOSITORY RESOURCES or SECURITY EDITOR views, right-click a universe based on this selection and select RUN QUERY to run a query on this universe. In the query panel that opens, the REFRESH button is not displayed.

▶ Web Intelligence: Refresh a document based on a universe based on this connection; an error message is displayed.

Download connection locally

This right allows the tools running on desktop to retrieve all the connection parameters from the CMS repository.

If the right is denied

The different tools can retrieve only a sub-set of the connection parameters. For any request to the database, they no longer use local middleware, but they need to contact the Connection Server hosted on the server. The Connection Server then runs the request and returns the result to the client tools. Thus, the connection most sensitive parameters (username, password) remain on the CMS repository and are not stored on the client machine. Consider these potential impacts for these desktop tools:

▶ In Web Intelligence Desktop, the connection parameters cannot be downloaded on the cache. Thus, in Web Intelligence Desktop, in offline mode, it is no longer possible to run query based on a universe based on this connection (see Section 5.19.2).

▶ In Information Design Tool, open the Repository Resources view. Navigate in the "Connections" tree and select the connection. Double-click the connection or select the open button in the toolbar. The connection editor opens:

  ▶ Only the parameters that are not considered sensible are displayed: connectivity type, DBMS, network layer, authentication mode.

  ▶ The EDIT and CHANGE DRIVER buttons are disabled, preventing you from editing this connection.

▶ In Universe Design Tool, in the menu bar, in the TOOLS menu, select CONNECTIONS or, in the STANDARD toolbar, click the CONNECTIONS button to open the CONNECTION PANEL dialog box. In this dialog box:

  ▶ The EDIT CONNECTION and EDIT DESCRIPTION buttons are disabled, preventing you from editing the connection.

  ▶ Click the PROPERTY button to open the CONNECTION PROPERTIES dialog box. This dialog box does not contain any value for sensitive parameters like USER NAME, DATA SOURCE NAME, or other configuration parameters.

Use connection for stored procedures

This right is deprecated and no longer used.

5.21.2 OLAP Connection Rights

OLAP Connection InfoObject type is the connection used by Information Design Tool, SAP Direct Access (supported by Web Intelligence, Crystal Reports for Enterprise, and Dashboards) and Analysis, Edition for OLAP. It supports only general rights, without the scheduling rights set.

5.21.3 Data Federator Data Source Rights

This InfoObject is used for relational SAP NetWeaver BW or SAS connections created in Information Design Tool and based on Data Federator Query Server. It can be used only with universes created in Information Design Tool.

It supports general rights and some specific rights, described next.

Data access

This right allows you to retrieve data from the database defined in this connection.

If the right is denied

Any workflow that needs access to the database referenced by the connection fails, both in metadata design tools and reporting tools. See the examples in Section 5.21.1, which covers relational connections.

Use connection for stored procedures

This right is deprecated and no longer used.

5.21.4 Connection Rights

Connection InfoObject type is the connection used by Crystal Reports 2011 for business views. Its file format is different from the relational connection (see Section 5.21.1) and thus these connections are not compatible. Such a connection can be created only in Business View Manager and cannot be used in Universe Design Tool or Information Design Tool. It supports general rights, without the scheduling rights set and one specific right, described next. These rights can also be set only in Business View Manager and not in the CMC.

Data access

This right allows you to retrieve data from the database defined in this connection.

If the right is denied

You are not able to retrieve data from the connection.

5.22   Note Rights

A Note includes the discussion threads you can create in BI Launch Pad for objects that support them. By default, this capability is disabled since the new collaboration tool is now SAP StreamWork (see Section 5.15). To use discussions, you need to explicitly enable them in the CMC: in the APPLICATIONS tab, in the BI Launch Pad application's property, select the ENABLE DISCUSSIONS checkbox.

A Note can exist only if it is attached to another InfoObject. It is not possible to directly assigned rights to a Note InfoObject. When you set advanced rights for an object that supports discussion, Note is listed in the list of content InfoObjects whose rights can be set for this object, as shown in Figure 5.5.

Note supports general rights but also a specific right, described next.

Allow discussion threads

This right allows you to create and contribute to discussion threads.

If the right is denied

In BI Launch Pad, in the DOCUMENTS tab, select a folder in the left pane. In the right pane, select an object that supports Notes: Web Intelligence or Crystal Reports document, BI workspace, information space, and so on. In the toolbar, click the DETAILS button or right-click the object and in the contextual menu, and select DETAILS. The DETAILS pane opens in the right pane, but the DISCUSSIONS section is disabled and you cannot create and post new notes or see the ones already posted.

5.23   Schedule Output Format

Adobe Acrobat, Microsoft Excel, Microsoft Word, Rich Text, and Text are special InfoObjects type since they can be output of a scheduled Web Intelligence or Crystal Reports document.

When they are generated, instances are created below the original scheduled document, which can be seen as a container for these instances. For this reason, when you set rights for Web Intelligence or Crystal Reports documents, in addition to Note (see Section 5.22), you can set rights for the following content InfoObjects, which are the possible scheduling outputs:

▶ For Web Intelligence document: Adobe Acrobat and Microsoft Excel

▶ For Crystal Reports document: Adobe Acrobat, Microsoft Excel, Microsoft Word, Rich Text, and Text (as shown in Figure 5.5)

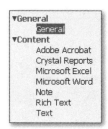

Figure 5.5   InfoObject Types Rights for Crystal Reports Document

You can select Adobe Acrobat and Microsoft Excel to modify the rights applied to the corresponding instances generated from the Web Intelligence document. It is not possible to set right individually to an instance, but you can set rights to all instances of the same format:

▶ If you deny the "View document instances" right to a user for an InfoObject type, then this user does not see instances of this type any longer.

▶ If you deny the "View objects" right to a user for an InfoObject type, then the user can still see instances of this type.

> **Note**
>
> If you deny the "View document instances" general right to a user, then in BI Launch Pad the HISTORY menu is not displayed.

5.24 Summary

In the CMS repository, all InfoObjects follow the same security rights framework. In addition, on the general rights that apply almost identically to all objects (both application, system, or content), these objects can enforce a set of specific rights to secure their behavior.

This chapter describes the different applications that can be managed in the CMC and the specific rights enforced by these applications and by the objects they generate. Among these applications, two are special from a security perspective:

▶ Explorer, where navigation in information space can be limited by universe object access level for facets and personalization, for the data in the facet.

▶ Web Intelligence, whose numerous features are secured by a large number of security rights and whose deployment modes, especially the offline mode, require additional control on the connections.

Additionally, in this chapter we covered specific rights for some system and content InfoObjects: users, connections, Note, and file formats that can be generated from schedule.

This chapter has covered connections from rights points of view. Because it is also important to secure these connections and define how they access databases, the next chapter covers these topics.

Connections are the keys to the database containing your production data. Different types of connections support different reporting tools and authentication modes.

6 Connections and Database Authentications

In the BI 4.0 system, a connection is an object containing the parameters used to connect to the database containing the data to query. For this reason, a connection is mandatory for any workflows where you need to access this database.

Because of the different evolutions in SAP BusinessObjects releases, different connections exist in BI 4.0, based on different components; there are some that have existed for several releases and some that have been introduced to support new technologies.

In all cases, the databases that a connection references contain your production and sensitive data; therefore, you need to make sure that this connection is properly secured in order to avoid misuse of the databases.

This chapter focuses on the different connections in BI 4.0:

▶ Those that can exist in a CMS repository

▶ The local connections the authoring tools can manage

▶ The different authentication modes used by the connections to authenticate to the database

▶ The use of credentials mapping for single sign-on

▶ The different workflows in Information Design Tool, Universe Design Tool, and the Central Management Console to manage connections

Let's begin by exploring secured connections.

6.1 Secured Connections

A secured connection is a connection that has been saved in the CMS repository. Connections saved in the CMS repository give you the benefit of a security framework that controls who can view this connection and use it to query the database. Furthermore, because the connection is stored on a server, its access is more secure than if it were saved locally on a file system.

Different connections exist in the CMS repository:

▸ Relational connection used for the universe (created by Universe Design Tool and Information Design Tool)

▸ Relational connection used by Crystal Reports 2011 only and their business views

▸ Data Federator data source created with Information Design Tool (uses Data Federator technology to access two specific databases: SAP NetWeaver BW and SAS)

▸ OLAP connection used by OLAP universes (created by Universe Design Tool)

▸ OLAP connection created by Information Design Tool or the Central Management Console to refer to OLAP databases such as SAP NetWeaver BW, Microsoft SSAS, and so on. This connection is used by Analysis, Edition for OLAP, Web Intelligence, Crystal Reports for Enterprise, Dashboard, and multidimensional universes created by Information Design Tool

Since the BI 4.0 release, except for the relational connections used by Crystal Reports 2011, these connections are all located under the same Connections top-root folder. Furthermore, sub-folders can be created in this folder to make managing connections easier.

Let's spend some time on each type of connection.

6.1.1 Relational Connections

Relational connections are the historical file format for relational connections supported by SAP BusinessObjects products. They are initially created by Universe Design Tool and cover a wide range of relational databases. They have also been extended to file text format, Java Bean, and others.

In BI 4.0, these relational connections are common to Universe Design Tool and Information Design Tool, in order to support interoperability between these two tools. A relational connection can be created in either the Information Design Tool or Universe Design Tool and subsequently used by a universe in either tool.

However, there are very slight differences between the database vendors and versions supported by the two tools. Refer to the Product Availability Matrix (PAM), available at *http://service.sap.com/pam* to check the databases supported by each tool.

For example, for relational connections, some databases or versions supported by Universe Design Tool are not supported by Information Design Tool. Similarly, some new databases or versions are supported by Information Design Tool but not by Universe Design Tool.

These connections are operated by a connection server component. This component is available in two modes:

▸ In server mode, in which the connection server is running server-side and answer requests

▸ In library mode, in which it is embedded in other applications

In the CMS repository, these connections (even the OLAP ones) are saved as relational connection InfoObjects.

> **Warning!**
>
> To set security rights at folder level and to have them inherited by these relational connections, you need to set them for the relational connection InfoObject and not for the connection InfoObject.

6.1.2 Data Federator Data Sources

Data Federator data sources were introduced in BI 4.0 with the integration of Data Federator technology. This data source InfoObject is the format used by Information Design Tool to store the connections to some relational drivers that require the use of the Data Federator technology in the CMS repository. These connections can be used to access two different databases:

▸ The underlying relational model of SAP NetWeaver BW

▸ SAS

These connections can be used only for relational universes created in Information Design Tool. These connections rely on the Data Federator Query Server, so when you create such a universe, you need to explicitly choose to create a multi-source data foundation used by a multi-source universe.

Furthermore, in contrast to the other connections you can create in Information Design Tool, Data Federator data sources can be created only in the CMS repository, and not locally on your file system.

6.1.3   OLAP Connections (Universe Design Tool)

With the introduction of the OLAP universe in Universe Design Tool (see Chapter 7, Section 7.1.2), the relational connection created in Universe Design Tool and based on the Connection Server component was extended to OLAP databases.

This OLAP connection can be created only in Universe Design Tool and used by OLAP universes created in Universe Design Tool. Information Design Tool does not support this connection.

For BI 4.0, we recommend that you use new multidimensional universes (UNX) and OLAP connections created in Information Design Tool (see Section 6.1.4) rather than OLAP universes created in Universe Design Tool. Using OLAP universes and connections in Universe Design Tool can be done for existing projects or if Information Design Tool does not support the equivalent feature.

6.1.4   OLAP Connections (Information Design Tool/CMC)

In XI 3.x, Voyager (which is the predecessor of Analysis, Edition for OLAP) relies on an OLAP connection different from the one used for OLAP universe and used to access OLAP databases.

Unlike the OLAP connections created in Universe Design Tool, these OLAP connections benefit from the hierarchical dimensions in the OLAP database.

In BI 4.0, this OLAP connection has been extended and can be used both for Analysis, Edition for OLAP, and multidimensional universes created in Information Design Tool.

This OLAP connection covers two connections:

▶ SAP NetWeaver BW connection, which are based on the SAP Java Connector driver: This connection can be used only for direct access from reporting tools (Web Intelligence; Crystal Reports for Enterprise; Analysis, Edition for OLAP;

Dashboard). It is not possible to create a universe on top of it. It is more fully described in Chapter 10.

▶ OLAP connections for other OLAP databases different than SAP NetWeaver BW, such as Microsoft SQL Server Analysis Services and Essbase: This connection is used by Analysis, Edition for OLAP, and multidimensional universes created in Information Design Tool.

Both of these OLAP connections can be created both in Information Design Tool and CMC. They are interoperable, even if some differences exist:

▶ The list of OLAP databases supported by Information Design Tool and the CMC slightly differs. Refer to the PAM for more details.

▶ The authentication modes supported when creating the connection in the two tools are different (see Section 6.3).

Note that an OLAP connection can refer to an OLAP server or a cube on this server:

▶ If the connection refers to an OLAP server, then when the connection must be used in Information Design Tool or any reporting tool supporting this OLAP connection, users must select one cube on this server.

▶ If the connection refers to a cube, then the connection is self-sufficient and the reporting tool can directly query the cube referenced by the connection.

6.1.5   Relational Connections (Business View Manager)

Crystal Reports 2011 uses connections based on its own drivers. These connections are directly saved in the Crystal Reports documents and cannot be saved as standalone objects.

In the CMS repository, Crystal Reports 2011 also uses connections on which it can create business views. These connections are manageable only in Business View Manager: creation, edition, security rights setting. Even if they are published in the CMS repository, they cannot be viewed in the CMC.

In Crystal Reports for Enterprise, business views are replaced by universes created with Information Design Tool. We don't spend any more time on these connections in this chapter.

6.1.6 Product Consumptions

Because of the different connection types and technologies used, not all connections are supported in the same manner by the different reporting tools.

Table 6.1 lists the connections the reporting tools support and how they use them. In this table, UNV designates universes created with Universe Design Tool and UNX designates universes created with Information Design Tool.

Note that this table does not cover the OLAP SAP NetWeaver BW connection (which is instead covered in Chapter 10) or relational connections used by Crystal Reports 2011 for business views.

	Relational connection (Universe Design Tool or Information Design Tool)	Data Federator data source (Information Design Tool)	OLAP connection (Universe Design Tool)	OLAP connection, except SAP NetWeaver BW (CMC or Information Design Tool)
Analysis, Edition for OLAP	N/A	N/A	N/A	▶ Direct access
Crystal Reports 2011	▶ Relational UNV	N/A	N/A	N/A
Crystal Reports for Enterprise	▶ Relational monosource UNX ▶ Relational multi-source UNX	▶ Relational multi-source UNX	N/A	▶ Multi-dimensional UNX
Dashboard	▶ Relational monosource UNX ▶ Relational multi-source UNX ▶ Relational UNV, through Query as a Web Service	▶ Relational multi-source UNX	N/A	▶ Multi-dimensional UNX

Table 6.1 Connections and How Reporting Tools Use Them

	Relational connection (Universe Design Tool or Information Design Tool)	Data Federator data source (Information Design Tool)	OLAP connection (Universe Design Tool)	OLAP connection, except SAP NetWeaver BW (CMC or Information Design Tool)
Explorer	▸ Relational monosource UNX ▸ Relational multi-source UNX	▸ Relational multi-source UNX	N/A	N/A
Live Office	▸ Relational UNV, through Web Intelligence	N/A	▸ OLAP UNV, through Web Intelligence	N/A
Web Intelligence	▸ Relational monosource UNX ▸ Relational monosource UNV ▸ Relational multi-source UNX	▸ Relational multi-source UNX	▸ OLAP UNV	▸ Multi-dimensional UNX

Table 6.1 Connections and How Reporting Tools Use Them (Cont.)

6.2 Local Connections

In addition to the secured connections saved in the CMS repository, Information Design Tool and Universe Design Tool can also create local connections for local use.

6.2.1 Information Design Tool

With Information Design Tool, you can create connections in a local project stored in your file system. In Information Design Tool, local projects are used only for authoring mode when you create different resources that are merged to create the universe: data foundation and business layer (Chapter 8, Section 8.1 covers this topic in more detail).

In local projects, connections that rely on a server component can't be created, so you can only create two kinds of connections with Information Design Tool in local projects:

▶ Relational connections, except the SAP NetWeaver BW and SAS that are based on Data Federator data sources

▶ OLAP connections

When you can create a local connection, you can select any authentication mode from among the ones supported by Information Design Tool for the database (fixed credentials, credentials mapping, or single sign-on). But because as credentials mapping or single sign-on require to retrieve credentials from the server, to use this connection in Information Design Tool, you need to open a session to a BI 4.0 system.

A local connection created in Information Design Tool can only be used in Information Design Tool. It is used by a universe when you generate and publish the universe from the resources that makes it (connection, data foundation, and business layer).

When you publish a universe locally, the connection is embedded in the generated universe that can be directly used by Web Intelligence Desktop interface (see Chapter 5, Section 5.19).

When you publish a universe in a CMS repository, it must rely on a secured connection already published in the CMS repository. You can do two things: Create the connection directly in the CMS repository or create the connection in a local project and then publish it in the CMS repository.

In both cases, you must create a *connection shortcut* from the connection stored in the CMS repository. This connection shortcut is used to reference a connection in a CMS repository. Before publishing the universe in the CMS repository, its data foundation (if it is a relational universe) or its business layer (if it is a multidimensional universe) must be linked to this connection shortcut so it knows which connection (or connections) to use once the universe is published in the CMS repository.

6.2.2 Universe Design Tool

In addition to the secured connections you can create in Universe Design Tool (see Section 6.1), you can create two types of local connections:

▶ *Personal*: This connection is saved locally in the list of connections Universe Design Tool maintains and can be used only by the local user.

▶ *Shared*: This connection is saved locally in the list of connections Universe Design Tool maintains, but it can be shared by several users.

Once a connection is saved, it is not possible to modify its type (personal, shared, or secured). Unlike secured connections, Universe Design Tool does not classify connections through folders.

Local connections are used to create local universes that can be used by Web Intelligence Desktop mode. But when you export a local in the CMS repository, you must link it to a connection saved in this CMS repository.

In contrast, when you import a universe from a CMS repository, it remains secured if it is attached to its secured connection. To save a universe for all users, it must reference a local connection, in order to remove the links it may have with the CMS repository.

You can also create local connections when you open Universe Design Tool in standalone mode, without being connected to a CMS repository. In this mode, you can create locally the same connections as those connected to a CMS repository. But you cannot select the authentication modes that require a session to a CMS: single sign-on or credentials mapping. We'll cover these next.

6.3 Connection Authentication Mode

A database has its own security repository. The connection authentication mode defines how the connection authenticates to the database when it needs to connect to it. We'll next describe these existing authentication modes:

▶ Fixed credentials

▶ Credentials mapping

▶ Prompted authentication

▶ Single sign-on

However, due to the different technologies used, not all connections and products support the same list of authentication modes. This list is presented in Table 6.2.

Connection	Fixed	Mapping	Prompted	Single Sign-On
Relational connections (see Section 6.1.1)	Supported	Supported	Not supported	Partly supported (see Section 6.3.4)
OLAP connections created in Universe Design Tool (see Section 6.1.1)	Supported	Supported	Not supported	
OLAP Connections created in Information Design Tool or CMC (see Section 6.1.4)	Supported	Supported, except by CMC and Analysis, Edition for OLAP	Supported only by CMC and Analysis, Edition for OLAP	
Data Sources (see Section 6.1.2)	Supported	Supported	Not supported	

Table 6.2 Connections and Supported Authentication Modes

Let's begin with the most basic authentication mode—fixed credentials.

6.3.1 Fixed Credentials

This is the simplest authentication mode because the credentials you use in order to connect to the database are stored in the connection. This account created at database level must be dedicated to the BI 4.0 system. We recommend that you grant this account read-only rights at database level because for reporting use, this authentication mode does not require the rights to write in the database. These credentials are always used when the connection must be used, whenever the user calls it.

The fixed credentials authentication mode does not allow you to trace who has sent different requests at the database level in detail. But we consider this authentication mode to be relatively less secure because it directly contains the credentials.

If a connection with fixed credentials authentication mode is saved locally, then it can be seen as vulnerable and, for this reason, it should contain only parameters to test database rather than production database.

When it is published in the CMS repository, it can be secured with CMS security framework. Starting with BI 4.0 FP3, for relational connections stored in the CMS repository, you can deny the "Download connection locally" connection right in order to force database queries to be run on the server and prevent the connection credentials from being retrieved on client machines.

In Universe Design Tool, it is possible to use @VARIABLE ('DBUSER') or @VARIABLE ('DBPASS') as fixed credentials in order to have a dynamic user name and password, but this mode should be replaced by credentials mapping.

6.3.2 Credentials Mapping

This authentication mode is available only when the connection is used with a session opened to the CMS repository. The connection does not store any credentials to connect to the database, but they are saved as a user's properties.

You can define a different set of credentials for each user. However, each user only gets assigned one set of database credentials, meaning that the same credentials are used for a user if he tries to authenticate through different connections that use this authentication mode.

> **Note**
>
> Depending on the context, credentials mapping is also called secondary credentials, SAP BusinessObjects credentials mapping, user's database credentials, or user's data source credentials.

Connections can use a user's database credentials to authenticate in two ways:

▶ By using credentials mapping authentication mode. In this case, when the connection tries to connect to the database, it retrieves database credentials saved as properties of the logged on user. These credentials are used by the connection to authenticate to the database.

▶ By using fixed credentials authentication mode and by setting @VARIABLE ('DBUSER') as the user name to use by fixed credentials and @VARIABLE ('DBPASS') as the password to use by fixed credentials.

This substitution is supported in Universe Design Tool and universes created with it. But it is no longer supported in Information Design Tool.

You can enable or disable credentials mapping for each different user. If credentials mapping is disabled for a user, then the user cannot use connections whose authentication mode is credentials mapping.

You can define this authentication mode for any relational or OLAP connections. But because it is not supported by Analysis, Edition for OLAP, it is not possible to set this authentication mode when you create this connection in the CMC. On the other hand, even if you set this authentication mode for an OLAP connection in Information Design Tool, it is not supported by Analysis, Edition for OLAP.

Defining User's Database Credentials

To define user's credentials mapping in the CMC, follow these steps:

1. Go to the USERS AND GROUPS tab in the CMC.

2. In the left pane, navigate in the USER LIST, GROUP LIST or GROUP HIERARCHY branch in order to display the list of users or of groups in the right pane.

3. In the menu bar, select MANAGE • PROPERTIES or right-click the user and, in the contextual menu, select PROPERTIES. The PROPERTIES panel opens.

4. In the DATABASE CREDENTIALS section, as shown in Figure 6.1, select the ENABLE checkbox.

5. In the ACCOUNT NAME text field, enter the username to use for this user.

6. In the PASSWORD and CONFIRM text fields, enter the password to use for this user.

7. Click the SAVE & CLOSE button to close the panel and save the database credentials.

These steps must be done for each user who needs to authenticate with credentials mapping. As this task may be tedious, you can either use SDK to automate it or use an option to fill credentials mapping when users log on (see Section 6.4).

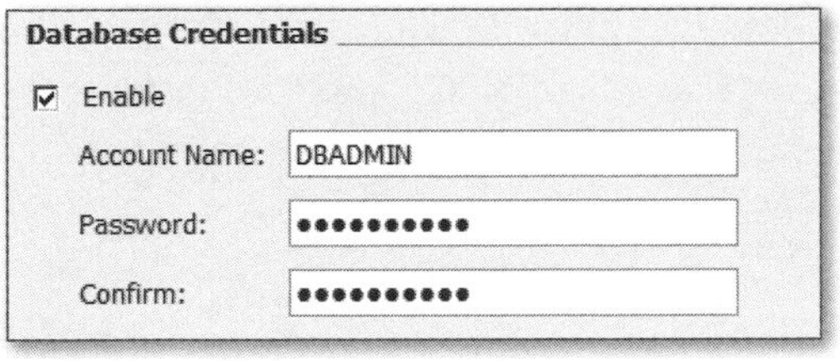

Figure 6.1 Database Credentials Parameters in User's Properties

Credentials Mapping Evolution

In SAP BusinessObjects Enterprise 6.x, it was possible to define a connection and use the @VARIABLE ('BOUSER') and @VARIABLE ('BOPASS') as the user name and password used by the connection to authenticate to the database. When the connection had to connect to the database, these variables were substituted by the username and password of the user logged on to the SAP BusinessObjects system. This method was a simple way to implement a single sign-on.

In XI R2, this capability was no longer possible since the system did not allow the retrieval of the password. For this reason, in order to support a similar workflow for a customer who didn't want to deploy a full single sign-on infrastructure, this set of credentials has been introduced as user's properties. This property can be used as @VARIABLE ('DBUSER') and @VARIABLE ('DBPASS') in fixed credentials.

However, in BI 4.0, Information Design Tool does not support the use of these variables in fixed credentials, so you must explicitly use credentials mapping.

6.3.3 Prompted Authentication

In this mode, when the connection must connect to the database, the user is prompted to explicitly provide some database credentials to authenticate to the database. It means the database credentials must be given to all users who need to query the database and that they must provide these credentials to connect to the database.

As for credentials mapping, this connection does not explicitly store database credentials. However, it requires giving users the credentials they need to provide when querying the database.

This authentication mode is supported only for OLAP connections created in the CMC. Usually, OLAP connections created in Information Design Tool and in CMC are compatible, except for OLAP connection with prompted authentication mode, which can be created and edited only in CMC (see Section 6.5). Furthermore, only Analysis, Edition for OLAP can use this connection to query data from the database.

6.3.4 Single Sign-On

This authentication mode is also called *single sign-on to database* in order to avoid confusion with the single sign-on used to log on to BI 4.0 products (see Chapter 3, Section 3.1).

If the connection authentication mode is single sign-on to database, then the credentials used to connect to the BI 4.0 are reused by the connection to authenticate to the database and query data from it. It means the database and the BI 4.0 system must share the same authentication information.

Single sign-on is supported only for a limited set of databases and in specific configurations, as described in Table 6.3.

Database	Middleware	Operating System	Comment
MS SQL Server Analysis Services	XMLA	Windows	The BI 4.0 system and the database have been configured to authenticate with Windows Active Directory and Kerberos (see Chapter 3, Section 3.8).
MS SQL Server	ODBC OLE DB	Windows	
Oracle	Oracle Client	Windows	The BI 4.0 system and the database have been configured to authenticate with LDAP.
Oracle EBS	Oracle Client	All	The BI 4.0 system has been configured to authenticate with the Oracle EBS. The Oracle EBS account is used to connect to BI 4.0 and is then passed to the connection to connect to the Oracle EBS database.

Table 6.3 Databases for Which Single Sign-On Is Supported

Database	Middleware	Operating System	Comment
SAP NetWeaver BW	OLAP BAPI	All	The BI 4.0 system has been configured to authenticate with the SAP NetWeaver BW database (see Chapter 10, Section 10.2).
SAP ERP	SAP Java Connectivity	All	The BI 4.0 system has been configured to authenticate with the SAP system (see Chapter 10, Section 10.2).
SAP HANA	JDBC	Windows Linux	The BI 4.0 system and the database have been configured to authenticate with Windows Active Directory and Kerberos (see Chapter 3, Section 3.8).

Table 6.3 Databases for Which Single Sign-On Is Supported (Cont.)

To work, single sign-on requires the authentication to be available. When you connect to BI 4.0 and use a connection defined with single sign-on authentication to query a database, the credentials you have used to connect can be passed to the database (through a token, for example) because you are already connected.

But single sign-on won't work in workflows where you are no longer connected. This is the case for scheduling or publishing workflows. In scheduling, if the schedule happens when you are no longer connected, then the refresh cannot happen. When publishing, if the report bursting option requires the recipient credentials to run the publication in its name, the credentials for the recipient are also not available.

In any case supported by single sign-on, you can only refresh when you are logged on. To work around this restriction, you may either use credentials mappings adapted for single sign-on (see Section 6.4) or, for SAP NetWeaver BW connections, configure SNC or STS (see Chapter 10, Section 10.6).

6.4   Using Credentials Mapping for Single Sign-On

For the different data sources where single sign-on is not supported, an option based on credentials mapping can be used to achieve single sign-on. This option assumes that the CMS repository and the database share the same authentication information. This can be achieved either through a replication process that synchronizes the users and passwords between the two systems, or a common authentication system (Active Directory or LDAP).

Then, if your BI 4.0 system uses enterprise authentication mode or has been configured to authenticate with Active Directory or LDAP, you can use the use credentials mapping for single sign-on.

In this method, when a user logs on to any BI 4.0 product by authenticating with the CMS repository, his username and password are saved in the database credentials parameters for this user (even if the "Enable Database Credentials" option has not been selected for this user).

So when a user needs access to the database through a connection defined with secondary credentials as the authentication mode, then these database credentials can be reused to authenticate the user to the database

Furthermore, even if the user logs off the BI 4.0 system, his credentials remain saved in his database credentials settings. Thus, they can also be used for scheduling or publication workflows, when the user is no longer logged on. However, if the user has not yet logged on to the system since the option was set, then his credentials are not saved, and scheduling or publication workflows fail.

Setting Credentials Mapping for Single Sign-On Option

To use credentials mapping for single sign-on, you can set this option for any authentication mode that supports it:

1. Log on to the CMC, and go to the AUTHENTICATION tab.
2. Double-click the ENTERPRISE, LDAP, or WINDOWS AD line to open the panel used to configure the corresponding authentication mode.
3. In this pane, select the ENABLE AND UPDATE USER'S DATA SOURCE CREDENTIALS AT LOGON TIME checkbox.
4. Click the UPDATE button to save this change and close the panel.

Once this option has been set, two things happen when a user logs on to the system using the corresponding authentication mode:

- His "Enable Database Credentials" parameter is enabled.

- The credentials he has provided to log on are saved in his "Database Credentials Account Name" and "Database Credentials Password" parameters.

6.5 Managing Connections

Depending on the connection you use, you can create and manage it either in Information Design Tool, Universe Design Tool, or the CMC.

Specific workflows to create an SAP NetWeaver BW connection are described in Chapter 10, Section 10.4.

6.5.1 Managing Connections in Information Design Tool

To manage secured connections in Information Design Tool, you must have the Information Design Tool "Create, modify, or delete connections" right granted. To create a secured connection, you also need the "Add objects to the folder" right for the folder where you create the connection. To edit a secured connection, you also need the "Edit objects" right.

Creating a Secured Connection

To create a secured connection in Information Design Tool, follow these steps:

1. Open the REPOSITORY RESOURCES view.

2. Open a predefined session to the CMS, or, if it does not exist, create and open one.

3. In the "Connections" tree folder, select the folder where the connection must be created.

4. In the REPOSITORY RESOURCES toolbar:

   - Select INSERT RELATIONAL CONNECTION to open the NEW RELATIONAL CONNECTION dialog box and create a relational connection.

   - Select INSERT OLAP CONNECTION to open the NEW OLAP CONNECTION dialog box and create an OLAP connection.

5. In this dialog box, in the RESOURCE NAME text field, enter the name of the connection.

6. Click the NEXT button to display the DATABASE MIDDLEWARE DRIVER SELECTION page. This page displays the list of databases, versions, and middlewares supported by Information Design Tool, as shown in Figure 6.2.

Figure 6.2 Databases Supported in Information Design Tool

7. In the DATABASE MIDDLEWARE DRIVER SELECTION page, select the driver for the database you want to access from among the ones supported by Information Design Tool. Use the HIERARCHICAL LIST or FLAT LIST radio buttons to display these drivers as a tree or as a list.

8. Click the NEXT button.

9. In the AUTHENTICATION MODE dropdown list, select the authentication mode (if it is supported by the connection):

   ▶ USE SPECIFIED USER NAME AND PASSWORD for fixed credentials

   ▶ USE SINGLE SIGN-ON WHEN REFRESHING REPORTS AT VIEW TIME for single sign-on

   ▶ USE BUSINESSOBJECTS CREDENTIALS MAPPING for credentials mapping

10. Enter the different parameters that identify the connection. These parameters depend on the connection.

11. Click the NEXT button. Depending on the connection to create, you may have additional parameters to enter. For example, if you are creating an OLAP

connection, in the CUBE SELECTION page, select the DO NOT SPECIFY A CUBE IN THE CONNECTION radio button if you want the connection to refer the database server. Otherwise, select the SPECIFY A CUBE IN THE CONNECTION radio button and, in the tree list, navigate in the server content to select the cube the connection must refer, as shown in Figure 6.3.

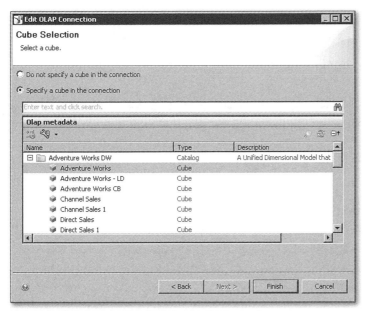

Figure 6.3 Cube Selection Page for OLAP Connection

12. Click the FINISH button to close the connection wizard and create the connection in the selected folder. In the right pane, a tab for the newly created connection is opened. This tab displays this connection parameters.

Table 6.4 presents connections icons displayed in Information Design Tool by type.

Icon	Connection Type
	Relational connection
	OLAP connection
	Data Federator data source

Table 6.4 Connection Icons in Information Design Tool

Creating a Local Connection

To create a local connection in Information Design Tool, follow these steps:

1. Open the LOCAL PROJECTS view.

2. Select the project and, if needed, the folder where the connection must be created.

3. Right-click the project or the folder where the connection must be created and, in the contextual menu:

   ▶ Click NEW • RELATIONAL CONNECTION to open the NEW RELATIONAL CONNECTION dialog box and create a relational connection.

   ▶ Click NEW • OLAP CONNECTION to open the NEW OLAP CONNECTION dialog box and create an OLAP connection.

4. The dialog box that opens is similar to the one used to create a secured connection. Follow the same workflow used when creating a connection to modify the connection parameters.

5. Click the FINISH button to close the connection wizard and create the connection in the selected project or folder. In the right pane, a tab for the newly created connection is opened. This tab displays this connection parameters.

Publishing a Connection

Another way to create a secured connection is to create it locally and then publish it in a CMS repository. The connection is created with the same parameters as the local project. To do so, follow these steps:

1. In the LOCAL PROJECTS view, select the local connection to publish.

2. Right-click this connection and, in the contextual menu, select PUBLISH CONNECTION TO A REPOSITORY to open the PUBLISH CONNECTION TO A REPOSITORY dialog box.

   In this dialog box, select a session to the CMS repository where the connection must be published. Type the session password to open it if it is not yet opened.

3. Click the NEXT button.

4. In the Connections tree folder, select the folder where the connection must be published. You must have the "Add objects to the folder" right granted for this folder.

5. Click the FINISH button to close this dialog box and publish the connection in the CMS repository.

6. When you are asked whether to create a shortcut, click either YES or NO. The shortcut is created in the same folder as the local connection.

Another method to publish a connection is to drag and drop it from the LOCAL PROJECTS view to the destination folder in the Repository Resources view.

Creating a Connection Shortcut

At the end of the connection publication, Information Design Tool offers you a way to create a connection shortcut to this connection. You can also explicitly create it by following these steps:

1. In the Repository Resources view, open a session to the CMS repository containing the secured connection.

2. Navigate in the Connections tree folder to select the connection. Right-click it and, in the contextual menu, select CREATE CONNECTION SHORTCUT to open the SELECT A LOCAL PROJECT dialog box.

   In this dialog box, select the project and folder where the connection must be created.

3. Click OK to close this dialog box and create the connection shortcut. It appears in the LOCAL PROJECTS view. If you double-click it, a tab opens with this connection shortcut parameters, as shown in Figure 6.4.

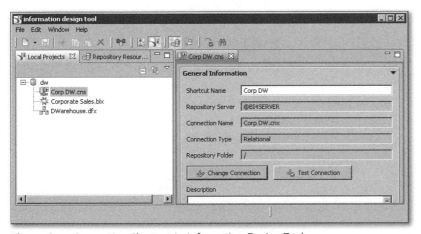

Figure 6.4 Connection Shortcut in Information Design Tool

Editing a Connection

To edit a local or secured connection, follow these steps:

1. From the Published Resources or Local Projects views, select your connection and double-click it to open a tab for this connection in the right pane.

2. In this tab, click the EDIT button to open the connection dialog box. This dialog box is the same as the one used to create the connection. Use the dialog box to modify the connection parameters.

3. Click the FINISH button to save close the connection wizard. The modified parameters are updated in the tab containing the connection parameters.

4. In the toolbar, click the SAVE button to save your changes.

To edit secured connection, you must have the Information Design Tool "Create, modify, or delete connections" right granted. You must also have the connection "Edit objects" right granted.

If you have the "Download connection locally" right denied for the relational connection, then the connection parameters remain on the server and only a limited set of parameters that are considered as not sensitive (authentication mode, driver, database) are displayed in the connection tab in the right pane. Furthermore, you cannot edit this connection.

Navigating in the Database

In Information Design Tool, the connection editor allows you to navigate in the database in order to get samples of the data it contains. For relational connections, if the "Data Access" right for the connection is not denied to you, you can even directly type some SQL scripts and send them to the database.

In a relational connection editor tab, select the SHOW VALUES tab. In this tab, you can:

▶ Navigate in the database content using the CATALOG tree field.

▶ Type an SQL command in the SHOW VALUES text field and click the REFRESH button. The result of the query is displayed in the VALUES tab, as seen in Figure 6.5.

You have also the same capability for an OLAP connection (except for the SAP NetWeaver BW OLAP connection) in the QUERY tab, where you can type some commands in MDX to send to the database.

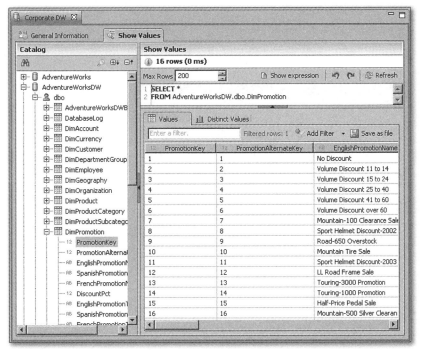

Figure 6.5 Show Values Tab for a Relational Connection

These capabilities can be handy to quickly analyze data contained in the database. However, the query is directly sent to the database. For this reason, we recommend that you carefully choose the database accounts dedicated to BI 4.0. If you want to avoid user changes in the database through this capability, use only accounts that have read-only privileges on the database. Additionally, check that the security defined at database level allows these accounts to see only the data they are allowed to see.

6.5.2 Managing Connections in Universe Design Tool

To manage secured connections in Universe Design Tool, you must have the Universe Design Tool "Create, modify, or delete connections" right granted.

Creating a Connection

To create a connection in Universe Design Tool, follow these steps:

1. In the menu bar, in the TOOLS menu, select CONNECTIONS or, in the STANDARD toolbar, click the CONNECTIONS button to open the CONNECTION PANEL dialog box, as shown in Figure 6.6.

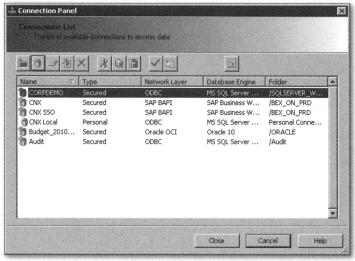

Figure 6.6 Connection Panel in Universe Design Tool

2. In this dialog box toolbar, click the NEW CONNECTION button to open the DEFINE A NEW CONNECTION dialog box.

3. In this dialog box, use the CONNECTION TYPE dropdown list to select the connection type to create: SECURED, SHARED, or PERSONAL.

4. In the CONNECTION NAME text field, enter the connection name.

5. If you have selected to create a secured connection, in the CONNECTION FOLDER text field, enter the connection folder where the connection must be created. You can click the FOLDER button to open the BROWSE CONNECTION FOLDER dialog box and select a connection folder.

6. Click the NEXT button to display the DATABASE MIDDLEWARE SELECTION page. This page contains the list of database vendors, databases, versions, and middleware supported by Universe Design Tool, as shown in Figure 6.7.

7. In this screen, select your database vendor, name, version, and the middleware to use to access it.

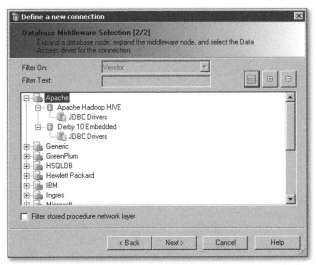

Figure 6.7 Databases Supported in Universe Design Tool

8. Click the NEXT button.

9. In the LOGIN PARAMETERS pane, use the AUTHENTICATION MODE dropdown list to select the authentication mode for this connection, if it is supported:

   ▶ USE SPECIFIED USERNAME AND PASSWORD for fixed credentials

   ▶ USE BUSINESSOBJECTS CREDENTIALS MAPPINGS for single sign-on

   ▶ USE SINGLE SIGN-ON WHEN REFRESHING REPORTS AT VIEW TIME for secondary credentials

10. If you have selected fixed credentials, enter the username and password used by the connection to authenticate to the database.

11. Follow the dialog box to enter the remaining parameters used to define the connection. The additional parameters to enter may depend on the connection you create.

12. Click the FINISH button to close the connection wizard and create the connection in the selected folder. The newly created connection is added to the list of connections.

Table 6.5 displays connections icons displayed in Universe Design Tool by type.

Icon	Connection Type
	Secured connection
	Personal connection
	Shared connection

Table 6.5 Connection Icons in Universe Design Tool

Editing a Connection

To edit a connection in Universe Design Tool, follow these steps:

1. In the menu bar, in the TOOLS menu, select CONNECTIONS or, in the STANDARD toolbar, click the CONNECTIONS button to open the CONNECTION PANEL dialog box.

2. Select the connection to edit in the connection list.

3. In the dialog box toolbar, click the EDIT CONNECTION button to open the EDIT CONNECTION dialog box. This dialog is similar to the one used to create the connection.

4. Modify the parameters in the dialog box and go to the last pane of dialog box to click the FINISH button and save the modified connection.

6.5.3 Managing Connections in the CMC

The CMC contains two tabs for connections:

▶ One CONNECTIONS tab, which is used to display, delete, and set security for all connections, except the connections used by Crystal Reports 2011 (see Section 6.1.5). In this tab, you cannot create or edit any connection.

▶ One OLAP CONNECTIONS tab, which is used to display, create, copy, edit, delete, and set security to OLAP connections compatible with Information Design Tool (see Section 6.1.4).

> **Note**
>
> In XI 3.x, relational connections used by Universe Designer and OLAP connections used by Voyager are stored in two different top-root folders, thus the two tabs. In BI 4.0, all connections have been gathered under the same Connections top-root folder for better interoperability between the reporting tools. But the tabs in the CMC have not been merged. These two tabs offer two different views of the same "Connections" top-root folder.

Creating a Connection

To create an OLAP connection in the CMC, follow these steps:

1. Log on to the CMC and go to the OLAP CONNECTIONS tab.

2. In the left pane, select the folder where the connection must be created.

3. In the toolbar, click the NEW CONNECTION button to open the panel where you can enter connection parameters, as shown in Figure 6.8.

Figure 6.8 OLAP Connection Panel in CMC

4. In the NAME text field, enter the name for the connection.

5. In the PROVIDER dropdown list, select the database to connect.

6. The list of parameters to enter is updated depending on the selected database provider. Enter the requested parameters to identify the database to query.

7. If your connection must point only to the database server, go to the next step. Otherwise, if your connection must point to a cube, click the CONNECT button:

   ▶ The LOG ON TO THE DATA SOURCE dialog box opens. Enter a user name and password to authenticate to the database, and then click OK.

   ▶ In the CUBE BROWSER dialog box, select the cube the connection must point to.

   ▶ Click the SELECT button to close this dialog box.

   The selected cube and its location are displayed in the CUBE and CATALOG text fields.

8. In the AUTHENTICATION dropdown list, select the authentication mode:

   ▶ PREDEFINED for fixed credentials (in which case, enter the user name and password this connection must use to authenticate to the database in the USER and PASSWORD text fields)

   ▶ SSO for single sign-on

   ▶ PROMPT for prompted credentials

9. Click the SAVE button to save the connection and return to the connection list.

Editing a Connection

To edit an OLAP connection in the CMC, follow these steps:

1. Log on to the CMC and go to the OLAP CONNECTIONS tab.

2. In the left pane, select the folder containing the connection to edit. The list of connections contained in this folder is displayed in the right pane.

3. In the right pane, select the connection to edit.

4. In the toolbar, click the EDIT CONNECTION button to open the panel where you can edit connection parameters. Modify the connection parameters.

5. Click the SAVE button to save your changes and return to the connection list.

6.6   Summary

Connections contain the parameters used to connect to the database you want to query through reporting tools. The database contains its own security repository and, in addition to the database parameters you need, the connection must contain authentication information to log on to this database.

Because of the different products and technologies embedded in BI 4.0, there are different types of connections. The most commonly used are the relational connections, the Data Federator data sources, and the OLAP connections.

Because the connection contains sensitive data (credentials, server name, and so on), it must be properly secured by saving it in the CMS repository. In addition to explicitly saving some credentials in the connection, you can use three other authentication modes for these connections: credentials mapping, prompted authentication, and single sign-on. Because single sign-on is only supported by a limited set of databases and drivers, it is possible to use the credentials mapping to simulate single sign-on.

Depending on the connection type, you can use Universe Design Tool, Information Design Tool, or the CMC to administrate connections.

With connections, security is defined at database level. With the use of the universe, described in the next chapter, security can be defined at a higher level.

The universe is a concept invented by BusinessObjects to provide easy access to data. Universe Design Tool offers different techniques—filters, auto-joins, access restrictions, and object access level—to secure this layer.

7 Universe Security in Universe Design Tool

Once upon a time, SAP BusinessObjects relied on Universe Design Tool as its metadata design tool. However, BI 4.0 contains Universe Design Tool's successor: Information Design Tool, described in Chapter 8. Most investments and new features are now dedicated to Information Design Tool, so, when possible, we recommend that you use Information Design Tool to create universes—especially for new projects.

Nevertheless, in order to allow a smooth transition from Universe Design Tool and classic universes to Information Design Tool and new universes, BI 4.0 continues to support Universe Design Tool and classic universes.

Consequently, a single BI 4.0 installation can contain both of the following:

▶ Universes created with Information Design Tool and consumed by reporting tools (Web Intelligence, Crystal Reports for Enterprise, Dashboard, Explorer)

▶ Universes created with BI 4.0 version of Universe Design Tool or migrated from previous releases (XI R2 or XI 3.x) and consumed by the reporting tools that still support them (Web Intelligence, Crystal Reports 2011)

After a short presentation of universes, this chapter focuses on the different options to secure them in the Universe Design Tool:

▶ Through filters

▶ Through access restrictions

▶ Through object access level

7.1   Universe

Historically, universes were created to hide the complexity of relational databases (tables, columns, joins, SQL, and so on) behind concepts that are easier for end users to understand: business objects.

These business objects must be named based on the business vocabulary of the targeted end user. For this reason, the universe is also called the Semantic Layer because it acts as a layer between the user and the database. For example, a universe used by a financial analyst may contain objects such as Profit Margin or Return on Investment, while a universe used by a human resources director may contain objects named Employee, Age, Level, and Salary, and so on. Each object contains the SQL fragment used to retrieve the corresponding data from the database.

Reporting tools that take advantage of the universe and query data through that universe implement a *query panel*, which is a graphical user interface that allows the user to select the objects defined in the universe through drag and drop. For example, Figure 7.1 shows the Web Intelligence query panel, where you can select the objects of the universe in the left pane, add them into the RESULT OBJECTS pane, and click the REFRESH button to retrieve data corresponding to these objects in the DATA PREVIEW pane.

Once the objects for which the user wants to retrieve data are selected, the query panel automatically generates the query by combining the SQL contained in the objects' definition. The resulting SQL is sent to the database, which returns the data requested by the user.

Universes and query panels offer more advanced features to query data (for example, prompts and filters), but their description goes beyond the scope of this book.

The person responsible for creating universes, called the designer, uses the Universe Design Tool graphical interface (as shown in Figure 7.2) to create universes and then publishes them either locally or in the CMS repository.

Universe Design Tool supports two types of universes, depending on the type of databases it queries: relational or OLAP. Let's briefly explore these two universes before reviewing some security concepts related to the universes.

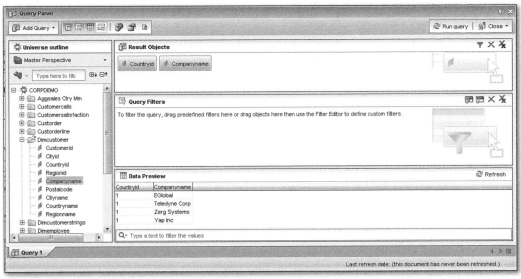

Figure 7.1 Web Intelligence Query Panel Showing Universe Content

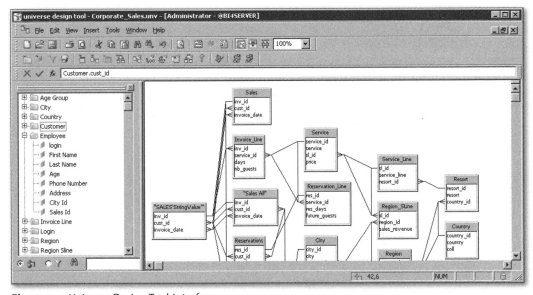

Figure 7.2 Universe Design Tool Interface

7.1.1 Relational Universe

To create a *relational universe* (based on a relational database), the universe designer must provide the following information:

▶ A connection to the relational database.

▶ A schema (the tables and the joins between these tables) from this database that is consumed by this universe. This schema contains the database complexity and is hidden from the user through the business objects.

▶ The business objects, organized in classes and sub-classes, based on the previous schema. Each object is defined by the SQL statement used to retrieve the data from the database. These objects and classes are exposed to the user through the query panel.

> **Note**
>
> Before SAP BusinessObjects' acquisition of Crystal Decisions, the business view was seen as the equivalent of universe for Crystal Reports, as it provided also an abstraction layer between the database and the reporting tool.
>
> After the acquisition, Crystal Reports was able to use both classic universe and business view. But business view has finally been deprecated in order to focus on classic universe only. Two versions of Crystal Reports are delivered with BI 4.0:
>
> ▶ Crystal Reports 2011, which supports universes created by Universe Design Tool and business views created with Business View Manager
>
> ▶ Crystal Reports for Enterprise, which supports only new universes created by Information Design Tool
>
> Compared to business view, view time security is a capability that Crystal Reports still doesn't support with new universes. Such a gap should be filled to achieve iso-functionality between business views and new universes.

7.1.2 OLAP Universe

With the spread of multidimensional databases, OLAP universes have been introduced in order to query OLAP databases. These universes can be created on an OLAP connection from Universe Design Tool, but you can't use an OLAP connection created in the Central Management Console or Information Design Tool.

Being relational by design, universes created in Universe Design Tool do not benefit from all multidimensional capabilities. For example, the multidimensional hierarchies exposed by the OLAP cube are flattened in the universe.

However, OLAP universes benefit from Universe Design Tool capabilities:

► Metadata exposed by the OLAP databases can be renamed, reorganized, or hidden through the universe classes and objects.

► Security (such as CMC rights and universe security concepts) can also be applied to OLAP universe.

A multidimensional database does not expose any tables; consequently, an OLAP universe does not contain any relational schema and does not enforce concepts related to tables and joins. As shown in Figure 7.3, an OLAP universe in Universe Design Tool does not expose any tables or joins.

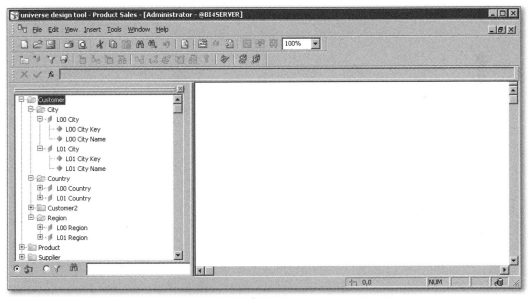

Figure 7.3 OLAP Universe in Universe Design Tool

Note

OLAP universes were introduced in XI 3.x Universe Designer. Although they are still supported in BI 4.0 Universe Design Tool, you should use Information Design Tool to create multidimensional universes. Multidimensional universes created with Information Design Tool take full advantage of multidimensional metadata.

7.1.3   Universe Security

As mentioned, relational and OLAP universes are very powerful tools to easily access and retrieve data from the database in order to query and analyze them through BusinessObjects reporting tools. For this reason, it is mandatory to properly secure universe capabilities as well as the users and groups who can access them.

To secure this universe, you can export it into a CMS repository, where it can benefit from CMS framework security. These security rights provide the framework to authorize users to view, edit, and use this universe, as seen in Chapters 4 and 5.

To export a universe into a CMS repository, you must be logged on with Universe Design Tool to this CMS repository and the universe must be attached to a secured connection stored in this CMS repository. In the CMS repository, the universe is secured since a user must be logged on to this CMS repository to access it. In this CMS repository, his security rights are checked in order to determine the actions he is allowed to do with this universe.

To work on a universe that has been exported to a CMS repository, a designer must import it locally in Universe Design Tool. This creates a secured copy of the universe. To open this local copy later with Universe Design Tool, the designer must authenticate to its source CMS repository.

The designer can also save this universe for all users. In this case, the universe must first be attached to a shared or personal connection. Once saved locally for all users, the universe is no longer secure, and it is not mandatory to authenticate to the CMS to open it.

Once a universe is exported in the CMS repository, several other techniques in addition to universe rights can be used to secure a universe's behavior:

▶ Using variables associated with the session

▶ Defining a filter on a table, an object, a class, or a universe

▶ Defining and assigning access restriction, also known as universe overload

▶ Defining the access level for universe objects and for users and groups

This chapter explores these techniques. Before moving to using filters on a table, object, class, or universe, let's make sure your understanding of variables is solid.

7.1.4 @VARIABLE

Universe Design Tool supports a predefined list of variables supported by universe. These are some of these variables:

▶ BOUSER: Login name used to log on to the CMS repository and currently using the universe to query data

▶ DBUSER: Database user name for secondary credentials authentication (see Chapter 6, Section 6.3)

▶ DOCNAME: Document name using this universe

▶ DPNAME: Data provider name

▶ DPTYPE: Data provider type

▶ UNNAME: Universe name

▶ UNVID: Universe ID

These variables can be used in the object, table, or join definition by using the @VARIABLE function. At query time, this function returns the variable value, depending on the context.

These variables, especially the ones that return values from the user session, are often used to secure the universes. This is the case for BOUSER and DBUSER since they can be used to create filters on user name and filter data to return only authorized data. If the universe is local, then these variables associated with CMS sessions return empty strings.

> **Note**
>
> Since the release of BI 4.0 SP4, it is possible to extend this list of variables and consume them in the New Semantic Layer and Information Design Tool (see discussion of user attributes in Chapter 8, Section 8.8).

7.2   Using Filters on Table, Object, Class, or Universe

One method to secure a universe is to use a WHERE clause in order to explicitly restrict data retrieved from the database. Such clauses can be defined in several places:

- On a table, through an auto-join
- An object, in its definition
- Through a mandatory filter

Let's examine each of these options more closely.

7.2.1 Table Auto-join

In Universe Design Tool, a join defines which WHERE clause to add to the generated query when two columns in two tables in the universe schema share the same value.

In case of an auto-join, the join applies to only one table, and the WHERE clause is always added to the generated query. The WHERE clause defined in the auto-join can be used to filter the data returned by the query, and thus to prevent users from accessing them.

> **Warning!**
>
> An auto-join defined on a table is not applied on an alias or a derived table created from this table, so the auto-join must be re-created on any alias or derived table based on the table.

If the universe is local, even if the table has been secured with this auto-join, the environment is not considered. It is easy for someone who has enough knowledge of Universe Design Tool to open it, edit the universe in order to remove the filter, and get unfiltered data.

If the universe is saved in the CMS repository, editing the universe is more difficult, especially if the right to edit the universe has been denied (see Chapter 4, Section 4.5). In addition, if the universe is saved in the CMS, then the filters can use variables to implement security (for example, @VARIABLE('BOUSER')).

> **Example**
>
> A table Employee with a column ID containing a user login in the CMS can be filtered with the following auto-join:
>
> WHERE Employee.ID = @VARIABLE ('BOUSER')
>
> When this table is used in a query, this filter is automatically added. At query time, the variable is replaced by the user login, and the user can see only the table rows containing his CMS login.

7.2.2   Object Filters

You can add a WHERE clause in the object definition. This WHERE clause is added to the query when the object is selected and will filter the data returned by the query. As in auto-join, this WHERE clause can be complex and can also include @VARIABLEs.

When you display the generated SQL in the query panel, you can see the WHERE clause added through the selected objects.

7.2.3   Mandatory Filters

A mandatory filter is similar to a filter that a universe designer creates and exposes in the universe through the query panel. It is expressed as a WHERE clause that is added to the query when this filter is added. This WHERE clause can be complex and uses some functions like @VARIABLE.

When you define a mandatory filter, you can set it at either *universe level* or at a *class level*. If the mandatory filter is defined at universe level, then it is always included in the query. If the mandatory filter is defined at a class level, then this filter is always added to the query if an object or a filter contained in the class or in one of its sub-class is used in the query.

A mandatory filter is hidden: it is not displayed in query panel and cannot be selected by the query creator. However, when the query is generated, the mandatory filter is added to the query and can be seen if the user displays the generated script to send to the database.

If different mandatory filters apply in a query, they are aggregated with the AND operator.

> **Warning!**
>
> A class mandatory filter is not inherited. It is not applied if you add in the query an object or a filter that does not belong to its class but that references an object of the class mandatory filter with the @SELECT or @WHERE functions.

7.3   Using Filters in Universe Design Tool

The filters described in the previous sections can be useful to filter data retrieved from the database. To prevent users from changing these filters, it is better to have them saved in the CMS repository. Let's review how to create them in Universe Design Tool and how to export a universe in the CMS repository to secure it.

7.3.1   Defining an Auto-join

You can define an auto-join on a table by following these steps:

1. Open your universe in Universe Design Tool.

2. In the menu bar, select INSERT • JOIN. The EDIT JOIN dialog box opens.

3. In the TABLE 1 dropdown list, select the table for which you want to create the auto-join. The list of column of this table is displayed in the list below.

4. Select a column.

5. In the TABLE 2 dropdown list, select the same table, then select the same column than in TABLE 1.

6. Edit the EXPRESSION text field to add the filter to apply on this table. For example, as shown in Figure 7.4, to filter rows and display only values for a specific tag saved in the column `country_id` in the table `Country`, type

    `Country.country_id = 'FR'`

    You can also click the >> button to open the JOIN SQL DEFINITION dialog box. This dialog box allows you to type your SQL and propose a list of available tables, columns, operators or functions. You can click them to directly insert them into the SQL you type.

    To close the JOIN SQL DEFINITION dialog box, click OK. The SQL you have typed in this dialog box is copied in the WHERE CLAUSE field.

7. Set a 1-to-1 cardinality in order to prevent error messages when detecting contexts.

8. Click the PARSE button to run validity checks on the SQL you have typed.

9. Click OK to close the EDIT JOIN dialog box.

10. Click the SAVE button to save the universe's changes.

If, in the auto-join expression, you have used variables (like `BOUSER`) attached to user's CMS session, then this universe must be published in the CMS repository.

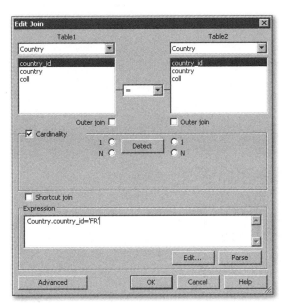

Figure 7.4 Editing an Auto-join

7.3.2 Defining a WHERE Clause on an Object

To define the WHERE clause for an object:

1. Open your universe in Universe Design Tool.

2. Select an object.

3. Right-click this object and select OBJECT PROPERTIES. The EDIT PROPERTIES OF <OBJECT NAME> dialog box opens.

4. In the WHERE text field, type the clause to add to the SQL generated to retrieve this object data. For example, as shown in Figure 7.5, to filter the values returned by the object Country Id, by a specific tag, type

```
Country.country_id = 'FR'
```

You can also click the >> button to open the EDIT WHERE CLAUSE OF '<OBJECT NAME>' dialog box.

This dialog box allows you to type your SQL and offers a list of available tables, columns, classes, objects, operators, or functions. You can click on them to directly insert them into the SQL you type.

To close this dialog box, click OK. The SQL you have typed in this dialog box is copied in the WHERE text field.

5. Click OK to close the EDIT PROPERTIES OF <OBJECT NAME> dialog box.

6. Click the SAVE button to save the universe's changes.

If, in the filter expression, you have used variables (like BOUSER) attached to user's CMS session, then this universe must be published in the CMS repository.

Figure 7.5 Object Properties Dialog Box

7.3.3 Defining a Mandatory Filter

To create a mandatory filter:

1. Open your universe in Universe Design Tool.

2. Select the class where the filter is created.

3. In the menu bar, select INSERT • CONDITION. The EDIT PROPERTIES OF CONDITION<X> dialog box opens, as shown in Figure 7.6.

4. Fill in the NAME, DESCRIPTION and WHERE text fields as for any filter. You may click the >> button to open the PREDEFINED FILTER OF 'CONDITION<X>' dialog box.

5. Check the USE FILTER AS MANDATORY IN QUERY checkbox.

6. Choose between the APPLY ON UNIVERSE or APPLY ON CLASS radio button, depending on the mandatory filter you seek to create.

7. Click OK to close the EDIT PROPERTIES OF CONDITION<X> dialog box. The new filter is added to the selected class.

8. Click the SAVE button to save the universe's changes.

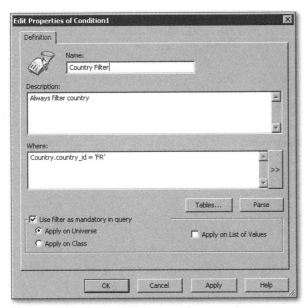

Figure 7.6 Defining a Mandatory Filter

7.3.4 Exporting a Universe in a CMS Repository

To export a universe in the CMS repository, you must be logged on to a CMS repository in Universe Design Tool. The universe must be linked to a secured connection stored in this CMS repository. Then you need to follow these steps:

1. In the Universe Design Tool toolbar, select FILE • SAVE to save the universe locally.

2. In the Universe Design Tool toolbar, select FILE • EXPORT to open the EXPORT UNIVERSE dialog box.

3. Near the DOMAIN text field, click the BROWSE button to open the SELECT A UNIVERSE FOLDER dialog box.

4. In this dialog box, select a folder in the CMS repository where the universe will be saved.

5. Click OK to close the SELECT A UNIVERSE FOLDER dialog box.

6. The GROUPS list contains all groups existing in the CMS repository. Select one or several groups; several groups can be selected by pressing the ⌈Ctrl⌋ key. When the universe is published, these groups are assigned some advanced rights for this universe.

7. Click OK to confirm. The EXPORT UNIVERSE dialog box closes and a confirmation window opens.

8. Click OK to close it. The universe is exported in the CMS repository in the selected folder. The name of the InfoObject for this universe is the universe name.

Having covered the use of filters and their definition in the user interface, let's turn our attention to access restriction, which is another technique used to secure a universe's behavior.

7.4   Access Restriction Definition

The use of auto-joins and filters, as described in Section 7.2, can resolve some security requirements, but it is not flexible, even with the use of @VARIABLE. The formula is unconditionally applied and cannot be modified. In contrast, access restrictions offer more options to secure the universe, with more flexibility when applied to users or groups.

Access restriction can be defined only for universes published in the CMS repository and can be assigned to users or groups. When a user that has been assigned an access restriction uses this universe, then the settings defined in the access restriction apply.

When a universe is imported in Universe Design Tool and re-exported to the CMS repository, it does not modify the access restrictions defined for this universe.

When you republish a universe with inconsistency between the universe and the access restriction (for example, a table or object referenced in the access restriction that does not exist any longer), no check is done. But when the query is created from this universe, an error may be raised if the access restriction adds to the query a table that does not exist any longer.

When a universe is deleted, all access restrictions created for this universe are also deleted.

For a relational universe, six different security concepts can be defined in an access restriction:

- Connection
- Controls
- SQL
- Objects
- Rows
- Table mapping

For an OLAP universe, this list of possible access restrictions is restricted to connection, controls, and objects.

Let's explore each of these security concepts further.

7.4.1 Connection

Connection access restriction is also known as connection overload. With this access restriction, you can select a connection from the Connections folder or sub-folders in the CMS repository that replaces the default universe connection. Only connections supported by Universe Design Tool can be selected (OLAP, relational SAP NetWeaver BW or SAS connections created in Information Design Tool or CMC are not supported).

When this access restriction is applied, any query is sent to the database referenced by the replacement connection instead of the original connection.

This can be useful when you want to prevent a user from seeing a table and the data it contains. To do so, you can do the following with this access restriction applied:

1. In your database, create another schema with the same structure as the original database and fill it with fake data.
2. Create a connection to this new database containing fake data.

3. For a universe that uses the connection to the original database, create a connection access restriction to replace this source connection by this new connection.

4. Assign this access restriction to the user or user group.

When the user creates a query on top of this universe, then the query is sent to the database containing the fake data. This fake data is returned, instead of the actual data from the original database.

The two databases must have the same structure. This is not checked when the connection access restriction is created. But at query time, an error will be raised if the objects used in the query reference tables that are not found in the replacement database.

> **Warning!**
>
> When assigning a connection access restriction to a user or a group, you should check that the users or groups are granted the connection security rights they need to query the database with this replacement connection (see Chapter 5, Section 5.21).

7.4.2 Controls

Controls access restriction is used to replace universe parameters defined to limit the size of the result set and query execution time. Table 7.1 outlines these parameters.

Parameter Name	Description
Limit size of result set to	This option stops the query once it has returned the specified number of rows.
Limit execution time to	This option stops the query once it exceeds the specified number of minutes.
Warn if cost estimate exceeds	This parameter is used only by Web Intelligence for Teradata databases. If this option is selected, a confirmation message is displayed to the effect that the query may last more than the specified number of minutes.
Limit size of long text objects to	This parameter is deprecated. It was used only by Desktop Intelligence, which is no longer released in BI 4.0.

Table 7.1 Parameters Covered by Controls Access Restriction

This access restriction can be used if you want to define some conservative values for a universe in order to prevent most users from downgrading the system but extend these limits for a specific set of users.

7.4.3 SQL

This access restriction overrides universe parameters used to generate the SQL sent to the database. Table 7.2 outlines these parameters.

Parameter Name	Description
Allow use of subqueries	This parameter enables the creation of sub-queries when defining filters in the query panel. If this option is denied, then the icon to add a sub-query is disabled in the query panel.
Allow use of union, intersect and minus operators	This parameter enables combination of queries using data set operators (union, intersect, and minus) to obtain one set of results. If this option is denied, then the button to add combined queries is disabled in the query panel.
Allow complex operands in query panel	This parameter enables the use of the Both and Except operators when defining query filters in query panel. If this option is denied, then these two operators are not displayed in the available operators.
Multiple SQL statements for each context	This parameter enables a query to be split into multiple SQL statements if it contains objects from different contexts. If this option is denied, an error message is displayed when queries containing objects from different contexts are run.
Multiple SQL statements for each measure	This parameter forces a query to be split into multiple SQL queries if it contains measures based on different tables. To split the SQL even if the measures come from the same table, you may create an alias table, which is considered a different table. If this option is denied, then only one query is sent to the database.

Table 7.2 Parameters Covered by SQL Access Restriction

Parameter Name	Description
Allow selection of multiple contexts	This parameter enables end users to create queries on objects in more than one context and to generate one set of results from multiple contexts. Do not select this parameter if the universe contains contexts to resolve join path problems such as loops, chasm traps, and fan traps.
Cartesian product: ▶ Prevent ▶ Warn	A Cartesian product is the set of all rows that can be created by merging all rows from tables. Using Cartesian products can generate queries that return large result set and impact the overall system performance. For this reason, it can be useful to prevent users from generating such a Cartesian product. If you opt to prevent a Cartesian product, then an error message is raised if the generated query contains a Cartesian product.

Table 7.2 Parameters Covered by SQL Access Restriction (Cont.)

7.4.4 Objects

The objects access restriction allows you to deny some classes and objects from the universe. If a class is denied, then all objects in the class are also denied.

When objects and classes are denied through an objects access restriction, several things happen:

▶ The object does not appear in the query panel.

▶ The object is removed from the query when the query is generated.

In Web Intelligence, removing an object from the query before a refresh may lead to some unexpected behaviors if it modifies the document structure.

For this reason, the universe AUTO_UPDATE_QUERY parameter is used to prevent the refreshing of a report containing an object denied by an objects access restriction.

If this parameter is set to No, then the query is not executed, the report is not displayed, and an error message is displayed. This is the default value for this parameter.

If this parameter is set to Yes, then the report is refreshed but the object is denied from data point of view. There are several ramifications of the denial of such an object:

▶ The query specification is not modified but the object disappears from the execution plan, as well as calculated measures, variables depending on it.

▶ Predefined filters used in the query and containing this denied object are removed from the conditions tree of the execution plan.

▶ Data corresponding to this object are no longer retrieved from the data and are thus removed from the report.

7.4.5 Rows

Rows restrictions are the most used access restriction. They allow you to define a conditional WHERE clause to be added to the query generated and sent to the database if a conditional table is used in the query. This WHERE clause is often used to give a condition used to filter the data.

When the SQL query to retrieve data is generated, this WHERE clause is added to the query if it contains the table secured by the row access restriction.

It is possible to use any table from the universe, including an alias table or a derived table.

Example

A table Customer contains the column Country. If you want some users to access only the data for customers whose country is France, you may create a row restriction, based on the Customer table and with the following WHERE clause:

```
WHERE Customer.Country = 'France'
```

The WHERE clause in the row restriction can contain very complex SQL. For example, it is possible to use @VARIABLE, which supports only predefined variables supported by Universe Design Tool. It does not support the user attributes that are supported only by Information Design Tool and new universes (see Chapter 8, Section 8.8).

A row restriction triggered by a table is not triggered by an alias or derived table created from this table. If needed, the row restriction must be re-created on any alias or derived table based on this table.

> **Example**
>
> In the previous example, if you create a `Premium_Customer` table derived from the `Customer` table, then the row restriction created for `Customer` table is not applied if the query contains the `Premium_Customer` table. You need to explicitly re-create the same row restriction on the `Premium_Customer` table.

7.4.6 Table Mapping

Table mapping can be used to replace a table with another table. When the query to send to the database is generated, any occurrence of the source table is replaced by the replacement table.

This can be useful when you want to prevent a user or a users group from seeing a table and the data it contains. You can do the following using table mapping:

1. Create a table in your database with the same structure as the original table and fill it with fake data.

2. For a universe using this table, create a table mapping access restriction to replace the source table by this fake table.

3. Assign this access restriction to a user or a group.

When the user creates a query that contains this table, then the table is replaced by the replacement table and the system returns fake data from the replacement table instead of actual data.

Both the original and replacement tables can be any tables or alias tables but not derived tables.

> **Warning!**
>
> A table mapping access restriction defined on a table won't apply if the query contains an alias or a derived table created from this source table.

When you enter the replacement table, Universe Design Tool offers the flexibility to enter a formula containing @VARIABLE or @PROMPT, and thus define dynamic table mapping. You can use this flexibility to support functional requirements rather than security needs.

7.5 Access Restriction Aggregation

As seen in previous sections, you can define several access restrictions for a universe and assign the same access restriction to different groups or users. But only one access restriction can be assigned to the same group or user. When a user belongs to different groups that are assigned access restrictions, these access restrictions are inherited. But some settings defined in these different access restrictions may conflict. The next sections describe the different aggregation rules that define how to compute the effective settings to apply when the user uses this universe.

Note that if no access restriction is defined, then the universe default behavior is used.

> **Warning!**
>
> In order to compute the list of access restrictions that apply to a user, this user must be given the "View objects" right for all groups from which he can inherit access restrictions. If a user cannot see the groups he belongs to, he cannot get the list of access restrictions that apply to him.

7.5.1 Connection, SQL, Controls, and Table Mapping

For a universe, you can prioritize the list of groups that are assigned an access restriction. By default, these groups are prioritized in chronological order of assignment. When a new group is assigned an access restriction, it has the lowest priority.

This priority list is used to compute effective values for connection, SQL, controls, and table access restriction. For each individual parameter that you can modify in these access restrictions, two rules apply:

- If there is an access restriction assigned to the user who modifies this parameter, then its value becomes the effective value for this parameter.

- Otherwise, its effective value is taken from the access restriction with the highest priority that modifies this setting.

7.5.2 Objects

Any object or class denied in an objects access restriction inherited by the user or directly assigned to him is denied to the user.

7.5.3 Row Restriction

For row restriction, all WHERE clauses are taken into consideration to compute the effective one applied to a user. There are two methods to aggregate them, as described next:

1. The AND aggregation—the default method—involves aggregating all of the WHERE clauses with an AND operator. It is quite restrictive, because all WHERE clauses must be true to display a row.

2. The less-restrictive ANDOR aggregation involves aggregating these WHERE clauses with two operators:

   ▶ With an AND operator in the case of parent-child direct inheritance aggregation, as shown in Figure 7.7 ❶.

   ▶ With an OR operator in the case of aggregation from multiple parents, as shown in Figure 7.7 ❷.

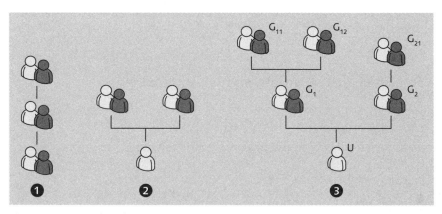

Figure 7.7 Examples of Rows Restriction Aggregation

Example

In the group inheritance model depicted in Figure 7.7 ❸, the aggregated clause for the user U is:

▶ R(U) AND R(G1) AND R(G11) AND R(G12) AND R(G2) AND R(G21), if the aggregation is done with the AND algorithm

> ▸ R(U) AND [(R(G1) AND (R(G11) OR R(G12))) OR (R(G2) AND R(G 21))], if the aggregation is done with the ANDOR algorithm
>
> R (X) returns the WHERE clause of the rows restriction access restriction assigned to user or group X.

7.6   Managing Access Restrictions in Universe Design Tool

The previous section described access restrictions and how they can be used to secure universe. Next we explain how to manage these access restrictions in Universe Design Tool.

7.6.1   Opening the Manage Access Restrictions Dialog Box

Managing access restrictions can be done only on a universe published in a CMS repository. Universe Design Tool can manage access restrictions for only one universe once. This universe must have been imported first from the CMS repository, which you can do by following five steps:

1. Connect to the CMS repository where the universe is stored by logging in to Universe Design Tool.

2. In the menu bar, select FILE • IMPORT.

3. In the IMPORT UNIVERSE dialog box, select the universe to import. Click the BROWSE button to change the universe folder in the SELECT A UNIVERSE FOLDER dialog box.

4. Once you have selected a universe, click OK. The IMPORT UNIVERSE dialog box closes. The universe is imported and displayed.

5. In the menu bar, select TOOLS • MANAGE SECURITY • MANAGE ACCESS RESTRICTIONS. The MANAGE ACCESS RESTRICTIONS dialog box shown in Figure 7.8 opens.

In this dialog box you can do several things, which are detailed in upcoming sections:

▸ Create or edit access restrictions

▸ Assign or un-assign access restrictions

▸ Set group priorities

- ▶ Set row restriction aggregation option
- ▶ Preview aggregated access restrictions
- ▶ Delete access restrictions

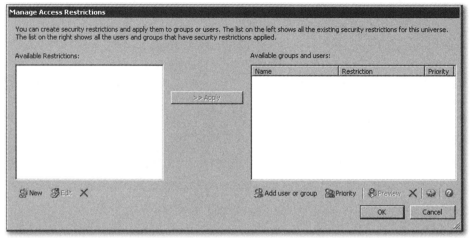

Figure 7.8 Manage Access Restrictions Dialog Box

By default, any changes done in the Manage Access Restrictions dialog box are not committed in the CMS repository and are kept locally by Universe Design Tool. Once you are finished, click OK to close the editor and to commit the changes in the CMS repository. If you click the Cancel button, all your changes will be lost.

7.6.2 Creating and Editing Access Restrictions

Once you are in the Manage Access Restrictions dialog box (see Section 7.6.1), follow these steps to create a new access restriction:

1. Click the New button. The Edit Restriction dialog box opens.

2. Type a name in the Restriction Name text field.

3. For each security to define, select the corresponding tab. The panels of each tab are described in the sections below. Use the panels to set the access restriction behavior.

4. Click OK to close the Edit Restriction dialog box. The new access restriction is displayed in the Available Restrictions list.

To edit an existing access restriction, after you have opened the MANAGE ACCESS RESTRICTIONS dialog box (see Section 7.6.1), follow these steps:

1. Select the access restriction in the AVAILABLE RESTRICTIONS list.

2. Click the EDIT button. The EDIT RESTRICTION dialog box opens.

3. For each security to define, select the corresponding tab. The parameters of each tab are described in the sections below. Edit these parameters to set the access restriction behavior.

4. Click OK to close the EDIT RESTRICTION dialog box.

Connection

To define a connection overload in the access restriction:

1. In the access restriction editor, select the CONNECTION tab, which is shown in Figure 7.9.

2. In the CONNECTION dropdown menu, select the connection to use as the replacement connection. The connection name appears in a red font to highlight that the default connection has been changed.

3. Click OK to close the EDIT ACCESS RESTRICTION dialog box or select another tab in the editor to define another security type in the access restriction.

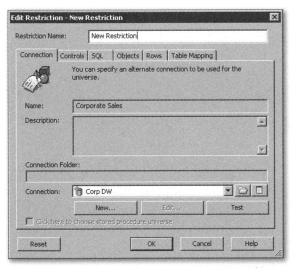

Figure 7.9 Connection Tab in Access Restriction Editor

> **Warning!**
>
> When you select the replacement connection, Universe Design Tool does not check that this connection is a valid one.
>
> If the universe is relational, it does not check that this replacement connection is relational and that the schema exposed by the original connection and the replacement connection are similar. You can save the access restriction, but when this access restriction applies, the query may fail because of inconsistency between the query and the database referenced by the replacement connection.
>
> Similarly, if the universe is OLAP, Universe Design Tool does not check that the replacement connection is an OLAP connection.

Controls and SQL

To define controls or SQL parameters to overload in the access restriction, follow these steps:

1. In the access restriction editor, select the CONTROLS or SQL tab. These tabs are shown in Figure 7.10 and Figure 7.11, respectively.

2. Modify any settings displayed in the tab. The modified settings appear in red font.

3. Click OK to close the EDIT ACCESS RESTRICTION dialog box or select another tab in the editor to define another security type in the access restriction.

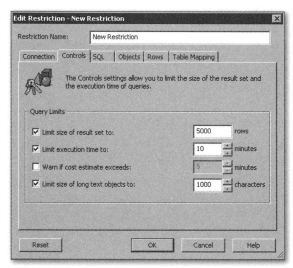

Figure 7.10 Controls Tab in Access Restriction Editor

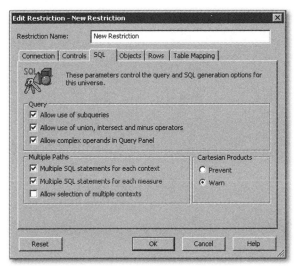

Figure 7.11 SQL Tab in Access Restriction Editor

Objects

To define objects and classes to restrict in the access restriction, follow these steps:

1. In the access restriction editor, select the OBJECTS tab.

2. Click the ADD button to open the NEW RESTRICTED OBJECT dialog box.

3. Click the SELECT button to open the OBJECT BROWSER dialog box, as shown in Figure 7.12.

4. Select a class or an object in the universe objects, and then click OK. The OBJECT BROWSER dialog box closes and the selected object or class is displayed in the OBJECT NAME text field, as shown in Figure 7.13. You can also explicitly type a class or an object name.

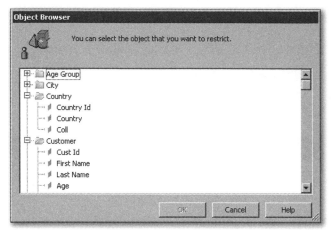

Figure 7.12 Object Browser Dialog Box to Select Restricted Object or Class

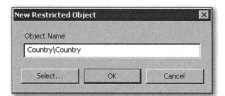

Figure 7.13 Select Object or Class to Restrict

5. Click OK to close the NEW RESTRICTED OBJECT dialog box. The selected object or class is displayed in the list of denied objects, as shown in Figure 7.14.

6. Click the CHECK ALL button to run a validation on each object denied by the access restriction. This is useful, for example, for detecting objects that no longer exist in the universe if it has been modified.

7. Click OK to close the EDIT ACCESS RESTRICTION dialog box or select another tab in the editor to define another security type in the access restriction.

Rows

To define a rows restriction in the access restriction, follow these steps:

1. In the access restriction editor, select the Rows tab.

2. Click the ADD button to open the NEW ROW RESTRICTION dialog box.

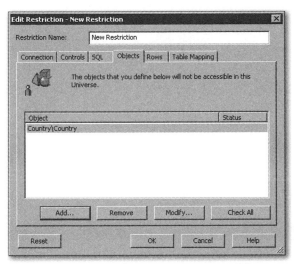

Figure 7.14 OBJECTS Tab in Access Restriction Editor

3. Type a table name the TABLE field. This table will trigger the row restriction. You can also click the >> button to select the table in the list of tables used by the universe.

4. Type the WHERE clause in the WHERE CLAUSE field. You can also click the >> button to open the WHERE CLAUSE DEFINITION dialog box.

   This dialog box is similar to any SQL editor used to define SQL in Universe Design Tool. It allows you to type your SQL and offers a list of possible tables, columns, operators, or functions. You can click on them to directly insert them into the SQL you type.

   Click OK to close the WHERE CLAUSE DEFINITION dialog box. The SQL you have typed in this dialog box is copied in the WHERE CLAUSE field.

5. Click OK to close the NEW ROW RESTRICTION dialog box. The row restriction is displayed in the row restriction array, as shown in Figure 7.15. Repeat these steps for each row restriction to define in this access restriction.

6. If needed, click the CHECK ALL button to run some validity checks on the SQL you have entered.

7. Click OK to close the EDIT ACCESS RESTRICTION dialog box or select another tab in the editor to define another security type in the access restriction.

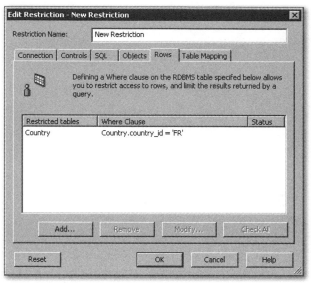

Figure 7.15 Rows Tab in Access Restriction Editor

Table Mapping

To define a table mapping in the access restriction, follow these steps:

1. In the access restriction editor, select the TABLE MAPPING tab.

2. Click the ADD button. The NEW TABLE MAPPING dialog box opens.

3. Type the original table name in the ORIGINAL TABLE field. You can also click the SELECT button to select the table in the list of tables used by the universe.

4. In the REPLACEMENT TABLE field, type the replacement table name or some formula using @VARIABLE. You can also click the SELECT button to select the table in the list of tables used by the universe.

5. Click OK to close the NEW TABLE MAPPING dialog box. The table mapping is displayed in the table mapping array, as shown in Figure 7.16. Repeat these steps for each table mapping to define in this access restriction.

6. Click the CHECK ALL button to validate the different table mappings you have entered.

7. Click OK to close the EDIT ACCESS RESTRICTION dialog box or select another tab in the editor to define another security type in the access restriction.

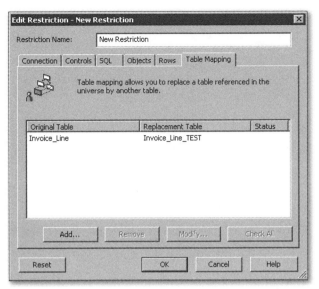

Figure 7.16 Table Mapping Tab in Access Restriction Editor

7.6.3 Assigning Access Restrictions

In the MANAGE ACCESS RESTRICTIONS dialog box (see Section 7.6.1), follow these steps to assign an access restriction to a user or to a group:

1. If the group or user is not listed in the AVAILABLE GROUPS OR USERS list, you first need to add it. Click the ADD USER OR GROUP button. The SELECT USERS AND GROUPS dialog box opens.

2. Select the user or the group in the AVAILABLE GROUPS AND USERS array. Several users or groups can be selected simultaneously by pressing the Ctrl key.

3. Click the > button to move the selected user(s) or group(s) in the SELECTED GROUPS AND USERS array.

4. Click OK to close the SELECT USERS AND GROUPS dialog box.

5. In the AVAILABLE RESTRICTIONS array, select the access restriction to assign.

6. In the AVAILABLE GROUPS OR USERS array, select the user or the group to assign the access restriction. Several users or groups can be selected by pressing the Ctrl key.

7. Click the >>APPLY button. The access restriction is displayed in the RESTRICTION column for the selected user(s) or group(s).

8. Click OK to make your changes in the CMS repository and to close the MANAGE ACCESS RESTRICTIONS dialog box. The new access restrictions assignments are saved in the CMS repository.

> **Note**
>
> Only one access restriction can be assigned to a user or a group. So if you assign an access restriction to a user or a group that was already assigned an access restriction, you'll replace the previously assigned access restriction with the new one.

7.6.4 Un-Assigning Access Restrictions

You can un-assign an access restriction in the MANAGE ACCESS RESTRICTIONS dialog box by following these steps (see Section 7.6.1):

1. In the AVAILABLE GROUPS OR USERS array, select the user or group to un-assign the access restriction. Several users or groups can be selected by pressing the `Ctrl` key.

2. Click the REMOVE THE RESTRICTIONS FROM THE SELECTED USERS OR GROUPS button. The users or groups are removed from the AVAILABLE GROUPS OR USERS array.

3. Click OK to make your changes in the CMS repository final and to close the MANAGE ACCESS RESTRICTIONS dialog box. The access restriction are then unassigned to the selected users and groups.

You can also un-assign an access restriction by assigning another access restriction to the user or to the group (see Section 7.6.3) or by deleting the assigned access restriction (see Section 7.6.8).

7.6.5 Defining Group Priority for Access Restrictions

You can define access restrictions priority in the MANAGE ACCESS RESTRICTIONS dialog box by following these steps (see Section 7.6.1):

1. Click the PRIORITY button to open the SET GROUP PRIORITY dialog box, as shown in Figure 7.17. The groups with applied access restrictions for this universe are listed, the highest priority on top.

2. To increase a group priority, select the group, then click the MOVE UP button until it reaches the expected priority in the list.

3. To decrease a group priority, select the group, then click the MOVE DOWN button until it reaches the expected priority in the list.

4. Click OK to make your changes in the CMS repository and to close the MANAGE ACCESS RESTRICTIONS dialog box. The new access restrictions priority is then saved in the CMS repository.

Figure 7.17 Set Group Priority Dialog Box

7.6.6 Setting Row Restriction Aggregation

In the MANAGE ACCESS RESTRICTIONS dialog box, follow these steps to define row restrictions aggregation option (see Section 7.5.3):

1. Click the RESTRICTION OPTIONS button to open the RESTRICTIONS OPTIONS dialog box.

2. To select the row restriction aggregation option, choose one of two radio buttons, as shown in Figure 7.18:

   ▸ COMBINE ROW RESTRICTIONS USING AND to select the AND algorithm

   ▸ COMBINE ROW RESTRICTIONS USING AND WITHIN GROUP HIERARCHIES AND OR BETWEEN GROUPS to select the ANDOR algorithm.

3. Click OK to close the RESTRICTION OPTIONS dialog box.

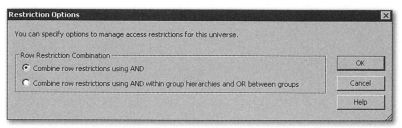

Figure 7.18 Row Restriction Aggregation Selection

7.6.7 Preview Net Results

The previewing net result functionality is useful to get an overview of the access restriction actually applied to a user or a group through inheritance, priority, and aggregation options. There are two methods to display the restriction: via the MANAGE ACCESS RESTRICTIONS dialog box or directly from the Universe Design Tool menu bar.

In the MANAGE ACCESS RESTRICTIONS dialog box (see Section 7.6.1), follow these steps to preview aggregated access restrictions:

1. In the AVAILABLE GROUPS OR USERS array, select a user or a group.

2. Click the PREVIEW button below this array.

   If some access restriction applies to this user or group, the RESTRICTION PREVIEW FOR '<USER NAME>' dialog box opens, as shown in Figure 7.19. This dialog box is similar to the access restriction editor. However, it displays only the tabs for the access restriction types that apply and highlights in red the options modified for this user or group. Click the CLOSE button to close this dialog box.

   If no access restriction applies to the user or group, then a warning message is displayed. Click the CLOSE button to close it.

Unless you have edited the content of an access restriction, this computation takes the access restrictions in the MANAGE ACCESS RESTRICTIONS dialog box into consideration, even if they have not yet been committed in the CMS repository.

If you have modified the settings of an access restriction, we recommend that you click OK to save MANAGE ACCESS RESTRICTIONS changes and then preview the effective access restriction.

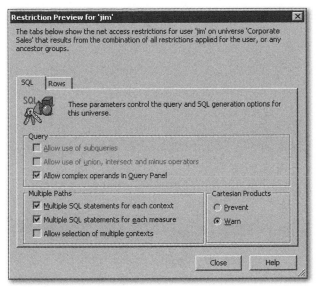

Figure 7.19 Preview Result Overview

To preview net results with the method described previously, the selected user or group must be listed in the MANAGE ACCESS RESTRICTIONS dialog box. If it is not the case, you can still preview net results directly from the menu bar by following these steps:

1. In Universe Design Tool menu bar, select TOOLS • MANAGE SECURITY • PREVIEW NET ACCESS RESTRICTIONS. The PREVIEW NET ACCESS RESTRICTIONS FOR USERS OR GROUPS dialog box opens, which is shown in Figure 7.20.

2. In the AVAILABLE GROUPS OR USERS array, select a user or a group.

3. Click the PREVIEW button.

   If some access restriction applies to this user or group, the RESTRICTION PREVIEW FOR <USER NAME> dialog box opens. This dialog box is similar to the access restriction editor. However, it displays only the tabs for the access restriction types that apply to this user or group and highlights in red the options modified for this user or group. Click the CLOSE button to close this dialog box.

   If no access restriction applies to the user or the group, then a warning message is displayed.

4. Click the Close button to close the Preview net access restrictions for users or groups dialog box.

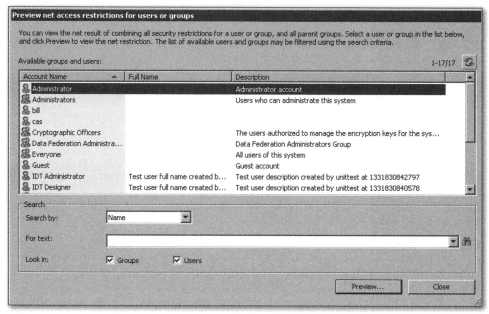

Figure 7.20 User or Group Selection for Preview

7.6.8 Deleting Access Restrictions

In the Manage Access Restrictions dialog box (see Section 7.6.1), you can delete an access restriction by following these steps:

1. Select the access restriction in the Available Restrictions list.

2. Click the Delete the selected restriction button, below the Available Restrictions list.

3. If the access restriction is assigned to a user or a group, a confirmation message is displayed. Click the Yes button to confirm.

4. The access restriction is removed from the Available Restrictions list. It is also removed from the Restriction column in the Available groups and users array, if some users or groups were assigned this access restriction.

5. Click OK to make your changes in the CMS repository final and to close the MANAGE ACCESS RESTRICTIONS dialog box. The access restriction is then removed from the CMS repository and is no longer assigned to any users or groups.

7.6.9   Setting AUTO_UPDATE_QUERY Parameter

Follow these steps to set a value to the AUTO_UPDATE_QUERY parameter for a universe:

1. Open the universe in Universe Design Tool.

2. Select FILE • PARAMETERS to open the UNIVERSE PARAMETERS dialog box.

3. Click the PARAMETER tab, which is shown in Figure 7.21. The PARAMETER array displays the list of parameters.

4. Select the AUTO_UPDATE_QUERY line if it exists in the array. In PROPERTY section, AUTO_UPDATE_QUERY is displayed. Enter its value (Yes or No) in the VALUE text field.

   If this parameter does *not* exist in the array, follow these additional steps:

   ▶ Type AUTO_UPDATE_QUERY in the NAME text field

   ▶ Enter its value (Yes or No) in the VALUE text field.

   ▶ Click the ADD button.

5. Click OK to close the UNIVERSE PARAMETERS dialog box.

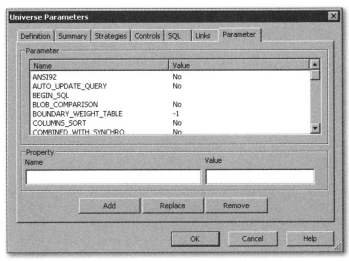

Figure 7.21 Universe Parameters Dialog Box

7.7 Object Access Level

In addition to the access restrictions described in the two previous sections, Universe Design Tool offers another concept called object access level.

Access level is a business object property (dimensions, measures, attributes) that defines its level of confidentiality. Access level can take the following values, in increasing order of confidentiality:

- ▶ Public (the default value and the least confidential)
- ▶ Controlled
- ▶ Restricted
- ▶ Confidential
- ▶ Private (the most confidential)

In addition, each user can be assigned an access level for each universe. A user can see only objects whose access level is lower or equal to his own access level.

Example

If you have the restricted access level for a universe, you can see only objects of this universe with public, controlled, and restricted object access level.

If an object is denied to you through an object access level, it means:

- ▶ In the query panel, you do not see this object in the list of objects exposed by the universe.
- ▶ When you refresh a query containing this object, the query fails and no data are retrieved from the database.

If no access level is explicitly assigned to a user for a universe, then it can be inherited through group or universes folder:

- ▶ A group can be assigned an access level for a universe: this object access level is inherited by all groups and users it contains.
- ▶ A user can also be assigned an access level for a universe folder: this access level is inherited by the universes and sub-folders this folder contains.

▶ A group can be assigned an access level for a universe folder: this object access level is inherited by all groups and users it contains for all universes and folders this folder contains.

If an access level is explicitly assigned to a user for a universe, then this access level is used, without taking into consideration the inherited ones.

> **Note**
>
> The access levels defined for folders are also inherited and used for objects access level for universes created in Information Design Tool (see Chapter 8, Section 8.7).

When you install BI 4.0, the following access levels are assigned to the "Universes" root folder:

▶ Public for the Everyone group

▶ Private for the Administrator group

So, if no access level is assigned to a user, these user access levels apply.

This security comes in addition to the security set through object access restriction.

> **Warning!**
>
> Universe object access level must not be confused with CMC rights access level (see Chapter 4, Section 4.8). Although they share the same name, these two access levels refer to completely different concepts:
>
> ▶ Object access levels are related to the universe and have been introduced in classic SAP BusinessObjects releases.
>
> ▶ Rights access levels are related to CMC rights and have been introduced in classic Crystal Reports releases.

7.8   Managing Object Access Levels

The previous section described universe access level. In this section, we explain how to define object access levels in Universe Design Tool and users and groups' access levels in the CMC.

7.8.1 Defining Object Access Levels in Universe Design Tool

Follow these steps to define an object access level:

1. Open your universe in Universe Design Tool.

2. In the universe, select an object.

3. Right-click this object and select OBJECT PROPERTIES or select EDIT • OBJECT PROPERTIES in the menu bar. The EDIT PROPERTIES OF <OBJECT NAME> dialog box opens.

4. Click the ADVANCED tab.

5. In the SECURITY ACCESS LEVEL section, use the dropdown list to select the access level value, as shown in Figure 7.22.

6. Click OK to close the EDIT PROPERTIES OF <OBJECT NAME> dialog box.

7. Repeat these steps for all objects to modify.

8. Save your universe and export it in the CMS repository (see Section 7.3.4).

Figure 7.22 Advanced Tab for Selecting Object Access Level

7.8.2 Defining User Access Levels in CMC

To define a user or a group access level for a universe or a universes folder, follow these steps:

1. Log on to the CMC.

2. Click the UNIVERSES tab in order to access the universes' page.

3. Select the universe or the universes folder.

4. Right-click it and, in the contextual menu, select UNIVERSE SECURITY or, in the toolbar, select ACTIONS • UNIVERSE SECURITY. The UNIVERSE SECURITY panel, which is shown in Figure 7.23, opens. It lists the users and groups that are assigned an access level for this universe or folder. The NET SECURITY column displays for users and groups the aggregated access level for this user, by computing inheritance.

5. If the user or group is not listed, follow these additional steps:

   ▶ Click the ADD button to display the AVAILABLE USERS/GROUPS list.

   ▶ Select the user or group, then click the >> button to move the selected user or group into the SELECTED USERS/GROUPS.

   ▶ Click OK. The user or group is added to the list, with the default Public value.

6. Select the access level value in the dropdown list in the OBJECT LEVEL SECURITY column.

7. Click the UPDATE button to save your changes; otherwise your changes are not saved when you close the UNIVERSE SECURITY panel.

8. Click the cross icon in the UNIVERSE SECURITY panel header to close it.

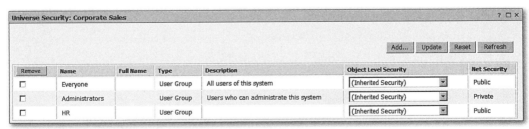

Remove	Name	Full Name	Type	Description	Object Level Security		Net Security
☐	Everyone		User Group	All users of this system	(Inherited Security)	▾	Public
☐	Administrators		User Group	Users who can administrate this system	(Inherited Security)	▾	Private
☐	HR		User Group		(Inherited Security)	▾	Public

Figure 7.23 Universe Security Panel for Selecting User Access Level

7.8.3   Editing User Access Levels in CMC

Follow these steps to modify an access level explicitly assigned to a user or a group for a universe or a folder:

1. In the CMC, open the UNIVERSE SECURITY panel for this universe or this folder as described in Section 7.8.2.

2. In the OBJECT LEVEL SECURITY column, if the value is not (INHERITED SECURITY) for this user or group, it means that the access level is explicitly assigned to the user or group. You can select a different value from this dropdown menu.

3. Click this UPDATE button. The effective value is updated in the NET SECURITY column.

4. Click the cross icon in the UNIVERSE SECURITY panel header to close it.

> **Note**
>
> The UNIVERSE SECURITY panel displays access levels explicitly assigned to user or group or inherited. If the access level is inherited, it is displayed as (INHERITED SECURITY) in the OBJECT LEVEL SECURITY column and it is not possible to directly edit it. You must edit this access level from the group or folder it is explicitly assigned to.

7.8.4   Removing User Access Levels in CMC

Follow these steps to remove an access level explicitly assigned to a user or a group for a universe or a folder:

1. In the CMC, open the UNIVERSE SECURITY panel for this universe as described in Section 7.8.2.

2. In the left column, below the REMOVE button, select the checkbox for every user or group to remove his access level.

3. Click the REMOVE button. Access levels are removed for the selected users and groups. They are no longer displayed in the list of users and groups that have an access level for this universe.

4. Click the cross icon in the UNIVERSE SECURITY panel header to close it.

> **Note**
>
> The Universe Security panel displays access levels explicitly assigned to user or group or inherited. If the access level is inherited, it is displayed as (Inherited Security) in the Object Level Security column and it is not possible to directly remove this access level. You must remove this access level from the group or folder it is explicitly assigned to.

7.9   Summary

Historically, universe designers created universes with the metadata design tool called Universe Design Tool. These universes expose an easy-to-use abstraction of the database through a high-level layer based on objects related to business use. You can secure and control data returned by universes through the following security concepts:

▶ WHERE clauses can be used to filter data returned by the query. Such WHERE clauses are supported in a table auto-join, an object's WHERE clause, or a mandatory filter.

▶ @VARIABLE function, to customize the query sent to the database

▶ Access restrictions, which offer different options:

  ▶ Connection overload, which replaces the universe connection by another one

  ▶ Controls and SQL parameters overload, which replaces some universe parameters

  ▶ Objects, which deny objects and classes exposed by the universe and returning data

  ▶ Rows restriction, which filters data retrieved from the database with a WHERE clause added at query time

  ▶ Table mapping, which replaces a table with another table

▶ Object and user access level, to define some confidentiality level to object and user. User can see objects only if their access level is lower or equal to his own access level.

While Universe Design Tool can effectively be used in BI 4.0—as discussed in this chapter—we recommend that you use its successor, Information Design Tool, for creating new universe and other projects. In Chapter 8, we turn our attention to Information Design Tool and its important features, such as semantic layer security.

Information Design Tool extends the Universe Design Tool security concepts. It introduces new security capabilities with security profiles, the Security Editor to administer them, and user attributes.

8 Universe Security in Information Design Tool

BI 4.0 contains the first version of Information Design Tool, the successor to Universe Design Tool for metadata design. This new application extends the universes with new capabilities and supports the following new features:

▶ *Multi-source universe*, to query data from different relational databases

▶ *Multidimensional universe*, to take full advantage of OLAP databases

▶ Improved user interface, to create universes more efficiently

▶ Separation between authoring and consumption workflows

However, the same concepts popularized by Universe Design Tool are still valid, as with the security model: Its bases are similar to the Universe Design Tool security model, but it has been extended to comply with new Information Design Tool features and to provide more capabilities.

After an introduction to universes in Information Design Tool, this chapter describes how to secure these universes and touches on the following topics:

▶ The user of filters in table auto-join and object definition

▶ Data security profiles, which are the equivalent of access restrictions

▶ The business security profile, which is a new security concept enforced by universes created in Information Design Tool

▶ The Security Editor's management of these security profiles

▶ Object access level, which is identical to Universe Design Tool object access level

▶ User attributes, which can be used to define new parameters for users; these parameters can be filled from an external source

Notice that these concepts are similar to the ones in Universe Design Tool; Appendix A offers a comparison of these two tools.

8.1   Introduction to New Universe

In Information Design Tool, there is a strong distinction between authored resources and published resources.

When you create a universe, you must author the different resources that make up this universe—the database connection, the data foundation (if the universe is relational), and the business layer.

To generate a universe that can be consumed by the reporting tools, you must merge these different resources. This operation, called *publication*, allows you to generate and save this universe locally or in a CMS repository. The reverse operation, called *retrieval*, can be used to extract the database connection, the data foundation, and the business layer from the published universe. If the universe is retrieved from a CMS repository, then a connection shortcut is generated instead of a connection.

Because Chapter 6 describes the connections and their shortcuts, we quickly review the data foundation and the business layer before turning our attention to securing them.

8.1.1   Data Foundation

Data foundations are needed only for relational universes; they do not exist for multidimensional universes. As shown in Figure 8.1, a data foundation contains the relational schema used by the universe: tables, joins, contexts, alias tables, derived tables, and so on.

Furthermore, a data foundation can be multi-source and be linked to different connections or data sources in order to query different relational databases.

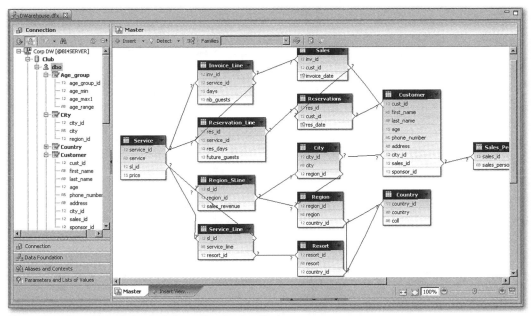

Figure 8.1 Data Foundation in Information Design Tool

A data foundation can be reused by different business layers. This feature has the following advantages:

▶ When you create a new universe, you can reuse the data foundation of an existing universe that uses the same databases.

▶ Any changes in the data foundation can be shared by all business layers created from this data foundation. They are taken into consideration by the universes when you republish them.

8.1.2 Business Layer

The business layer contains the list of objects exposed by the universe and displayed in reporting tools' query panel. The business layer contains the universe's Semantic Layer, as shown in Figure 8.2. Objects are organized in folders—previously called classes in Universe Design Tool.

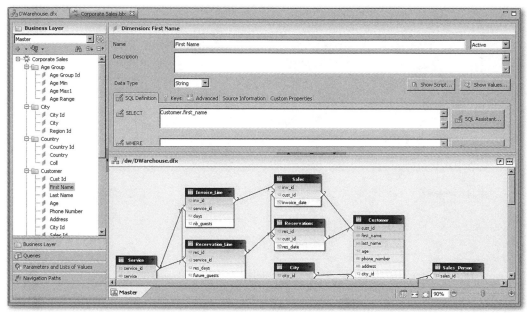

Figure 8.2 Business Layer in Information Design Tool

The business layer exists for both relational and multidimensional universes. For relational universes, the business layer must be created from a data foundation. This data foundation can be monosource or multi-source. In the case of a multi-source data foundation, the resulting universe is able to query multiple databases. In both cases, the business layer considers the data foundation to be a schema containing tables and joins, whatever databases they are coming from.

For multidimensional universes, the business layer relies only on an OLAP connection. When the business layer is created, the metadata are retrieved from the OLAP database and are used to generate the multidimensional objects of the business layer. In multidimensional universes, the business layer supports objects that take advantage of the multidimensional metadata: hierarchies, levels, and member sets.

In the business layer, you can define *views*. A view is a subset of business layer objects and folders, which generally have a meaning together. By default, a business layer has only one view, the *master view*, containing all the business layer's objects and folders.

These views introduce two functional features:

▶ When you edit a business layer in Information Design Tool, you can select a view. Only the folders and objects it contains are displayed, which allows you to focus only on them. In some cases, views can be used to replace linked universes that are no longer supported in Information Design Tool.

▶ When a user creates a query in the query panel, he can select the view and thus its objects to display. Information Design Tool allows you to secure these views and thus to grant or deny your users the ability to see these views (see Section 8.5.1).

8.1.3 Security Model

As in Universe Design Tool, you can secure the universe by defining a WHERE clause defined at table, object, folder, or universe level in order to filter the data retrieved from the database.

If the universe is published in the CMS repository, then it takes advantage of the rights framework (see Chapter 4 for an in-depth explanation of rights frameworks) and of the following universe security concepts:

▶ *Security profiles*, which can be seen as the evolution of Universe Design Tool's access restrictions. Security profiles define security at two different levels:

  ▶ A data security profile replicates the behavior of classic universes' access restrictions, except the objects access restriction, whose security is now managed in business security profile. A data security profile handles security related to database schemas, connections, and some universe parameters and can be seen as low-level security.

  ▶ A business security profile secures objects defined in the business layer. It also includes the behavior of classic universes' objects access restriction.

▶ Object access level, similar to the ones you can set in Universe Design Tool.

▶ *User attributes*, which are a new feature introduced in BI 4.0 FP3.

In the next few sections we cover these security concepts, beginning with defining the WHERE clauses and filters and then moving on to the various relevant security profiles.

8.2 Defining WHERE Clauses and Filters in Information Design Tool

The same techniques described in Chapter 7 to secure universe in Universe Design Tool also apply to Information Design Tool. These techniques rely on the use of a filter defined on a table, an object, a folder, or the universe. This filter is added to the generated query if the associated table, object, folder, or universe is used.

- ▶ Table auto-join: Used to add a WHERE clause to the generated query when a specific table is used in a query. This method can be used only for a relational universe and not for a multidimensional universe.

- ▶ Object filters: Used to add a WHERE clause to the generated query when a specific object is used in the query. If the universe is relational, the WHERE clause must be expressed in SQL; if the universe is multidimensional, it must be expressed in MDX.

- ▶ Mandatory filters: Used to force a filter defined in the business layer to be always applied (*universe filter*) or to be applied when the query uses one object of a specified folder (*folder filter*). Note that you can create two types of filters in a business layer:

  - ▶ *Native filter*, which is defined by using an SQL expression. A native filter cannot be created for multidimensional universe.

  - ▶ *Business filter*, which is defined by using some objects of the business layer.

  Both filters can be used to define a mandatory filter.

These techniques are easy to define and are defined in the universe itself. They always apply and can be customized by using the @VARIABLE function (see Chapter 7, Section 7.1).

As for Universe Design Tool, if the universe has been published locally, even if it has been secured with such a filter, it remains vulnerable. It is easy for someone who has access to this universe to retrieve it with Information Design Tool and edit the corresponding data foundation and/or business layer in order to remove the filter and republish the universe. The resulting universe can be used to query unfiltered data.

If the universe is published in the CMS repository, editing the universe can be denied by setting a security right (see Chapter 5, Section 5.12.2). In addition, if the universe is saved in the CMS, then these filters can use @VARIABLE function and variables associated with the CMS session to implement security. These variables can be:

► The predefined ones supported by Information Design Tool (for example, BOUSER)

► The user attributes that you define yourself (see Section 8.8)

These filters can be used to secure data retrieved from the database. Let's review how to define them in Information Design Tool and how to publish the universe in the CMS repository in order to prevent someone from removing them.

8.2.1 Defining an Auto-join in Information Design Tool

You can define an auto-join on a table by following these steps:

1. Open your data foundation.

2. Select a table and the column to filter.

3. Right-click this column and select INSERT FILTER. The EDIT JOIN dialog box opens.

   In the EXPRESSION text field, type the filter to apply to this column. For example, to filter rows and display only values for a specific tag saved in the column country_id in the table Country, type

   Country.country_id = 'FR'

4. Click OK to close the EDIT JOIN dialog. In the table, a filter icon appears in front of the column name, as shown in Figure 8.3.

5. Click the SAVE button to save the data foundation's changes.

Figure 8.3 Country Table with Auto-Join Defined on country_id Column

8.2.2 Defining a WHERE Clause on an Object

You can define the WHERE clause of an object by following these steps:

1. Open the universe's business layer in Information Design Tool.

2. Select a business object by clicking it to open its editor.

3. In the WHERE text field, type the WHERE clause to add to the SQL generated to retrieve this object data. For example, as shown in Figure 8.4, if you want to filter the values returned by the object Country Id, by a specific tag, type

   `Country.country_id = 'FR'`

   You can also click the SQL ASSISTANT button to open the SQL EXPRESSION EDITOR ON <…> dialog box.

   ▶ This dialog box allows you to type your SQL and offers a list of available tables, columns, classes, objects, operators, or functions. You can click on them to directly insert them into the SQL you type.

   ▶ Click OK to close this dialog box. The SQL you have typed in this dialog box is copied in the WHERE text field.

4. Click OK to close the EDIT PROPERTIES OF <…> dialog box.

5. Click the SAVE button to save the universe's changes.

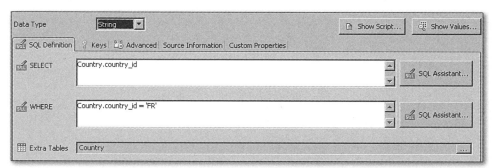

Figure 8.4 WHERE Clause for Object in Relational Business Layer

8.2.3 Defining a Mandatory Filter

You can create a mandatory filter on a relational or a multidimensional universe by following these steps:

1. Open the universe's business layer in Information Design Tool.

2. Select the folder where the filter will be created.

3. Right-click the folder and, in the contextual menu bar, select NEW • FILTER. A new filter is added into the folder. Its FILTER PROPERTIES pane is opened in the right side of the business layer editor.

4. Fill in the NAME and DESCRIPTION text fields.

5. Select the NATIVE or BUSINESS radio button, as shown in Figure 8.5, depending on the filter type you want to create:

   ▶ Native, available only if the universe is relational: to define the filter using an SQL expression. Type the SQL expression in the `WHERE` text field.

   ▶ Business: to define the filter using objects of the business layer. Click the EDIT FILTER button to open the EDIT BUSINESS FILTER panel. Use this panel to create your filter by selecting and dropping objects and setting the values to filter.

6. Click the PROPERTIES tab.

7. Check the USE FILTER AS MANDATORY IN QUERY checkbox.

8. Choose the APPLY ON UNIVERSE or APPLY ON FOLDER radio button, depending on the mandatory filter you want to create.

9. Check the APPLY ON LIST OF VALUES checkbox to apply this filter when computing list of values as well.

10. In the toolbar, click the SAVE button to save the business layer's changes.

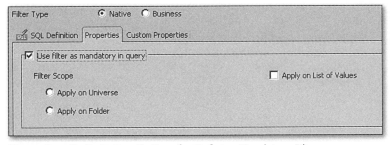

Figure 8.5 Radio Button Options for Defining Mandatory Filter

8.2.4 Publishing a Universe in CMS Repository

You must merge the different resources you have authored in Information Design Tool to generate a universe that the reporting tools can use. In order to publish this universe in a CMS repository, run the following steps:

1. Select the business layer in the Local Projects view.

2. Right-click this business layer and, in the contextual menu, select PUBLISH • TO A REPOSITORY.... The PUBLISH UNIVERSE dialog box opens.

3. You can scan the data foundation and the business layer to look for errors. If you do not need to run the integrity check, click the NEXT button, but if you need to run this optional step:

   ▸ Select some rules in the RULES tree by clicking the checkbox in front of them.

   ▸ Click CHECK INTEGRITY to run the scan. Once it is completed, any found errors and warnings are displayed in the dialog box.

   ▸ When you have reviewed these messages, click the NEXT button to continue the publication or click CANCEL to cancel the publication so you can correct any issues if needed.

4. Select the folder in the CMS repository where the universe is saved.

5. Click the FINISH button. The universe is published and a success message is displayed. The published universe is named from the business layer's name.

6. Click the CLOSE button to close the PUBLISH UNIVERSE dialog box.

8.3   Security Profiles

Recall that in Information Design Tool, data security profiles and business security profiles are an extension of Universe Design Tool's access restrictions. Security profiles can be seen as a super-set of access restrictions:

▸ The concepts are similar and access restrictions can be mapped into data and business security profiles. However, security profiles offer some new capabilities.

▸ You can create data security profiles only for relational universes, whereas you can create business security profiles for both relational and multidimensional universes, as shown in Figure 8.6 and Figure 8.7.

This section details common characteristics of security profiles; Section 8.4 and Section 8.5 focus on data and business security profiles, respectively.

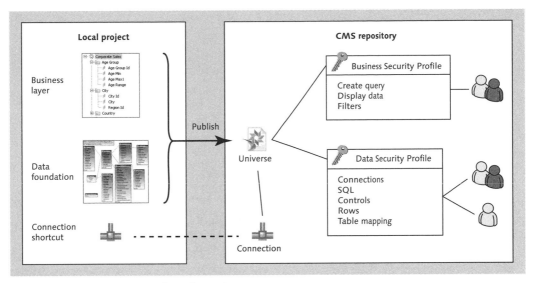

Figure 8.6 Security Overview for Relational Universe

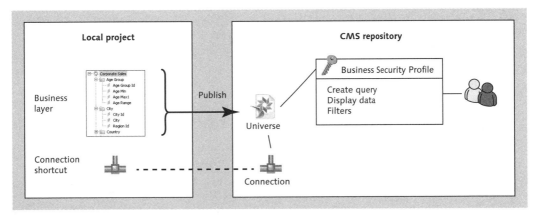

Figure 8.7 Security Overview for Multidimensional Universe

8.3.1 Assigned Users and Groups

Data and business security profiles can only be created once the universe has been published in a CMS repository. By default, no data security profiles and no business security profiles are created for this universe or assigned to users or groups. The universe is not considered secured and no security profile applies.

You can secure the universe by creating data and business security profiles and by assigning them to users or groups. Remember that a data or business security profile assigned to a user applies to the *user*, and a data or business security profile assigned to a group applies to *all users and groups it contains*.

A data or business security profile can be attached to only one universe and applies only to this universe. It is possible to assign several security profiles to the same user or group.

In the CMS repository, security profiles are created and stored as InfoObjects linked to the universe they secure. They are also linked to the users and groups they are assigned to. Thus, these security profiles and their assigned users and groups are not changed if the universe is modified and republished.

Identically, a change in a data or business security profile definition does not modify its assigned users or groups.

> **Warning!**
>
> As for Universe Design Tool, in order to compute the list of security profiles that apply to a user, this user must be given the "View objects" right for all groups from which he can inherit security profiles. If a user cannot see the groups he belongs to, he cannot get the list of security profiles that apply to him.

The next section details how aggregation is computed when several data or business security profiles must be applied to the same user or group.

8.3.2   Aggregations

As for access restrictions (see Chapter 7, Section 7.5), several data and/or business security profiles of the same universe can be applied to the same user. Several different cases can occur:

▶ *Parent-child* (Figure 8.8, ❶): The user belongs to a group. Both the user and the groups are assigned a data and/or business security profile.

▶ *Multiple-parents* (Figure 8.8, ❷): The user belongs to different groups that are assigned a data and/or business security profile.

▶ *Multiple-assignments* (Figure 8.8, ❸): Several data and/or business security profiles are assigned to the same user or group.

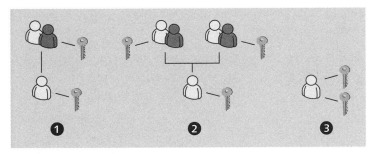

Figure 8.8 Various Aggregation Cases

These aggregations rules depend on the data security profile and the business security profile type. There are two main aggregation methods:

▶ Priority, used to aggregate some data security profiles: Priority is defined at the data security profile level. This priority is absolute and applies to all data security profiles. For security profile aggregated by priority, the value to apply is always the one defined in the data security profile with the higher priority, even if one or several data security profiles are directly applied to a user.

▶ The AND, ANDOR, or OR algorithms and their adaptations: These will be described in the next section.

When a security profile type supports several aggregation options, you can select one to define how security profiles are aggregated.

8.3.3   AND, ANDOR, and OR Aggregation

In Universe Design Tool, the AND and ANDOR algorithms define how security is aggregated for rows access restrictions. Information Design Tool extends these algorithms in two ways:

▶ By adding a new algorithm that uses only the OR operator for all possible inheritances and aggregations. From a security point of view, this algorithm, called OR, is less restrictive than the AND and ANDOR algorithms.

▶ By using these algorithms to aggregate more security types: business security profiles, controls and SQL data security profiles.

The AND, ANDOR, and OR algorithms are also respectively called "Very restrictive," "Moderately restrictive," and "Less restrictive" algorithms.

These algorithms are generic and can be used to aggregate different types of security profiles. Specification is done through two operators:

▶ A restrictive one, which requires the two security profiles to be enforced. Depending on the security profiles type, the actual operator to apply is AND, MIN, or intersection.

▶ A permissive one, which requires at least one security profile to be applied. Depending on the security profiles type, the actual operator to apply is OR, MAX, or union.

To compute the effective value of any parameter that can be modified by a security profile, rewind the group inheritance tree for the user. If a security profile modifies this parameter, the following scenarios apply:

▶ In parent-child (profiles inherited from one parent to a child) or multiple-assignment (profiles assigned to the same user or group) cases:

  ▶ If the aggregation is "Very restrictive (AND)" or "Moderately restrictive (ANDOR)," then the aggregation operator is a restrictive one.

  ▶ If the aggregation is "Less restrictive (OR)," then the aggregation operator is a permissive one.

▶ In multiple-parents (profiles that aggregate from different groups at same level) case:

  ▶ If the aggregation is "Very restrictive (AND)," then the aggregation operator is a restrictive one.

  ▶ If the aggregation is "Moderately restrictive (ANDOR)" or "Less restrictive (OR)," then the aggregation operator is a permissive one.

Example

In the group inheritance model depicted in Figure 8.9, for any parameter secured by security profiles, the aggregated value for user U is:

▶ $R(U)$ AND $R(G_1)$ AND $R(G_{11})$ AND $R(G_{12})$ AND $R(G_2)$ AND $R(G_{21})$, for the "Very restrictive (AND)" algorithm.

▶ $R(U)$ AND [($R(G_1)$ AND ($R(G_{11})$ OR $R(G_{12})$)) OR ($R(G_2)$ AND $R(G_{21})$)], for the "Moderately restrictive (ANDOR)" algorithm.

▶ $R(U)$ OR $R(G_1)$ OR $R(G_{11})$ OR $R(G_{12})$ OR $R(G_2)$ OR $R(G_{21})$, for the "Less restrictive (OR)" algorithm.

$R(X)$ returns the value set for the parameter by the security profile assigned to the user or group X. AND represents the restrictive operator, whereas OR is the permissive operator.

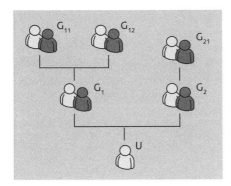

Figure 8.9 Inheritance Example

8.3.4 Consumption

Once the effective data and business security profiles that must apply to a user have been computed from aggregation options, they must be applied. In Information Design Tool, security profiles apply depending on how you run a query:

▶ In authoring mode, when you run a query directly from the business layer editor, data and business security profiles do not apply.

▶ Information Design Tool allows you to run secured queries (see Section 8.10). When you run a query on top of a published universe from the Published Resources or Security Editor view, the query takes into consideration the data and business security profiles that apply to the user whose account has been used to open the CMS session.

When a reporting tool uses a universe to query data from database, security profiles are applied for any request to the database, at query time:

▶ During the query itself

▶ When retrieving list of values, if the table on which the rows restriction is based is involved in the computation of the list of values

8.4 Data Security Profiles

Data security profiles can be created only for relational universes. It is not possible to create them for multidimensional universes.

In Information Design Tool, relational universes rely on a data foundation that is the database abstraction used by universes.

Data foundation concepts are secured by data security profiles that cover almost the same concepts and behaviors as Universe Design Tool's access restrictions, except objects access restriction, whose equivalent is supported by business security profile (see Section 8.5):

- Connections data security profile, similar to the connection access restriction
- Controls data security profile, similar to the controls access restriction
- SQL data security profile, similar to the SQL access restriction
- Rows data security profile, similar to the rows access restriction
- Tables data security profile, similar to the table mapping access restriction

Furthermore, they have been adapted to take multi-source universes into consideration.

> **Warning!**
>
> The rows and tables data security profiles do not apply if the user has directly edited the generated SQL, for example, in Web Intelligence. For this reason, it is important to secure the ability to edit SQL in Web Intelligence through the "Query script: Enable editing (SQL, MDX, ...)" right or the document "Edit script" right (see Chapter 5, Section 5.19).

8.4.1 Connections

The connections data security profile is used to define alternate secured connections for a user. When this user runs a query on top of the universe, the connection defined at data security profile is used instead of the one defined by default for this universe.

To select the replacement connection, you can drill into the CMS connection folders. When designing security, you must be connected and authenticated to the CMS repository. Thus, CMS rights apply to you: You can see only the connections for which you have the "View objects" right granted.

This data security profile applies only to relational universes. Only relational connections can be selected as alternate connections. If the universe is a multi-source universe, the connections data security profile allows the overload of each individual connection used in the multi-source universe.

A connection can be replaced only by a connection of the same type:

▶ If the original connection is an SAP NetWeaver BW data source, then only an SAP NetWeaver BW data source can replace it.

▶ If the original connection is an SAS data source, then only an SAS data source can replace it.

▶ If the original connection is a relational connection of another type, then any relational connections *except* SAP NetWeaver BW and SAS can replace it.

Aggregation

If one connection can be replaced by several connections data security profiles, then the replacement connection that applies is the one defined by the data security profile with the highest priority (see Section 8.3.2).

For multi-source universe, each replacement connection is computed independently of the other connections.

8.4.2 Controls

In relational universes, the controls data security profile is used to override some parameters defined at the universe level. Users and groups who have been assigned this controls data security profile use these parameters instead of the ones defined in the universe.

These parameters are related to time-outs and limits when retrieving data from databases. These parameters are described in Table 8.1.

Parameter Name	Description
Limit size of result set to	This option stops the query once it has returned the specified number of rows.
Limit execution time to	This option stops the query once it exceeds the specified number of minutes.
Warn if cost estimates exceeds	This parameter is used only by Web Intelligence for Teradata databases. If this option is selected, a confirmation message is displayed before a notification that the query may last more than the specified number of minutes.

Table 8.1 Parameters Covered by Controls Data Security Profile

These parameters are typically used to secure the reporting servers and make sure they do not freeze by limiting the set of data they have to handle. In the universe, these parameters are defined in the business layer.

This data security profile can be used if you want to define some conservative values for a universe in order to prevent most users from downgrading the system but extend these limits for a specific set of users.

Aggregation

The following are possible aggregation options for controls business security profile:

▶ Priority: the value of the parameter is the value in the data security profile with the highest priority is used. This is the default aggregation option.

▶ The "Very restrictive (AND)," "Moderately restrictive (ANDOR)," and "Less restrictive (OR)" algorithms, described in Section 8.3.3. In these algorithms, to aggregate the same option defined in two data security profiles:

  ▶ If the parameter is disabled in both security profiles, then the aggregated parameter is also disabled.

  ▶ If the parameter is enabled in both security profiles, then the aggregated parameter is also enabled. The value for the value of the parameter is the smaller value for a restrictive aggregation and the greater value for a permissive aggregation.

  ▶ If the parameter is enabled in one security profile and disabled in the other, then the aggregated parameter is also enabled if the aggregation is restrictive and disabled if the aggregation is permissive.

The aggregation you choose for controls data security profile is also the aggregation of SQL data security profile (see Section 8.4.3).

8.4.3 SQL

The SQL data security profile is used to override some parameters defined at the universe level. Users and groups who have been assigned this SQL data security profile use these parameters instead of the ones defined at the universe level. Table 8.2 describes these parameters, which are related to the operations that are allowed when generating the SQL query. Because SQL data security profiles are similar to SQL access restrictions, the parameters they enforce are almost identical (see Chapter 7, Table 7.2).

Parameter Name	Description
Allow use of sub-queries	Enables the creation of sub-queries when defining filters in the query panel. If this option is denied, then the icon to add a sub-query is disabled in the query panel.
Allow use of union, intersect and minus operators	Enables combination of queries using data set operators (union, intersect, and minus) to obtain one set of results. If this option is denied, then the button to add combined queries is disabled in the query panel.
Allow complex operands in query panel	Enables the use of the Both and Except operators when defining query filters in query panel. If this option is denied, then these two operators are not displayed in the available operators.
Multiple SQL statements for each context	Enables a query to be split into multiple SQL statements if it contains objects from different contexts. If this option is denied, an error message is displayed when queries containing objects from different contexts are run.
Multiple SQL statements for each measure	Forces a query to be split into multiple SQL queries if it contains measures based on different tables.
Allow Cartesian products	If you choose to prevent a Cartesian product, then an error message is raised if the generated query contains a Cartesian product.

Table 8.2 Parameters Covered by SQL Data Security Profile

In the universe, these parameters are defined in the business layer, except "Multiple SQL statements for each context" and "Allow Cartesian products," which must be defined in the data foundation.

Aggregation

The following are the possible aggregation options for SQL data security profile:

► Priority: The value of the parameter in the data security profile with the highest priority is used. This is the default aggregation option.

▶ The "Very restrictive (AND)," "Moderately restrictive (ANDOR)," and "Less restrictive (OR)" algorithms, described in Section 8.3.3. In these algorithms, to aggregate the same option defined in two data security profiles:

   ▶ If the parameter is similar in both security profiles, then the aggregated parameter has also the same value.

   ▶ If the parameter is enabled in one security profile and disabled in the other one, then the aggregated parameter is enabled if the aggregation is permissive or disabled if the aggregation is restrictive.

For the "Allow Cartesian Products" parameter, the aggregation rules are:

▶ The aggregation of two "Allow" values returns "Allow."

▶ The aggregation of two "Prevent" values returns "Prevent."

▶ The aggregation of "Allow" and "Prevent" values returns "Allow" if the aggregation is permissive and "Prevent" if the aggregation is restrictive.

The aggregation you choose for SQL data security profile is also the aggregation of controls data security profile (see Section 8.4.2).

8.4.4 Rows

Rows data security profiles are used to associate a WHERE clause with a table. This WHERE clause is added to the SQL generated for the query if this table is used in the query. Through this WHERE clause, it is possible to filter the data retrieved from the database and thus prevent a user from seeing unauthorized data.

If no rows data security profile is defined for any user, no WHERE clause is added to the queries generated. The data retrieved by the query are not filtered. If a rows data security profile is assigned to a user, then the queries are post fixed with the WHERE clause. The data retrieved by the queries are filtered by this clause and only data that comply with this filter are seen by the user. For other users who do not have any rows data security profile assigned, they continue to see data without the filter applied.

For example, a [WHERE Country.country_id = 'FR'] rows data security profile associated with the Country table filters and returns only lines that fulfill the WHERE condition when accessing the Country table.

As in Universe Design Tool, this security is widely used to secure universes.

The SQL request that can be used in the WHERE clause can be very flexible and very complex:

▶ It can reference and query another table containing some security definition.

▶ It supports built-in Information Design Tool functions, such as @VARIABLE. In addition, @VARIABLE function now supports user attributes (see Section 8.9.1).

In the first releases of BI 4.0, you could not select the alias and derived tables as the table to trigger the WHERE clause of the rows data security profile. Since BI 4.0 SP4, it is possible to select the alias and derived tables as this conditional table. Calculated columns are not supported and so cannot be used in the WHERE clause of a rows data security profile.

In a multi-source universe, the WHERE clause can reference tables in any databases used in it.

Aggregation

The possible options to aggregate the WHERE clauses triggered by the same table by rows data security profile are the "Very restrictive (AND)" (the default one), "Moderately restrictive (ANDOR)," and "Less restrictive (OR)" algorithms, described in Section 8.3.3.

In these algorithms, the WHERE clauses are aggregated in the generated SQL:

▶ For the restrictive aggregation, with the AND operator

▶ For the permissive aggregation, with the OR operator

Once the rows restrictions that apply to the same tables are aggregated, the resulting rows restrictions are all aggregated with the AND operator.

A rows data security profile and filters business security profile (see Section 8.5.3) both generate the WHERE clause to filter the query. If both a rows data security profile and filters business security profile are applied, these two resulting WHERE clause are aggregated with the AND operator.

8.4.5 Tables

Tables data security profiles allow you to define a replacement table instead of a table defined in the data foundation. When a query is run against the database, any occurrence of this table is replaced by its corresponding replacement table in the generated SQL.

When you define the replacement table, you must give the name of an actual table. As opposed to Universe Design Tool, it is no longer possible to enter an expression (based on @VARIABLE, for example) for the name of this replacement table.

To set the owner and qualifier of the table, you must explicitly enter them as such and not as part of the table name. In Universe Design Tool, it is easy to get mislead if the table name contains a dot in its name.

In a multi-source universe, the replacement table can be a table from any databases used by the multi-source universe. It is not possible to select an alias table as a replacement table or to select a derived table as a source or replacement table.

In the first releases of BI 4.0, alias tables could not be selected as the original table. As of BI 4.0 SP4, this is possible.

Aggregation

If one table is overloaded by several tables data security profiles, then the replacement table to apply is the one defined by the data security profile with the higher priority (see Section 8.3.2).

In a universe, several tables can be secured by tables data security profile. In this case, each replacement table is computed independently of the other tables.

8.5   Business Security Profiles

Business security profiles secure different concepts in the business layer. They are common in relational and multidimensional universes.

Consider the following different business security profile types:

- *Create query*: To grant or deny views, objects, and folders in the query panel
- *Display data*: To grant or deny objects that can actually retrieve data from the database
- *Filters*: To filter data returned by the query
  - For a relational universe, data are filtered by a predefined condition

> ▸ For a multidimensional universe, data are filtered by a member set on a hierarchy

Display data and filters business security profiles actually secure the data retrieved from the database, whereas a create query business security profile secures the metadata in the query panel.

Create query and display data business security profiles are both the equivalent of Universe Design Tool objects access restriction for classic universe. But an objects access restriction denies objects at both metadata and data level, and it is not possible to distinguish between the two behaviors:

▸ The object is available in the query panel.

▸ The object can retrieve data from the database.

With a business security profile, the two concepts can be independently secured in order to support the following scenario:

▸ A designer can create a query, but he is not allowed to query the data behind.

▸ A user can refresh data in reports, but he is not allowed to select this object in the query panel, to create new queries with this object, for example.

Because the business layer is common to all universes, business security profiles are common to all universes except filters business security profiles, whose definitions are different for relational and multidimensional universes.

In the next sections, we detail each type of business security profile and how it can be used.

8.5.1 Create Query

This business security profile secures the business layer views and objects users can access when they create a query in the query panel.

Authoring

When you create a create query data security profile, you can independently secure two levels:

▸ View: Defines whether a business layer view is displayed in the query panel's view list and whether the user can select it. You can explicitly grant or explicitly deny any view (including the master view).

- ▸ You can also define whether all views are by default denied or granted, through the "All views" shortcut.

- ▸ If the master view is defined as hidden, then it cannot be selected in the business security profile (it is not displayed in the view list).

▸ Object: Defines whether an object is displayed in the query panel and whether a user can select it to create a query. You can explicitly grant or explicitly deny any object of the business layer (dimension, attribute, measure, filter, member set, folder, analysis dimension, and hierarchy, and so on) except level and calculated measure.

- ▸ It is not possible to secure an individual level. All levels must be granted or denied as a whole through the hierarchy.

- ▸ You can also define whether all objects are by default denied or granted, through the "All objects" shortcut.

- ▸ It is possible to select hidden and deprecated objects, but if the object is hidden, then it is not displayed in the query panel, even if it has been granted by a business security profile.

All objects and views available in the business layer can be selected in the create query business security profile. There is no security applied to check whether the user is allowed to see and select them in the definition of a business security profile.

Default Values

If no create query business security profile is assigned to any user or group, then no create query security is applied. Users can see all objects and all views in the query panel for this universe. If a create query business security profile is assigned to a user, all views become by default denied to this user by default. Then you can explicitly grant some views in the create query business security profile.

By default, because all views are denied when a business security profile is created, the user cannot see the objects in these views. But if a view is granted, then all objects it contains are granted by default: A user is allowed to see all of them, except the ones you may explicitly deny in the create query business security profile.

Other users who do not have any create query business security profile that applies to them (directly assigned or inherited) keep seeing all objects and views in the query panel.

When you create a business security profile, it is important to grant some objects and views for both create query and display data business security profiles. By default, this new business security profile denies all objects and all views. Thus, unless this is the expected behavior, any user and group assigned this business security profile sees an empty query panel and cannot retrieve data from the database.

In a create query business security profile, a value set to "All views" defines the default value for all views. This value can be explicitly modified for other views:

► If in the same create query business security profile, "All views" is granted and some views are denied, then this security profile grants all views except the ones explicitly denied.

► If in the same create query business security profile, "All views" is denied and some views are granted, then this security profile denies all views except the ones explicitly granted.

In a create query business security profile, a value set to "All objects" defines the default value for all objects. This value can be explicitly modified for other objects:

► If in the same create query business security profile, "All objects" is granted and some objects are denied, then this security profile grants all objects except the ones explicitly denied. However, if these objects are contained, the objects they contain are also denied and are not displayed in the query panel.

► If in the same create query business security profile, "All objects" is denied and some objects are granted, then this security profile denies all objects except the ones explicitly granted. However, to grant an object, you need to explicitly grant its parent objects until the root folder as well.

Example

A business layer contains the following folder hierarchy: FOLDER1 • FOLDER2 • MYDIMENSION.

If "All objects" is denied, then to grant MYDIMENSION, you need to explicitly grant the two folders and the object:

► FOLDER1

► FOLDER1 • FOLDER2

► FOLDER1 • FOLDER2 • MYDIMENSION

> **Example**
>
> If "All objects" is granted, then by denying FOLDER1, you also deny all the objects it contains (FOLDER2 and MyDimension).

Using "All views" or "All objects" avoids selecting explicitly all views or all objects. Furthermore, if the list of views or objects evolves, "All views" and "All objects" dynamically covers them.

Aggregation

The possible aggregation options for create query business security profile are the "Very restrictive (AND)" (the default one), "Moderately restrictive (OR)," and "Less restrictive (ANDOR)" algorithms, described in Section 8.3.3. The chosen aggregation is also the aggregation of display data business security profile.

In these algorithms, you use two operators:

▶ Objects and views *intersection*, for the restrictive aggregation (AND): An object or a view is granted if it is granted in both security profiles to aggregate or if it is granted in one but not specified in the other.

▶ Objects and views *union*, for the permissive aggregation (OR): An object or a view is granted if it is granted in one of the security profiles to aggregate or if it is granted in one but not specified in the other.

Query Panel Impact

The create query business security profile impacts only the query panel and the views and objects it displays.

The list of views available in the query panel is computed using the aggregation option since several create query business security profiles may set different values for this view. Each view is considered independently:

▶ If the value aggregated from all security profiles is granted, then the view is displayed in the query panel.

▶ If this aggregated value is denied, then the view is not displayed.

▶ If this aggregated value is not defined, then it is also considered denied and it is not displayed.

If all views are denied, then the user is not authorized to see any view—and, indirectly, any object—in the query panel. The list of objects available in the query panel is also computed using the aggregation option.

If the value aggregated from all security profiles is granted, then the object is displayed in the views that contain this object, if all its parent folders until the root folder are also granted. If one of its parents is effectively denied, then the object is not displayed.

If this aggregated value is denied or not defined, then the object is not displayed in the views that contain it.

As a consequence, the following scenarios arise after the aggregation of all create query security profiles:

▶ In a view, an object is displayed if:

  ▶ It belongs to this view.

  ▶ It is effectively granted.

  ▶ It is not hidden or deprecated in the business layer.

  ▶ All its parent folders till the root folder are also effectively granted.

▶ An object is not displayed if one of its parents is denied.

▶ If a container is set as denied, all objects and sub-containers below are denied, whatever their status is.

▶ An object granted in a view is not necessarily displayed in all views.

Example
View1 contains Object1, Object2 and Object3.
View2 contains Object1, Object4 and Object5.
View1 and View2 are granted:
▶ When View1 is selected, it lists Object1, Object2 and Object3, but not Object5.
▶ When View1 is selected, it lists Object1, Object4 and Object5, but not Object3.

8.5.2 Display Data

The create query business security profile seen in Section 8.5.1 secures the views and objects in the business layer that user can see in the query panel. A display data business security profile secures the actual data retrieved by the query.

The philosophy behind a display data business security profile is similar to the that of a create query business security profile, both in authoring workflows, default values, aggregation rules, and effectively granted objects computation.

Authoring

When creating a display data security profile, you can grant or deny objects of the business layer that retrieve data:

▶ Single objects: dimensions, attributes, measures, calculated measures, levels, calculated members, and named sets, but not levels and calculated measures

▶ Containers that may contain single objects or other containers: folders, analysis dimensions, and hierarchies

It is also possible to explicitly set no status, explicitly grant a status, or explicitly deny a status to "All objects" (itself a shortcut to represent all objects).

All objects from the business layer that return data can be selected in the display data business security profile. There is no security applied to check whether the user is allowed to see and select them in the definition of a display data business security profile.

Default Values

If no display data business security profile is defined for any user, no security is applied and user can see data from all objects. If a display data business security profile is assigned to a user, then all objects become by default denied to this user, except the ones granted in the display data business security profile. An empty display data business security profile denies all objects by default.

In a display data business security profile, a value set to "All objects" defines the default value for all objects. This value can be explicitly modified for other objects:

▶ If, in the display data query business security profile, "All objects" is granted and some objects are denied, then this security profile grants all objects except the ones explicitly denied. However, if these objects are container, the objects they contain are also denied and are not displayed in the query panel.

▶ If, in the same display data business security profile, "All objects" is denied and some objects are granted, then this security profile denies all objects except the ones explicitly granted. However, to grant an object, you need to explicitly grant its parent objects until the root folder as well.

Aggregation

The possible aggregation options for a display data business security profile are the "Very restrictive (AND)" (the default one), "Moderately restrictive (ANDOR)," and "Less restrictive (OR)" algorithms, described in Section 8.3.3. The chosen aggregation is also the aggregation of create query business security profiles.

In these algorithms, you use these operators:

- Objects intersection, for the restrictive aggregation (AND): an object is granted if it is granted in both security profiles to aggregate or if it is granted in one but not specified in the other.

- Objects union, for the permissive aggregation (OR): an object is granted if it is granted in one of the security profiles to aggregate or if it is granted in one but not specified in the other.

Consumption

If an object is included in a query, then this object can actually query data if after the aggregation of all business security profiles:

- The object is effectively granted.

- And if all its parent folders till the root folder are also effectively granted.

As a consequence, after aggregation of all display data business security profiles:

- An object is not displayed if one of his parent is denied (an object cannot have more rights than its parents).

- If a container is set as denied, all objects and sub-containers below are denied, whatever their status is.

In Web Intelligence, the refresh of a document containing an object denied by security may lead to some unexpected behaviors since removing an object from the query may modify the document structure. As in Universe Design Tool (see Chapter 7, Section 7.4), the AUTO_UPDATE_QUERY parameter is used to define how to manage the refresh of a document based on a universe with an object denied by a display data business security profile:

▶ If this parameter is set to false, then the query is not executed, the report is not displayed, and an error message is displayed.

▶ If this parameter is set to true, then the report is refreshed, but the object is not taken into consideration:

  ▶ The object is removed from the run query, as well as predefined filters, calculated measures, and variables depending on it.

  ▶ Data corresponding to this object are no longer retrieved from the database and are thus removed from the report.

8.5.3 Filters (Relational Universe)

With filters business security profile, you can filter data retrieved from relational universe through a filter defined with objects from the business layer.

Authoring

Filters business security profile can be seen as the equivalent of the rows data security profile (see Section 8.4.4), but defined at the business layer level. Instead of explicitly writing the WHERE clause to apply, it is defined using a business filter similar to the one that can be created in the business layer.

A business layer supports two types of filters:

▶ Native filter: defined using an SQL expression

▶ Business filter: defined using some objects of the business layer

But only a business filter can be used in a filters business security profile. This business filter can be created using the same user interface as the one used in the query panel. For this reason, the possible filter can be complex:

▶ You can select any object (measure, dimension, or attribute) available in the business layer, except the objects whose state is hidden. There is no security applied to check whether you are allowed to use them in the definition of a business security profile.

▶ You can use any operator (equal, not equal, in list, etc.) supported by business filters on these objects. Furthermore, you can also use sub-queries.

▶ The filters operand can be a constant, a list of values, or an object. But it cannot be a prompt. In case of constant, it can use the @VARIABLE operator and user attributes (see Section 8.8).

This filter is created in the filters business security profile. This filter is attached to this security profile and is accessible only from it:

▶ It is not possible to reuse a filter created in the business layer.

▶ If the business security profile is deleted, this filter is deleted as well.

Query

Compared to a rows data security profile that applies only if a table is used in a query, a filters business security profile always applies at query time, whatever the objects selected in the query are.

If no filters business security profile is assigned or inherited by a user, no business filter is applied to the data retrieved by queries. If a filters business security profile applies to a user, then the business filter is converted into a WHERE clause. This WHERE clause is added to the query to send to the database. Thus data retrieved by the query are filtered by the business filter and only data that comply with this filter are returned.

No business filter is applied to other users who do not have any assigned or inherited filters business security profile.

Aggregation

The possible aggregation options for filters business security profile are the "Very restrictive (AND)" (the default one), "Moderately restrictive (ANDOR)," and "Less restrictive (OR)" algorithms, described in Section 8.3.3.

In these algorithms, the resulting WHERE clause generated from the filters are aggregated with:

▶ An AND operator for the restrictive aggregation

▶ An OR operator for the permissive aggregation

Rows data security profiles and filters business security profiles (see Section 8.5.3) both generate a WHERE clause to filter the query. If both a rows data security profile and a filters business security profile are applied, these two resulting WHERE clauses are aggregated with the AND operator.

8.5.4 Filters (Multidimensional Universe)

Multidimensional universes do not support the relational filters business security profiles described above. But they support another filters business security profiles type that takes advantage of the multidimensional universe.

Authoring

For multidimensional universes, the filters business security profile is used to grant or deny members of a multidimensional hierarchy. When you define such a filters business security profile, you create a newly named set that defines the granted members. This named set is created in the filters business security profile. It is attached to this security profile and is accessible only from it. Additionally, it is not possible to reuse this named set outside this security profile, and if the business security profile is deleted, this named set is deleted as well.

Business layer supports two types of named sets:

▶ Native member set: defined using an MDX expression
▶ Business filter: defined using some objects of the business layer; only a business filter can be used in the definition of business security profile

The named set you can create in a business filter is similar to the member sets you can create in the query panel when you select members in a hierarchy since both workflows use the same Member Selector.

Especially, it supports the selection of members in a hierarchy through level selection, which selects all members in the selected levels, and the explicit selection of members. To select these members, you can also use the multidimensional operators listed in Table 8.3.

Operator	Description
SELF	The selected member.
CHILDREN	The selected member's direct children (+1).

Table 8.3 Multidimensional Operators

Operator	Description
DESCENDANTS	All children of the selected member and their children, until the hierarchy bottom.
DESCENDANTS UNTIL NAMED LEVEL • *<level name>*	All children of the selected member and their children, until the level *<level name>* in the hierarchy.
DESCENDANTS UNTIL • + *<integer>*	All children of the selected member and their children, until the *nth* occurrence.
PARENT	The selected member's direct parent.
ANCESTORS	All parents of the selected member, until the hierarchy root.
SIBLINGS	All members whose parent is the parent's selected member.

Table 8.3 Multidimensional Operators (Cont.)

All the hierarchies of the business layer can be selected in the definition of a filters business security profile, even if they are hidden, deprecated, or denied by a create query business security profile.

Query

In the query panel, when you create the query, the member selector does not take filters security profiles into consideration. Thus, all members are displayed when you select hierarchy members, even if some are denied through filters business security profiles.

But filters business security profiles are applied at query time. If no filters business security profile is assigned to you, then you can see all members of the hierarchy if you select it in your query. Otherwise, the effective filters business security profiles defines the members you can see in the hierarchy if it is added to the query. The corresponding MDX code to filter the hierarchy with the effective filters business security profile is generated and added to the query sent to the database. In practice, the MDX intersects the member set defined by the effective filters business security profile with the member set returned by the hierarchy.

In a multidimensional database, the action to keep only a sub-set in a hierarchy is called *slicing*. Measures corresponding to the members that are not granted by the filters business security profile are not retrieved at query time. Slicing does not modify the aggregated values since it is only a visual filter.

Depending on the database, the default member returned by a hierarchy can be the "All members" member or the first member. This member intersects with the member set defined in the effective filters business security profile in order to guarantee that he cannot see the members he is not allowed to see.

If the member set defined in the security profile contains selected members other than the default member, the intersection returns an empty set, and the resulting query returns no value. To avoid this, when you select a hierarchy in a query, you should explicitly select all or some members in this hierarchy.

For example, a filters business security profile grants "AMER" and "EMEA" members in the Geography hierarchy, whose default member is the "All members" member.

If you use the Geography hierarchy in a query but do not select any member, then the hierarchy returns the default member and its intersection with the named set defined in the filters business security profile is empty, as shown in the top half of Figure 8.10.

But if, in the Geography hierarchy, you explicitly select several members, including "AMER" and "EMEA," then the intersection with the member set defined in the filters business security profile returns "AMER" and "EMEA" members, as shown in the bottom half of Figure 8.10.

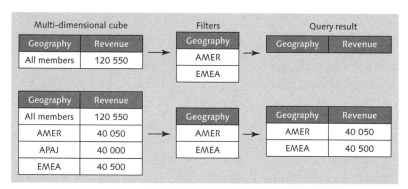

Figure 8.10 Filtering through Multidimensional Filters

For the same reason, if you want to add a prompt to select the values of the hierarchy to query, it is better to add it in the hierarchy member selector rather than adding a specific filter based on a prompt on this hierarchy. If the hierarchy is not selected in the query, the filter is not applied.

Aggregation

The possible aggregation options for filters business security profile are the "Very restrictive (AND)" (the default), "Moderately restrictive (ANDOR)," and "Less restrictive (OR)" algorithms, described in Section 8.3.3.

In these algorithms, you use these operators:

▶ Member set intersection, for the restrictive aggregation (AND): the resulting filter contains the members that are granted in both filters.

▶ Member set union, for the permissive aggregation (OR): the resulting filter contains the members that are granted in either of the filters.

8.6   Managing Security Profiles in Information Design Tool

In Information Design Tool, both the data and business security profiles described in the previous sections are managed in the Security Editor, which does the following:

▶ It is dedicated to security administrators who can manage security and focus on their security tasks without having to handle universe edition. This new Security Editor clearly separates the tasks and the two corresponding user personas.

▶ It provides an overview of all universes and users/groups in the CMS repository.

▶ It displays more easily security applied to principals: security profiles explicitly assigned, inherited, and the security that actually applies.

The Security Editor does *not* display universes created with Universe Design Tool.

The Security Editor is secured by the Central Management Console (CMC) rights related to security profiles (see Chapter 5, Section 5.12):

▶ You can access it only if Information Design Tool's "Administer security profiles" right has been granted to you.

▶ It does not display a universe if this universe's "View objects" right is denied to you.

▶ It does not allow you to edit or assign a universe's security profiles if this universe's "Edit security profiles" or "Assign security profiles" rights are denied to you.

8.6.1 Opening the Security Editor

To open the Security Editor in Information Design Tool:

1. In the menu bar, select WINDOW • SECURITY EDITOR or in the tool bar; click the SECURITY EDITOR button to open the OPEN SESSION dialog box.

2. In the SESSIONS dropdown list, select the predefined session to use to connect to the CMS repository where the security must be edited.

   ▶ If this session is not yet opened, fill in the PASSWORD text field to authenticate the user defined in the predefined session.

   ▶ If your session does not appear in the list of predefined sessions, select the NEW SESSION choice, and then type in the session parameters.

3. Click OK to submit your credentials. If the "Administer security profiles" right is granted to you, then the SECURITY EDITOR opens, as shown in Figure 8.11; otherwise, an error message is displayed.

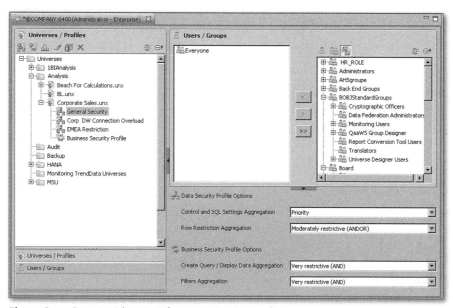

Figure 8.11 Security Editor in Information Design Tool

The Security Editor appears as a tab in the Information Design Tool window. Several Security Editors can be opened in parallel for different CMS repositories. In this case, there is one tab for each Security Editor.

Once connected to the Security Editor, you can perform the following tasks for security profiles administration:

▶ Create or edit security profiles (see Sections 8.6.3 to 8.6.6).

▶ Assign or unassign security profile (see Section 8.6.7).

▶ Show assigned security profiles (see Section 8.6.8).

▶ Set security profile aggregation options and priorities (see Sections 8.6.9 and 8.6.10).

▶ Delete a security profile (see Section 8.6.11).

▶ Show security profiles inheritance or aggregated security profile (see Sections 8.6.12 and 8.6.13).

▶ Check integrity (see Section 8.6.14).

It is also possible to run a secured query, as described in Section 8.10.

By default, any changes done in the Security Editor are not committed in the CMS repository and are kept in memory by Information Design Tool. The SECURITY EDITOR tab indicates any outstanding changes; in this case, a star (*) prefixes the cluster name, as shown in Figure 8.12.

Figure 8.12 Outstanding Changes in Security Editor

These changes are saved when:

▶ You explicitly save these changes by clicking the SAVE button in the toolbar.

▶ You close the Security Editor, you are asked to save or not to save these changes.

When you save these changes, all modified universes security (security profiles, assigned users and groups, data security profiles priority, aggregation options) are updated in the CMS repository. If several designers work on the same universe on their own machines, the last save with the Security Editor overwrites previous saves.

It is recommended that you save your work on a regular basis to avoid losing it.

8.6.2 Switching Universe-Centric View and User-Centric View

Security involves working on universes and users/groups. Depending on the tasks to perform, you may prefer to start from a universe or from a user or a group. For this reason, the Security Editor offers two views:

▶ The *universe-centric view* is more oriented to the security profiles' administration. It is more appropriate for the tasks where the starting point is the universe and its security profiles: administering them or assigning them to principals.

▶ The *user-centric view* is more oriented to display the security profiles assigned to a principal.

You can do almost the same tasks in the two views (assign a principal to a security profile, create a security profile), but some tasks are available only in one view: for example, aggregation options are available only in the universe-centric view.

The universe-centric view is made up of two sections, as shown in Figure 8.11:

▶ The Universes/Profiles section displays the universes published in the CMS repository as a tree of universes folders and sub-folders. If a folder contains sub-folders or universes, it can be elapsed or collapsed to show or hide them. A universe's data and business security profiles are listed below this universe; data security profiles are listed before business security profiles.

▶ The Users/Groups section

  ▶ The Assigned Users/Groups list, which displays all users and groups explicitly assigned to the data or business security profile selected in the Universes Browser tree

  ▶ The Users/Groups Browser, which displays all users and groups in the CMS repository

The Aggregation Options section defines how data or business security profiles aggregate for the universe selected in the Universes/Profiles section.

The user-centric view is also made up of three sections, as shown in Figure 8.13:

▶ The Users/Groups Browser section displays all users and groups in the CMS repository. You can navigate in these users and groups to select the user or the group to work on.

▶ The Universes Browser section displays universes published in the CMS repository as a tree of universes folder and sub-folders. If a folder contains sub-folders or universes, it can be elapsed or collapsed to show or hide them. You can choose to display all universes or only universes for which at least one data or business security profile is assigned to the selected user or group (see Section 8.6.8).

▶ The Security Profiles section lists the selected universe's data and business security profiles and is used to assign or unassign them to the selected user or group. This section has two panes:

  ▶ The Data Security Profiles pane displays the selected universe's data security profiles.

  ▶ The Business Security Profiles pane displays the selected universe's business security profiles.

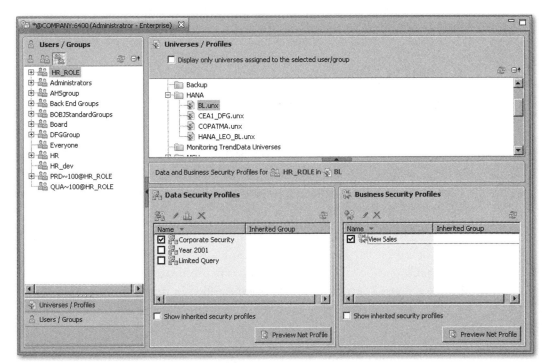

Figure 8.13 User-Centric View in Security Editor

You can switch from one view to another by clicking the corresponding button in the SECURITY EDITOR left navigation dock, as shown in Figure 8.14.

Figure 8.14 Universe-Centric or User-centric View Selection

Both universe-centric and user-centric views contain the USERS/GROUPS BROWSER. In this browser, you can navigate in the list of users and groups stored in the CMS repository. These users and groups can be displayed in three different ways:

▶ The flat list of users

▶ The list of groups with the users they contain

▶ The hierarchy of groups with the users and groups they contain

You can switch from one display to another by clicking the buttons in the USERS/GROUPS BROWSER toolbar.

8.6.3   Creating a Data Security Profile

In the universe-centric view, to create a data security profile for a universe:

1. Select the Security Editor universe-centric view.

2. Select the universe in the UNIVERSES/PROFILES section.

3. Click the INSERT DATA SECURITY PROFILE button in the UNIVERSES/PROFILES tool-bar or right-click the universe and select INSERT DATA SECURITY PROFILE. The DEFINE DATA SECURITY PROFILE dialog opens.

   This dialog box is used to create, view, and edit a data security profile. It is very similar to the one used in Universe Design Tool for access restriction. It contains several tabs, one for each type of data security profile: CONNECTIONS, CONTROLS, SQL, ROWS, and TABLES. These tabs are described in next sub-sections.

4. Type a name in the DATA SECURITY PROFILE NAME box.

5. Select any tab and set the data security profile's parameters. The parameters in each tab are described below.

6. Click OK to close the dialog box. The data security profile is created and is displayed below its universe.

7. Click the SAVE button in the main toolbar to save your changes.

Although not the most common way to do this, it is also possible to create a data security profile for a universe in the user-centric view. To do so:

1. Select the Security Editor user-centric view.

2. Select a user or a group in the USERS/GROUPS BROWSER.

3. Select a relational universe in the UNIVERSES BROWSER.

4. Click the INSERT DATA SECURITY PROFILE button in the DATA SECURITY PROFILES toolbar. The DEFINE DATA SECURITY PROFILE dialog box opens.

5. Type a name in the DATA SECURITY PROFILE NAME box.

6. Select any tab and modify the data security profile's parameters. The parameters in each tab are described below.

7. Click OK to close this dialog box and create the data security profile. This new data security profile is displayed in the DATA SECURITY PROFILES panel.

8. Click the SAVE button in the main toolbar to save your changes.

Connections

To define a replacement connection for a connection:

1. In the data security profile editor, select the CONNECTIONS tab shown in Figure 8.15. This tab contains several items of note:

    ▶ Some read-only details on the universe: its data foundation and its business layer.

    ▶ The REPLACEMENT CONNECTIONS list that contains all connections used by this universe.

2. Select a connection in the REPLACEMENT CONNECTIONS list.

3. Click EDIT to open the DEFINE REPLACEMENT CONNECTIONS dialog box where you can select or change the replacement connection associated with this connection.

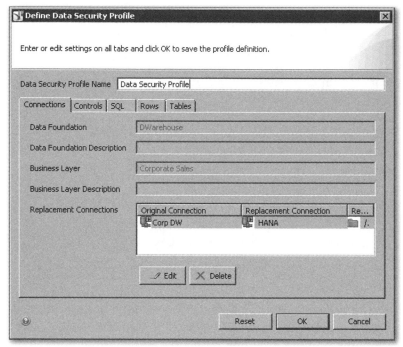

Figure 8.15 Connections Data Security Profile

4. The DEFINE REPLACEMENT CONNECTIONS dialog box lists the Connections folders and sub-folders in the CMS repository, as shown in Figure 8.16. You may drill into these folders and select a replacement connection:

   ▶ If the original connection is an SAP NetWeaver BW data source, then only SAP NetWeaver BW data sources are displayed and can be selected.

   ▶ If the original connection is an SAS data source, then only SAS data sources are displayed and can be selected.

   ▶ If the original connection is relational connection of another type, then any relational connections, except SAP NetWeaver BW and SAS, are displayed and can be selected.

5. Click OK to close the DEFINE REPLACEMENT CONNECTION dialog box. The selected connection is displayed in the connection list, in the REPLACEMENT CONNECTION column.

6. Click OK to close the DEFINE DATA SECURITY PROFILE dialog box or select another tab in the editor to edit another security type in the data security profile.

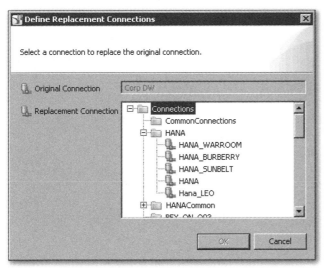

Figure 8.16 Replacement Connection Selection

To edit or remove a replacement connection, follow these steps:

1. Select a connection that is overloaded in the REPLACEMENT CONNECTIONS list.

2. Click the EDIT button to open the DEFINE REPLACEMENT CONNECTIONS dialog box and edit the selected connection overload or click the DELETE button to remove this connection overload.

3. Click OK to close the DEFINE DATA SECURITY PROFILE dialog box or select another tab in the editor to edit another security type in the data security profile.

Controls and SQL

To define new parameters to overload in the controls and SQL data security profile, follow these steps:

1. In the data security profile editor, select the CONTROLS or SQL tab. These tabs are shown in Figure 8.17 and Figure 8.18, respectively. By default, these tabs display the values defined for the universe.

2. Modify any settings displayed in these tabs. The modified settings appear in blue and bold font.

3. Even if you reset a modified parameter with its initial value, the parameter remains displayed in blue and bold font. This means that the parameter remains explicitly overridden, even if it is overridden by the same value defined by

default for the universe. Such a configuration can be useful in case of aggregations of this parameter.

To remove the override, you must click the RESET button, which resets the complete data security profile.

4. Click OK to close the DEFINE DATA SECURITY PROFILE dialog box or select another tab in the editor to edit another security type in the data security profile.

Figure 8.17 Controls Data Security Profile

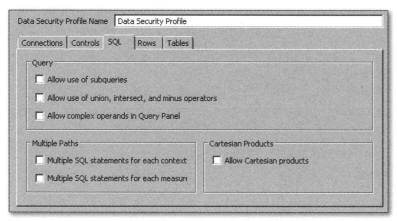

Figure 8.18 SQL Data Security Profile

Rows

To define a row restriction in the data security profile editor, follow these steps:

1. In the data security profile editor, select the ROWS tab.

2. Click the INSERT button to open the DEFINE ROW RESTRICTION dialog box, as shown in Figure 8.19.

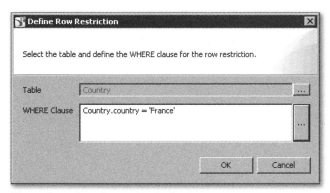

Figure 8.19 Row Restriction Definition

3. In the DEFINE ROW RESTRICTION dialog box, click the … button near the TABLE text field to open the SELECT A TABLE dialog box where you can select the conditional table, as shown in Figure 8.20:

   ▶ If the data foundation used by the universe is monosource, then you can select any table from the data foundation. Since BI 4.0 SP4, this also includes alias and derived tables, which was not the case before.

   ▶ If the data foundation is multi-source, then you can select any table from any databases the universe queries from the connections or data sources.

Figure 8.20 Table Selection for Monosource Universe

4. In the SELECT A TABLE dialog box, select the conditional table.

5. Click OK to close the SELECT A TABLE dialog box. The selected table is displayed in the TABLE text field.

6. Type the WHERE clause in the WHERE CLAUSE text field. You may also click the ... button near WHERE CLAUSE text field to open the DEFINE WHERE CLAUSE editor that can help you to type the SQL.

7. Click OK to close the DEFINE ROW RESTRICTION dialog box. The row restriction is now listed in the ROWS tab.

8. Click OK to close the DEFINE DATA SECURITY PROFILE dialog box or select another tab in the editor to edit another security type in the data security profile.

To edit or remove a row restriction, follow these steps:

1. Select a row restriction listed in the ROWS tab.

2. Click the EDIT button to open the DEFINE ROW RESTRICTION dialog box and edit the selected row restriction or click the DELETE button to remove this row restriction.

3. Click OK to close the DEFINE DATA SECURITY PROFILE dialog box or select another tab in the editor to edit another security type in the data security profile.

Tables

To define a table mapping in the data security profile editor, follow these steps:

1. In the data security profile editor, select the TABLES tab.

2. Click the INSERT button to open the DEFINE REPLACEMENT TABLE dialog box, as shown in Figure 8.21.

3. In the DEFINE REPLACEMENT TABLE dialog box, near the ORIGINAL text field, click the ... button to open the SELECT A TABLE dialog box that displays data foundation's table.

4. In the SELECT A TABLE dialog box, select the original table.

5. Click OK to close the SELECT A TABLE dialog box. The selected table is displayed in the ORIGINAL TABLE text field.

6. In the REPLACEMENT section, click the SELECT A TABLE button. The SELECT A TABLE dialog box contains any tables available in the databases.

7. Click OK to close the SELECT A TABLE dialog box. The selected table is displayed in the REPLACEMENT section.

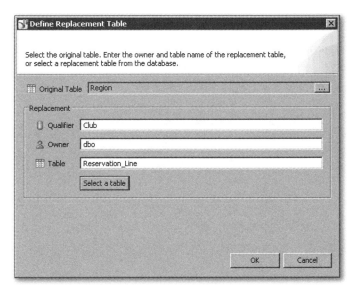

Figure 8.21 Replacement Table Selection

8. Click OK to close the DEFINE REPLACEMENT TABLE dialog box. The original table and its replacement table are now listed in the TABLES tab.

9. Click OK to close the DEFINE DATA SECURITY PROFILE dialog box or select another tab in the editor to edit another security type in the data security profile.

To edit or remove the table mapping, follow these steps:

1. Select a table mapping listed in the TABLES tab.

2. Click the EDIT button to open the DEFINE REPLACEMENT TABLE dialog box and edit the selected table mapping or click the DELETE button to remove this table mapping.

3. Click OK to close the DEFINE DATA SECURITY PROFILE dialog box or select another tab in the editor to edit another security type in the data security profile.

8.6.4 Editing a Data Security Profile

In the universe-centric view, to edit a data security profile for a universe, follow these steps:

1. Select the Security Editor universe-centric view.

2. Select the data security profile.

3. Click the EDIT DATA SECURITY PROFILE button in the UNIVERSES/PROFILES panel toolbar. The DEFINE DATA SECURITY PROFILE dialog box opens.

4. Select any tab and modify the data security profile's parameters. These tabs are described in Section 8.6.3.

5. When you have completed your changes, click OK to close the DEFINE DATA SECURITY PROFILE dialog box.

It is also possible to edit a data security profile in the user-centric view, follow these steps:

1. Select the Security Editor user-centric view.

2. Select a user or a group in the USERS/GROUPS BROWSER.

3. Select a universe in the UNIVERSES BROWSER.

4. In the DATA SECURITY PROFILES panel, select the data security profile.

5. In the DATA SECURITY PROFILES toolbar, click the EDIT DATA SECURITY PROFILE button. The DEFINE DATA SECURITY PROFILE dialog box opens.

6. Select any tab and modify the data security profile's parameters. These tabs are described in Section 8.6.3.

7. When you have completed your changes, click OK to close the DEFINE DATA SECURITY PROFILE dialog box.

> **Note**
>
> Editing a data security profile does not modify its assigned users and groups.

8.6.5 Creating a Business Security Profile

In the universe-centric view, to create a business security profile for a universe, follow these steps:

1. Select the Security Editor universe-centric view.

2. Select the universe in the UNIVERSES/PROFILES section.

3. Click the INSERT BUSINESS SECURITY PROFILE button in the UNIVERSES/PROFILES toolbar or right-click the universe and select INSERT DATA SECURITY PROFILE. The DEFINE BUSINESS SECURITY PROFILE dialog opens.

   This dialog box is used to create, view, and edit a business security profile. It is very similar to the one used to create and edit data security profile. It contains several tabs, one for each type of business security profile: CREATE QUERY, DISPLAY DATA, and FILTERS. These tabs are described in the next sub-sections.

4. Type a name in the BUSINESS SECURITY PROFILE NAME box.

5. Select any tab to modify the business security profile's parameters. The parameters in each tab are described below.

6. Click OK to close this dialog box and create the business security profile. It is displayed below its universe.

7. Click the SAVE button in the main toolbar to save your changes.

It is not the most common way to achieve this, but it is also possible to create a business security profile for a universe in the user-centric view. To do so:

1. Select the SECURITY EDITOR user-centric view.

2. Select a user or a group in the USERS/GROUPS BROWSER.

3. Select a universe in the UNIVERSES BROWSER.

4. Click the INSERT BUSINESS SECURITY PROFILE button in the BUSINESS SECURITY PROFILES toolbar. The DEFINE BUSINESS SECURITY PROFILE dialog box opens.

5. Type a name in the BUSINESS SECURITY PROFILE NAME box.

6. Select any tab to modify the business security profile's parameters. The parameters in each tab are described below.

7. Click OK to close this dialog box and create the business security profile. This new business security profile is displayed in the BUSINESS SECURITY PROFILES panel.

8. Click the SAVE button in the main toolbar to save your changes.

Create Query

In the business security editor, the CREATE QUERY tab allows you to define views and objects to explicitly grant or deny in the create query business security profile.

This tab contains two panes: one that lists granted and denied views and one that list granted and denied objects, as shown in Figure 8.22.

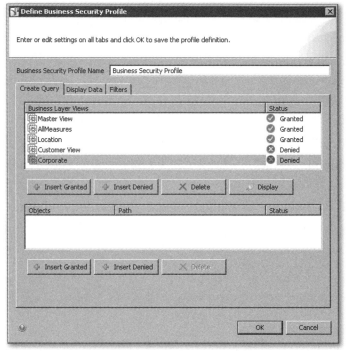

Figure 8.22 Create Query Tab in Business Security Profile Editor

In the BUSINESS LAYER VIEWS table, each line of the table is the name of a view that is either explicitly granted or denied. It can also contain ALL VIEWS to explicitly grant or deny all views. Each line contains the following data:

▶ BUSINESS LAYER VIEWS: The view's name or ALL VIEWS.

▶ STATUS: The field will say GRANTED if the view is granted or DENIED if the view is denied.

You can grant a view in the business security profile by following these steps:

1. If the view is already denied by this security profile and listed in the BUSINESS LAYER VIEWS table, select it, right-click it and, in the contextual menu, select GRANT.

2. Otherwise, click the Insert Granted button below the Business Layer Views table to open the Select a Business Layer View dialog box, as shown in Figure 8.23.

3. Select the views to grant. Press the Ctrl key to select several views. You can select all views by clicking the All business layer views checkbox.

4. Click OK. The Select a Business Layer View dialog box closes and the selected view(s) are displayed in the Business Layer Views table with the Granted status.

To deny a view in the business security profile, follow these steps:

1. If the view is already granted by this security profile and listed in the Business Layer Views table, select it, right-click it and, in the contextual menu, select Deny.

2. Otherwise, click the Insert Denied button below the Business Layer Views table to open the Select a Business Layer View dialog box, as shown in Figure 8.23.

3. Select the views to deny. Press the Ctrl key to select several views. You can select all views by clicking the All business layer views checkbox.

4. Click OK. The Select a Business Layer View dialog box closes and the selected view(s) are displayed in the Business Layer Views table with the Denied status.

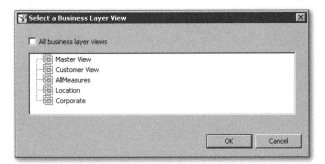

Figure 8.23 Views Selection

To remove a view that is granted or denied by this security profile:

1. Select the view in the Business Layer Views table. Press the Ctrl key to select several views.

2. Click the REMOVE button below the BUSINESS LAYER VIEWS table or right-click the selected view(s) and select REMOVE. The view(s) are removed from the VIEWS table.

To list the objects contained in a view granted or denied by this security profile, follow these steps:

1. Select the view in the BUSINESS LAYER VIEWS table.

2. Click the VIEW button below the BUSINESS LAYER VIEWS table or right-click the view and select VIEW. A dialog box opens with the list of objects contained in the selected view.

In the OBJECTS table, each line of the table is the name of an object that is either explicitly granted or denied. It can also contain "All objects" to explicitly grant or deny all objects. Each line contains the following data:

▶ OBJECTS: The object name or ALL OBJECTS.

▶ STATUS: The field says GRANTED if the object has been granted or DENIED if the object has been denied.

To grant an object in the business security profile, follow these steps:

1. If the object is already denied by this security profile and listed in the OBJECTS table, select it, right-click it and, in the contextual menu, select GRANT.

2. Otherwise, click the INSERT GRANTED button below the OBJECTS table to open the SELECT AN OBJECT dialog box, as shown in Figure 8.24.

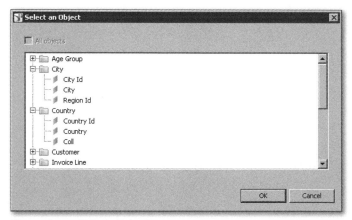

Figure 8.24 Objects Selection

3. Select the objects to grant. Press the ⌈Ctrl⌋ key to select several objects. You can select all objects by clicking the ALL OBJECTS checkbox.

4. Click OK. The SELECT AN OBJECT dialog box closes and the selected object(s) are displayed in the BUSINESS LAYER VIEWS table with the GRANTED status.

To deny an object in the business security profile, follow these steps:

1. If the object is already granted by this security profile and listed in the OBJECTS table, select it, right-click it and, in the contextual menu, select DENY.

2. Otherwise, click the INSERT DENIED button below the OBJECTS table to open the SELECT AN OBJECT dialog box, as shown in Figure 8.24.

3. Select the objects to deny. Press the ⌈Ctrl⌋ key to select several objects. You can select all objects by clicking the ALL OBJECTS checkbox.

4. Click OK. The SELECT AN OBJECT dialog box closes and the selected object(s) are displayed in the BUSINESS LAYER VIEWS table with the DENIED status.

To remove an object that is granted or denied by this security profile, follow these steps:

1. Select the object in the OBJECTS table. Press the ⌈Ctrl⌋ key to select several objects.

2. Click the REMOVE button below the OBJECTS table or right-click the object and select REMOVE. The object(s) are removed from the OBJECTS table.

Display Data

In the business security editor, you can define in the DISPLAY DATA tab the objects to explicitly grant or deny in the display data business security profile. This tab contains one table listing these objects, as shown in Figure 8.25.

In the OBJECTS table, each line of the table is the name of an object that is either explicitly granted or denied. It can also contain ALL OBJECTS to explicitly grant or deny all objects. Each line contains the following data:

▶ OBJECTS: The object name or ALL OBJECTS.

▶ STATUS: The field says GRANTED if the object has been granted or DENIED if the object has been denied.

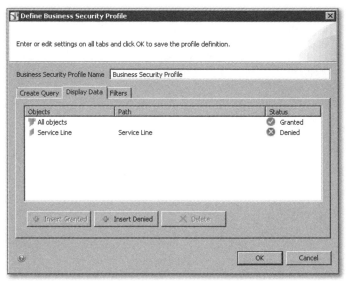

Figure 8.25 Display Data Business Security Profile

To grant an object in the business security profile, follow these steps:

1. If the object is already denied by this security profile and listed in the Objects table, select it, right-click it and, in the contextual menu, select Grant.

2. Otherwise, click the Insert Granted button below the Objects table to open the Select an Object dialog box, as shown in Figure 8.24.

3. Select the objects to grant. Press the Ctrl key to select several objects. You can select all objects by clicking the All objects checkbox.

4. Click OK. The Select an Object dialog box closes and the selected object(s) are displayed in the Business Layer Views table with the Granted status.

To deny an object in the business security profile, follow these steps:

1. If the object is already granted by this security profile and listed in the Objects table, select it, right-click it and, in the contextual menu, select Deny.

2. Otherwise, click the Insert Denied button below the Objects table to open the Select an Object dialog box, as shown in Figure 8.24.

3. Select the objects to deny. Press the Ctrl key to select several objects. You can select all objects by clicking the All objects checkbox.

4. Click OK. The SELECT AN OBJECT dialog box closes and the selected object(s) are displayed in the BUSINESS LAYER VIEWS table with the DENIED status.

To remove an object that is granted or denied by this security profile:

1. Select the object in the OBJECTS table. Press the ⌞Ctrl⌟ key to select several objects.

2. Click the REMOVE button below the OBJECTS table or right-click the object and select REMOVE. The object(s) are removed from the OBJECTS table.

Filters (Relational Universe)

In the business security editor, if the universe is relational, the FILTERS tab allows you to define relational filters.

To add a filter in the business security profile, follow these steps:

1. In the business security profile editor, select the FILTERS tab, as shown in Figure 8.26.

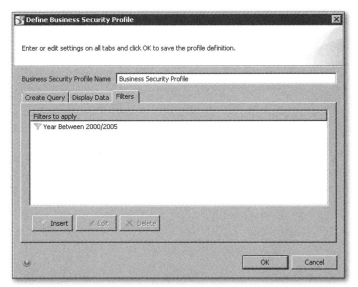

Figure 8.26 Filters Business Security Profile (Relational Universe)

2. Click the INSERT button to open the DEFINE FILTER dialog box.

3. You may enter a name and a description for this filter in the NAME and DESCRIPTION text fields.

4. Click the EDIT FILTER button to open the EDIT BUSINESS FILTER panel. This panel, as shown in Figure 8.27, is the same used in the business layer to create a business filter. In the left part, it contains the objects of the business layer.

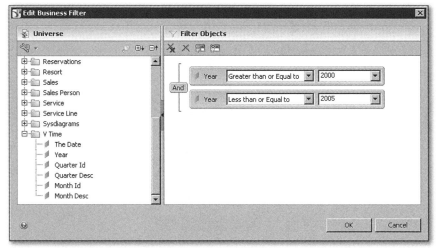

Figure 8.27 Filter Editor (Relational Universe)

5. Select the object to use in the filter and drag and drop in the right part. The filter appears in the right panel with a default operator and default operand.

6. In the filter, use the dropdown menu listing all possible operators to select the operator to use in the filter.

7. In the filter, use the dropdown menu listing all possible operands to select the operand to use in the filter.

   ▶ If you select CONSTANT, you may type any value. Since BI 4.0, you may also use @VARIABLE function to personalize the filter and use any predefined variables or user attributes (see Section 8.8).

   ▶ If you select LIST OF VALUE, then the SELECT PARAMETER VALUES dialog box opens, where you can select the available values for the selected object. Once selected, these values are saved in the filter as its operands.

▶ If you select OBJECT, you can then select an object from the left panel and add it in the operand field in order to compare two object values in the filter.

8. If needed, repeat these steps to create complex filters based on several objects.

9. Click OK to close the EDIT BUSINESS FILTER panel. The filter is displayed in the DEFINE FILTER dialog box.

10. Click OK to close the DEFINE FILTER dialog box. The name of the newly created filter is displayed in the FILTERS tab.

11. Click OK to close the DEFINE BUSINESS SECURITY PROFILE dialog box or select another tab in the editor to edit another security type in the business security profile.

To edit or remove a filter, follow these steps:

1. Select the filter in the business security profile.

2. You can either:

▶ Click the EDIT button to open the DEFINE FILTER dialog box and edit the selected filter, as described below.

▶ Click the DELETE button to remove this filter.

3. Click OK to close the DEFINE BUSINESS SECURITY PROFILE dialog box or select another tab in the editor to edit another security type in the business security profile.

Filters (Multidimensional Universe)

In the business security editor, if the universe is multidimensional, the FILTERS tab allows you to define filters based on hierarchy.

To add a filter in the business security profile for a multidimensional universe, follow these steps:

1. In the business security profile editor, select the FILTERS tab.

2. Click the INSERT button to open the DEFINE MEMBER SET dialog box.

3. Enter a name and an optional description for this filter in the NAME and DESCRIPTION text fields.

4. In the HIERARCHY text field, click the … button to open the SELECT A HIERARCHY dialog box. This dialog box displays all hierarchies defined in this multidimensional universe, as shown in Figure 8.28.

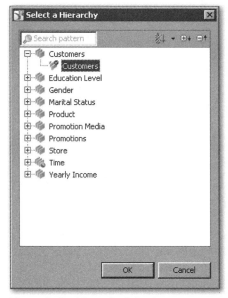

Figure 8.28 Hierarchy Selection

5. Select a hierarchy and click OK to close the SELECT A HIERARCHY dialog box. The hierarchy is displayed in the HIERARCHY text field.

6. Click the EDIT MEMBERS button to open the MEMBER SELECTOR dialog box, as shown in Figure 8.29. This dialog box is similar to the one used in the Query panel to select member set when querying a multidimensional universe.

7. You can define the members to add in the filter by following one of these methods:

By explicitly defining member or operator. To do so:

▶ If it is not selected, click the MEMBERS button. The hierarchy members are displayed as a tree.

▶ Expand the tree to select a member.

▶ Right-click on this member. The contextual menu lists the multidimensional operators you can choose to add this member or other members returned by these operators from this member. This list is detailed in Table 8.3.

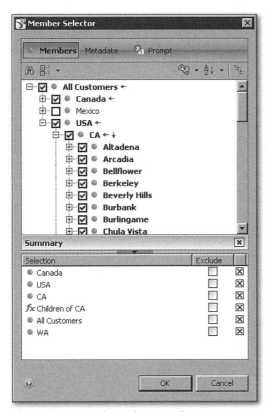

Figure 8.29 Member Selector Dialog Box

▶ In the same contextual menu, EXCLUDE opens another menu containing the same multidimensional operators (Table 8.3). You can use them to exclude some members from the member set. Select one of these operators to exclude this member or other members returned by these operators from this member.

By selecting levels in the hierarchy. To do so:

▶ Click the METADATA button to display the different levels in the hierarchy.

▶ To explicitly grant a level, click the checkbox before it. It appears in the SELECTION list.

▶ To explicitly deny a level, you first need to grant it as described below. Then, when it is listed in the SELECTION list, select the checkbox for this level in the EXCLUDE column to deny it.

8. Click OK to close the MEMBER SELECTOR dialog box. The selected member set is displayed in the DEFINE MEMBER SET dialog box, as shown in Figure 8.30.

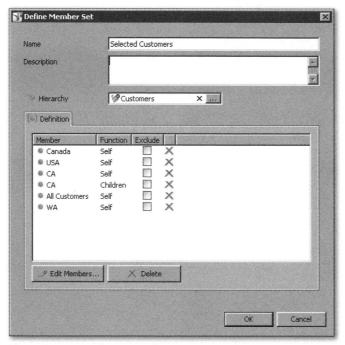

Figure 8.30 Member Set Definition

9. Click OK to close the DEFINE MEMBER SET dialog box. The new member set is listed in the FILTERS TO APPLY list, as shown in Figure 8.31.

10. Click OK to close the DEFINE BUSINESS SECURITY PROFILE dialog box or select another tab in the editor to edit another security type in the business security profile.

To edit or remove a filter, follow these steps:

1. In the FILTERS TO APPLY list, select the named set used to define this filter.

2. You can either:

   ▸ Click the EDIT button to open the DEFINE MEMBER SET dialog box and edit the members, as described below.

   ▸ Click the DELETE button to remove this named set.

3. Click OK to close the DEFINE BUSINESS SECURITY PROFILE dialog box or select another tab in the editor to edit another security type in the business security profile.

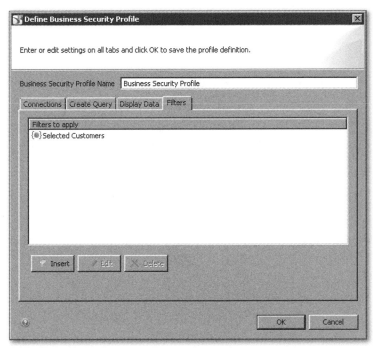

Figure 8.31 Filters Business Security Profile (Multidimensional Universe)

8.6.6 Editing a Business Security Profile

In the universe-centric view, follow these steps to edit a data security profile for a universe:

1. Select the Security Editor universe-centric view.

2. Select the business security profile below its universe.

3. Click the EDIT BUSINESS SECURITY PROFILE button in the UNIVERSES/PROFILES panel toolbar. The BUSINESS SECURITY PROFILE dialog box opens.

4. Select any tab in this editor to edit the various security parameters. These tabs are described in Section 8.6.5.

5. When you have completed your changes, click OK to close the DEFINE BUSINESS SECURITY PROFILE dialog box.

It is also possible to edit a data security profile in the user-centric view. Follow these steps:

1. Select the Security Editor user-centric view.

2. Select a user or a group in the Users/Groups Browser.

3. Select a universe in the Universes Browser.

4. In the Business Security Profiles panel, select the data security profile.

5. In the Business Security Profiles toolbar, click the Edit Business Security Profile button.

6. The Define Business Security Profile dialog box opens.

7. Select any tab in this dialog box to edit the various security parameters. These tabs are described in Section 8.6.5.

8. When you have completed your changes, click OK to close the Define Business Security Profile dialog box.

> **Note**
>
> Editing a business security profile does not modify its assigned users and groups.

8.6.7 Assigning and Unassigning a Security Profile

Assigning and unassigning a security profile to a user or a group can be done in both the universe-centric view and the user-centric view (see Section 8.6.2).

In the universe-centric view, follow these steps to assign a security profile:

1. Select the Security Editor universe-centric view.

2. Select a universe in the Universes/Profiles Browser tree.

3. Select a data security profile or a business security profile below this universe. In the Assigned Users/Groups list, the users or groups already assigned to this security profile are listed.

4. Select one or several users or groups in the Users/Groups Browser. Several users or groups can be selected by pressing the Ctrl key.

5. Click the < button to add the selected users and groups to the list of assigned users or groups.

6. Click the Save button in the main toolbar to save your changes.

In the universe-centric view, follow these steps to unassign a security profile:

1. Select the Security Editor universe-centric view.

2. Select a universe in the Universes/Profiles Browser tree.

3. Select a data security profile or a business security profile below this universe. In the Assigned Users/Groups list, the users or groups already assigned to this security profile are listed.

4. Select one or several users or groups in the Users/Groups Browser. Several users or groups can be selected by pressing the Ctrl key.

5. Click the > button to remove the selected users and groups from this list.

6. You can also click the Unassign All button to directly unassign the security profile from all users and groups.

7. Click the Save button in the main toolbar to save your changes.

In the user-centric view, to assign a security profile, follow these steps:

1. Select the Security Editor user-centric view.

2. Make sure the Display only universes assigned to the selected user/group checkbox is not selected; otherwise, universes with security profiles not assigned to selected user or group are not displayed (see Section 8.6.8).

3. Select a user or a group in the Users/Groups Browser.

4. Select a universe in the Universes/Profiles Browser. The list of data security profiles are displayed in the Data Security Profiles list. The ones already assigned to the user have a checkbox selected in their line in front of each data and business security profile.

5. Select the checkboxes for the data and business security profiles to assign them to the selected user or group.

6. Click the Save button in the main toolbar to save your changes.

In the user-centric view, follow these steps to unassign a security profile:

1. Select the Security Editor user-centric view.

2. Select a user or a group in the Users/Groups Browser.

3. Select a universe in the Universes/Profiles Browser. The list of data security profiles is displayed in the Data Security Profiles list. The ones already assigned

to the user have a checkbox selected in their line in front of each data and business security profile.

4. Unselect the checkboxes for the data and business security profiles to unassign them to the selected user or group.

5. Click the SAVE button in the main toolbar to save your changes.

8.6.8   Show Universes with Assigned Security Profiles

In the Security Editor user-centric view, you may display only universes that have a data or business security profile explicitly assigned to a user or a group. This can be useful when you are designing or checking security for a specific user or group. To do so:

1. Select the Security Editor user-centric view.

2. Select a user or a group in the USERS/GROUPS BROWSER.

3. In the UNIVERSES BROWSER, select the DISPLAY ONLY UNIVERSES ASSIGNED TO THE SELECTED USER/GROUP checkbox, as shown in Figure 8.32. The universes tree is filtered and only:

   ▶ Universes with data or business security profiles explicitly assigned to the selected user or group are displayed.

   ▶ Folders containing such universes are displayed.

Figure 8.32   Option to Display Only Universes with Assigned Security Profiles

8.6.9   Setting Aggregation Options

Setting data and business security profiles aggregation options can be done only in the universe-centric view (see Section 8.6.2). To do so:

1. Select the Security Editor universe-centric view.

2. Select a universe in the UNIVERSES BROWSER.

3. In the AGGREGATION OPTIONS pane, as shown in Figure 8.33, if the universe is relational, use the following dropdown lists to modify data security profiles aggregation options:

▶ CONTROL AND SQL SETTINGS AGGREGATION for controls and SQL data security profiles

▶ ROW RESTRICTION AGGREGATION for rows data security profiles

4. Use the following dropdown lists to modify business security profiles aggregation options:

▶ CREATE QUERY/DISPLAY DATA AGGREGATION for create query and display data business security profiles

▶ FILTERS AGGREGATION for filters business security profiles

5. Click the SAVE button in the main toolbar to save your changes.

The possible values in each dropdown list are the ones supported by each type of data security profile and business security profile aggregation.

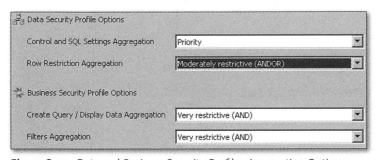

Figure 8.33 Data and Business Security Profiles Aggregation Options

8.6.10 Setting Data Security Profile Priorities

In the Security Editor, you can define priority for data security profiles that are aggregated using priority, as seen in Section 8.3.2. This is done in the SET PRIORITY dialog box.

To open this SET PRIORITY dialog box in the universe-centric view (see Section 8.6.2), follow these steps:

1. In the universe-centric view, in the UNIVERSES/PROFILES panel, select a universe.

2. In the UNIVERSES/PROFILES toolbar, click the CHANGE DATA SECURITY PROFILE PRIORITY or right-click the universe, and, in the contextual menu, select CHANGE DATA SECURITY PROFILE PRIORITY. The SET PRIORITY dialog box opens.

Follow these steps to open the SET PRIORITY dialog box in the user-centric view (see Section 8.6.2):

1. In the user-centric view, in the USERS/GROUPS panel, select a user or a group.

2. In the UNIVERSES/PROFILES panel, select the universe.

3. In the CHANGE DATA SECURITY PROFILES panel toolbar, click the CHANGE DATA SECURITY PROFILE PRIORITY. The SET PRIORITY dialog box opens.

Once it is open, this SET PRIORITY dialog box displays universe's data security profiles, sorted by priority, as shown in Figure 8.34. The data security profile with highest security is displayed at the top of the list, whereas the one with lowest priority is at the bottom of the list.

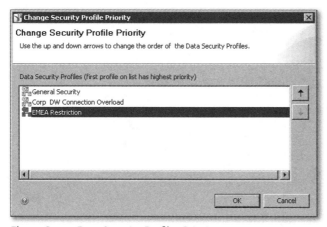

Figure 8.34 Data Security Profiles Priority

You can change these priorities:

1. Select a data security profile.

2. Click the INCREASE PRIORITY button (up arrow) to increase its priority. In the list, the data security profile is moved up.

3. Click THE DECREASE PRIORITY button (down arrow) to decrease its priority. In the list, the data security profile is moved down.

4. Repeat these steps for each data security profile until the priorities are properly set.

5. Click OK to close the SET PRIORITY dialog box.

6. Click the SAVE button in the main toolbar to save your changes.

8.6.11 Deleting Security Profiles

To delete a data or business security profile in the universe-centric view (see Section 8.6.2), follow these steps:

1. Select the Security Editor universe-centric view.

2. In the UNIVERSES/PROFILES BROWSER, select the universe containing the security profiles to delete, and elapse its branches to display its security profiles.

3. Select the security profiles to delete. Several security profiles can be selected by pressing the `Ctrl` key, even if they belong to different universes.

4. Click the DELETE button in the toolbar or right-click the security profile(s) and select DELETE DATA SECURITY PROFILE or DELETE BUSINESS SECURITY PROFILE in the contextual menu. A confirmation window opens.

5. Click the YES button to confirm. The security profile(s) are removed from the UNIVERSES/PROFILES BROWSER.

6. Click the SAVE button in the main toolbar to save your changes.

Follow these steps to delete a data or business security profile in the user-centric view (see Section 8.6.2):

1. Select the Security Editor user-centric view.

2. Select any user or group in the USERS/GROUPS BROWSER.

3. Select a universe in the UNIVERSES BROWSER.

4. Select the data security profiles to delete in the DATA SECURITY PROFILES pane. Several data security profiles can be selected by pressing the `Ctrl` key.

5. Click the DELETE button in the DATA SECURITY PROFILES pane's toolbar or right-click the data security profile(s) and select DELETE DATA SECURITY PROFILE in the contextual menu. The data security profile(s) are removed from the DATA SECURITY PROFILES pane.

6. Repeat the same steps in the Business Security Profiles pane to delete business security profiles.

7. Click the Save button in the main toolbar to save your changes.

8.6.12 Show Inherited Security Profiles

In order to ease security profiles administration, it is possible to display security profiles inherited by a user or a group. This option, disabled by default, is available only in the user-centric view (see Section 8.6.2). Follow these steps to enable it and to show the security profiles inherited from other groups:

1. Select the Security Editor user-centric view.

2. Select a user or a group in the Users/Groups Browser.

3. Select a universe in the Universes Browser.

4. In the Data Security Profiles pane, select the Show inherited security profiles checkbox. All data security profiles inherited by the selected user or group are redisplayed once again. The group they inherit from is listed in the Inherited Group column, as shown in Figure 8.35.

5. Repeat the same steps in the Business Security Profiles pane to show inherited business security profiles.

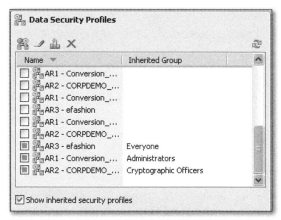

Figure 8.35 Inherited Security Profiles

8.6.13 Preview Net Result

In order to check aggregation options and group inheritance rules, it is possible to display the aggregated data or business security profile to apply to a user or a group.

To display the effective data or business security profile, follow these steps:

1. Select the Security Editor user-centric view.

2. Select a user or a group in the USERS/GROUPS BROWSER.

3. Select a universe in the UNIVERSES BROWSER.

4. In the DATA SECURITY PROFILES pane, click the PREVIEW NET PROFILE button. A dialog box similar to the one used to create data security profile opens (see Section 8.6.3). This dialog box is in read-only mode and it is not possible to edit its content.

5. Click the different tabs to check the different aggregated values for the selected user or group:

    ▶ The CONNECTIONS tab displays the effective replacement connection, if any. If no overload applies, then the universe connection(s) are displayed

    ▶ The CONTROLS and SQL tabs display the effective values used by a query. If no overload applies, then the universe parameters are displayed.

    ▶ The ROWS tab displays the aggregated WHERE clause to use. If no row restriction applies, then the tab is empty.

    ▶ The TABLES tab displays the effective replacement table. If no table mapping applies, then the tab is empty.

6. Click OK to close the dialog box.

7. In the BUSINESS SECURITY PROFILES pane, click the PREVIEW NET PROFILE button. A dialog box similar to the one used to create business security profile opens (see Section 8.6.5). This dialog box is in read-only mode and it is not possible to edit its content.

8. Click the different tabs to check the different aggregated values for the selected user or group:

    ▶ The CREATE QUERY tab displays the list of views and objects granted and denied after aggregation. If no create query security profile applies, then the tab is empty.

► The DISPLAY DATA tab displays the list of objects granted and denied after aggregation. If no display data business security profile applies, then the tab is empty.

► For a relational universe, the FILTERS tab displays the filters to apply. For a multidimensional universe, displays the member sets used the filter the hierarchy. If no filters business security profile applies, then the tab is empty.

9. Click OK to close the dialog box.

8.6.14   Check Integrity

From time to time, it is interesting to check that the security profiles are still valid and that they are still synchronized with the published universe they secure. This integrity check can be run only in the universe-centric view (see Section 8.6.2). To do so:

1. Select the Security Editor universe-centric view.

2. Select a universe in the UNIVERSES BROWSER.

3. Right-click the universe and select CHECK INTEGRITY in the contextual menu. The CHECK INTEGRITY dialog box opens.

4. Select the CHECK DATA SECURITY PROFILE and CHECK BUSINESS SECURITY PROFILE checkboxes.

5. Click the CHECK INTEGRITY button. The integrity rules are parsed and the results are displayed in the DESCRIPTION pane, as shown in Figure 8.36. These integrity rules can help you to detect invalid connections, objects, or tables referenced in security profiles.

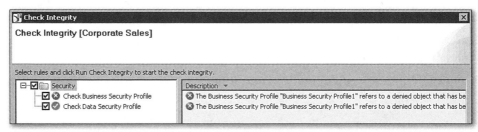

Figure 8.36   Security Profiles Check Integrity

6. If any error messages appear, review them and decide how to correct the published universe or security profiles. You may save this list of errors in a text file by clicking the EXPORT button.

7. Click the CLOSE button to close the CHECK INTEGRITY dialog box.

> **Note**
>
> In the SECURITY EDITOR, the integrity check tests only the security profiles assigned to the selected universe. To run other rules, select CHECK INTEGRITY from the REPOSITORY RESOURCES panel. However, from this panel the integrity check does not test security profiles.

8.7 Object Access Level

As for classic universes created with Universe Design Tool (see Chapter 7, Section 7.7), it is also possible to assign access level to objects of universes created with Information Design Tool.

8.7.1 Object Access Level Overview

An access level is a property that can be set to objects defining the business layer:

▶ For a relational universe, these are dimensions, measures, attributes.

▶ For a multidimensional universe, these are dimensions, attributes, measures, calculated measures, filters, member sets.

The access level defines the object level of confidentiality. It can take the following values, in increasing order of confidentiality:

▶ Public (the default value and the least confidential)

▶ Controlled

▶ Restricted

▶ Confidential

▶ Private (the most confidential)

In addition, in the CMS repository, a user or a group can be assigned an access level for a universe or a universe folder: public, controlled, restricted, confidential, or private. An object access level set at a group level is inherited by its children. A user can see only objects whose access levels are lower than or equal to his own access level.

If an object is denied to you through an object access level, it means:

▶ In the query panel, you do not see this object in the list of objects exposed by the universe.

▶ When you refresh a query containing this object, then the query fails and no data is retrieved from the database.

This security comes in addition to the one set through create query business security profiles; to be displayed in the query panel, an object must be granted both through create query business security profile and object access level.

8.7.2 User Access Level

If no access level is explicitly assigned to a user for a universe, it can be inherited through group or universes folder:

▶ A group can be assigned an access level for a universe. This object access level is inherited by all groups and users it contains.

▶ A user can also be assigned an access level for a universe folder. This access level is inherited by the universes and sub-folders this folder contains.

▶ A group can be assigned an access level for a universe folder. This object access level is inherited by all groups and users it contains for all universes and folders this folder contains.

If an access level is explicitly assigned to a user for a universe, this access level is used, without taking the inherited ones into consideration.

> **Note**
>
> The access levels defined for folders are also inherited by universes created in both Universe Design Tool and Information Design Tool.

When you install BI 4.0, the following access levels are assigned to the Universes root folder:

▶ Public for Everyone group

▶ Private for Administrator group

Therefore, if no access level is assigned to a user, these user access levels apply.

Defining user access level is described in Chapter 7, Section 7.8. It is done in the CMC, and these settings that apply for a user can also be defined for a new universe.

8.7.3 Defining Object Access Level in Information Design Tool

To define object access level in Information Design Tool, follow these steps:

1. Open your business layer in Information Design Tool.

2. In the business layer's list of objects, select an object by clicking it. This object editor opens.

3. In the object editor, select the ADVANCED tab.

4. In the ACCESS LEVEL section, use the dropdown list to select a value for this object access level, as shown in Figure 8.37.

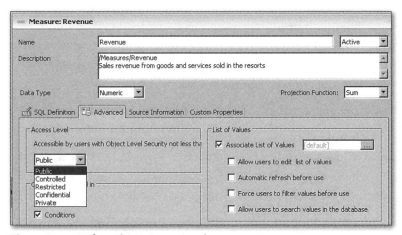

Figure 8.37 Define Object Access Level

5. Click the SAVE button in the main toolbar to save your changes.

To enforce these objects' access levels, you need to publish your universe in a CMS repository (see Section 8.2.4).

8.8   User Attributes

As seen for filters or security profiles, the @VARIABLE function is a useful way to personalize security. However, the list of variables attached to a CMS session and supported by default is limited; the most-used variable is BOUSER. In order to extend this list, user attributes have been introduced in BI 4.0 FP3.

8.8.1   Defining User Attributes

Through this new feature supported by Information Design Tool, you can define new variables for users defined in the CMS repository. When you define these user attributes, you also define how these attributes must get their value for each user. These values can be:

▶ Explicitly set in the CMS repository for each user. In this case, the user attribute is called Enterprise.

▶ Retrieved from an SAP NetWeaver BW, LDAP, or Active Directory system used by the CMS for authentication. By using an external system, you can benefit and reuse attributes already contained in this external system.

To define a user attribute that retrieves values from an external system, your CMS system must first have been configured to support authentication to this external system (see Chapter 3, Sections 3.7 and 3.8 for LDAP and Active Directory and Chapter 10, Section 10.8 for SAP NetWeaver BW).

When you define the user attribute, you need to give the name of the attribute in the external system that must be used to retrieve the values from the external system.

Furthermore, you need this capability both globally for this authentication mode and for each individual user.

User attributes can be defined in the CMC. To add some values for Enterprise user attributes to a user, you must have the "Add or edit user attributes" right for this user.

8.8.2   Using User Attributes

User attributes are recognized by Information Design Tool but not by Universe Design Tool.

You can use user attributes in any script definition where you can use the @VARIABLE function:

► In a join or an object definition.

► In a derived table or calculated column definition.

► In a rows data security profile.

  In a relational filter or in a relational filters business security profile. (However, multidimensional filters business security profiles do not support the use of @ VARIABLE and thus do not support user attributes.)

The use of @VARIABLE operand in relational filters business security profiles has been added in BI 4.0 FP3. Before, it was not possible to use @VARIABLE, even for variables already supported, such as BOUSER.

When using @VARIABLE, you must provide the user attribute internal name. This internal name is given in the CMC when you define it (see Section 8.9.1); it is the name of the user attribute prefixed by SI_.

Example

To use a user attribute called COUNTRY, you need to call it @VARIABLE('SI_COUNTRY').

8.8.3 User Attributes Substitution

In the universe, user attributes used in @VARIABLE functions are replaced by their values for the connected user when the query is sent to the database. These user attributes values are retrieved from the CMS repository when the user logs on to the CMS repository.

It is possible to create several user attributes with the same name, as long as they have different types: Enterprise, SAP, LDAP, or Active Directory. These user attributes defined for external authentications can be prioritized by giving a rank to these parameters, which are defined when configuring each authentication mode:

► "Set priority of SAP attribute binding relative to other attributes bindings" for SAP authentication

▶ "Set priority of LDAP attribute binding relative to other attributes bindings" for LDAP authentication

▶ "Set priority of Active Directory attribute binding relative to other attributes bindings" for Active Directory authentication

If a user with several aliases connects, and if the user attribute name has been defined for different authentications modes, the one to use is the one defined for the authentication mode whose value for the "Set priority of..." parameter is the lowest.

If user attributes has been disabled for external authentications or for this user, then the value used is the one set for the user attribute defined for Enterprise authentication.

8.9 Managing User Attributes in the CMC

User attributes were introduced in the previous section. Let's see how to manage them in the CMC.

8.9.1 Defining User Attributes in the CMC

If you plan to create user attributes from external sources, you first need to allow the retrieval of these user attributes from the external source. To do so, follow these steps:

1. Log on to the CMC and go to the AUTHENTICATION tab.

2. Double-click the LDAP, SAP, or WINDOWS AD line depending on your external authentication mode

3. If you have clicked SAP and the SAP authentication has already been configured, then the SAP authentication panel displays.

   ▶ In this panel, click the OPTIONS tab to display SAP authentication options.

   ▶ In the ATTRIBUTE BINDING OPTIONS section, make sure the IMPORT FULL NAME, EMAIL ADDRESS, AND OTHER ATTRIBUTES checkbox is properly selected.

▶ Use the SET PRIORITY OF SAP ATTRIBUTE BINDING RELATIVE TO OTHER ATTRIBUTES BINDINGS dropdown list to assign a priority to the user attributes retrieved from the SAP system.

▶ Click the UPDATE button to save your changes.

4. If you have clicked LDAP or WINDOWS AD and if this authentication has already been configured, then the corresponding authentication panel displays.

▶ In the ATTRIBUTE BINDING OPTIONS section, make sure the IMPORT FULL NAME, EMAIL ADDRESS, AND OTHER ATTRIBUTES checkbox is properly selected.

▶ Use the dropdown list to assign a priority to the user attributes retrieved from this external system.

▶ Click the UPDATE button to save your changes.

You can define a user attribute in the CMC by following these steps:

1. Log on to the CMC and go to the USER ATTRIBUTE MANAGEMENT tab.

2. In the toolbar, click the ADD A NEW CUSTOM MAPPED ATTRIBUTE button.

3. The ADD ATTRIBUTE panel opens.

4. In the NAME text field, type the user attribute name.

5. In the ADD A NEW SOURCE FOR dropdown list, select the user attribute type.

▶ If you have not configured your CMS to authenticate with an SAP, LDAP, or Active Directory system, then only the ENTERPRISE choice is available.

▶ If you have configured your CMS to authenticate with an SAP, LDAP, or Active Directory system, then you can select SAP, LDAP, or WINDOWS AD type.

6. Click the ADD button to add the source for the user attribute.

7. If your source is an external system, then type in the ATTRIBUTE SOURCE text field, the external attribute to map to your attribute. For example, if your external source is LDAP, to map the LDAP `city` attribute to your user attribute, type `city`, as shown in Figure 8.38.

8. Click OK to close the ADD ATTRIBUTE panel and to create the user attribute. The ADD ATTRIBUTE page closes and the new user attribute is displayed in the list of user attributes defined in this CMS repository.

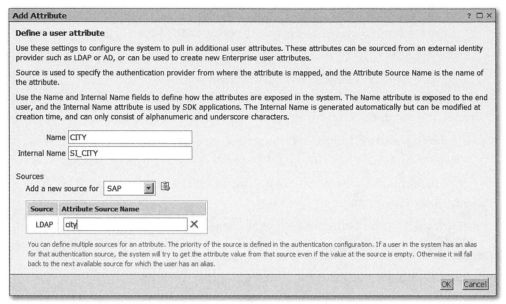

Figure 8.38 Define LDAP User Attribute in CMC

8.9.2 Setting User Attributes Value in the CMC

Once an Enterprise user attribute has been created, you can set value for this attribute for each individual user by following these steps:

1. In the CMC, open the USERS AND GROUPS tab.

2. Select a user then click the MANAGE • PROPERTIES button in the toolbar or right-click it and select PROPERTIES. The PROPERTIES: <USER NAME> panel opens. The ADDITIONAL USER PROPERTIES section contains text fields for all user attributes that have been defined, as shown in Figure 8.39.

3. Type the values of the Enterprise user attributes for this user. LDAP, Active Directory, and SAP user attributes are filled with the values retrieved from the external system and cannot be modified, if the ATTRIBUTE BINDING • IMPORT FULL NAME, EMAIL ADDRESS, AND OTHER ATTRIBUTES checkbox has been selected for this user.

4. Click the SAVE button to save these values.

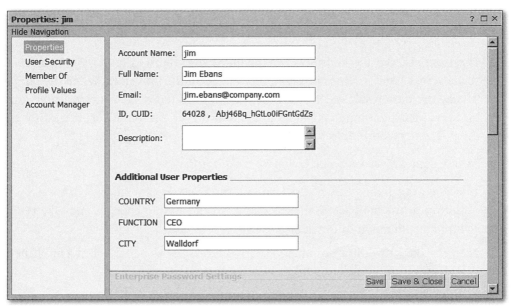

Figure 8.39 User Attributes Values in User Properties Panel

8.9.3 Deleting User Attributes in the CMC

You can delete a user attribute by following these steps:

1. In the CMC, open the USER ATTRIBUTE MANAGEMENT tab.

2. Select the user attribute in the list of user attributes. You can select several user attributes by pressing the Ctrl key.

3. Click the DELETE SELECTED ATTRIBUTES button in the toolbar. The user attributes are deleted and are removed from the list.

When an Enterprise user attribute is deleted, then all values of this attribute that have been defined for users are also deleted.

8.10 Running a Secured Query

When you are defining security on your universe, you might find it useful to test it. For this purpose, Information Design Tool allows you to run a query that takes into consideration the security you have defined. This can be done from the Security Editor or the Published Resources views.

These panels take into consideration the following security rights: "View objects," "Data access," and "Create and edit query on top of the universe." When the query is run, the data result set is filtered by the aggregated data security profile and business security profile that apply to the user logged on to the Security Editor or the PUBLISHED RESOURCES panel.

To test your universe's security, follow these steps:

1. If you are running this secured query from the Security Editor, click the SAVE button in the toolbar in order to save any outstanding changes and take them into consideration in the query.

2. In the Security Editor or in the REPOSITORY RESOURCES panel, select a published universe and right-click it to open its contextual menu.

3. Select RUN QUERY. The query panel opens. It takes into consideration the object access level and aggregated business security profile that apply to the logged on user:

   ▶ The objects denied through object access level are not displayed.

   ▶ The views and objects denied by the create query business security profile are not displayed.

4. Create a query by selecting objects in the pane containing the universe objects and by moving them into the RESULT OBJECTS FOR QUERY pane.

5. Click the VIEW SCRIPT button to display the generated SQL or MDX and check that it has been properly modified and that it takes into consideration:

   ▶ Rows and tables data security profiles (if the universe is relational)

   ▶ Filters business security profiles

   ▶ Aggregation options

6. Click the REFRESH button to run the query. The query takes into consideration the aggregated data and business security profile that apply to the logged on user and the result set displayed by the query panel once the query is done is secured by these security profiles:

   ▶ Connections data security profiles

   ▶ Display data business security profiles

- ▶ User attributes values
- ▶ Object access levels

7. Click the CLOSE button to close the query panel.

> **Warning!**
>
> When you edit a business layer in Information Design Tool, it is also possible to run a query on top of this business layer. This query is not protected by any data or business security profiles or any right, except the connection rights if this business layer still refers to a secured connection saved in the CMS repository.
>
> If you have been able to retrieve a business layer from a universe published in the CMS repository, Information Design Tool assumes that you have the rights to do so and the business layer retrieved locally is no longer impacted by the universe's security profiles.

8.11 Summary

Information Design Tool is the successor to Universe Design Tool. This new metadata design tool delivered in BI 4.0 can create universes enforcing New Semantic Layer capabilities. These universes have been designed in the continuity of universes created with Universe Design Tool in order to ensure a smooth transition.

The security concepts supported by Information Design Tool are also an extension of Universe Design Tool's concepts:

- ▶ The WHERE clause is used in a table auto-join, in an object definition, or in a folder or universe filter.
- ▶ The @VARIABLE customizes the security with variables associated with the user's session.
- ▶ Object access levels define confidentiality level for objects and users.

Furthermore, Information Design Tool offers some enhancements on these security concepts:

- ▶ Access restrictions have been extended to data and business security profiles:
  - ▶ Data security profiles support previous access restriction's security concepts but have been adapted to support multi-source universe

► Business security profiles are common to relational and multidimensional universes and secure the business layer content.

► It contains a new editor dedicated to administration of these security profiles. It is also possible to run queries from published universes. These queries are secured by CMS rights and security profiles.

► User attributes provide the ability to define dynamic variables that can be used in security definition. These attributes can be used in joins, objects, filters, or security profiles definition. They can be explicitly set in the CMS repository or retrieved from an SAP, LDAP, or Active Directory system.

Thus, universes offer a way to define metadata security. For publishing workflows, universe metadata can also be used to personalize data. This method to filter data received by recipients is described in the next chapter, which covers scheduling and publishing.

Scheduling and publishing capabilities allow you to send documents at specified times. Different options define the security to apply, such as Schedule For and External Recipients. Data in publication can also be personalized through the use of profiles.

9   Scheduling and Publishing

BI 4.0 supports scheduling and publishing capabilities that are useful for sharing documents by sending them to different users. Scheduling and publishing offer many attractive advantages:

▶ If your document refresh takes a long time, or if you need to send a document to a large number of users, scheduling allows you to run the document during low server workload peaks, such as during the night.

▶ If your data source is also updated during the night, you can schedule a document and reports refresh that uses this data source just after its update so your end users can immediately access the refreshed instances of documents when they arrive at the office.

▶ Many different options are available, such as sending your document to users who are not part of the BI 4.0 environment, or filtering data and showing the end user only the data they are interested in.

This chapter covers the following scheduling and publishing security concepts:

▶ The scheduling and publishing framework

▶ The scheduling options and the capability to schedule in the name of other users

▶ An introduction to publication

▶ Publication recipients, especially dynamic recipients

▶ Data personalization through publication

▶ Publication options for report bursting

Let's begin by deconstructing the scheduling and publishing framework to better understand its underpinnings.

9.1   Scheduling and Publishing Framework

In scheduling and publishing workflows, various contributors play a role:

▸ The Web Intelligence or Crystal Reports *document designer* creates the document(s) to schedule or to publish.

▸ The *administrator* defines publication profiles.

▸ The *schedule designer* creates the schedule.

▸ The *publication designer* creates the publication. This publication can be run by another user.

▸ The *sender* runs the schedule/publication. He can be different from the schedule/publication designer.

▸ The *recipient* receives the scheduled or published document(s). He can also subscribe to and unsubscribe from publications.

9.1.1   Support for Schedule and Publication

Support for scheduling and publishing varies. You can schedule or publish a document from BI Launch Pad or from the Central Management Console (CMC), but only Web Intelligence, Crystal Reports 2011, and Crystal Reports for Enterprise documents and publications can be scheduled. Additionally, only Web Intelligence, Crystal Reports 2011, Crystal Reports for Enterprise documents, and agnostic documents such as Microsoft Office (Word, PowerPoint, and Excel), PDF, TXT documents can be published. Dashboards, Analysis workspaces, and BI workspaces cannot be scheduled or published. Explorer also uses its own schedule for indexing, but it is not covered in this chapter.

9.1.2   Refresh During Schedule or Publication

Unless you schedule or publish a file that can't be refreshed (such as text files), or unless you explicitly deny it in case of a publication, then a document is refreshed in the name of the sender whenever it is scheduled or published. You can change this setting through the Schedule For option covered in Section 9.2.2.

The security enforced for this sender—either security rights or universe security—applies when the refresh happens.

However, for the connection authentication mode, the single sign-on authentication mode cannot be used since it requires a token of the logged-on user to be passed to the database. By design, this sender is not likely to be connected during a schedule or a publication.

Relying on the database security and single sign-on to filter retrieved data can only be done in two different situations:

▶ If you are using the credential mapping for single sign-on option (see Chapter 6, Section 6.4).

▶ If you are using SAP authentication and have defined STS or SNC. In this case, even if the full user's credentials are not available, it is possible to log on to the SAP NetWeaver BW system.

After the data refresh, the document contains data that the sender's profile is allowed to see. These data can then be filtered through personalization (see Section 9.5) before the document is delivered the recipients.

9.2   Scheduling

The schedule objective is to send a document refreshed to users with a different format and at a specific date and hour. During the schedule, the document is refreshed with the right of the sender, and the recipient receives it with the data of the sender. Because there is no view time security, and if your report lacks the option to refresh upon open, the recipient is able to see the data of the sender.

Once he has received this document, if the recipient refreshes it, he can only see the data his rights allow him to see. Therefore, if some restrictions (SSO connection or row-level security in the connection or on the universes objects) are applied to this user, they are applied during this refresh.

9.2.1   Scheduling Parameters

When you create a schedule for a document, you can provide a set of parameters that define this schedule. These parameters are listed in Table 9.1. Most parameters are common to Web Intelligence and Crystal Reports, though some are exclusive to one of these tools. All parameters are available when scheduling from the BI

Launch Pad and CMC, except "Schedule For," "Web Intelligence Process Settings," and "Notification," which are available only in the CMC.

Parameters	Supported by	Description
Instance title	Web Intelligence Crystal Reports	Specifies names of the generated instances.
Recurrence	Web Intelligence Crystal Reports	Defines the occurrence for scheduling (now, hourly, daily, weekly, and so on)
Schedule For	Web Intelligence Crystal Reports	Defines the sender who runs the schedule (see Section 9.2.2).
Notification	Web Intelligence Crystal Reports	Defines audit and email notification about a publication status (successful or failed).
Database logon	Crystal Reports 2011	Allows you to use another set of credentials for the connection used by the Crystal Reports document. If the document relies on a universe, then its connection is not updated.
Prompts	Web Intelligence Crystal Reports	If the document contains prompts, this parameter defines the values for these prompts.
Filters	Crystal Reports	Defines the filters to apply.
Formats	Web Intelligence Crystal Reports	Defines output file format (Microsoft Excel, Adobe Acrobat, CSV, text files, XML, and so on) of the scheduled document. The list of supported file formats depends on the scheduled document type.
Caching	Web Intelligence	When scheduling, this parameter defines options to cache the documents. Thus, if several users open the same scheduled document, it remains preloaded in the cache.

Table 9.1 Scheduling Parameters

Parameters	Supported by	Description
Destinations	Web Intelligence Crystal Reports	Defines where the generated instance of the scheduled document is sent (BI Inbox, Email, FTP server, and so on).
Print settings	Crystal Reports	Defines options to print the scheduled document.
Events	Web Intelligence Crystal Reports	Defines events that can trigger the publication or to be triggered once the publication is done.
Scheduling Server Group	Web Intelligence Crystal Reports	Defines the servers to use to process the schedule.
View Server Group	Crystal Reports	Defines the Crystal Reports server group to use when a scheduled document is opened by recipients.
Web Intelligence Process Settings	Web Intelligence	Defines the Web Intelligence server group to use when a scheduled document is opened by recipients.
Thumbnail	Crystal Reports	Enables or disables the reports preview.
Languages	Crystal Reports	Defines the languages to use for the scheduling.

Table 9.1 Scheduling Parameters (Cont.)

9.2.2 Schedule For Option

In the CMC, you have the option to schedule, refresh, and send a document on behalf of someone else to the recipient you want. In this case, the schedule is impersonified, and the user used in the *Schedule For* option is used to compute security:

► CMS security rights
► Universe overload
► User object access level
► Connection credentials

For connection credentials, if the connection uses Enterprise credentials or database credentials, the refresh is successful. But if the connection uses SSO, the schedule is "failed" because the user password for the connection is not stored in the CMS. There is one exception: if the connection is accessing SAP NetWeaver BW data and if the SNC/STS is enabled (see Chapter 10). In this case, due to the impersonalization option, the schedule is successful.

This capability is very powerful since it allows a user to refresh a document in the name of any other user. For this reason, you should ensure that you give this capability only to users who must explicitly be given this right for well identified documents.

To prevent a user from scheduling a document on behalf on other users, you must deny him the "Schedule on behalf of other users" right for this document. You can also deny the right at folder level in order to have this right inherited by all objects in this folder.

Schedule For in the CMC

Schedule For can be done only in the CMC. To do so, follow these steps:

1. In the CMC, go to the Folders, Inbox, or Favorites tab.
2. Select the document to schedule.
3. Right-click it and, in the contextual menu, select Schedule to open the Schedule pane.
4. In its left pane, select the Schedule For section.
5. In the right pane, select the Schedule for specified users and user groups radio button, as shown in Figure 9.1.
6. In the Available list, select one or several users or groups:
   - If you select several users, the document is scheduled once for each selected user.
   - If you select a group, the document is scheduled once for each user who belongs to the selected group.
7. Define the other parameters for the schedule in the other sections (Recurrence, Formats, and so on) of the left pane.
8. Click the Schedule button to close the Schedule dialog box and save the schedule options.

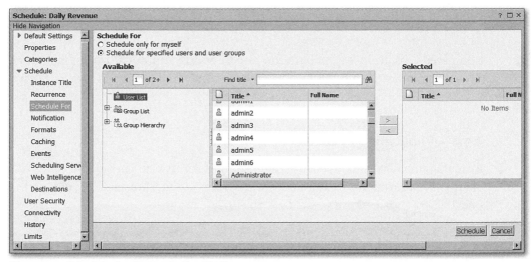

Figure 9.1 Schedule For Option in the CMC

Having considered some of the options available for scheduling, let's turn our attention to publishing.

9.3 Publishing

The main purpose of the publishing is to be able to refresh one of multiple documents, to "personalize" them, and finally to distribute them to a large number of recipients (inside or outside the CMS). These two actions (refresh and personalize) combined are called *report bursting;* when the publication is distributed to large audience, it is also called *mass publication*.

9.3.1 Publishing vs. Scheduling

Publication offers more options and possibilities than scheduling. These are the main additional features that publication offers:

▶ Multiple source documents: including different documents in the publication

▶ Dynamic recipients: sending a publication to users who are external to the system and identified by their email (see Section 9.4)

▶ Personalization: filtering data in the documents during the publication (see Section 9.5)

▶ Report bursting options: defining the method to run the processing (see Section 9.6)

Compared to scheduling, publication also supports additional capabilities, such as delivery rules, merged PDFs, or languages, but they are supported by Crystal Reports publication only.

9.3.2 Publication Parameters

All parameters are available when publishing from BI Launch Pad and the CMC, except "Publication Extension" and "Notification," which are available only in the CMC. These parameters are listed in Table 9.2.

Sections	Supported by	Description
Source Documents	Web Intelligence Crystal Reports	Defines the set of documents to add in the publication and the order of processing. The documents can be a Web Intelligence, Crystal Reports, or agnostic document, but it is not possible to mix both Web Intelligence and Crystal Reports documents. You can also define whether the documents must be refreshed during publication.
Enterprise Recipients	Web Intelligence Crystal Reports	Defines Enterprise recipients, meaning the recipients that exist in the BI 4.0 system and thus can receive the published document in their inbox or Favorites folder.
Dynamic Recipients	Web Intelligence Crystal Reports	Defines the dynamic recipients (see Section 9.4).
Personalization	Web Intelligence Crystal Reports	Defines the local profiles (see Section 9.5).
Formats	Web Intelligence Crystal Reports	Defines the output file format in which the publication is sent. The list of supported file formats depends on the document type (Microsoft Excel, Adobe Acrobat, CSV, text files, XML, and so on).

Table 9.2 Publication Parameters

Sections	Supported by	Description
Print Settings	Crystal Reports	Defines options to print the published document.
Delivery Rules	Crystal Reports	Defines some conditions to deliver the document.
Merged PDF Options	Crystal Reports	Defines some options to merge generated PDFs.
Destinations	Web Intelligence Crystal Reports	Defines where the publication is sent (BI Inbox, email, FTP server, etc.) and how to deliver it (ZIP file, shortcut, and so on).
Prompts	Web Intelligence Crystal Reports	Defines the values for prompts if the document contains them.
Publication Extension	Web Intelligence Crystal Reports	Programmatically adds some tasks to be run after publication processing or publication delivery (this parameter is a dynamically loaded library of code).
Recurrence	Web Intelligence Crystal Reports	Defines the occurrence for publication (now, hourly, daily, weekly, and so on).
Notification	Web Intelligence Crystal Reports	Defines audit and email notification about a publication status (successful or failed).
Events	Web Intelligence Crystal Reports	Defines events that can trigger the publication or to be triggered once the publication is done.
Scheduling Server Group	Web Intelligence Crystal Reports	Defines the servers to use to process the publication.
Advanced	Web Intelligence Crystal Reports	These parameters are used for report bursting (see Section 9.6).

Table 9.2 Publication Parameters (Cont.)

9.4 Publication Recipients

When scheduling a document, only users from the BI 4.0 system can be added as recipients. When publishing a document, however, you can send it to two different users:

▸ *Enterprise recipients*, or users who exist in the BI 4.0 system. As for scheduling, the published document can be sent to a user's inbox or Favorites folder in the CMS repository or in the Public Folders folder.

▸ *Dynamic recipients*, or users who don't belong to the CMS repository. You can send to these users as long as they have an email where they can received the publication.

When you create or edit your publication, you can add Enterprise recipients, dynamic recipients, or both.

9.4.1 Dynamic Recipient Document

To add dynamic recipients to a publication, you need to create a Web Intelligence or Crystal Reports document containing the list of users to send the documents. This document must be saved in the CMS repository.

The data can come from all types of data source supported by Web Intelligence or Crystal Reports: relational database, text files, and so on. The document can be static or refreshable, but only the data contained when the publication is run are used to list the dynamic recipients.

This document needs to have at least three columns, one for each of the following:

▸ The user's unique identifier; it can be any integer as long as it is unique

▸ The user's email address where he receives the publication (since these users are external to the BI 4.0 system, they are not necessarily able to log on to it and have personal folders in it such as the inbox or Favorites folder)

▸ The user's full name

You may also add additional columns containing values for these dynamic recipients for local profiles to map to local filters (see Section 9.5.2).

If you have dynamic recipients, the report bursting option "one database fetch per recipient" (see Section 9.6.2) is not available. Because these external users do not exist in the BI 4.0, they have no rights and the publication cannot apply any rights to these users.

Furthermore, because these recipients are external, they are unlikely to have access to a BI 4.0 system, so the published document must instead be generated using a non-BusinessObjects file format, like PDF or Excel.

9.4.2 Add Dynamic Recipients to a Publication

To add dynamic recipients to your publication, you must first create the recipients document containing the parameters used to identify these recipients and publish it in the CMS repository. Then, in BI Launch Pad or in the CMC, follow these steps:

1. In the CMC or in BI Launch Pad, navigate in the folders to select a publication.

2. Right-click it and, in the contextual menu, select PROPERTIES to open the PROPERTIES pane.

3. In its left pane, select the DYNAMIC RECIPIENTS section to select the source for the dynamic recipients document, as shown in Figure 9.2.

4. In the CHOOSE THE SOURCE FOR THE DYNAMIC RECIPIENTS dropdown list, select one of the following:

   ▸ WEB INTELLIGENCE REPORT DYNAMIC RECIPIENT PROVIDER in order to use a Web Intelligence document for the dynamic recipient document

   ▸ CRYSTAL REPORTS DYNAMIC RECIPIENT PROVIDER in order to use a Crystal Report document for the dynamic recipient document

5. In the left pane, navigate in the folder tree to reach the folder containing this recipient document and select this document.

6. Click OK below this tree to select this document, close the tree, and display the name of the selected document.

7. If the recipient document type is Web Intelligence, select the query of the document to use in the SELECT THE DATASOURCE NAME FOR THE DOCUMENT dropdown list.

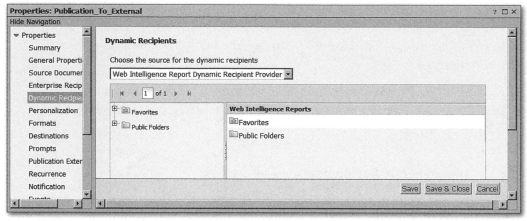

Figure 9.2 Dynamic Recipients Document Selection

8. For each of the three parameters needed to create the dynamic recipients list, select the column in the document that is used to returns these values in the dropdown list, as shown in Figure 9.3.

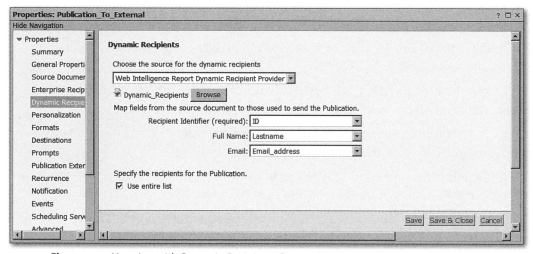

Figure 9.3 Mapping with Dynamic Recipients Document

9. To use the full document content as the recipient list, click the SAVE & CLOSE button to close the PROPERTIES dialog box and use the list of users it contains in the publication.

10. Otherwise, unselect the USE ENTIRE LIST checkbox to explicitly select some users from the list. The rows contained in the document are displayed.

11. In the AVAILABLE list, select some users. Click the > button to move these users to the SELECTED list, as shown in Figure 9.4.

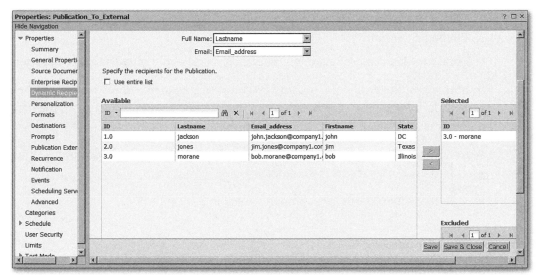

Figure 9.4 Dynamic Users Selection

12. Click the SAVE & CLOSE button to close the PROPERTIES dialog box and use the selected list of users for dynamic recipients.

9.4.3 Subscription and Unsubscription to a Publication

Subscription, which can be done in the CMC or in BI Launch Pad, allows you to add yourself to the list of recipients of a publication. To subscribe to a publication, you must have the "Subscribe to objects" right and follow these steps:

1. Select the publication you want to subscribe to.

2. Right-click it and, in the contextual menu, select SUBSCRIBE.

3. You are added to the list of these publication recipients.

You can also subscribe or unsubscribe from the history page of the publication instances.

9.5   Publication Personalization and Profile

When publication is sent to recipients, you can filter the data contained in the published document received by each individual recipient. This is done through personalization, that you can define using:

▶ Global profiles that are saved as Profile InfoObject in the CMS repository (see Chapter 5, Section 5.2)

▶ Local profiles that are saved in a publication and apply only to this publication

In both cases, the profile defines an object, called the *target*, which is used to filter some values for some recipients. Before a publication is sent to a recipient, the data it contains are filtered through these profiles.

Personalization is more a functional feature than a security method, but it can be used to deny a user access to some data.

In the following sections, we compare global and local profiles.

9.5.1   Global Profile

A global profile defines personalization based on an object from a universe created with Universe Design Tool or Information Design Tool. It is not possible to create a global profile for Crystal Reports on top of business views. Thus, the personalization can only apply to a document created on top of this universe, and must query this object.

A profile is defined by a list of *profile targets*, which are the parameters used to filter the data for the users and groups defined in the profile. Such a target must be an object of a universe. For each target, you can define users and groups that are assigned different *profile values*. These values are the ones used to filter the publication data for the corresponding user.

> **Example**
>
> A profile can have the Country object as its target. This profile can also define:
>
> ▶ France as a profile value for the user herve.
> ▶ US as a profile value for the user bill.
>
> If this profile is used to personalize the publication of a document based on this universe, then, through the publication, herve receives only data filtered for the Country object France, whereas the bill document is filtered for the Country object US.

The global profile is created in the CMC and is stored in the CMS repository as a system InfoObject. The same profile can be reused for several publications.

9.5.2 Local Profile

The local profile is defined only in the publication to which it applies. The local profile target is based column of your document that can be based on either a dimension for a Web Intelligence document, or a field or parameter for a Crystal Reports document.

This profile target is compared to some values used to filter the rows in the document depending. Depending on the recipient types, you have two methods to get these values:

▶ If the recipients of your publication are Enterprise recipients, you can reuse the personalization defined in a global profile. However, the target in the local profile is compared to all values in the global profile for this Enterprise recipient, whatever the target in this global profile is.

▶ If the recipients of your publication are dynamic recipients, the document used to create these dynamic recipients must contain a column for these values. When defining the local profile, you select this column name. The target in the local profile is compared to the value in this column and used to filter data for each recipient.

The same local profile can define personalization for both Enterprise and dynamic recipients.

Example

A local profile uses `State` as its profile target.

For Enterprise recipients, if the local profile is based on a global profile that defines the following personalization:

▶ `herve: State = France`
▶ `herve: City = Paris`

Then, when the local profile is applied to the user `herve`, the local profile target `State` is compared to any personalization of the global profile for `herve: France and Paris`.

For dynamic recipients, you can add a column in the recipients document containing this state for dynamic recipients. If, in the local profile, you select to use this column, when personalization is done, it retrieves the profile value for external users from this document, as shown in Figure 9.5.

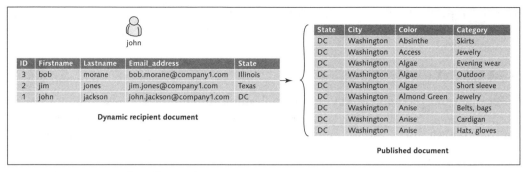

Figure 9.5 Local Profile Based on a Recipient Document

9.5.3 Creating a Global Profile

To create a global profile, follow these steps:

1. In the CMC, go to the PROFILES tab.

2. In the menu bar, select MANAGE • NEW • NEW PROFILE to open the CREATE NEW PROFILE pane.

3. In this pane, in the TITLE text field, enter a name for your profile.

4. Click OK to close this pane and create the profile. The profile is displayed in the profiles list.

5. Double-click the profile to open the PROPERTIES pane for this profile.

6. In the left pane, select the PROFILE TARGETS section to define the objects on which the profile is based.

7. In the right pane, click the ADD button to select the universe and the object.

8. In the UNIVERSE NAME dropdown list, select the universe to use. If you select a folder name and click the SHOW SUBFOLDER button, then the dropdown list is updated with the content of this subfolder where you can select the universe.

9. Once you have selected the universe, click the SELECT OBJECT FROM THE UNIVERSE button to open the UNIVERSE OBJECT SELECTION dialog box that lists the objects of the universe, as shown in Figure 9.6.

10. Select the object to use for the profile and click OK to close the dialog box. The object and its parent folder are displayed in the VARIABLE NAME and CLASS NAME text fields.

11. Click OK to return to the list of profiles targets.

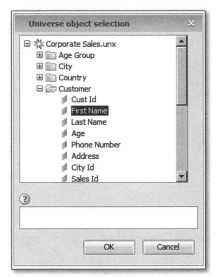

Figure 9.6 Universe Object Selection

12. In the left pane, click the PROFILE VALUES section to display the pane to select target values, as shown in Figure 9.7.

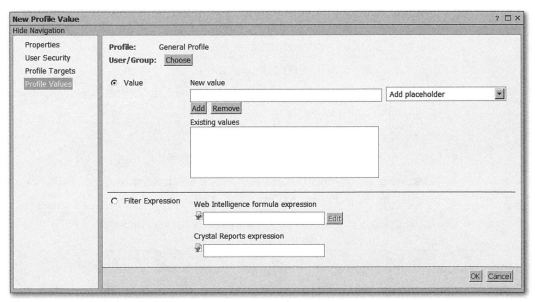

Figure 9.7 Profile Values Definition

13. In the right pane, click the Choose button to select the user or group to which the profiles apply. The list of users and groups is displayed.

14. Navigate in this list to select the user or the group.

15. Click the > button to add it to the list on the right.

16. Click OK to return to the value selection.

17. To enter a value for this user or group, you can either add it manually or use the filter expression. To enter the value explicitly:

   ▶ Select the Value radio button, if it is not yet selected.

   ▶ Type a value in the New value text field.

   ▶ Click the Add button.

   ▶ The value is added to the Existing values list. Repeat for each value you want to add.

18. Instead of typing directly the value, you can also use the filter expression:

   ▶ Select the Filter Expression radio button.

   ▶ Click the Edit button to open the Formula Editor dialog box.

   ▶ In this dialog box, in the dropdown list, select the object to filter, and then click the Formula Editor button to open the Profile list of value dialog box, as shown in Figure 9.8. This dialog box allows you to write this expression by picking objects and showing you the associated values.

   ▶ In the dropdown list, select the operator to use to compute the profile.

   ▶ In the left list containing the possible values for the object, select the value to use when computing the profile.

   ▶ Click the > button to move this value to the list on the right.

   ▶ Click OK to close the Profile list of values dialog box.

   ▶ Click the cross in Formula Editor dialog box header to close it. The value is added as formula expression.

19. Click OK to close the profile editor and save your changes.

> **Warning!**
>
> If you use Web Intelligence formula expression, this Profile list of values works only with universes created with Universe Design Tool. If the target is a universe created with Information Design Tool, it remains empty. As a workaround, you may explicitly type in the values.

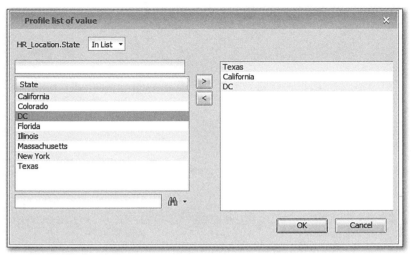

Figure 9.8 Profile Value Selection

9.5.4 Setting Profiles to a Publication

Setting a global profile to a publication or defining a local profile for a publication is done in the same panel. To do so:

1. Create a publication.

2. In the publication PROPERTIES panel, click the PERSONALIZATION section in the left pane to display the PERSONALIZATION pane.

3. To use a global profile to personalize this publication, in the GLOBAL PROFILES section, in the ENTERPRISE RECIPIENT MAPPING dropdown list, select the profile to apply. Once a profile has been assigned, a new dropdown list appears, allowing you to assign another global profile to this publication.

4. To define a local profile based on a global profile for Enterprise recipients:

   ▶ In the LOCAL PROFILES section, in the REPORT FIELD column, in the dropdown list, select a dimension object of the report to be used to filter data.

   ▶ In the ENTERPRISE RECIPIENT MAPPING column, in the dropdown list, select a global profile from among the ones created in the CMS repository, as shown in Figure 9.9. The personalization defined in this profile is applied to the object selected in the REPORT FIELD column.

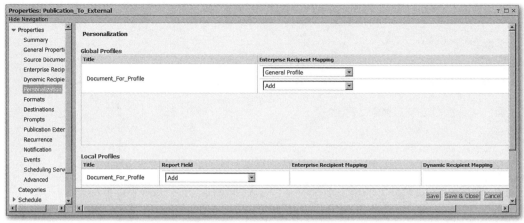

Figure 9.9   Global Profile Selection

5. To define a local profile based on the recipient document for dynamic recipients:

▸ In the LOCAL PROFILES section, in the REPORT FIELD column, in the dropdown list, select a dimension object of the report to be used to personalize data.

▸ In the DYNAMIC RECIPIENT MAPPING column, in the dropdown list, select a column in the dynamic recipient document, as shown in Figure 9.10. For each dynamic recipient, this column contains the values to use with the local profile target in order to personalize data.

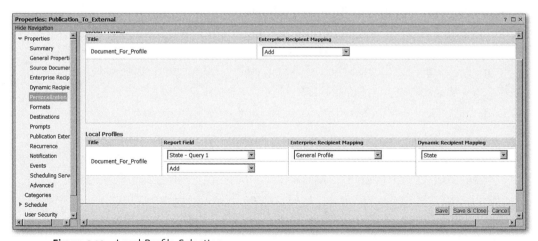

Figure 9.10   Local Profile Selection

6. Click the SAVE & CLOSE button to save the personalization and close the PROPER-TIES dialog box.

9.6 Report Bursting Options

When creating the publication, you can choose from among three methods to process the publication:

▸ One database fetch for all recipients

▸ One database fetch per recipient

▸ One database fetch for each batch of recipients

These options define how the document is refreshed and personalized before being sent to the publication recipients. We cover each option in this section.

These options can be set in the ADVANCED section in the publication PROPERTIES panel.

9.6.1 One Database Fetch for All Recipients

With this option, the data inside the document are refreshed once, even if you have multiple recipients. Later, the documents are personalized and published to each recipient, as shown in Figure 9.11. In this method, the report bursting uses the data source logon credentials of the sender to refresh data.

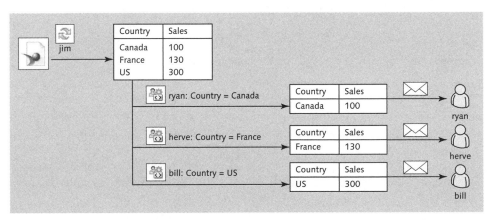

Figure 9.11 Report Refreshed Once but Personalized for Each Recipient

We recommend this option in order to minimize the impact on the data source, because the data source is refreshed only once, thus minimizing the number of database queries.

This is the default option for Web Intelligence. For Web Intelligence, this option is done by simply applying a report filter on top of the report. All data are still in the report. If you publish a report in a Web Intelligence format, your recipient can remove the filter and access all the data, if he can edit the report in design mode. In order to prevent this filter from being removed, it is always better to publish your report in PDF format.

9.6.2 One Database Fetch per Recipient

With this option, the document is refreshed for every recipient. Then it is personalized for each recipient with its profile, before being sent to the recipient, as shown in Figure 9.12. In this method, the report bursting uses the CMS recipient logon credentials of each recipient to refresh data.

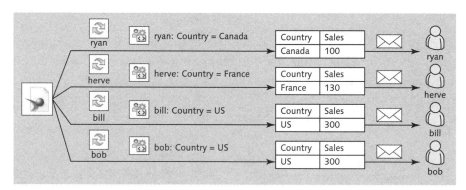

Figure 9.12 Report Refreshed and Personalized Once for Each Recipient

This option is recommended in order to have maximum security, if you have set some security through universes or business views. But it may have a huge impact on your data source, especially if you have lot of recipients, because the document is refreshed as many times as you have recipients.

Dynamic recipients do not exist in the CMS, so this report bursting method cannot use their data source logon credentials to refresh the published document.

If the recipients of the publication are dynamic recipients (See Section 9.4.1):

▶ In Web Intelligence, then this "One Database Fetch per Recipient" option is not available.

▶ In Crystal Reports, the publication is run using the sender's data source logon credentials.

9.6.3 One Database Fetch for Each Batch of Recipients

With this option, the document is refreshed once by the sender. Then personalization and the publishing is done by factorizing the recipients who share the same personalization values (see Section 9.5). Personalization is done once for each possible value and the resulting output is sent to all recipients who have the same personalization values, as shown in Figure 9.13.

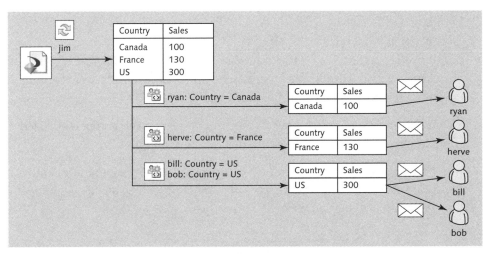

Figure 9.13 Report Refreshed and Personalized Once per Recipient Batch

This option, though not available for Web Intelligence documents, is the default option for Crystal Reports and is recommended for large documents because the data source is refreshed only once. With this option, you can execute the personalization and send actions concurrently on different BI 4.0 servers. Splitting the load across multiple servers helps decrease the time required for large publications.

9.7 Summary

Scheduling and publishing are two core capabilities for collaboration that are offered by BI 4.0. Because they are powerful, proper security is of paramount importance.

Scheduling enforces a set of rights in BI 4.0 system; the Schedule For option allows a user to schedule a document in the name of another user.

Publication offers additional options beyond those available for scheduling: multiple documents, dynamic recipients, personalization, and report bursting. With dynamic recipients, publications can be sent to external users who do not have accounts in the CMS repository.

Additionally, data in publications can be filtered through two kinds of profiles:

▸ Global profiles, which are based on a universe objects and filter values for these objects for specified users and groups

▸ Local profiles, which, depending on the recipient type, rely on values retrieved either from a global profile for Enterprise recipients or from the document containing dynamic recipients for dynamic recipients

Report bursting options define how the document is refreshed and personalized—another important collaborative feature that is offered by BI 4.0.

With scheduling and publishing, this chapter concludes the presentation of how to secure a BI 4.0 system. The next chapter focuses on their specific use when using SAP NetWeaver BW data sources.

SAP NetWeaver BW implements its own security repository. If BI 4.0 is configured to authenticate with SAP NetWeaver BW, some specificities can be used when querying data from SAP NetWeaver BW: connections, single sign-on, and user attributes.

10 Security for SAP NetWeaver BW Data Sources

The previous chapters describe how to set up security in your BI 4.0 system. BI 4.0 reporting tools can also query the SAP NetWeaver BW system and use it as a data source. This SAP NetWeaver BW system also has the specificity to contain its own security repository that can be used by BI 4.0 as an external source for authentication.

This chapter covers how to secure your BI 4.0 system using the SAP NetWeaver BW system as an external authentication system. As it walks through BI 4.0 security, it addresses the following topics:

▶ An overview of SAP authentication

▶ How to configure SAP authentication

▶ The different database connections to an SAP NetWeaver BW system

▶ Single sign-on to SAP NetWeaver BW database, and how to use Secure Network Communications (SNC) and Security Token Service (STS)

▶ How to configure STS

▶ The SAP user attributes that can be enforced in universes

Note
This chapter does not describe the integration of SAP Crystal Reports 2011 into SAP NetWeaver BW or the SNC configuration.

10.1 SAP Authentication

Recall the Chapter 3, Section 3.1 coverage of external authentication. SAP NetWeaver BW authentication follows those same principles, which we summarize here.

10.1.1 SAP NetWeaver BW System Parameters

The SAP NetWeaver BW system differs from the other databases in terms of the parameters needed to identify and connect to it. Different workflows require the parameters listed in Table 10.1 when authenticating to an SAP system.

SAP NetWeaver BW Parameter	Parameter Description
System ID	This parameter comprises of three letters that identify the SAP NetWeaver BW system name.
Client	This parameter comprises of three numbers that identify the SAP NetWeaver BW client.
Message Server Logon Group	If your SAP NetWeaver BW system has been clusterized, you need to provide the message server name and the name of its logon group.
Application Server System Number	If your SAP NetWeaver BW system has *not* been clusterized, you need to provide the application server name and the system number. The system number is a number between 00 and 99.
Username Password	User account and password are used to connect to the SAP NetWeaver BW system.
Language	This parameter identifies the language used to retrieve data.

Table 10.1 Parameters to Access SAP NetWeaver BW System

You may ask your SAP NetWeaver BW administrator to give you these parameters so you can connect to the system.

10.1.2 SAP Authentication Principles

In SAP BusinessObjects XI 3.x, in order to authenticate with SAP, you must install the BusinessObjects Integration Kit for SAP Solutions on all client and server installations. This kit contains the SAP NetWeaver BW MDX driver and libraries used to connect to the SAP NetWeaver BW server.

As of BI 4.0, you no longer need to install this integration kit because out-of-the-box SAP authentication is available by default in client and server installers. But you still need to configure SAP authentication and define the SAP systems used for authentication.

To set up this SAP authentication, you need to make sure that your SAP NetWeaver BW system meets the minimum requirements. Refer to the Product Availability Matrix (PAM) at *http://service.sap.com/pam* to confirm that your configuration is supported.

This section details how to configure the SAP authentication. It does not describe how to store Crystal Reports 2011 or Dashboard in the SAP NetWeaver BW system. With BI 4.0, tight integration to SAP NetWeaver BW, Crystal Reports 2011, and Dashboards are stored in the BI 4.0 CMS repository rather than in the SAP NetWeaver BW repository. Furthermore, this capability is not supported in Crystal Reports for Enterprise.

SAP authentication is used for:

▶ The logon process, allowing SAP NetWeaver BW users to log on to the CMS repository using the same credentials they use to authenticate to the SAP NetWeaver BW system.

▶ The SAP BusinessObjects reports refresh, for retrieving data from this SAP NetWeaver BW system. The SAP authentication controls access to the data, and retrieves only the data users are allowed to see.

Authenticating to the SAP NetWeaver BW system has the following advantages:

▶ **It eases user management (creation of users, password modifications)**
This user management for both systems is done in only one place: the SAP NetWeaver BW server. All modifications done in the SAP NetWeaver BW system are automatically and dynamically replicated in the BI 4.0 system because SAP NetWeaver BW users are mapped to BI 4.0 users.

▶ **It preserves and leverages all your SAP NetWeaver BW authorizations.** Since you've already defined an SAP NetWeaver BW authorization matrix, you don't want to modify this matrix. You are leveraging this matrix when refreshing BI 4.0 reports based on SAP NetWeaver BW data. The BI 4.0 system delegates all the authorization parts to the SAP NetWeaver BW system. So the SAP NetWeaver BW system validates your BI 4.0 requests and the BI 4.0 users retrieve only the SAP NetWeaver BW data they are allowed to see.

As for LDAP and Active Directory authentications, in order to authenticate to an external SAP system, you need to replicate SAP NetWeaver BW users into the CMS repository.

10.1.3 Role and User Mapping

As described in Chapter 3, Section 3.5, external authentication is done by mapping users and groups from the external system to users and groups defined in the CMS repository. In the SAP authentication case:

▶ SAP NetWeaver BW roles are considered and imported as groups into the CMS repository.

▶ SAP NetWeaver BW users who belong to an imported SAP NetWeaver BW role can also be imported in the CMS repository as users under the group mapped to the SAP NetWeaver BW role.

When an SAP NetWeaver BW role is imported into the CMS repository, a group is created in the CMS repository; its name follows this syntax:

```
<SAP System ID>~<SAP client Number>/<SAP role>
```

Once the SAP NetWeaver BW role is imported in the CMS repository as a group, all SAP NetWeaver BW users who belong to this role can log on to the BI 4.0 system using their SAP NetWeaver BW user name and password.

When an SAP NetWeaver BW user is imported into the CMS repository, a user is created in the CMS repository; that user's SAP alias (see Chapter 3, Section 3.5) follows this syntax:

```
<SAP System ID>~<SAP client number>/<SAP user name>
```

Only the user's name is stored in the CMS repository; the password remains in the SAP NetWeaver BW system and is not duplicated in the CMS repository.

For example, in the SAP NetWeaver BW system identified by the system ID PRD and the client number 100, the role HR_ROLE is created in the CMS repository as the group PRD~100@HR_ROLE, as shown in Figure 10.1.

From the same system, the user jim is created in the CMS repository as the user PRD~100/JIM.

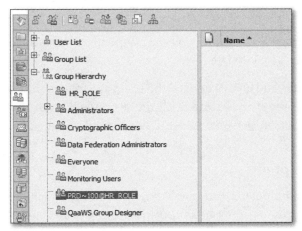

Figure 10.1 Role Imported into the CMS Repository

When these new groups are imported from the SAP NetWeaver BW roles, they don't belong to any other group. Thus, the users imported and created from the SAP NetWeaver BW system belong only to these mapped groups and the Everyone group. If this Everyone group has been given only a few rights, these users inherit only those rights.

Therefore, once these groups are imported to the CMS repository, you need to give corresponding rights to these groups so they can access connections, universes, public folders and applications, depending on your users' needs (see Chapter 4, Section 4.7).

10.1.4 Users and Groups Updates

Changes may occur in the SAP NetWeaver BW system so you need to update the users created from this system. The different cases are described in Chapter 3, Section 3.5.4. However, in SAP authentication, it is not possible to disable the alias creation at user login. A new alias is always created when the user logs on if it does not exist in the BI 4.0 system.

You can also schedule these groups updates to run at times when active system use is low, and thereby avoid adding to its workload during peak activities. Furthermore, by defining the schedule frequency, you can make sure your system is regularly synchronized with the external system.

The scheduling recurrence options are the same as the ones supported by the BI 4.0 to schedule a report. To define and run these schedules, you need to have an Adaptive Job Server up and running in your servers.

You can schedule a roles update or both a roles and users update. A scheduled update can take the same settings as an update.

Once you have scheduled the roles and aliases update, the users are created under the corresponding groups. Once the user is created, all the dependencies of this user are also created: the inbox folder, personal folder, and personal categories.

10.1.5 SAP Authentication Options

The SAP authentication can be parameterized through several options, which are described in Table 10.2. These options apply to all SAP system registered in the CMS and used for authentication.

Authentication Option	Description
Enable SAP authentication	If this option is disabled, then external authentication to all SAP NetWeaver BW systems is disabled.
Content folder root	This parameter defines the folder used as a root when replicating the SAP NetWeaver BW folder structure for Crystal Reports publication. By default, it is *Folders/SAP/2.0*. If you change this value to another folder, you must also change it in the Content Administration Workbench.
Default system	Select the default SAP NetWeaver BW to log on to the BI 4.0 system. You can use this default system to avoid requiring a user to type his whole identity if he already has been authenticated to this system. If he authenticates to this default system, then he can just type his user name, instead of his user name prefixed by the SAP system name. Otherwise, if you do not specify a particular SAP system in the logon dialog box, then user must also enter his user name prefixed by the SAP system name.

Table 10.2 SAP Authentication Options, without SSO Options

Authentication Option	Description
Max. number of failed attempts to access entitlement system	This parameter defines the number of times the server tries to connect to the SAP system to authenticate a user. If this value is -1, then there is no limit: The server keeps trying to connect to the SAP NetWeaver BW system until it succeeds. If this value is 0, then the server tries only once.
Keep entitlement system disabled [seconds]	This parameter defines the number of seconds before retrying an authentication against the SAP system after a failed authentication.
Max. concurrent connections per system	This parameter defines the number of concurrent connections that can be opened with the SAP NetWeaver BW system from this CMS repository.
Number of uses per connection	This parameter defines the number of logons a connection to an SAP NetWeaver BW system can handle.
Concurrent users and named users	When users are imported from the SAP NetWeaver BW, this parameter defines licenses used by the newly created users. You can choose between concurrent users or named users.
Import full name, email address and other attributes	When users are imported from the SAP NetWeaver BW, then, if this parameter is selected, some user properties are retrieved as well. These include full name and email address and also the attributes used for user attributes (see Section 10.8). If this option is not selected, then these user attributes are not retrieved from the SAP NetWeaver BW.
Set priority of SAP attribute binding relative to other attributes binding	When a user account has aliases from different external authentication systems (SAP, Active Directory, or LDAP), you need to use this parameter to define what system is used to retrieve attributes (full name, email address, and user attributes) to attach to the user account. The value with the highest priority is 1, whereas 3 is the value with the lowest priority. See also Chapter 8, Section 8.8 for more information on user attributes priority.

Table 10.2 SAP Authentication Options, without SSO Options (Cont.)

As shown in Figure 10.2, to log on to the CMS repository from client tools using SAP authentication, follow these steps on the BI 4.0 products logon page:

1. Enter the CMS repository name.

2. Enter the user name as it was created in the CMS repository:

   `<SAP System ID>~<SAP client number>/<SAP user name>`

3. Enter the SAP NetWeaver BW password.

4. Select SAP for the authentication mode.

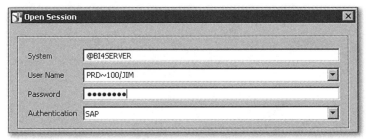

Figure 10.2 Logon Dialog Box with SAP Authentication

But if your system has been configured to authenticate to only one SAP NetWeaver BW system, then, for the user name, instead of typing the full user name as it was created by default in the CMS repository, you can type only the `<SAP user name>`. You have selected the SAP authentication mode and, because there is no ambiguity, the system is able to resolve the user name.

Similarly, if your system has been configured to authenticate to several SAP NetWeaver BW systems for authentication, and if you have defined a default system (see the "Default System" parameter in Table 10.2), then to authenticate to this system, you can also enter just `<SAP user name>`.

However, to authenticate to a system different from the default one, you must enter the user name in its long form.

If you are logging on from BI Launch Pad or CMC, you can directly type the SAP system parameters in the dedicated text fields, as seen in Figure 10.3.

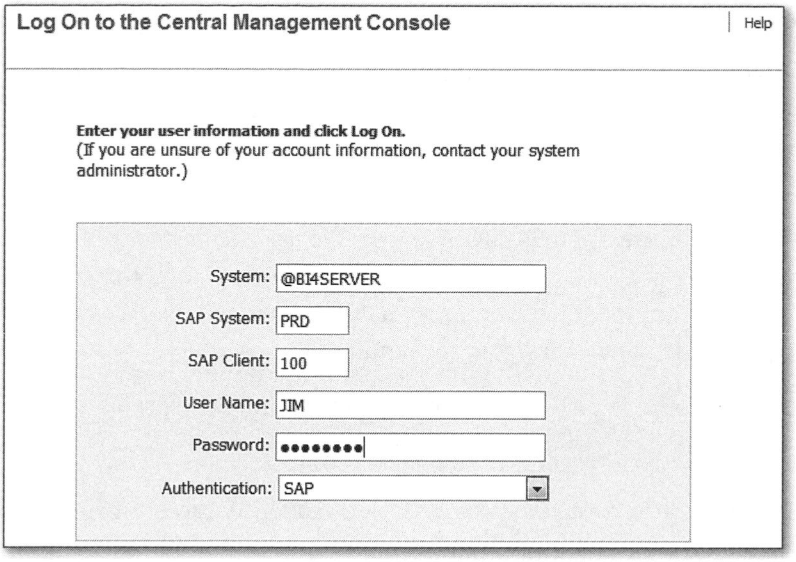

Figure 10.3 CMC Logon Dialog Box with SAP Authentication

10.2 Configuring SAP Authentication

As explained in the previous section, SAP authentication is done by replicating SAP NetWeaver BW roles and users in the CMS repository. This configuration is done mainly in the CMC, through the following steps:

1. Create an account in the SAP NetWeaver BW system, used to connect to this system.

2. In the CMC, declare the SAP NetWeaver BW system.

3. Set SAP authentication options.

4. Import SAP NetWeaver BW roles.

5. Update SAP NetWeaver BW users and roles.

Let's walk through each one.

10.2.1 Creating a Dedicated SAP NetWeaver BW Account

To manage the configuration between the BI 4.0 system and the SAP NetWeaver BW system, you need to use an SAP NetWeaver BW account to read, validate, and authorize the users and roles to import into the CMS repository.

You can use an existing SAP NetWeaver BW account if it has enough rights, but we recommend that you create an SAP NetWeaver BW user dedicated to this task to avoid sharing an account for multiple different tasks. Furthermore, this account can be given only the minimum requested rights. Ask your SAP NetWeaver BW administrator to help define which rights are required.

To create this new account in SAP NetWeaver BW, follow these steps:

1. Connect to your SAP NetWeaver BW using SAP Logon.

2. Use Transaction SU01 to create this new SAP NetWeaver BW account and associate it with a role.

3. Use Transaction PFCG01 to give some authorizations to the role where this user belongs and give this role these authorization objects: S_DATASET, S_RFC and S_USER_GROUP.

If necessary, ask your SAP NetWeaver BW administrator to create this account and to assign it the minimum requested rights.

10.2.2 Registering the SAP System

To configure the SAP authentication, you must register the SAP NetWeaver BW system in the CMC by following these steps:

1. Go to the Authentication tab in the CMC.

2. Double-click the SAP line to open the SAP authentication wizard.

3. In the Entitlement Systems tab, enter the parameters that define your SAP NetWeaver BW system, as shown in Figure 10.4.

   ▶ In the Logical system name text field, enter a name to identify this SAP NetWeaver BW system.

   ▶ Enter the various parameters to define the SAP NetWeaver BW system, as described in Table 10.1.

   ▶ In the User name and Password text fields, enter the credentials of the SAP NetWeaver BW user account created previously (see Section 10.2.1).

▶ In the LANGUAGE text field, enter the language to query the SAP NetWeaver BW system.

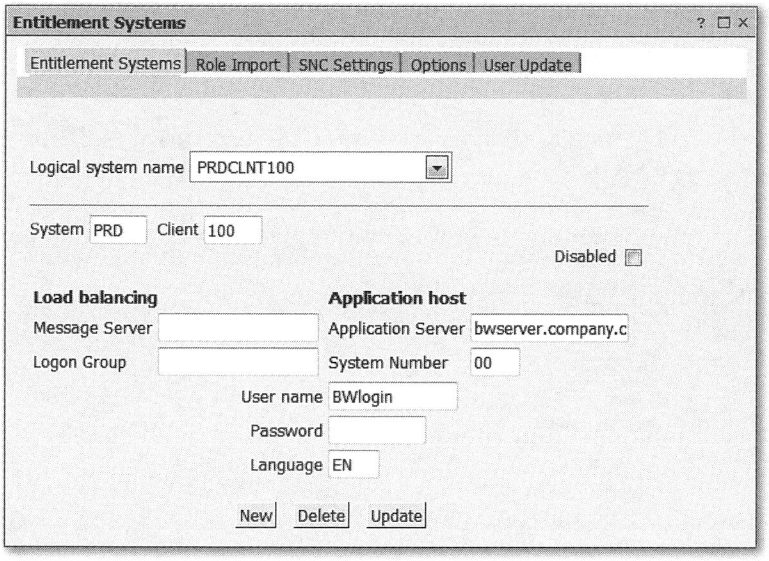

Figure 10.4 SAP NetWeaver BW System Parameters

4. Make sure the DISABLED checkbox is unchecked. If you check the DISABLED checkbox, then the authentication to this SAP NetWeaver BW system will be disabled and the users can no longer log on. If you have added other authentication systems, the other systems remain available.

5. Click the NEW button to enter this system into the CMS. This particular SAP NetWeaver BW system is added to the list of SAP NetWeaver BW systems.

You can add another SAP NetWeaver BW system by repeating these steps.

To modify the parameters of an SAP NetWeaver BW system you have already added into the CMS repository, follow these steps:

1. Open the ENTITLEMENT SYSTEMS tab in the SAP Authentication wizard, as described at the beginning of this section.

2. Select the system to update in the LOGICAL SYSTEM NAME dropdown list.

3. Modify the parameters of this system.

4. Click the UPDATE button to modify the SAP NetWeaver BW parameters.

10.2.3   Defining Authentication Options

Once the SAP NetWeaver BW system has been registered, you can set the SAP authentication options described in Table 10.2 by following these steps:

1. Open the ENTITLEMENT SYSTEMS tab in the SAP Authentication wizard, as described in Section 10.2.2.

2. Click the OPTIONS tab. This tab, shown in Figure 10.5, contains the different options described in Table 10.2.

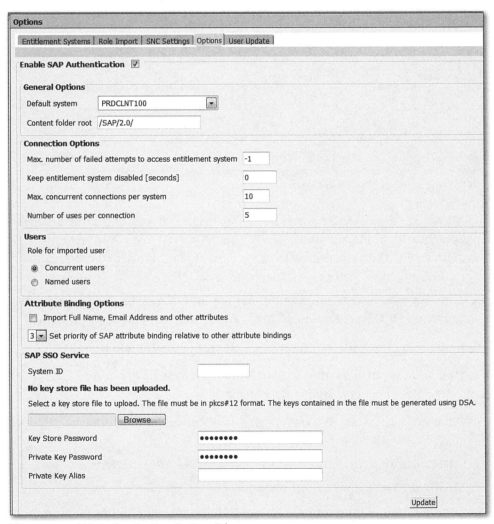

Figure 10.5   SAP Authentication Options Tab

3. Modify these options, except for the options listed in the SAP SSO Service that are not mandatory for SAP authentication. These options are detailed in Section 10.7.4, in the description of STS configuration.

4. To completely enable or disable SAP authentication to all SAP systems, check or uncheck the Enable SAP Authentication checkbox.

5. Click the Update button to save these parameters.

10.2.4 Importing Roles

In the SAP NetWeaver BW system, every user belongs to a role. Once the SAP system has been defined in the CMC, you can import roles from this SAP system by following these steps:

1. Go to the CMC and open the SAP authentication wizard, as described in Section 10.2.2.

2. Click the Role Import tab. In this tab, as shown in Figure 10.6, select the SAP NetWeaver BW roles to import into the CMS repository.

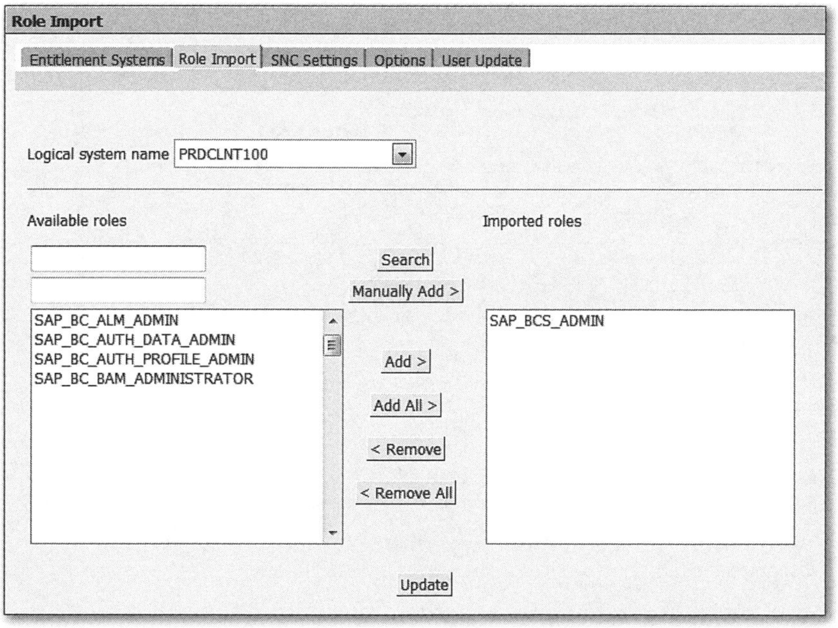

Figure 10.6 Roles Selection

3. In the LOGICAL SYSTEM NAME dropdown list, select an SAP system you have configured and enabled in the ENTITLEMENT SYSTEMS tab.

4. In the AVAILABLE ROLES list, select the roles to import (use the ⌈Ctrl⌉ key to select several roles).

5. Click the ADD button to move these roles into the IMPORTED ROLES list.

6. Click the UPDATE button to create a group in the CMS repository for each selected role.

10.2.5 Updating Users and Roles

The list of users and groups in the SAP NetWeaver BW system may evolve. For this reason, you may schedule automatic updates between the SAP NetWeaver BW system and your CMS repository to ensure that the mapping of roles and users remains synchronized. To do so, follow these steps:

1. Go to the SAP AUTHENTICATION page, as described in Section 10.2.2.

2. Click the USER UPDATE tab. In this tab, as shown in Figure 10.7, you can set up how users are updated.

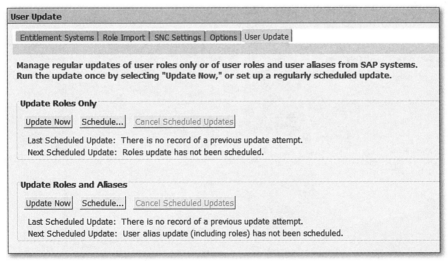

Figure 10.7 User Update Tab

3. To update mapped groups, click:

▶ The UPDATE NOW button in the UPDATE ROLES ONLY section to update only groups created from SAP NetWeaver BW roles.

▶ The UPDATE NOW button in the UPDATE ROLES AND ALIASES section to update only groups and users created from the SAP NetWeaver BW roles and users.

4. To schedule this update, click:

▶ The SCHEDULE button in the UPDATE ROLES ONLY section to update only groups created from SAP NetWeaver BW roles.

▶ The SCHEDULE button in the UPDATE ROLES AND ALIASES section to update only groups and users created from the SAP NetWeaver BW roles and users.

Whichever schedule update option you choose, the SCHEDULE: UPDATE AUTHENTICATION GROUP MEMBERSHIP dialog box opens, which is where you can define the schedule options. As shown in Figure 10.8, these options are the same as the ones supported by the platform for scheduling any job or document.

Figure 10.8 Scheduling Options for Mapped Groups and Users Schedule

10.2.6 Validating the SAP Authentication Configuration

To validate that the users and groups have been properly created, you can go to the USERS AND GROUPS tab in the CMC. If the groups have been created, then the BI 4.0 system was able to connect to the SAP NetWeaver BW system and add enough rights to import and create the user groups in the BI 4.0 system. This means that the authentication configuration were successful.

After granting rights to some applications and some rights to the imported groups, you can also try to log on to any BI 4.0 application (products or tools) using an imported user. If you can log on to any of these applications, then your SAP authentication is well configured.

10.3   SAP Connections

After configuring the CMS repository to authenticate with SAP NetWeaver BW, you can also use the same SAP NetWeaver BW system as a data source for the various reporting tools. To do this, you need to create a connection to this SAP NetWeaver BW system.

As described in Chapter 6, which covers connections in detail, BI 4.0 supports various technologies to enforce these connections. There are four different possible connections for the SAP NetWeaver BW system:

▶ OLAP connection created with Information Design Tool or the CMC

▶ Relational connection created with Information Design Tool

▶ Relational connection created with Universe Design Tool

We do not cover Crystal Reports 2011 since it uses a connection that it is the only one to support. Furthermore, where possible, Crystal Reports for Enterprise should now be privileged against Crystal Reports 2011.

Table 10.3 details the technology and connection type each product can use to access the SAP NetWeaver BW system.

Connection Type	Product	Technology
OLAP connection created with Information Design Tool or CMC	▶ Web Intelligence ▶ Crystal Reports for Enterprise ▶ Dashboard	SAP Direct Access
	▶ Analysis, Edition for OLAP	Direct access through BICS
Relational Data Federator data source created with Information Design Tool	▶ Web Intelligence ▶ Crystal Reports for Enterprise ▶ Explorer ▶ Dashboard	Multi-source relational universe created with Information Design Tool

Table 10.3   Technology and Connection to SAP NetWeaver BW Used by Various Products

Connection Type	Product	Technology
Relational connection created with Universe Design Tool	▶ Web Intelligence ▶ Live Office (through Web Intelligence) ▶ Dashboard (through Query as a Web Service)	OLAP universe created with Universe Design Tool

Table 10.3 Technology and Connection to SAP NetWeaver BW Used by Various Products (Cont.)

These different connections are described in the next sections, but their creation is described in Section 10.4.

10.3.1 OLAP Connection Created in Information Design Tool or CMC

This connection relies on the BICS component and can be used in two workflows:

▶ By OLAP analysis to directly access BEx query

▶ By Web Intelligence, Crystal Reports for Enterprise, or Dashboard to directly query a BEx query, without the need for UNX (in this case, it is called *SAP Direct Access*)

This connection is a real multidimensional connection—it allows you to access normal hierarchies and to select hierarchy member (native hierarchy format). Such a connection is used by reporting tools to retrieve data from a BEx query. It supports key BEx query metadata such as structures, variables, restricted and calculated key figures.

This connection can refer to an SAP NetWeaver BW server, a cube on this server or a BEx query based on a cube of this server.

▶ If the connection refers to a BEx query, then the query can be run only on this query.

▶ If the connection refers to a cube, then users must select one of the BEx queries in the reporting tool created on this cube to retrieve data from it.

▶ If the connection refers to a server, then users must select one of the BEx queries in the reporting tool created on this cube on this server to retrieve data from it.

This connection can be created in Information Design Tool and in the CMC (see Chapter 6, Section 6.5). But in Information Design Tool, it is not possible to select prompted authentication as the authentication mode and, in the CMC, it is not possible to select credentials mapping as the authentication mode.

In the CMS repository, this connection is stored as an OLAP Connection InfoObject and supports only general rights.

10.3.2 Relational Data Federator Data Source Created in Information Design Tool

This connection relies on the Data Federator and can be used only for universes created by Information Design Tool.

This connection, and thus universes created from this connection, does not support SAP NetWeaver BW hierarchies, structures, or restricted and calculated key figures.

You cannot create this connection in a local project; you need to create it directly in the CMS repository through the PUBLISHED RESOURCES view. It relies on the Data Federator Query Server.

When you create a universe from this connection, you need to do the following:

1. Create the connection in the CMS repository.
2. Create a connection shortcut from this connection in your local project.
3. Create a multi-source data foundation, even if you intend to access only this single data source.

This connection accesses the InfoProvider (InfoCube, DataStore Object, Master Data InfoProvider, MultiProvider, etc.) from the SAP NetWeaver BW system using SQL language. However, it does not support BEx queries.

When you create this connection, you select an InfoProvider that is used as a fact table when a data foundation is created on this connection.

In the CMS repository, such a data source is stored as a Data Federator data source InfoObject, and it supports general and custom rights.

10.3.3 Relational Connection Created in Universe Design Tool

This type of connection is inherited from XI 3.x. You use a monosource relational universe (UNV), which accesses the BEx query or the BW Cube but in a flat view.

To create a universe with Universe Design Tool on top of an SAP NetWeaver BW system, you need to create an OLAP connection to this SAP NetWeaver BW system in Universe Design Tool.

This universe is monosource and is relational (that is, it flattens the dimensions coming from the OLAP database, as described in Chapter 7, Section 7.1.2).

In the CMS repository, such a connection is stored as a Relational Connection InfoObject and it supports general and custom rights.

10.3.4 Authentication Modes

As for other connections, the SAP NetWeaver BW connections support the following authentication modes, which are more fully detailed in Chapter 6, Section 6.3:

▶ Fixed credentials: The username and password are explicitly saved in the connection. When accessing the SAP NetWeaver BW system to query data, these credentials are always used.

▶ Credentials mapping: The connection does not store any credentials. They are saved as user's properties and saved in the CMS repository. When accessing the SAP NetWeaver BW system, the credentials are retrieved from the user's properties.

▶ Prompted authentication: No credentials are saved in the connection. When accessing the SAP NetWeaver BW system (to refresh a report, for example), the credentials are requested from the user.

▶ Single sign-on: No credentials are saved in the connection. The credentials provided to log on to the CMS repository are used to connect to the SAP NetWeaver BW system.

These authentication modes and connections are not identically supported by all products. Table 10.4 lists the authentications and connections supported by various products. In this table, UNV indicates universes created with Universe Design Tool, and UNX indicates universes created with Information Design Tool.

Connection Type	Product	Technology
OLAP connection created with Information Design Tool or CMC	▶ Web Intelligence ▶ Crystal Reports for Enterprise ▶ Dashboard	SAP Direct Access ▶ Fixed ▶ Credentials mapping ▶ SSO
	▶ Analysis, Edition for OLAP	Direct access through BICS ▶ Fixed ▶ Prompted ▶ SSO
Relational Data Federator data source created with Information Design Tool	▶ Web Intelligence ▶ Crystal Reports for Enterprise ▶ Explorer ▶ Dashboard	Multi-source relational universe created with Information Design Tool ▶ Fixed ▶ Credentials mapping ▶ SSO
Relational connection created with Universe Design Tool	▶ Web Intelligence ▶ Live Office (through Web Intelligence) ▶ Dashboard (through Query as a Web Service)	OLAP universe created with Universe Design Tool ▶ Fixed ▶ Credentials mapping ▶ SSO

Table 10.4 Supported SAP NetWeaver BW Connections for Various Products

10.4 Creating SAP NetWeaver BW Connections

Depending on the connection type you want to create, you need to use different tools. These workflows to create these connections in these tools are described in the following sections.

10.4.1 Creating an OLAP Connection in Information Design Tool

To create an SAP NetWeaver BW OLAP connection in Information Design Tool, follow these steps:

1. As described in Chapter 6, Section 6.5.1, open the OLAP CONNECTION wizard, give a name to the new connection, and go to the DRIVER SELECTION pane.

2. In the OLAP MIDDLEWARE DRIVER SELECTION page, select SAP • SAP NETWEAVER BI 7.x • SAP BICS CLIENT.

3. Click the NEXT button.

4. In the PARAMETERS FOR SAP NETWEAVER BI 7.x page shown in Figure 10.9, in the AUTHENTICATION dropdown list, select the authentication mode:

   ▶ USE SPECIFIED USER NAME AND PASSWORD for fixed credentials

   ▶ USE SINGLE SIGN ON for single sign-on

   ▶ USE BUSINESSOBJECTS CREDENTIAL MAPPING for secondary credentials

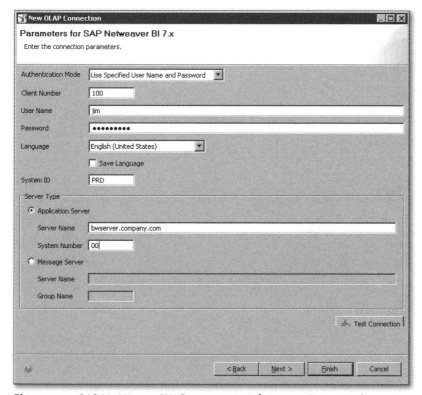

Figure 10.9 SAP NetWeaver BW Parameters in Information Design Tool

5. Enter the parameters that identify the SAP NetWeaver BW system. These parameters are described in Table 10.1.

6. Click the NEXT button.

7. In the CUBE SELECTION page shown in Figure 10.10, select the DO NOT SPECIFY A CUBE IN THE CONNECTION radio button if you want the connection to refer to an SAP server. Otherwise, select the SPECIFY A CUBE IN THE CONNECTION radio button and, in the tree list, navigate in the server content to select a cube or a BEx query.

   To get the list of cubes, if the authentication mode is single sign-on, you need to authenticate to a CMS using an SAP authentication in order to use this session to connect to the SAP NetWeaver BW system.

8. Click the FINISH button to close the connection wizard and create the connection.

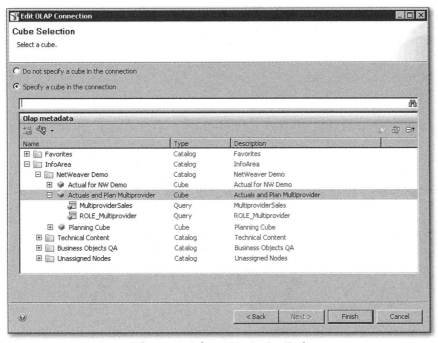

Figure 10.10 BEx Query Selection in Information Design Tool

10.4.2 Creating an OLAP Connection in CMC

The OLAP connection created in Information Design Tool can also be created in the CMC. To create an SAP NetWeaver BW OLAP connection in the CMS, follow these steps:

1. As described in Chapter 6, Section 6.5.3, go to the OLAP CONNECTIONS tab in the CMC and create a new OLAP connection.

2. Enter a name and, in the PROVIDER dropdown list, select SAP NETWEAVER BUSINESS WAREHOUSE. The panel updates to display the parameters to enter for an SAP NetWeaver BW system, as shown in Figure 10.11.

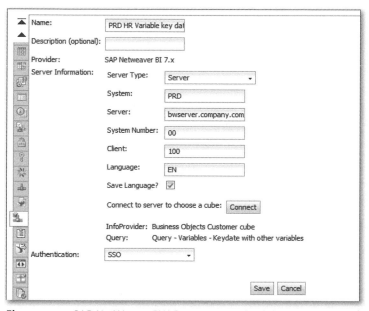

Figure 10.11   SAP NetWeaver BW Parameters in CMC Connection Wizard

3. Enter the parameters as described in Table 10.1.

4. If your connection simply refers to the SAP NetWeaver BW server, go to next step. Otherwise, to choose a BEx query or a cube, click the CONNECT button:

   ▶ The LOG ON TO THE DATA SOURCE dialog box opens. Enter a user name and password, and then click OK.

   ▶ In the CUBE BROWSER dialog box, shown in Figure 10.12, navigate to the list of cubes and BEx queries list and select a cube or a BEx query.

   ▶ Click the SELECT button to close this dialog box.

Figure 10.12 Cube or BEx Query Selection in the CMC

5. In the AUTHENTICATION dropdown list, select the authentication mode:

   ▶ SELECT PREDEFINED for fixed credentials. In this case, enter the user name and password this connection must use to authenticate to the database in the USER and PASSWORD text fields.

   ▶ SELECT SSO for single sign-on.

   ▶ SELECT PROMPT for prompted credentials.

6. Click the SAVE button to save the connection and return to the connection list.

10.4.3 Creating a Relational Data Federator Data Source in Information Design Tool

You can create an SAP NetWeaver BW relational connection for a multi-source universe only in Information Design Tool. This connection can be created only through the PUBLISHED RESOURCES view in the CMS repository. To create this connection, follow these steps:

1. As described in Chapter 6, Section 6.5.1, open the RELATIONAL CONNECTION dialog box in the REPOSITORY RESOURCES view in order to create a new secured relational connection. Name it and go to the DRIVER SELECTION pane.

2. In the DATABASE MIDDLEWARE DRIVER SELECTION page, expand the tree list and select SAP • SAP NETWEAVER BW • SAP JAVA CONNECTOR (WHICH IS ALSO KNOWN AS SAP JCO).

3. Click the NEXT button.

4. In the PARAMETERS FOR SAP NETWEAVER BW CONNECTION page, in the AUTHEN-TICATION MODE dropdown list, select the authentication mode:

   ▶ USE SPECIFIED USER NAME AND PASSWORD for fixed credentials

   ▶ USE SINGLE SIGN ON for single sign-on

   ▶ USE BUSINESSOBJECTS CREDENTIAL MAPPING for secondary credentials

5. If you select the single sign-on authentication mode, keep the USE SNC IF AVAILABLE checkbox unselected.

6. Enter the parameters that identify the SAP NetWeaver BW system, as described in Table 10.1.

7. To select the InfoProvider to query, click the ... button next to the INFOPROVIDER text field. The SELECT INFOPROVIDER FACT TABLE dialog box opens, as shown in Figure 10.13.

8. In this dialog box, select the InfoProvider to query.

9. Click OK to close this dialog box.

10. Click the FINISH button to close the connection wizard and create the connection.

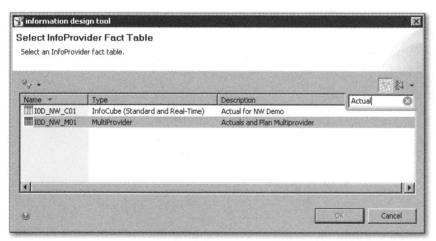

Figure 10.13 Select Fact Table for Relational SAP NetWeaver BW Connection Based on Data Federator

10.4.4 Creating a Relational Connection in Universe Design Tool

In Universe Design Tool, to create a universe on top of an SAP NetWeaver BW system, you need to create an OLAP connection to this SAP NetWeaver BW system. This created connection is relational, as it flattens the dimensions coming from the SAP NetWeaver BW system (as explained in Chapter 7, Section 7.1.2). To create this connection, follow these steps:

1. As described in Chapter 6, Section 6.5.2, open the CONNECTION PANEL dialog box in Universe Design Tool to create a new secured connection in the CMS repository. Name it and go to the DRIVER SELECTION pane.

2. In the DATABASE MIDDLEWARE SELECTION page, select the SAP • SAP BUSINESS WAREHOUSE • SAP CLIENT option.

3. Click the NEXT button to go to the LOGIN PARAMETERS page, as shown in Figure 10.14.

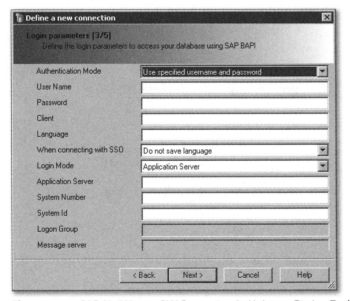

Figure 10.14 SAP NetWeaver BW Parameters in Universe Design Tool

4. In the LOGIN PARAMETERS page, in the AUTHENTICATION MODE dropdown list, select the authentication mode:

▶ USE SPECIFIED USERNAME AND PASSWORD for fixed credentials

▶ USE BUSINESSOBJECTS CREDENTIAL MAPPINGS for secondary mapping

▶ USE SINGLE SIGN ON WHEN REFRESHING REPORTS AT VIEW TIME for single sign-on

5. Enter the parameters to identify the SAP NetWeaver BW system, as described in Table 10.1.

6. Click the NEXT button to go to the CATALOG/DATABASE PARAMETERS page.

7. As shown in Figure 10.15, this page contains a list of cubes and BEx queries you can select from. Cubes are listed in the OLAP CUBES folder and BEx queries are listed below the cubes they query.

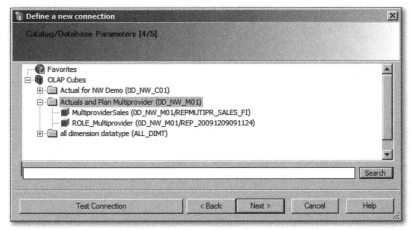

Figure 10.15 Cube or BEx Query Selection in Universe Design Tool

8. Select a cube to have the connection return data from the InfoProvider. Select a BEx query to have the connection return data from the BEx query.

9. Click on the TEST CONNECTION button to check the parameters you have entered.

10. Click the NEXT button to go to the CONFIGURATION PARAMETERS page.

11. This page contains some additional parameters for this connection. Review and modify them as needed, and then click the FINISH button to close the connection wizard and create the connection.

10.5   SAP Authentication and Single Sign-On

As explained in Section 10.1, SAP authentication allows users to log on to the BI 4.0 system by authenticating them to the SAP NetWeaver BW system. In addition to this SAP authentication, you can also set up single sign-on.

In this case, single sign-on is used during all workflows where you need to use this SAP authentication:

▶ If your BI Launch Pad portal is called from an SAP NetWeaver Enterprise portal that has already been authenticated with SAP, then you can reuse this authentication to log on to BI Launch Pad.

▶ If your connection references and queries data from the SAP NetWeaver BW system used to authenticate, you can define the connection authentication mode as single sign-on. In this case, when the connection needs to connect to the SAP NetWeaver BW system, it can reuse the credentials used by the user to log on to the BI 4.0 system. This method can be combined with the integration with SAP NetWeaver BW portal to achieve better integration with SAP NetWeaver BW system.

Note

This book does not cover SSO for publishing Crystal Reports documents, which is a capability that allows you to store Crystal Reports documents in the SAP NetWeaver BW system and was mainly used in XI 3.x. With BI 4.0's tight integration with SAP NetWeaver BW, Crystal Reports documents are stored in the BI 4.0 repository rather than in the SAP NetWeaver BW repository. Furthermore, this capability is not supported by Crystal Reports for Enterprise.

Like for other connections (see Chapter 6, Section 6.3), this single sign-on authentication mode has some limitations (for example, for scheduling and publishing). Single sign-on requires the user to be connected in order to reuse his credentials to pass them on to the SAP NetWeaver BW server.

To overcome these limitations, SAP authentication supports additional options for single sign-on. These options are useful for querying data from SAP NetWeaver BW using a connection defined with single sign-on authentication. Typical workflows include the following:

▶ When you schedule a document once you have logged out

▶ When you publish a document using report bursting, which delegates the refresh action to the recipient (user impersonification)

▶ When you log on to BI 4.0 using an authentication mode different from SAP but you want to use an SAP alias to authenticate to the SAP NetWeaver BW to query data

In these workflows, the simple single sign-on does not work because the user's full credentials for the SAP NetWeaver BW system are not available; thus, it's impossible to log on to the SAP NetWeaver BW system. By using SNC or STS, the SAP NetWeaver BW system relies on the BI 4.0 system and allows the user to log on, even if his full credentials are not available.

10.6 SNC and STS

This section describes the two other options that can be used with SAP authentication configuration: *Secure Network Communications* and *Security Token Service*.

10.6.1 Principles

Both SNC and STS are used to create trust between BI 4.0 and SAP NetWeaver BW. These two methods are supported in BI 4.0, but they do not apply to the same products:

▶ SNC is the method implemented since XI 3.x to overcome these limitations and, in BI 4.0, it is still supported by the products that previously supported it:

  ▶ Crystal Reports 2011

  ▶ Universes created with Universe Design Tool

  ▶ All clients that are using these universes

  Out-of-the-box SNC is not supported on the client side, but it is supported on the server side. In SNC, a certificate is created on both the BI 4.0 and SAP NetWeaver BW servers so it can be used by the other. SNC is also used to encrypt data exchange between server components.

▶ STS can be considered the successor to SNC. It has been implemented in BI 4.0 for reporting tools using SAP Direct Access (Web Intelligence, Crystal Reports for Enterprise, and Analysis, Edition for OLAP), and for universes created in

Information Design Tool (and all clients using these universes). In STS, a certificate is created on the BI 4.0 server and imported in the SAP NetWeaver BW server.

STS is supported on both the client and server sides.

Compared to SNC, STS is easier to set up:

▶ SNC relies on a certificate exchange between BI 4.0 and SAP NetWeaver BW.

▶ STS relies only on one certificate from BI 4.0 that is passed to SAP NetWeaver BW. Identification is done through a token.

10.6.2 Workflows

Table 10.5 defines which workflows can work with an SAP NetWeaver BW connection based with single sign-on authentication, depending on the SNC or STS configuration of your system. In this table, SAP Direct Access covers Web Intelligence, Crystal Reports for Enterprise, and Dashboards, and UNV is used for universes created with Universe Design Tool.

Configuration	Products	Results
User X logged on with an account that does not have SAP alias.	All products	Refresh fails because SAP credentials are not available.
User X logged on with SAP authentication.	All products	Refresh is successful because cached credentials are used.
User X logged with an authentication other different from SAP but has SAP alias.	Crystal Reports 2011 and document-based products on UNV server side	Refresh fails because SAP credentials are not available. Refresh is successful if SNC is configured.
User X logged with an authentication other different from but has SAP alias.	SAP Direct Access	Refresh fails because SAP credentials are not available. Refresh is successful if STS is configured.

Table 10.5 Workflows Based on Connection with Single Sign-On Authentication Mode

Configuration	Products	Results
Publication bursting to User X (with SAP alias), using one database fetch per recipient.	Crystal Reports 2011 and document-based products on UNV	Publication fails because there's no impersonification. Publication is successful if SNC is configured.
Publication bursting to User X (with SAP alias), using one database fetch per recipient.	SAP Direct Access	Publication fails because there's no impersonification. Publication is successful if STS is configured.
User X (with SAP alias) schedules a document and logout.	Crystal Reports 2011 and document-based products on UNV	Schedule fails because there's no impersonification. Schedule is successful if SNC is configured.
User X (with SAP alias) schedules a document and logout.	SAP Direct Access	Schedule fails because there's no impersonification. Schedule is successful if STS is configured.

Table 10.5 Workflows Based on Connection with Single Sign-On Authentication Mode (Cont.)

10.6.3 STS and SNC Coexistence

In the CMC, in the SAP authentication wizard, the SNC SETTINGS tab contains two checkboxes, as shown in Figure 10.16.

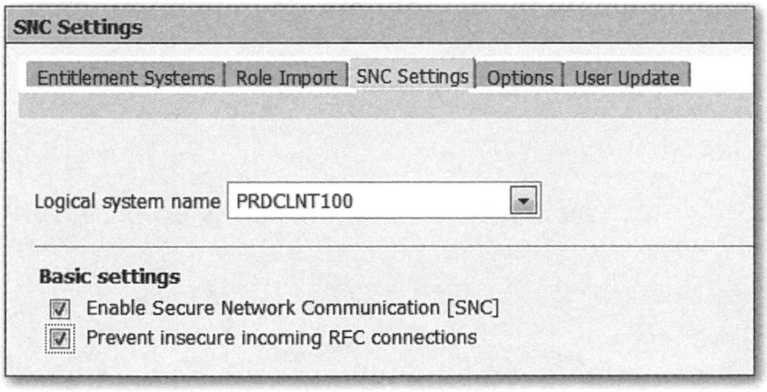

Figure 10.16 SNC Settings Tab

▶ ENABLE SECURE NETWORK COMMUNICATION [SNC]

▶ PREVENT INSECURE INCOMING RFC CONNECTIONS

By default, the PREVENT INSECURE INCOMING RFC CONNECTIONS is not checked. If you enable SNC by checking the ENABLE SECURE NETWORK COMMUNICATION [SNC] checkbox, this prevents the BICS connection from working with SAP Direct Access with Web Intelligence, Crystal Reports for Enterprise, and Dashboards.

Select the PREVENT INSECURE INCOMING RFC CONNECTIONS checkbox to make it work.

More generally, Table 10.6 shows in which cases SNC and STS work, depending on these checkboxes.

		Enable Secure Network Communication (SNC)	
		Not selected	Selected
Prevent Insecure Incoming RFC Connections	Not selected	SNC does not work STS works	SNC works STS does not work
	Selected	SNC does not work STS works	SNC works STS works

Table 10.6 Impact of SNC Settings Checkboxes

10.7 Configuring STS

To configure STS, you need to follow these steps:

1. On the machine running the BI 4.0 server, create a keystore file.

2. On the machine running the BI 4.0 server, create a certificate including this keystore file.

3. Import this certificate into the SAP NetWeaver BW system.

4. Import this keystore into the CMS repository.

Once all these steps have been done, you can check that the STS is properly running on the BI 4.0 system.

10.7.1 Creating a Keystore File

The first step in setting up the STS is to create a keystore file and a certificate from the BI 4.0 system. To generate this keystore, you must run a Java tool provided in BI 4.0 as a jar file named *PKCS12Tool.jar*.

On Windows, this jar file is located in the following folder:

<INSTALLDIR>\SAP BusinessObjects Enterprise XI 4.0\java\lib

On UNIX, it is located in the following folder:

<INSTALLDIR>/sap_bobj/enterprise_xi40/java/lib

Navigate to this directory and run the following command, as shown in Figure 10.17:

```
java —jar PKCS12Tool.jar -keystore <keystore> —alias <alias> —storepass
<storepass> —dname <dname> -validity <validity>
```

Figure 10.17 PKCS12Tool.jar Run in MS-DOS Windows

The arguments are defined in Table 10.7.

Argument Name	Argument Description
<keystore>	The file name for the generated keystore. By default, the generated file is named *keystore.p12*.
<alias>	An alias name for your BI 4.0 system. This alias is used in a later step in the CMC, in the PRIVATE KEY ALIAS text field.
<storepass>	The keystore password. The password will be requested when you will create the import keystore in the cert file.
<dname>	A distinguished name for your server. By default, this distinguished name is "CN=CA."

Table 10.7 Parameters for PKCS12Tool.jar

Argument Name	Argument Description
`<validity>`	Validity (in days) of your certificate. By default, this validity is 365 days.

Table 10.7 Parameters for PKCS12Tool.jar (Cont.)

This command generates two files in the directory from which you run the command:

▶ The keystore file: *keystore.p12*

▶ A default certificate named *cert.cert* that is regenerated in next step

10.7.2 Creating a Certificate

The second step in setting up the STS is to export the keystore you created before in the certificate. To export this keystore, use a program called `keytool.exe` on Windows or `keytool` on UNIX.

On Windows, this program is located in the following folder:

<INSTALLDIR>\SAP BusinessObjects Enterprise XI 4.0\ SAP BusinessObjects Enterprise XI 4.0\win64_x64\sapjvm\bin

On UNIX, it is located in the following folder:

<INSTALLDIR>/sap_bobj/enterprise_xi40/<UNIX version>/sapjvm/bin/

`<UNIX version>` must be replaced by the value corresponding to your UNIX: `linux`, `aix`, or `solaris`.

Go to the directory where the keystore has been generated and launch the following command, as shown in Figure 10.18:

```
keytool.exe -exportcert –keystore <keystore> –storetype pkcs12 –file
<certfile> -alias <alias>
```

Figure 10.18 keytool.exe Run in MS-DOS Windows

The arguments are defined in Table 10.8.

Argument Name	Argument Description
`<keystore>`	File name of the keystore generated in the previous step.
`<alias>`	The alias you gave to your server when generating the keystore.
`<certfile>`	The file name for the generated certificate file.

Table 10.8 Parameters for keytool.exe

When `keytool` prompts you for the keystore password, enter the storepass you used to create the keystore (see Section 10.7.1).

10.7.3 Importing the Certificate into the SAP NetWeaver BW Server

To perform the following steps, you need to access the SAP NetWeaver BW system with enough privileges (such as Administrator privileges) to perform this action on the SAP NetWeaver BW system.

1. Launch SAP GUI to access your SAP NetWeaver BW system.

2. Run Transaction STRUSTSSO2.

3. In the left pane, select the SYSTEM PSE folder to display the OWN CERTIFICATE, CERTIFICATE LIST, CERTIFICATE, LOGON TICKET sections in the right pane.

4. In the CERTIFICATE section, select the IMPORT button to open the IMPORT CERTIFICATE dialog box, as shown in Figure 10.19.

5. In the IMPORT CERTIFICATE dialog box, in the FILE PATH text field, enter the full path of the certificate generated on the BI 4.0 system (see Section 10.7.2).

6. In the FILE FORMAT section, select the BINARY radio button used to set the certificate file format.

7. At the bottom of the dialog box, click on the green checkmark to close this dialog box and import the certificate. The CERTIFICATE section is updated with the details contained in your certificate, as shown in Figure 10.20.

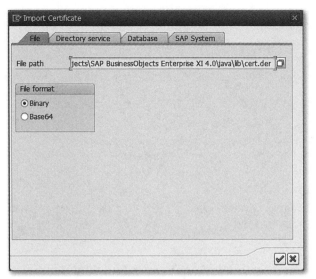

Figure 10.19 Import Certificate Dialog Box

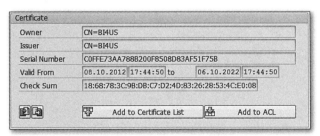

Figure 10.20 Certificate Details

8. In the CERTIFICATE section, click the ADD TO CERTIFICATE LIST button to add your system to the CERTIFICATE LIST section in the OWNER table, as shown in Figure 10.21.

Figure 10.21 Certificate List

9. In the CERTIFICATE section, click the ADD TO ACL button to open the ADD ENTRY TO SINGLE SIGN-ON ACCESS CONTROL LIST dialog box.

10. In this dialog box, in the SYSTEM ID text field, enter the system ID used to identify your BI 4.0 system.

11. In the CLIENT text field, enter 000, as shown in Figure 10.22.

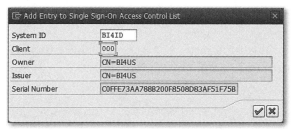

Figure 10.22 Add Entry to SSO Access Control List

12. Click the green checkmark button to close this dialog box and to add the certificate and the system ID of your BI 4.0 system to the SAP NetWeaver BW system. Your system appears in the LOGON TICKET section in the ACCESS CONTROL LIST table, as shown in Figure 10.23.

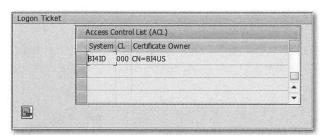

Figure 10.23 Logon Ticket

10.7.4 Importing the Keystore into the CMS Repository

Once the certificate has been imported into the SAP NetWeaver BW system, you need to configure your BI 4.0 system so the SAP NetWeaver BW system can trust it.

1. Go to the AUTHENTICATION tab in the CMC.

2. In the AUTHENTICATION tab, double-click on the SAP line to open the SAP AUTHENTICATION wizard.

3. Select the Options tab.

4. Because STS has not yet been configured, the SAP SSO Service section displays, No key store file has been uploaded.

Note

The name of the section may be confusing. It is called SAP SSO Service, but it is used only for STS configuration.

---

5. In the System ID text field, enter the same system ID used to identify the SAP system when importing the certificate into the SAP NetWeaver BW system (see Section 10.7.3). Enter this system ID without the CN= prefix.

6. To export the keystore you created on your BI 4.0 system keystore (see Section 10.7.2) to the CMS repository, click the Browse button and navigate in file folders to select it.

   By default, PKCS12Tool generates this keystore in the *<INSTALLDIR>\SAP Business-Objects Enterprise XI 4.0\java\lib* folder and its name is keystore.p12.

7. In the Key Store Password and Private Key Password text fields, enter the password used when creating the keystore file (see Section 10.7.1).

8. In the Private Key Alias text field, enter the alias used when creating the key-store file (see Section 10.7.1).

9. Click the Update button to save your parameters. Once the keystore has been imported, the message A key store file has been uploaded is displayed in the SAP SSO Service section, as shown in Figure 10.24.

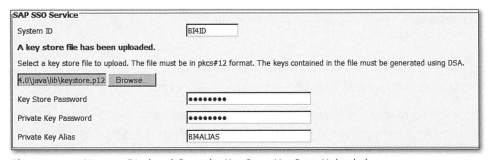

Figure 10.24 Message Displayed Once the Key Store Has Been Uploaded

10. Exit the window to close it.

To use STS, you need to validate that this service is available and working in your BI 4.0 system. By default, this server is part of the Adaptive Processing Server. As described in Chapter 2, Section 2.6, go to the SERVERS tab in the CMC and check that the Security Token Service is properly displayed in the AVAILABLE SERVICES list of the Adaptive Processing Server.

10.8   User Attributes

As described in Chapter 8, Section 8.8, it is possible to create user attributes to customize the universes created in Information Design Tool. So if you have configured SAP authentication, you can retrieve the attributes associated with the users saved in the SAP NetWeaver BW repository.

To retrieve these attributes from the SAP NetWeaver BW system, make sure the following parameters are properly set in the CMC:

▶ In the authentication option parameter (see Section 10.1.5), the IMPORT FULL NAME, EMAIL ADDRESS, AND OTHER ATTRIBUTES checkbox must be selected in order to grant these attributes to this SAP NetWeaver BW system.

▶ In the user properties panel, the IMPORT FULL NAME, EMAIL ADDRESS, AND OTHER ATTRIBUTES checkbox must be checked to grant this capability to this user.

10.9   Summary

With SAP NetWeaver BW system supporting its own security repository, it is possible to configure your BI 4.0 system to authenticate in the SAP NetWeaver BW system. As with LDAP and Active Directory authentication, SAP authentication is done by importing SAP NetWeaver BW roles and users into the CMS repositories and creating them as groups and users. CMS rights can then be defined for these users and groups.

To query data from the SAP NetWeaver BW system, you need to create connections. There are three SAP NetWeaver BW connections, each based on different technologies that are supported by different products:

- An OLAP connection created with Information Design Tool or CMC and used to query SAP BEx queries

- A relational connection created with Information Design Tool and used to create relational, monosource, or multi-source universes with Information Design Tool

- A relational connection created with Universe Design Tool and used to create relational universes with Universe Design Tool

In addition to SAP authentication, single sign-on can be configured to both log on to the BI Launch Pad and to query SAP NetWeaver BW data.

SAP authentication configuration provides two additional options to implement trust between BI 4.0 and SAP NetWeaver BW and to impersonate data refresh:

- Secure Network Communications (SNC), which was already available in XI 3.x

- Security Token Service (STS), which is the recommended option new to BI 4.0

Attributes associated with users saved in SAP NetWeaver BW system can also be retrieved in the BI 4.0 through user attributes. They can typically be used in universes created in Information Design Tool.

Let's see in next chapter how you can put in place the various methods we've introduced to set up security on your system.

Six of one, half-dozen of another? Let's turn our attention to important principles to follow when designing a BI 4.0 security model, regardless of your method.

11   Defining and Implementing a Security Model

Given all the concepts supported by BI 4.0, it is possible to find different methods to implement a security model and achieve the same objective. But remember that the overall objective is to define a model that is maintainable—easy to use for performing daily tasks, easy to enhance when new requirements arise, and easy to understand in the event of knowledge transfer.

For this reason, defining this security model must be done with care. It is important that some general rules are defined initially in order to ensure that the system remains secure throughout the process. Defining a security model is a long-term project. For large companies with thousands of users, it can be considered as a sub-project of the deployment project, so it's not surprising that it can take weeks to finalize.

This chapter offers some guiding principles that you should consider when defining your security model. It gives some tips and recommendations to successfully implement your security model, but we caution you against being too strict in their application. What is relevant in one situation might not apply to another, so you should adapt them according to your configuration and environment.

11.1   General Recommendations

The most complex task is to put in place a security framework that precisely defines what users can do and see in your system. Keep these general recommendations in mind when designing it:

▶ Keep it simple. The security model should achieve the requirement of securing the content and functionality of the platform, but no more.

▶ Make it restrictive by default. That is, access to content or functionality is denied by default and must be explicitly granted.

▶ Minimize user management administration. The granting of rights should be carried out between user groups and folders, rather than users and objects to minimize the number of rights assignments that need to be set up; this step also facilitates the addition of new users to the platform by requiring only that they are added to the appropriate user groups to have their rights set.

▶ The inheritance of rights from folders to sub-folders, from groups to sub-groups, and from groups to users should be used wherever possible to minimize the total number of rights assignments.

▶ Identify people in teams who can help you define user requirements in order to define the reporting products they need to use. These people can later become delegated administrators, or at least help you to identify others who can take on this role (see Section 11.8).

▶ Document your model. You can use spreadsheets to keep a list of rights assigned to access levels or to create arrays that list all access levels assigned to users.

▶ Use meaningful names and document them. Specific nomenclature conventions may apply when naming objects, access levels, groups, or folders. It's important to keep proper documentation because you—or someone else—may have to revisit the security framework later.

▶ For some specific requirements or repetitive tasks, you may use the software development kits (SDKs) provided with BI 4.0 to write them.

▶ Triple-check your work. The definitions of users, folders, rights, and access levels are tightly dependent and they may need several reviews before they can be finalized.

From an administration point of view, there are also a few general recommendations:

▶ Do not deploy the CMC on the same production server used by your reporting tools, in order to avoid administrative tasks getting tangled up by production access bottlenecks.

▶ Use the audit in order to track events that happen in your system and to detect abnormal behaviors.

▶ Put Secure Sockets Layer (SSL) protocol in place to secure HTTP communication.

There are different ways to implement a security framework. Before the introduction of access levels, one common security model was to set up two user groups hierarchies and assign rights for functionality access and resource access. (Thus, by adding a user to the appropriate groups, you could define this user security.)

In BI 4.0, it is more convenient to combine it with the access levels described in Chapter 4, Section 4.8. The following sections offer some recommendations for achieving security framework implementation.

11.2 Defining Users and Groups

Install a BI 4.0 server and clients. During server installation, set the administrator's default password to a complex password. The Administrator account should not be used for day-to-day administrative tasks and its password should be kept secret. Keep it for an emergency (for example, when you've lost another user password or locked its account).

Then, connect to the CMC to set security and create users and groups. Consider these recommendations when defining the users and groups:

▶ Create an administrator user to back up the Administrator predefined user.

▶ All users on the platform must have their own user identity within the platform, which means that there shouldn't be any anonymous access. This ensures that the platform can be expanded to other applications with different security requirements without affecting the current users.

▶ Make sure the Guest account, which allows anonymous access to the platform, is disabled. Disabling the account ensures that all users log on using a named account, thereby letting you audit of all activity on your system.

▶ List groups and users hierarchies. The objective is to define security at the group level and avoid setting rights at the user level. These groups can be organized:

  ▶ By replicating your organization structure (for example, Company > Business Unit > Department...)

  ▶ By mapping the hierarchical positions in your organization (for example, President > Director > Line Manager...)

- ▶ By mapping functional roles (for example, Report Designer, Metadata Architect, Data Analyst, Administrator…)

▶ Define password settings. A passwords policy covers some properties related to passwords, and might answer these questions: Does the password expire? Does it have to contain at least X number of characters? Define the rules to apply, and then set them in the AUTHENTICATION tab of the CMC.

▶ If you already use an external authentication provider, reuse it where possible to spare the users from having to remember an additional username and password to connect to BI 4.0. This also eliminates the overhead of having to maintain separate passwords and group memberships within the CMS repository (see Chapter 3, Section 3.5). In some cases, you may not have a choice, as it is a corporate policy.

▶ Use SDKs to write some applications to automate user creation.

▶ In the case of external authentication, map external groups from LDAP or Active Directory or roles from SAP NetWeaver BW to CMS groups.

▶ If necessary, configure external authentication. This may be tricky because of the different steps involved and the steps to run on the different external systems, so be sure to review your requirements with system administrator.

▶ When creating users, remember that the platform does not differentiate between upper case and lower case for users and group names, but it does for passwords.

Predefined Groups

The predefined groups that are created by default in the CMS repository are intended to be used for quick deployment. You may prefer to explicitly re-create yours and use only them. Thus, you can name them using your standard naming conventions and set explicitly known rights.

However, there is one group that always contains all users: the Everyone group. Any security setting defined for this group applies to all users.

▶ Remove rights from the Everyone group. In order to implement a shared secured environment, this group should not be given rights by default, and rights should be granted only through group membership. Check that this group is assigned the "No Access" access level for the Universe, Connections, and Folders top-root folders.

▶ Set the Everyone group to Not Specified for all advanced rights that are denied to regular users for applications such as the BI Launch Pad, CMC, or Information Design Tool.

In contrast, the Administrator group has a "Full Control" access level for all top-root folders. Although it can be convenient to use it for quick tests, this access level means that a user in this group has all rights granted, so use it with care.

11.3   Defining Folders and Objects

Once your users and groups structure has been defined, you may define the folder structure that contains BI resources. Consider these best practices:

▶ The folder structure should be consistent with any format categorization scheme that has been defined for your organization. Its purpose should be to categorize the content, rather than to provide some sort of filtering of the data.

▶ The folder structure that categorizes content should be closely aligned with the responsibility for that content. Whenever possible, the responsibility to manage and publish content to a particular folder should reside with one group only.

▶ The folder structure should be integrated and deal with all subject areas and applications consistently.

▶ The folder hierarchy must be able to deal with administrative considerations, such as supporting multiple environments (for example, development, test, and production). You can isolate end users from these folders by applying security, but take them into consideration in the design.

▶ Each document object should be published once, where possible. Use parameterization and filtering to allow the same report to provide information at multiple levels. Shortcuts can be used to allow the same document content to be available from multiple folders, where this is logical.

▶ Remember that in BI 4.0, you can create connection folders, which was not possible in previous releases.

▶ Define hierarchies folders in the "Public," "Universes," and "Connections" top-root folders. The folder structure defines the workflow by which users typically locate report content, so it should be aligned, where possible, with how users conceptualize the structure of information within the organization.

▸ The depth of the folder hierarchy should be minimal while still providing sufficient categorization to be understandable. The structure should be sufficiently granular to achieve functional needs but the depth of the folder hierarchy should not be larger than ten.

▸ Your CMS repository contains fewer universes and connections. Therefore, in the Universes and Connections top-root folders, the depth of the folder hierarchy should contain fewer levels than the Public top-root folder—five levels at most.

11.4 Defining Rights

Assuming you have already defined the products that fit your users' needs and installed them, you need to define exactly how these products will be used, what features to enable or disable, what deployment mode to authorize, and for which groups.

Indeed, although rights can be granted to users, we don't recommend this for two reasons:

▸ The security model can become difficult to maintain.

▸ Assigning rights to individual users may overwhelm the CMS repository.

For groups, define what rights should be granted to them. It is more convenient to define security at the group level and to have these rights inherited by the users for several reasons:

▸ The use of folders and groups is mandatory in order to avoid setting rights at the individual user and object level. It simplifies the maintenance approach as well as rights administration.

▸ In the case of external authentication, the external users are mapped to the BI platform through groups.

▸ Taking advantage of the folders and groups was recommended even before the introduction of access levels in the BI platform.

▸ Define the rights to assign to top-level folders. By default, these rights are inherited by all folders below these top-level folders; thus, how they are secured is also defined, by default.

► With the scope of rights and rights override, you should be able to avoid breaking inheritance. Any exceptions must be documented.

► The rights framework is quite flexible and allows different combinations to achieve the same goals. Define some policies to standardize your rights framework:

   ► There are many different general rights. You may decide to use only a sub-set of the most important (the rights to view, edit, delete, etc.) and deny the others.

   ► For public folders, the use of an owner right can limit users to managing only their own objects.

We recommend that you distribute the following rights with care because they are very powerful:

► **Top-root folders: "Delete objects"**
At least for public top-root folders or important objects saved in these public folders, we recommend that you deny this right to avoid erroneous deletion. The CMS repository does not have any temporary recycle bin from which you can recover a deleted object, and the only way to recover it is to use backup.

► **Documents: "Schedule on behalf of other users"**
For objects that can be scheduled, this right allows you to run a document under the account of any other user and thus see the data he is allowed to see.

► **CMC application: "Log on to the CMC and view this object in the CMC"**
Because the CMC is your system administration tool, only authorized users should be allowed to use it.

► **Web Intelligence application: "Query script: Enable editing (SQL, MDX, ...)"**
This right allows users to directly modify the generated SQL or MDX used to query the database. If you are using universes to secure data through access restrictions or security profiles, this right allows users to simply bypass them.

► **Web Intelligence application: "Documents: Disable automatic refresh on open"**
By denying this right, you force any Web Intelligence document to be refreshed when it is opened.

11.5   Defining Access Levels

Once you have defined the rights to set, instead of explicitly assigning them to groups using advanced rights, use access levels. As described in Chapter 4, Section 4.8, access levels are easier to set and to maintain. If you upgrade from a release where access levels are not available (XI R2) or if you still use advanced rights to grant security, you may also plan to re-implement these rights using access levels.

To define the access levels to create, follow these recommendations:

▶ With the exception of the "Full Control" access level that grants all rights, do not use predefined access levels. Create and use only access levels so you explicitly know the rights you have granted through these access levels.

▶ From the rights requirements, identify classes of rights that are distinct and create access levels from these classes.

▶ Define general guidelines to create access levels in order to avoid creating too many. These policies should help you limit the number of access levels by providing a framework. If you plan to duplicate an access level and create a new one simply to grant one right, then first check whether this right can be granted in the initial access level.

▶ Define the access level granularity:

  ▶ *Should one access level define a role, a product use, and so on?*

  ▶ *Should the rights defined in access levels be cumulative?* In this case, you define a set of access levels—the first one granting a limited set of rights and the last one granting maximum rights—with different variations between these two access levels. You then assign to users the access level corresponding to the rights they are granted.

  ▶ *Or should they be additive?* In this case, each access level grants a set or rights that other access levels do not grant. You then assign to users all the access levels that cover the rights they are granted.

▶ If you can identify similar models in your classes of rights, turn them into templates, and use them for specific cases with consistency. For example, for Web Intelligence and Crystal Reports, you may identify main actions, such as create, edit, refresh, and view, so you decide to define three access levels that grant the following actions:

- Create, edit, refresh, and view
- Refresh and view
- View

Keep the same definition of these access levels for Web Intelligence and Crystal Reports. If you need to create access levels to secure a folder content, keep the same access level definitions.

- Again, remember to use meaningful names. Perhaps define some conventions for naming the access levels so you can easily understand what they grant. For example: `<Product>_<Actions>` or `<Object>_<Actions>`, where

  - `<Object>` is the object type (for example UNX for universes and CNX for connections)

  - `<Product>` is the name of product.

  - `<Actions>` is a suite of letters (one letter per action granted: create, edit, refresh, view…)

With these conventions:

  - `Webi_CERV`: An access level that gives the rights to create, edit, refresh, and view Web Intelligence documents

  - `UNX_CERQ`: An access level that gives the rights to create (publish in universe context) a universe with Information Design Tool, edit (retrieve and remodify in universe context) it, refresh a query on top of this universe (Data Access right), or create a new query on this universe

- To be more explicit, you may also document these access levels in spreadsheets:

  - In an access level definition matrix, you can record the rights each access level grants, as shown in Figure 11.1.

  - In an access level assignment matrix, you can record the access levels assigned to groups, as shown in Figure 11.2. In this matrix, list your groups in the columns, and list your folders in the rows. At the intersection of these rows and columns, note the access level assigned to this group for this folder.

	Web Intelligence Create	Web Intelligence Refresh	Web Intelligence View	Universe Create
BI Launch Pad				
Log into	Granted	Granted	Granted	Granted
Edit	Not Specified	Not Specified	Not Specified	Not Specified
Modify rights	Not Specified	Not Specified	Not Specified	Not Specified
Securely modify rights	Not Specified	Not Specified	Not Specified	Not Specified
Organize	Granted	Granted	Granted	Granted
Send to email destination	Granted	Not Specified	Not Specified	Granted
Send to file location	Granted	Not Specified	Not Specified	Granted
Send to StreamWork	Granted	Not Specified	Not Specified	Granted
Web Intelligence				
Log into	Granted	Granted	Granted	Granted
Edit	Not Specified	Not Specified	Not Specified	Not Specified
Modify rights	Not Specified	Not Specified	Not Specified	Not Specified
Securely modify rights	Not Specified	Not Specified	Not Specified	Not Specified
Data - enable data tracking	Granted	Granted	Not Specified	Granted
Data - enable formatting of changed data	Granted	Granted	Not Specified	Granted
Desktop Interface - enable local data providers	Granted	Granted	Granted	Granted
Desktop interface - enable Web Intelligence Desktop	Granted	Granted	Granted	Granted

Figure 11.1 Access Levels Definition

	Connections RDBMS_DEV	Connections OLAP_DEV	Universes DataW	Universes Consolidated	Public Folders Reports
Everyone					
Administrators	C_IDT_CE	C_IDT_CE	U_IDT_CE	U_IDT_CE	P_WebI_CE
Universe Designers	C_IDT_CERV	C_IDT_CERV	U_IDT_CERQ	U_IDT_CERQ	P_WebI_CE
Sales	C_IDT_RV	C_IDT_RV			P_WebI_CERV P_CR_CERV
AMER	C_IDT_RV		U_IDT_RQ	U_IDT_R	P_WebI_RV
EMEA	C_IDT_RV	C_IDT_RV	U_IDT_RQ	U_IDT_RQ	P_WebI_RV P_CR_CERV
APAJ	C_IDT_RV		U_IDT_RQ	U_IDT_R	P_WebI_RV

Figure 11.2 Access Levels Assignment

Note

If you upgrade from BusinessObjects 5.x/6.x releases, a similar concept, named predefined settings, exists. But it is not possible to migrate from these releases directly. You need to upgrade first to XI 3.x first, then to BI 4.0. In any case, we won't recommend that you migrate security from 5.x/6x to XI R2/XI 3.x. The models of these releases are too different—security model is user-centric, while in XI releases, it is object-centric. Instead we recommend that you take the opportunity of the migration to redefine the security model to take advantage of the new XI model.

When you have defined this list of access levels you need, you can create them using the CMC. To facilitate access level creation, you may duplicate existing access levels.

11.6   Mandatory Rights for Common Workflows

When you are defining access levels, ensure that all rights needed to grant one particular action are actually granted. Indeed, one of the strengths of the rights framework is its granularity. Security can be set at different levels to meet different levels of security requirements. The drawback of this flexibility is the number of rights to set at different levels to grant one particular action.

The following sections describe these rights for some common actions.

11.6.1   Viewing a Web Intelligence Document

To view a document, the following rights must be granted:

▶ "Log on to Web Intelligence" right for Web Intelligence application

▶ "Log on to BI Launch Pad and view this object in the CMC" right for BI Launch Pad application if the document is accessed through BI Launch Pad

▶ "View objects" right for the folder containing the document

▶ "View objects" right for the document (optional, since it should be inherited from the folder)

11.6.2   Creating a Web Intelligence Document

To create a Web Intelligence document on a universe (created either by Information Design Tool or Universe Design Tool), the following rights must be granted:

▶ "Log on to Web Intelligence" right for Web Intelligence application

▶ "Log on to BI Launch Pad and view this object in the CMC" right for BI Launch Pad application if the document was created through BI Launch Pad

▶ "Documents: Enable creation" and "Reporting: Enable formatting" rights for Web Intelligence application

▶ "Create and edit queries based on the universe," "View objects," and "Data access" rights for the universe

▶ "View objects" and "Data access" rights for the connection used by the universe

11.6.3 Saving a Web Intelligence Document

To save a Web Intelligence document in the CMS repository, the following rights must be granted:

- "Edit objects" right for the document, if this action simply updates a document that already exists

- "Add objects to the folder" right for the folder where the document will be saved, if this creates a new document in this folder

- "Copy objects to another folder" right for the document if a new version of an existing file will be saved

At the application level, Web Intelligence does not offer any right to prevent users from saving documents. A workaround is to disable the "Add objects" right for each folder or disable it at the folder root level and make sure it is inherited by all folders. Thus, the SAVE button is displayed in Web Intelligence, but no folder is displayed in the folder list and the user cannot save reports.

11.6.4 Refreshing a Web Intelligence Document

To refresh a Web Intelligence document based on a universe and a connection, the following rights must be granted:

- "Log on to Web Intelligence" right for Web Intelligence

- "Log on to BI Launch Pad and view this object in the CMC" right for BI Launch Pad application if the document is accessed through BI Launch Pad

- "View objects" right for the document
  - "View objects" right for the folder containing the document; "View objects" and "Refresh the report's data" rights for the document
  - "View objects" right for the folder containing the document

- If the document is based on a relational monosource universe created with Information Design Tool or Universe Design Tool:
  - "View objects" and "Data Access" rights for the universe
  - "View objects" and "Data Access" rights for the connection

- ▶ If the document is based on a relational multi-source universe created with Information Design Tool:
  - ▶ "View objects" and "Data Access" rights for the universe
  - ▶ "View objects" and "Data Access" rights for the all connections
- ▶ If the document is based on a multidimensional universe created with Information Design Tool:
  - ▶ "View objects" and "Data Access" rights for the universe
  - ▶ "View objects" right for the OLAP connection
- ▶ If the document is based on an SAP Direct Access
  - ▶ "View objects" right for the OLAP connection

11.6.5 Editing a Web Intelligence Document

To edit a Web Intelligence document, the following rights must be granted:

- ▶ "Log on to Web Intelligence" right for Web Intelligence
- ▶ "Log on to BI Launch Pad and view this object in the CMC" right for BI Launch Pad if you access it from BI Launch Pad
- ▶ "View objects" and "Edit objects" rights for the document
- ▶ "View objects" right for the folder containing the document

If the data provider is a universe, the following rights must also be granted:

- ▶ "View objects" and "Data access" rights for the universe
- ▶ "View objects" and "Data access" rights for the connection

11.6.6 Moving a Category to Another Category

To move a category to a destination category, the following rights must be granted:

- ▶ "View objects," "Edit objects," and "Delete objects" rights for the category to move
- ▶ "View objects" and "Add objects to the folder" rights for the destination category

11.6.7   Adding a Document to a Category

To add a document into a category, the following rights must be granted:

▶ "View objects" and "Add objects to the folder" rights for the category

▶ "View objects" and "Edit objects" rights for the document

11.6.8   Scheduling a Document

Scheduling and publishing are enforced by the framework, and scheduling rights are controlled by general rights, although these general rights do not apply to objects that cannot be scheduled. So for all applications that use this scheduling framework (Web Intelligence and Crystal Reports) the following rights must be granted to schedule a document:

▶ "Log on to <application name> and view this object" in the CMC rights for CMC or BI Launch Pad, depending on the application where the schedule is created

▶ "View objects" right for the document

▶ "View document instances" for the document

▶ "Schedule document to run" right for the document

And the same universe and connection rights needed to refresh the document (see Section 11.6.4).

The document is refreshed when it is scheduled. Nevertheless, the "Refresh" right is not needed at the document level for Web Intelligence. Some additional rights must also be granted to change some schedule parameters:

▶ "Schedule to destinations" right for the document to change the schedule default destination

▶ "Add objects to Folder" and "View objects" rights for the destination Inbox folder, if the destination is an Inbox folder

▶ "Define server groups to process jobs" right to change the server groups that process the schedule

To manage scheduling, some general rights can also be useful at the document level: "Define server groups to process jobs," "Delete instances," "View document instances," "Pause and Resume document instances," "Reschedule instances," and "Schedule on behalf of other users."

11.6.9   Sending a Document to Inbox

Any file stored in the CMS, even the agnostic ones, can be sent to a user's Business-Objects Inbox. The file is sent as-is, without any refresh in the case of a Web Intelligence file. To send a document to a user's BusinessObjects Inbox, the following rights must be granted:

▶ "Send to BusinessObjects Inbox" right for BI Launch Pad application, if the document is sent from BI Launch Pad

▶ "Add objects to folder" and "View objects" rights for the destination Business-Objects Inbox folder

▶ "Copy objects to another folder" and "Schedule to destinations" rights for the object to send

11.6.10   Adding a User or a Group to Another Group

To add a user or a group to a destination group, the following rights must be granted:

▶ "View objects" and "Edit objects" rights for the destination group

▶ "View objects" and "Edit objects" rights for the source user or group

11.7   Setting Security for External Groups

When you configure your system for an external authentication system, BI 4.0 creates in the CMS repository some groups that are mapped to groups from this external authentication system. In order to define what these users may access by default (connections, universes, folders, and so on), you need to define security rights for the users in these groups.

As seen in previous sections, this security is set at the group level so it is inherited by these users. However, you should in fact set these rights to another group created in the CMS repository and include the imported groups in this group for several reasons.

The main reason to do this is to avoid loss of your rights setting. Indeed, you may define synchronization between the external groups and mapped groups. If for any reason the synchronization does not proceed properly and the mapped group is deleted, then your settings may be lost. You can avoid this problem if rights are set to a parent group.

In the case of SAP authentication, there is another reason related to Promotion Management. In a typical deployment process, you usually set up and use multiple BI 4.0 environments: one for development, one for qualification, and one for production. Each environment may connect to a dedicated SAP NetWeaver BW system, for example:

▶ DEV~100 for the development environment

▶ QUA~100 for the qualification environment

▶ PRD~100 for the production environment

As each system has a different system ID, each imported user group has a different name.

By using a group whose name remains identical in all environments, you ensure that this group is promoted from one CMS to another with the security rights defined for this group. Thus, the groups created from external groups that belong to this group always inherit from this group, as shown in Figure 11.3.

Figure 11.3   Parent Group Used To Contain Imported Groups

11.8   Delegated Administration

When you install BI 4.0, you must provide a password for the Administrator account. As the system administrator, you are responsible for keeping the account healthy, so to speak, and for answering users' requests.

But if your deployment contains thousands of users, you might find it hard to do everything well. That is, sometimes one administrator can't possibly perform all of the daily operational tasks: creating a new user, granting a user access to a resource, deleting resources, recovering backed-up files, and so on. Furthermore, you might not have the business knowledge about what all of the users are working on and what their needs are.

To help you with these tasks, define a few delegated users who can act as local administrators in some sub-groups of users and perform daily tasks in the scope of their group. By delegating these tasks to other users, you give yourself the time to run high-level requirements for the BI system.

11.8.1 Using Rights to Delegate Administration

To delegate tasks, you can add your delegated administrators to the Administrators group or give them administrative rights rather than sharing the Administrator user account. This guarantees traceability and the capability to track who has performed a task. Furthermore, it allows you to define each delegated administrator's scope of rights.

Indeed, a delegated administrator should be allowed to see and edit only the users and resources he is managing and not the resources he is not managing. We recommend you consider the following best practices:

▶ Grant them the "Add objects to the folder" right for the Users and Groups top-root folders to let them create new users and groups.

▶ Deny them the "Add objects to the folder" right for the groups where you do not want them to add groups.

▶ Give them the owner versions of the "Edit objects" and "Delete objects" rights (see Chapter 4, Section 4.4) to let them manage only the users and groups they manage.

▶ Give them the owner version of the "Change user password" rights so they can reset password for the users they manage.

▶ Deny them these rights for the groups and users they do not manage.

> **Note**
>
> If you have configured your system with external authentication, you've reduced the task of managing these users and groups directly in the BI 4.0 system.

The same principles can also be applied to the resources (Universes, Connections, Public) top-root folders. You can grant some limited rights to the top-root folders, but identify some sub-folders where you can grant higher rights. For folders shared by multiple users, you can either grant them only the owner version of the rights, or their non-owner versions.

More generally, you should also grant the "Securely modify the rights users have to objects" right instead of the "Modify the rights users have to objects" right so that your delegated administrators can only grant to other users rights they are themselves granted.

11.8.2 Restricting CMC Usage

Because your delegated administrators only need to log on to the CMC in order to perform some of the tasks you delegate them, they do not need to access all CMC capabilities. Through the application rights (see Chapter 5), you can define the features they are allowed to use in the CMC: version management, promotion management, monitoring, and so on.

However, by default, when users log on to the CMC, all CMC tabs are available to them. You can restrict the CMC tabs they can access in the CMC user interface by following these steps:

1. Log into the CMC with the Administrator account.

2. Go to the USERS AND GROUPS tab and select a user or a group.

3. Right-click this user or this group and in the contextual menu, select the CMC TAB ACCESS CONFIGURATION command to open the CONFIGURE CMC TAB ACCESS dialog box. This dialog box lists all tabs in the CMC, as seen in Figure 11.4.

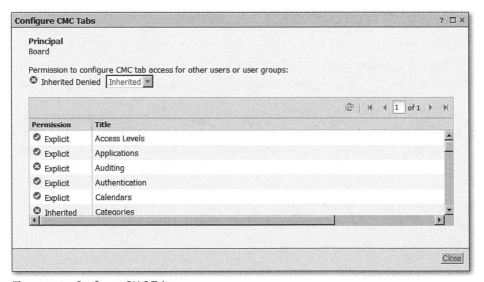

Figure 11.4 Configure CMC Tabs

4. To hide a tab for this user or group, select the name of a tab and, in the toolbar, click the DENY button.

5. Click the CLOSE button to close the dialog box and save your settings.

> **Note**
>
> Limiting the tab access is only a capability that affects the CMC user interface. It must be done in conjunction with security policies defined through rights.

11.9 Defining Database Filtering

Security rights secure resources in the CMS at the InfoObject level. Depending on the users, these rights may not be able to secure data. One method to implement such filtering is to rely on the database connection.

Databases can enforce their own security model—something you can take advantage of. By creating different accounts in the database, you can define in detail what these accounts are allowed to see (columns, rows, tables, and so on). For reporting usage, these accounts should have only read-only rights—it's not necessary to give them writing rights. In fact, to prevent users from erroneously typing SQL that modifies the database, it's important to restrict writing rights from them.

By using the appropriate credentials to access the database, you can define what data can be retrieved from the database. For reporting tools that directly access the database (Analysis for OLAP, Web Intelligence, and Crystal Reports with SAP Direct Access), this is the way to filter data.

11.9.1 Authentication Mode

To benefit from the database security, connections must be defined with an authentication mode different than fixed credentials, since fixed credentials use the same credentials for all users.

Recall from Chapter 6 that several other authentication modes can be used to authenticate users to the database using their own credentials:

► Single sign-on, when possible (it is not supported for all connectivities)

► Credentials mapping, where the credentials to connect to the database are retrieved from the CMS repository

▶ Prompted authentication, which is the simplest to define but it has two draw-backs:

  ▶ It is not supported by all the reporting tools.

  ▶ It forces reauthentication by asking the user to provide credentials.

Another advantage of using security defined at database level is that it limits the volume of data to be returned by the database and to be processed by BI 4.0 reporting products directly at the source.

11.9.2 Connection Overloads

If your reports are based on a relational universe, in some cases it is possible to use connection overloads to allow the database to apply security filtering:

▶ Connection access restriction for a relational universe created with Information Design Tool (see Chapter 7, Section 7.4.1)

▶ Connections data security profile for a relational universe created with Information Design Tool (see Chapter 8, Section 8.5.1)

It is difficult to implement this method for each user because in order to apply it for all users, you need to create a connection for every user. It can be easier to secure data by group of users. This can be done by following these steps:

1. Create a couple of accounts in the database. Data in the database is secured for this account through a role, a geographical location, or any other criteria that apply to a group of users.

2. Create several connections to the database (one for each account you have created in the database).

3. Create connection overloads for the universe (one for each connection).

4. Assign these connection overloads to the corresponding user groups, as shown in Figure 11.5.

When a user in these groups queries the database through this universe, then, at query time, the connection overload is applied and the query returns only data secured for the account used in the replacement connection definition.

In other situations, connection overload can be used to set a different authentication mode to a group of users; by default, a universe is based on a connection with fixed credentials authentication mode. For another group of users, you may define a connection to the same database but with another authentication mode (single sign-on, credentials mapping) that forces the user to authenticate to the database with his own credentials.

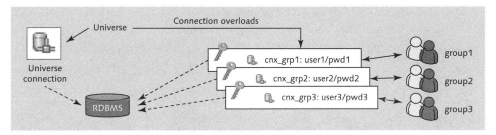

Figure 11.5 Connection Overloads Defined for Groups

11.10 Universe Security

When it is not possible to define security at the database level or when you want to define a more complex security, if you are using a universe, you might benefit from universe security.

11.10.1 Universe Scope

When you define security at the universe level (access restrictions, data and business security profiles), this security scope is limited to this universe and the reporting tools that use this universe.

You may need to discuss with your universe designer how to define the objects, tables, and values to grant or deny. As for right and access level assignment, assign access restrictions and security profiles to groups rather than to individual users to benefit from inheritance.

11.10.2 Row Filtering

In some cases, you can use table auto-joins, object filters, or mandatory filters to force a WHERE clause to be applied to the query (see Chapter 7, Section 7.2 and Chapter 8, Section 8.2). But even with the use of variables and with the extension of user attributes that allow you to define new user attributes or to retrieve them from an external authentication system (see Chapter 8, Section 8.8), the formula is unconditionally applied to all users and cannot be modified.

In practice, filtering is often done through universe security:

► Rows access restrictions for relational universes created with Universe Design Tool (see Chapter 7, Section 7.4.1) and data security profiles restrictions for those created with Information Design Tool (see Chapter 8, Section 8.4.4)

► Filters business security profiles for relational and multidimensional universes created with Information Design Tool (see Chapter 8, Sections 8.5.3 and 8.5.4)

Note

When you're defining business security profiles, all objects are denied by default in create query and display data business security profile. Don't forget to grant some views and objects in the appropriate tabs of the business security profile editor.

Despite these different aggregation options, there are some cases that rows restrictions cannot handle. For example, if you have defined two group hierarchies corresponding to dimensions to filter. Row restrictions assigned to the groups corresponding to the same hierarchy aggregate using the ANDOR algorithm, which is what is expected. But following this algorithm, rows restrictions between groups mapped to different dimensions are also aggregated with the OR operator. In practice, because the dimensions are disjoint, you might have assumed the restrictions are aggregated with AND.

Example

As shown in Figure 11.6, you have a group hierarchy Geography and a group hierarchy Products. Each group is attached to a row restriction on a universe whose aggregation is ANDOR:

► EMEA group is assigned the row restriction Country.region = 'EMEA'

► FR group is assigned the row restriction Country.name = 'FR'

► Sport group is assigned the row restriction Product.line = 'Sport'

► Shirt group is assigned the row restriction Product.name = 'Shirt'

If you add a user to the groups UK, CA, Desktop, and Shoes, the generated filter for this user is (Country.name='FR') OR (Country.name='CA') OR (Product.name = 'Desktop') OR (Product.name = 'Shirt') and not ((Country.name='FR') OR (Country.name='CA')) AND ((Product.name = 'Desktop') OR (Product.name = 'Shirt')).

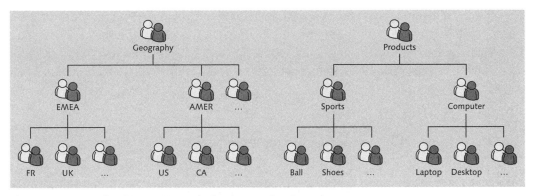

Figure 11.6 Example of Group Hierarchy for Aggregation Example

One workaround to this limitation is to create sub-groups for products below each group for countries or to create sub-groups for countries below each group for products, but this is not necessarily a good practice and might not have the rights to modify these group hierarchies.

Multidimensional Universe Example

In the same example seen previously, instead of row restrictions, you define multidimensional filters business security profiles for a multidimensional universe:

▸ EMEA group is assigned the filter on the member Geography.Region.'EMEA'

▸ France group is assigned the filter on the member Geography.Region.Country.'France'

▸ Sport group is assigned the filter on the member Product.line.'Sport'

▸ Shirt group is assigned the filter on the member Product.line.'Shirt'

▸ If the aggregation is ANDOR for filters business security profile, after the query returns data from the cube that correspond to the UK or CA countries and for the Desktop and Shirt products.

11.10.3 Consistency Between Products

If you define row level restriction on universes to filter data retrieved from the database and returned to users, make sure the row level restrictions you define are consistent with Explorer and Publishing.

For the data discovery product Explorer, the indexing is not necessarily done by the end users. To apply the same filtering when they access an information space, you may use information space personalization (see Chapter 5, Section 5.11).

For Publishing, if you use one data fetch for all recipients or one database fetch for each batch of recipients options, the document refresh is done not by the recipients but by the sender. Filtering defined for recipients at the universe level may not apply. For this reason, you can define personalization profiles (Chapter 9, Section 9.5).

11.10.4 User Attributes

Compared to Universe Design Tool, the use of user attributes in Information Design Tool should dramatically reduce the maintenance of universe security.

To filter rows through a parameter (country, for example) in Universe Design Tool, you must either:

▶ Create a rows access restriction per country (one for France, one for US, and so on) or

▶ Store these values in an additional table in the database and create a clause in the WHERE clause to retrieve the parameter value from this table for the user.

With Information Design Tool, this can be done by simply creating only one row data security profile that compares a value to the user attribute.

At query time, the user attribute is replaced by the appropriate value for the user and the WHERE clause is added with the filter to use for this user. If the user attributes are filled from an external system, which is often the case, this avoids having to maintain them at the BI 4.0 level since they are stored in one central location.

11.10.5 Business Layer Views

Information Design Tool does not support linked universes. In Universe Design Tool, these linked universes allow you to have a *core* universe used by and embedded into other universes, called *derived* universes.

A method to achieve one of the use-cases covered by these linked universes is to use business layer views. In your business layer, add all objects that were initially included in core and derived universes. Then create one view per derived universe. With create query business security profiles, you can secure these views and allow a user to see only some views.

More generally, using views and securing them with business security profiles can help to reduce the number of universes by maintaining only one universe but giving access only to a sub-set of it.

11.11   Combined Authentication

Even if you use SAP authentication, it is common to work on a Windows environment. In such an environment, you may need to access databases that authenticate with Active Directory. The following sections detail how to benefit from the two environments by combining both authentications.

11.11.1   Importing SAP NetWeaver BW Users

If a user exists in the CMS repository, when you import another user with another authentication mode but the same name, an alias to the first user is automatically created and attached to it.

By default, when they are imported, SAP users are created with the syntax

```
<SAP System ID>~<SAP client number>/<SAP user name>
```

Their names do not match the LDAP or Active Directory user names, so it is not possible to map them automatically.

A possible workaround is to remove the `<SAP System ID>~<SAP client number>/` prefix in the name of users created from the SAP NetWeaver BW system, so they will match the names of LDAP or Active Directory users if they are identical. This workaround requires two steps:

▶ Modifying the registry (so make sure to back it up first)

▶ Removing from the CMS repository all roles mapped from SAP NetWeaver BW

On a server running on Windows operating system, follow these steps to execute this workaround:

1. Launch the Central Configuration Manager to stop the SIA (see Chapter 3, Section 3.8.2).

2. Open the Registry Editor (`regedit`).

3. Browse to the registry key:

```
HKEY_LOCAL_MACHINE\SOFTWARE\SAPBusinessObjects\SuiteXI4.0\Enterprise\
Auth Plugins\secSAPR3\
```

4. Double-click `SimpleUsernameFormat` and change the value to `Yes`.

5. In the CCM, restart the SIA (see Chapter 3, Section 3.8.2).

On a server running a UNIX operating system, use this workflow:

1. Use the `stopservers` command to stop the SIA.

2. Open the `.registry` file located in the folder *<INSTALLDIR>/sap_bobj/data/.bobj/ registry/64/software/sap businessobjects/suite xi 4.0/enterprise/auth plugins/secsapr3*

3. Set the value for the parameter `SimpleUsernameFormat` to `Yes`, as in

```
"SimpleUsernameFormat"="Yes"
```

4. Save the file.

5. Use the `startservers` command to restart the SIA.

Then when you import SAP NetWeaver BW users, they are created only with their names, without the `<SAP System ID>~<SAP client number>/` prefix.

11.11.2 Single Sign-On with SAP NetWeaver BW and Active Directory

If your BI 4.0 system has been configured to authenticate to both Active Directory and SAP, you can configure it to use the Windows session and also to support single sign-on to database for SAP NetWeaver BW and for databases that authenticate to Active Directory, by following these steps:

1. Configure your system with Active Directory authentication and Kerberos and import your users from Active Directory.

2. Configure your system with SAP Authentication, set up SNC or STS, and also import your users from Active Directory.

3. Create aliases between users from Active Directory and SAP NetWeaver BW. You can create aliases manually one by one, but this may take too much time (unless you use the method described in Section 11.11.1 to import users from the SAP NetWeaver BW system so that they have the same names as in Active Directory).

Then users can log on to BI 4.0 products using their Windows session without having to type their passwords. If your connections to the databases (SAP NetWeaver

BW or the ones that authenticate with Active Directory) are defined with single sign-on authentication, then users can do the following, once connected:

▶ **Refresh reports based on these databases that authenticate with Active Directory.**
In this case, the Active Directory alias is used to log on with single sign-on to the database.

▶ **Refresh reports based on SAP NetWeaver BW.**
In this case, the SAP alias is used to authenticate to the SAP NetWeaver BW database. Even if the SAP password is not available, if SNC and/or STS have been configured, only the user name in SAP is checked in SAP NetWeaver BW to let the query run on the SAP system.

11.12   Testing a Security Model

Once your security model has been designed and implemented, you should test it to make sure that it behaves as expected. Consider these best practices when troubleshooting your security model:

▶ Check that external users can properly log on and that aliases are properly defined.

▶ Create some test users and test some workflows. There are no impersonifications possible to test security. You may need to create test users in typical groups. Give them the same rights as the user you want to test. If you have based your security model on inheritance and groups, this should be done only by assigning them to the appropriate groups from which they inherit rights. After your test, you may need to disable or delete these users if you don't want them to be exploited or allow others to maliciously enter the system.

▶ Problems in reporting are often caused by a security issue. Before troubleshooting your report or your universe, it is good practice to first check that the issue is not related to a denied right. Grant all rights for objects and applications involved in your workflow, and then re-test it. If it works fine, then you can investigate whether a security issue is causing the problem. Refer to Section 11.6 for a list of rights that are involved. If your workflow is not described, use a bottom-up approach to check that rights are properly defined at each level.

▶ Use Security Query to validate the rights that users are granted (see Chapter 4, Section 4.10).

▶ Create basic reports and check that they are working properly, if there is no security constraint.

▶ Improve your model by checking aggregation options and confirming that users in groups are actually granted what is requested.

▶ Save your security in an LCMBIAR file. Version the documents you create and save them in the LCMBIAR file.

11.13 Summary

Throughout this book, several concepts have been presented in order to support data and functional security in BI 4.0. Because the flexibility of this platform allows you to define security in different ways, this last chapter offers some recommendations for implementing a maintainable security model:

▶ Base the security rights on groups and folders rather than on users and objects in order to take advantage of inheritance.

▶ Use access levels to assign rights for folders and groups.

▶ If possible, take advantage of an external authentication system.

▶ Because all rights are dependent, check that the rights needed to run a workflow are properly set at all levels.

▶ Create additional administrators to whom you can delegate some daily tasks for the groups of users they maintain.

▶ If possible, leverage database security by implementing an authentication mode that can individually identify the user to the database.

▶ Data security can be implemented through universes. The most common are row access restrictions, row data security profiles, and filters business security profiles.

▶ Document your security and use matrix spreadsheets when possible.

These recommendations and the previous chapters should give you a better understanding of the underlying concepts used to functionally secure your BI 4.0 platform and then apply them in an SAP NetWeaver BW environment.

From a security point of view, Universe Design Tool and Information Design Tool share many concepts. However, you must take some differences—such as rights and security profiles—into consideration when converting universes.

A   Universe Comparison and Conversion

Previous chapters describe how universe security is managed in Universe Design Tool and Information Design Tool. Information Design Tool is the successor to Universe Design Tool, so most universe concepts, including security concepts, are common to both tools.

The security defined in Information Design Tool can be seen as a superset of the security defined in Universe Design Tool. However, there are some slight differences you need to know about when converting a universe created with Universe Design Tool to the new universe format if you expect the converted universe to behave like the original one. This appendix compares how security is managed in Universe Design Tool and Information Design Tool for several topics:

- Connections
- Security rights
- Access restrictions and security profiles

Finally, it describes how universe security is converted and how to run this conversion in Information Design Tool.

A.1   Connections

In authoring workflows, a connection is a mandatory resource to create a universe. The connection identifies the data source used to retrieve metadata and data.

A.1.1 Local and Secured Connection

Universe Design Tool uses three types of connections:

▶ Personal connection: The connection is created locally on the computer, and it can be used only by the universe creator on the computer on which it was created.

▶ Shared connection: The connection is created locally on the computer, but it can be used by all users.

▶ Secured connection: The connection is created in the CMS repository. You cannot create secured connection if you are connected in standalone mode.

Information Design Tool uses only two types of connections:

▶ Local connection: The connection is created in an Information Design Tool local project. This local connection covers the former personal and shared connections created in Universe Design Tool.

▶ Secured connection: The connection is created in the CMS repository and is similar to the one created in Universe Design Tool. To reference a secured connection in a local project, you must use connection shortcut.

In both tools, only connections stored in the CMS repository are considered truly secure. Other connections, created locally and thus more vulnerable, must be used only for testing or development purposes and not used in a production environment.

A.1.2 Connection Type

Table A.1 compares the different connections supported by Universe Design Tool and Information Design Tool.

Universe Design Tool	Information Design Tool
Does not support relational SAP NetWeaver BW and SAS connections based on Data Federator data source.	Supports relational SAP NetWeaver BW or SAS connections based on Data Federator data source. These connections can only be created in the CMS repository. It is not possible to create them locally.

Table A.1 Connection Support Comparison

Universe Design Tool	Information Design Tool
Supports relational connections based on Connection Server and created in Universe Design Tool or Information Design Tool.	Supports relational connections based on Connection Server and created in Universe Design Tool or Information Design Tool.
Supports OLAP connections based on Connection Server created in Universe Design Tool. It is possible to create OLAP universes on top of these connections.	Does not support OLAP connections based on Connection Server created in Universe Design Tool.
Does not support OLAP connections created in Information Design Tool or CMC.	Supports OLAP connections created in Information Design Tool or CMC. However, it is not possible to create universes on top of OLAP SAP NetWeaver BW connections.

Table A.1 Connection Support Comparison (Cont.)

A.2 Rights Comparison

When comparing Universe Design Tool and Information Design Tool from a security point of view, it is important to know the differences in the security rights supported by the two tools and the universes they generate.

The following sections compare these rights, but they do not detail them; their descriptions can be found in Chapter 5. Even if they are not explicitly mentioned, this comparison is valid for both the owner and non-owner right versions (see Chapter 4, Section 4.4 for detailed information on owner and non-owner right versions).

A.2.1 Application Rights

The authoring workflows in Universe Design Tool and Information Design Tool are different. This fact is reflected in the rights supported by Universe Design Tool and Information Design Tool.

Table A.2 compares and shows the equivalencies between these rights.

Universe Design Tool	Information Design Tool
Application general rights (see Chapter 4, Section 4.6)	Application general rights
Apply universe constraints	Administrate security profiles
N/A	Publish universes
N/A	Retrieve universes
Create, modify, or delete connections	Create, modify, or delete connections
Check universe integrity	N/A
Refresh structure window	N/A
Use table browser	N/A
Link universe	N/A
N/A	Use shared projects
N/A	Save for all users
N/A	Compute statistics

Table A.2 Rights Comparison

A.2.2 Universe Rights

As for design tools, the rights for universes created in Information Design Tool and Universe Design Tool differ.

Table A.3 compares and shows the equivalencies between these rights.

Rights of Universes Created with Universe Design Tool	Rights of Universes Created with Information Design Tool
All object general rights (see Chapter 4, Section 4.5)	All object general rights
Create and edit queries based on universe	Create and edit queries based on the universe
Edit access restrictions	Edit security profiles
	Assign security profiles

Table A.3 Universe Rights Comparison

Rights of Universes Created with Universe Design Tool	Rights of Universes Created with Information Design Tool
Data access	Data access
Unlock universe	N/A
New list of values	N/A
Print universe	N/A
Show table or object values	N/A
N/A	Retrieve universe

Table A.3 Universe Rights Comparison (Cont.)

A.2.3 Connection Rights

In Universe Design Tool, a universe can only be created on top of connections based on Connection Server. In Information Design Tool, universes can also be created on top of the same connections, so there's no need to convert these connections. Both the general and custom rights that these connections support are enforced similarly in the two tools.

Data Federator data sources and OLAP connections created in Information Design Tool or Central Management Console (CMC) are supported only in Information Design Tool, not in Universe Design Tool, as shown in Table A.1.

A.3 Universe Security Comparison

Compared to CMC rights, access restrictions are one of the universe specificities that make them so flexible and easy to use. In Information Design Tool, these access restrictions have been extended and replaced by security profiles. Let's see how they can compare with one another, in terms of their functional behavior and aggregation as well as their user interface.

A.3.1 Access Restrictions and Security Profiles (Relational Universe)

In Information Design Tool, access restrictions have been replaced and extended by data security profiles and business security profiles. Table A.4 points out the differences between the two concepts for a relational universe.

Universe Design Tool	Information Design Tool
Connection access restriction	Equivalent to connections data security profile. It has been extended in order to support multi-source universe.
Controls access restriction	Equivalent to controls data security profile. However, the "Limit size of long text objects to" parameter is no longer supported.
SQL access restriction	Equivalent to SQL data security profile, except the "Warn Cartesian product" option does not exist anymore.
Objects access restriction	The objects access restriction security is now supported by: ▶ Create query business security profile, to secure the objects to display in the query panel ▶ Display data business security profile, to secure the objects to query data Create query and display data business security profile can be independently set.
Objects access restriction is used to deny some objects. When it is assigned to a user, he can see all objects and classes in the universe, except the ones denied by the objects access restriction.	Create query and display data business security profiles can be used to grant or deny objects. When they are assigned to a user, all folders, business objects, and views, are, by default, denied to him. You can use create query and display data business security profiles to grant or deny him universe content.
N/A	Create query business security profile can secure business layer views that do not exist in Universe Design Tool.
Rows access restriction	Rows access restriction is equivalent to rows data security profile. For relational universe, filters business security profile is another way to filter data, by using objects from the business layer. However, filters business security profile is always applied to the query, while rows data security profile is added only if the conditional table is used in the query.

Table A.4 Relational Universe Security Comparison

Universe Design Tool	Information Design Tool
Rows access restriction does not support an alias table or derived table as the conditional table.	Since BI 4.0 SP4, rows data security profile supports an alias table and derived table as the conditional table. This was not the case before.
Table mapping access restriction	Equivalent to tables data security profile. It has been extended in order to support multi-source universe.
Table mapping access restriction supports an alias table as the source or replacement table.	Tables data security profile supports alias table as source table only since BI 4.0 FP3.
Table mapping access restriction support free text for the name of the replacement table.	Tables data security profile supports only the data foundation table as replacement table. It is no longer possible to type free text as the replacement table, and thus define dynamic table (use of @PROMPT or @VARIABLE).
@VARIABLE can be used in rows access restriction. It can substitute for predefined parameters.	@VARIABLE can be used in rows access restriction and filters business security profiles. It can substitute for predefined parameters and user attributes.

Table A.4 Relational Universe Security Comparison (Cont.)

A.3.2 Access Restrictions and Security Profiles (OLAP Universe)

In Universe Design Tool, the access restrictions you can define for an OLAP universe are a limited sub-set of access restrictions types supported by relational universes. Indeed, they secure generic database concepts without being specific to relational databases: connection, controls, and objects.

Information Design Tool does not convert the OLAP universe created with Universe Design Tool. However, the OLAP universe created in Information Design Tool can be secured by business security profiles. Table A.5 compares the security concepts enforced by the two tools.

Universe Design Tool	Information Design Tool
Connection access restriction	OLAP universe does not support the equivalent capability to replace an OLAP connection with another one.
Controls access restriction	OLAP universe does not support the equivalent capability to replace some query parameters.
Objects access restriction	The objects access restriction security is now supported by: ▶ Create query business security profile, to secure the objects to display in the query panel ▶ Display data business security profile, to secure the objects to query data Create query and display data business security profile can be independently set.
N/A	Create query business security profile can secure business layer views. This capability does not exist in Universe Design Tool.
Objects access restriction is used to deny some objects. When it is assigned to a user, he can see all objects and classes in the universe, except the ones denied by the objects access restriction.	Create query and display data business security profiles can be used to grant or deny objects. When they are assigned to a user, all folders, business objects, and views become denied to him. You can use create query and display data business security profiles to grant or deny him universe content.
N/A	Filters business security profile can secure members of hierarchies. This capability does not exist in Universe Design Tool for OLAP universe.

Table A.5 OLAP and Multidimensional Universe Security Comparison

A.3.3 Aggregation

In addition to the differences in the access restriction and security profiles behavior, Information Design Tool offers more options to aggregate security profiles. These differences are listed in Table A.6.

Universe Design Tool	Information Design Tool
Only one access restriction can be assigned to a user or a group.	Several data and business security profiles can be assigned to a user or a group.
Priority is defined at group level.	Priority is defined at data security profile level because setting priority at group level does not allow prioritizing two data security profiles assigned to the same user or group.
For access restriction aggregated by priority, the value to apply is this: In priority, the one defined in the access restriction assigned to the user, if any. Otherwise, the access restriction applied to the group with the highest priority.	For security profile aggregated by priority, the value to apply is always the one defined in the data security profile with the highest priority.
Connection access restriction can only be aggregated through priority.	Connection data security profiles can only be aggregated through data security profile priority.
Controls and SQL access restriction can only be aggregated through group priority.	Controls and SQL data security profiles can be aggregated through data security profiles priority but also through the AND, ANDOR, or OR algorithms.
Objects access restriction can only be aggregated with AND.	Create query business security profile and display data business security profile can independently aggregated through the AND, ANDOR, or OR algorithms.
Rows access restriction can be aggregated through the AND or ANDOR algorithms.	Rows data security profiles can be aggregated through the AND, ANDOR, or OR algorithms
N/A	Filters business security profiles for relational universes can be aggregated through the AND, ANDOR, or OR algorithms. The resulting WHERE clauses are merged using AND or OR operators.

Table A.6 Aggregation Comparison

Universe Design Tool	Information Design Tool
N/A	Filters business security profiles for OLAP universe can be aggregated through the AND, ANDOR, or OR algorithms adaptation. The member set to query data is computed though the union or intersection operators.
N/A	For relational universes, rows data security profiles and filter business security profiles are aggregated using the AND operator.
Table mapping access restriction can only be aggregated through priority.	Tables data security profiles can only be aggregated through data security profile priority.

Table A.6 Aggregation Comparison (Cont.)

A.3.4 Security Editor

Access restrictions in Universe Design Tool and security profiles in Information Design Tool must be created, edited, and managed. The Security Editor in Information Design Tool is much more complete and offers more capabilities than the dialog box you can use for this in Universe Design Tool. Table A.7 highlights these main enhancements.

Universe Design Tool	Information Design Tool
You can be connected to only one CMS repository at a time.	Connection to different CMS repositories is possible: You can open several Security Editor(s) connected to different CMS repositories and switch from one to another.
You must import the universe to edit its access restrictions and the user(s) and/or group(s) they are assigned to.	You do not need to retrieve universe to edit its security profiles and the user(s) and/or group(s) they are assigned to.
You can view and manage only one universe at a time.	The Security Editor offers you an overview of all CMS content and the security profiles defined for all your universes in the CMS repository.

Table A.7 Security Editors Comparison

Universe Design Tool	Information Design Tool
Editing access restrictions is protected by Universe Design Tool's "Apply universe constraint" right.	Editing security profiles is protected by the following CMC rights: ▶ Information Design Tool's "Administer security profiles" right ▶ Universe's "Edit security profiles" right
Assigning access restrictions to users and groups is protected by Universe Design Tool's "Apply universe constraint" right.	Assigning security profiles to users and groups is protected by the CMC rights: ▶ Information Design Tool's "Administer security profiles" right ▶ Universe's "Assign security profiles" right
You cannot run secured query.	You can run a query from a universe published in the CMS repository. Security assigned to the connected user applies to CMC rights, security profiles, user access level, @VARIABLE, and user attributes.
N/A	You can see security profiles inherited by a user or a group.
N/A	You can see all universes that have security profiles explicitly assigned to a user or a group.

Table A.7 Security Editors Comparison (Cont.)

A.3.5 Object Access Level

Both Universe Design Tool and Information Design Tool support object access level. Object access level can be defined for any business objects defined in classic universe (measures, dimensions, and attributes) and for any business objects defined in business layer of new universe (dimension, attribute, measure, calculated measure, member sets, etc.).

The different access levels are identical for both tools: public, controlled restricted, confidential, and private. The user access level you define in the CMC can be identically defined for a classic universe or a new universe.

User access levels inherited by a user from the groups it belongs to are also aggregated identically in Universe Design Tool and Information Design Tool.

A.4 Universe Conversion

In Information Design Tool, it is possible to convert a universe created with Universe Design Tool in order to save it in the new file format supported by Information Design Tool. Some universes cannot be converted: universes based on stored procedures and OLAP universes.

You can convert both local universes and universes saved in the CMS repository. The conversion of a local universe generates the corresponding connection, data foundation, and business layer in an Information Design Tool local project. Conversion of a universe stored in the CMS repository needs to take into consideration different aspects: its security rights, its access restrictions, the assigned users and groups, and the aggregation modes and priority, as described in the following sections.

A.4.1 Object Access Level

When a universe is converted, object access levels that are object properties are converted as well. The user access levels defined for this universe are also recreated for the converted universe, for the same user(s) and group(s).

A.4.2 Universe Rights Conversion

When a secured universe is converted, its security rights and its assignment to users and groups are also converted. Rights access levels assigned to the universe are also assigned to the converted universe for the same groups and users. Advanced rights assignments defined for the universe are also re-created for the converted universe for the same groups and users. However, because the rights differ between the source (classic) and target (new) universe, a mapping is done between these rights, as described in Table A.8.

Classic Universe Rights	New Universe Rights
All general rights	These rights are converted to the equivalent rights in the converted universe.
Create and edit queries based on this universe	This right is converted to the equivalent right in the converted universe.

Table A.8 Universe Rights Conversion

Classic Universe Rights	New Universe Rights
Data access	This right is converted to the equivalent right in the converted universe.
Edit access restrictions	This right does not exist anymore in Information Design Tool. Its value is set to "Edit security profiles" and "Assign security profiles" rights.
Unlock universe	These rights are no longer supported by Information Design Tool. Their values are not kept during conversion.
New list of values	
Print universe	
Show table or object values	

Table A.8 Universe Rights Conversion (Cont.)

A.4.3 Access Restriction Conversion

The security defined in Information Design Tool can be seen as a super-set of the security set in Universe Design Tool. Thus, the access restriction conversion into security profiles is quite simple. However, the slight differences between access restrictions and security profiles require some adaptation during the conversion phase in order to get the same behavior applied to the converted universe as in the original universe.

For each universe to convert, each access restriction generates one or several data security profiles and/or a business security profile.

By default, in Universe Design Tool, the access restriction is converted into a data business security profile, which is then assigned to a user or group. The name of this data security profile is the name of the access restriction. The definition of this data security profile is directly retrieved from the access restriction definition (connection, controls, SQL, rows and table mapping security).

However, in Information Design Tool, priority is no longer defined at the group level but at the data security profile level. If the access restriction is assigned to more than one user or group, and if this conversion does not allow the converted security to properly reflect the same security as in the source universe, then the access restriction is converted into several data security profiles, one for each user or group.

The names of these data security profiles are the names of the access restriction postfixed by the user or group names: <Access Restriction Name>_<user or group name>. The definitions of these data security profiles are all identical and are directly retrieved from the access restriction definitions (connection, controls, SQL, rows and table mapping security). These data security profiles are assigned to the same users and groups as their corresponding access restrictions and are prioritized using the group priority in Universe Design Tool.

If the access restriction defines object access restriction, then a business security profile is created and attached to the converted universe. This business security profile has these properties:

▶ It must define create query and display data security because they both cover the objects access restriction.

▶ Its name is the name of the access restriction.

▶ In create query security, master view is granted and all objects and classes denied in the access restriction are denied.

▶ In display data security, the "All objects" shortcut is used to grant all objects and classes denied in the access restriction are denied.

▶ It is assigned to the same users and groups as the access restriction.

A.4.4 Access Restriction Aggregation Option Conversion

When the universe is converted, its aggregation options are converted with these rules:

▶ The controls and SQL data security profile aggregation option is set to priority, since it is the only one available for controls and SQL access restriction.

▶ The rows data security profile aggregation option is the one defined for the original universe rows access restriction aggregation option:

  ▶ "Very restrictive (AND)" if it is AND.

  ▶ "Moderately restrictive (ANDOR)" if it is ANDOR.

▶ The create query and display data business security profile aggregation option is set to "Very restrictive (AND)" since it is the only one available for the objects access restriction aggregation option in Universe Design Tool.

▶ The filters business security profile aggregation mode is set to "Very restrictive (ANDOR)."

A.5   Running Conversion in Information Design Tool

Universe conversion can be run from Information Design Tool. This process converts both the universe content and the universe security, as described in the previous sections. To convert a secured universe, you need to follow these steps:

1. In the menu bar, select FILE • CONVERT UNIVERSE to open the CONVERT .UNV UNIVERSE dialog box.

2. In this dialog box, click the SELECT .UNV UNIVERSE FROM A REPOSITORY button to open the OPEN SESSION dialog box.

3. Select the CMS repository containing the universe to convert, type your credentials to authenticate to this CMS repository, and then click OK.

4. A dialog box opens in which you can navigate in the Universes folder and subfolders in the CMC repository. Select the universe to convert, and then click OK.

   The dialog box closes and the universe name to convert is displayed in the SELECT .UNV UNIVERSE TO CONVERT text field. Furthermore, the dialog box is updated, so you can add a destination repository folder, as shown in Figure 1.1.

5. Click the BROWSE button located near the DESTINATION REPOSITORY FOLDER.

6. A dialog box opens, where you can navigate in the Universes folders to select the folder where the converted universe is created. Select this folder then click OK. The dialog box closes and the folder name is displayed in the DESTINATION REPOSITORY FOLDER text field.

   Make sure you have the "Add objects to folder" right for the selected folder so you can create the converted universe.

7. You may optionally choose to retrieve the converted universe once the conversion is done:

   ▶ Click the BROWSE BUTTON NEAR THE DESTINATION LOCAL PROJECT FOLDER text field to open the SELECT LOCAL PROJECT dialog box.

   ▶ Select the project and a folder, and then click OK.

   ▶ The SELECT LOCAL PROJECT dialog box closes and the selected project and folder are displayed in the DESTINATION LOCAL PROJECT FOLDER text field.

8. Click OK to start the conversion. The converted universe is generated in the selected folder in the CMS repository. It has the same name as the original, except for its .UNV extension that is replaced by .UNX. If you have opted to retrieve the converted universe at the same time, it is also generated in the selected project and folder.

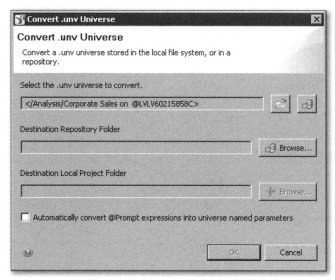

Figure A.1   Convert .UNV Universe Dialog Box

B The Authors

Christian Ah-Soon has worked for SAP BusinessObjects for 13 years as a program manager on transversal areas like administration, security, internationalization, and installation. For the last major release, SAP BusinessObjects BI 4.0, he worked on the Semantic Layer team. Christian holds a Ph.D. in computer science and graduated from TELECOM Nancy.

David François Gonzalez is an SAP BusinessObjects product expert engineer with the research and development group based in France. David has worked for SAP BusinessObjects for 13 years, starting with the BusinessObjects V5 and the Supervisor product and later managing a team in charge of BusinessObjects V6 suite testing. David shifted to customer contact with XI R2 and XI 3.1, where he was in charge of customer environment replication. Four years ago, he started working very close to both the field and the customers, providing best practices and white papers on internal and external websites. Since then, he has participated in conferences such as Utilisateurs SAP Francophones and TechEd, and he regularly helps customers troubleshoot site problems and implement SAP BusinessObjects solutions.

Photographs by Philippe Cuvillier

Index

■ Become an expert on the
principles and features of SAP
NetWeaver BW

■ Follow along with a step-by-step
case study that outlines a sales
analysis project from concept to
reality

Amol Palekar, Bharat Patel, Shiralkar Shreekant

SAP NetWeaver BW 7.3 — Practical Guide

Business analytics remains one of the hottest and most dynamic topics
in enterprise software — so don't be left behind. With this comprehensive
reference, you can get up to speed and stay up to date on the principles
of SAP NetWeaver BW 7.3, from the basics to the advanced concepts.
Thanks to a practical example that is carried throughout the course of the
book, you'll do more than learn what DSOs, InfoCubes, or InfoProviders
are: You'll learn what you can do with them, and how. If you want to
master BW, this book is what you need.

approx. 775 pp., 2. edition, 69,95 Euro / US$ 69.95
ISBN 978-1-59229-444-2, Nov 2012
www.sap-press.com

Galileo Press

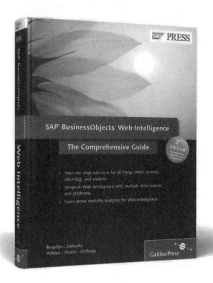

- Your one-stop reference for all things WebI: queries, reporting, and analysis

- Integrate Web Intelligence with multiple data sources and platforms

- Learn about mobility analytics for Web Intelligence

- 2nd edition updated and expanded for release 4.0

Jim Brogden, Heather Sinkwitz, Mac Holden, Dallas Marks, Gabriel Orthous

SAP BusinessObjects Web Intelligence

The Comprehensive Guide

Revolutionize your company's data presentation with SAP BusinessObjects Web Intelligence 4.0 with new flexibility and functionalities. This comprehensive guide will help you build a foundational understanding of WebI by beginning with the fundamentals; or you can jump straight into the advanced discussions that are new to the latest release, including advanced charting, advanced formula writing, and report scheduling and distribution.

591 pp., 2. edition 2012, 79,95 Euro / US$ 79.95
ISBN 978-1-59229-430-5
www.sap-press.com

- Provides 100 little-known time-saving tips and tricks

- Features detailed instructions and guiding screenshots

- Presents practical, expert advice for everyone working in BW

Andrew Joo, Buntic Georgian

SAP NetWeaver BW

100 Things You Should Know About...

If you're looking to take your knowledge of SAP NetWeaver BW to the next level, then this is the book for you! You'll benefit from expert information that reveals the secrets of SAP NetWeaver BW gurus as they provide the most useful tricks of working with the major task areas in SAP NetWeaver BW. These "100 Things" provide detailed screenshots, easy instructions, and a hands-on approach to quickly working with SAP NetWeaver BW.

approx. 350 pp., 49,95 Euro / US$ 49.95
ISBN 978-1-59229-447-3, Feb 2013
www.sap-press.com

Galileo Press